Palm Beach Babylon

Palm Beach
BABYLON

Sins, Scams, and Scandals

by Murray Weiss
and Bill Hoffmann

A Birch Lane Press Book
Published by Carol Publishing Group

A Birch Lane Press Book
Published by Carol Publishing Group
Birch Lane Press is a registered trademark of Carol Communications, Inc.
Editorial Offices: 600 Madison Avenue, New York, N.Y. 10022
Sales and Distribution offices: 120 Enterprise Avenue, Secaucus, N.J. 07094
In Canada: Canadian Manda Group, P.O. Box 920, Station U, Toronto, Ontario M8Z 5P9
Queries regarding rights and permissions should be addressed to
Carol Publishing Group, 600 Madison Avenue, New York, N.Y. 10022

Carol Publishing Group books are available at special discounts for
bulk purchases, for sales promotion, fund-raising, or educational
purposes. Special editions can be created to specifications. For
details, contact: Special Sales Department, Carol Publishing
Group, 120 Enterprise Avenue, Secaucus, N.J. 07094

Manufactured in the United States of America
10 9 8 7 6 5 4 3 2

Library of Congress Cataloging-in-Publication Data

Weiss, Murray.
    Palm Beach Babylon : sins, scams, and scandals / Murray Weiss &
Bill Hoffmann.
        p.   cm.
    "A Birch Lane Press book."
    ISBN1-55972-141-3
    1. Palm Beach (Fla.)—History.   2. Upper classes—Florida—Palm
Beach—History.   I. Hoffmann, Bill.   II. Title.
F319.P2W44   1992
975.9'32—dc20

                                                        92-21346
                                                        CIP

FOR MY PARENTS,
BEATRICE AND JERRY WEISS,
MY SISTER, RENEE,
HER FAMILY, JAY AND LAUREN,
AND
THE WONDERFUL AND PATIENT
ANNE WELDON

FOR MY PARENTS,
BILL AND NANCY HOFFMANN,
WHO MADE IT ALL POSSIBLE

Contents

Acknowledgments

The authors want to extend their sincere appreciation to the following people for their very special roles in making this book a reality:

Mel Juffe; Linda Marx; Jane Dystel, our literary agent; Edward Sears, editor, the *Palm Beach Post*; Pete Hamill; Lou Colasuonno, editor, the *New York Post*; Richard Gooding, metropolitan editor, the *New York Post*; Jim Willse, publisher, the New York *Daily News*; Hillel Black, our editor at Carol Publishing Group; Mary Kate Leming and the generous staff at the *Palm Beach Post* library; Mortimer Matz; Erica Browne; Elizabeth Hoffmann; Jerry Schmetterer; Johnny Fontana; Richard Hurley; Jack Cole; Malcolm Balfour; Milena Jovanovitch; Buddy Golan and staff at the Historical Society of Palm Beach County; Vernon Shibla, photo editor, the *New York Post*; Michael Lipack, photo editor, the New York *Daily News*; Merrill Sherr and the staff of the *New York Post* library; Faigi Rosenthal and staff of the New York *Daily News* library; Judy Terkel; Eric Figueroa; Ed Cafasso; Tony Burton; Maureen O'Sullivan; Joan Runkel curator, the Flagler Museum; Clive Barnes; Frank Andrews; Joe Amari; Dave Johnston; Dennis Wickman; John Langton; Charles Carillo; Joan Richardson; Mike Koleniak; Mickey and Jeanne Burns; Charles Wenzelberg; Carole Lee; Shay Williams, and Donald Trump, for approving a tour of Mar-a-Lago.

And to those who must remain anonymous, we offer our heartfelt thanks.

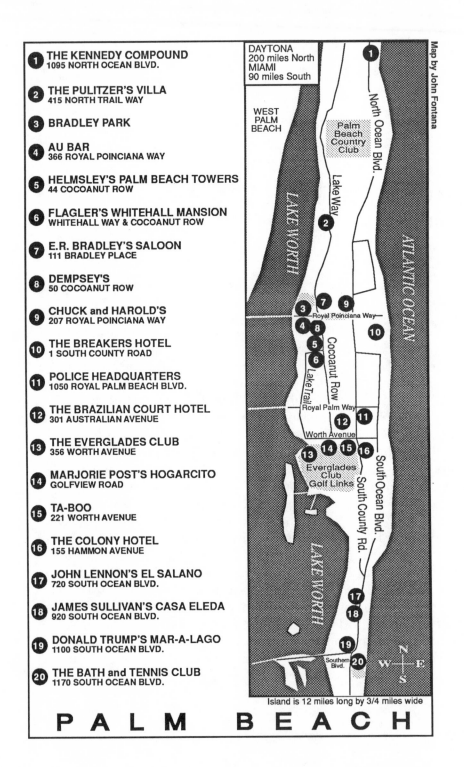

1. **THE KENNEDY COMPOUND**
   1095 NORTH OCEAN BLVD.

2. **THE PULITZER'S VILLA**
   415 NORTH TRAIL WAY

3. **BRADLEY PARK**

4. **AU BAR**
   366 ROYAL POINCIANA WAY

5. **HELMSLEY'S PALM BEACH TOWERS**
   44 COCOANUT ROW

6. **FLAGLER'S WHITEHALL MANSION**
   WHITEHALL WAY & COCOANUT ROW

7. **E.R. BRADLEY'S SALOON**
   111 BRADLEY PLACE

8. **DEMPSEY'S**
   50 COCOANUT ROW

9. **CHUCK and HAROLD'S**
   207 ROYAL POINCIANA WAY

10. **THE BREAKERS HOTEL**
    1 SOUTH COUNTY ROAD

11. **POLICE HEADQUARTERS**
    1050 ROYAL PALM BEACH BLVD.

12. **THE BRAZILIAN COURT HOTEL**
    301 AUSTRALIAN AVENUE

13. **THE EVERGLADES CLUB**
    356 WORTH AVENUE

14. **MARJORIE POST'S HOGARCITO**
    GOLFVIEW ROAD

15. **TA-BOO**
    221 WORTH AVENUE

16. **THE COLONY HOTEL**
    155 HAMMON AVENUE

17. **JOHN LENNON'S EL SALANO**
    720 SOUTH OCEAN BLVD.

18. **JAMES SULLIVAN'S CASA ELEDA**
    920 SOUTH OCEAN BLVD.

19. **DONALD TRUMP'S MAR-A-LAGO**
    1100 SOUTH OCEAN BLVD.

20. **THE BATH and TENNIS CLUB**
    1170 SOUTH OCEAN BLVD.

DAYTONA
200 miles North
MIAMI
90 miles South

WEST
PALM
BEACH

Palm
Beach
Country
Club

North Ocean Blvd.

Lake Way

LAKE WORTH

ATLANTIC OCEAN

Royal Poinciana Way

Cocoanut Row

Lake Trail

Royal Palm Way

Worth Avenue

South Ocean Blvd.

South County Rd.

Everglades
Club
Golf Links

LAKE WORTH

Southern
Blvd.

Map by John Fontana

Island is 12 miles long by 3/4 miles wide

P A L M   B E A C H

Palm Beach Babylon

1

Welcome to Babylon

The warm Florida breeze blew gently across Lake Worth from the mainland, softly rattling the fronds atop the swaying palm trees. As the warm night air embraced the tiny island, a trail of Rolls-Royces and Jaguars glided up to the doors of the newest nightspot on exclusive Palm Beach. Young valets in white sport shirts and tan shorts greeted each arriving car. It was Friday night, April 5, 1991, and the chic, trendy Au Bar was the center of one of the biggest scandals in America since Senator Ted Kennedy drove his car off the bridge at Chappaquiddick.

The imposing glass-and-wrought-iron doors swung open for each group of sleek, tanned partygoers entering the pulsing Au Bar. Beautiful young women were dressed in provocative miniskirts and body-hugging short dresses that displayed their bare legs and trim figures. For a touch of elegance, some set off their skimpy outfits with a single strand of pearls.

The older women in the crowd tended to wear loose-fitting silk shirts with pants. Several made the mistake of dressing in clothing designed for younger women—and they appeared sad and uninspired.

The men wore tasteful open-collared cotton sport shirts, slacks, and Gucci loafers. Several young men—their hair slick with gel—displayed gold chains around their necks, flashing smiles in every direction. The well-to-do Palm Beach men wore blazers, ascot or tie, and white trousers—without socks. Each clutched a cocktail while attempting to engage the younger women in conversation.

One distinguished-looking gentleman did not need to seek out companionship in the bustling crowd. He arrived with two beautiful, long-legged women who looked like models, one on each arm. With his silver hair neatly cut and his bushy gray mustache trimmed perfectly at the corners, the stately customer known only as "Neil" appeared to be the quintessential millionaire yachtsman. But he was no ordinary man-of-leisure. Neil was also wearing a short black miniskirt—cut fashionably at the thigh—and matching silk stockings, with a seam running up along the calves and high heel shoes.

Au Bar was swirling that evening with a raucous collection of celebrities and socialites, gawkers and reporters, hangers-on, and a cross-dresser or two. About two hundred people were seated around circular, candlelit tables, covered with white-and-peach-colored linen and surrounded with matching high-backed chairs. One week earlier, Senator Kennedy had sat at one of the tables, along with his twenty-three-year-old son, Patrick, and a nephew, William Kennedy Smith.

Another dozen people were comfortably ensconced on cushy floral-patterned sofas and couches that festively ringed a small dance floor. Champagne and wine buckets dotted the room. The wooden dance floor in the center of the room was crowded with couples gyrating to a robotic dance beat. "Did you ever make love on the backseat of a car?" singer Clarence Carter demanded. "I remember making love on the backseat of a car!" he announced, and then intoned, "I'm strokin' to the east. Strokin' to the west. Strokin' with the woman that I love the best. I'm strokin'!"

The elegant marble bar was surrounded three-deep with drinkers. People frantically exchanged credit cards or cash over the gray stone counter for flutes of champagne and cocktails. Several female patrons focused their gaze on the handsome tuxedoed bartenders, who happily provided them with another service. During "cigarette breaks," the employees—sometimes in small groups—took willing female patrons to an upstairs room for casual sex before returning to serve the next cocktail or Heineken beer.

When the partygoers at the bar were not reaching for beverages, they feverishly twisted in one direction and then the other to glimpse the action and keep track of the socialites and celebrities passing through the club.

Roxanne Pulitzer—who parlayed a ribald divorce from media heir Peter Pulitzer into three books, a nude *Playboy* magazine layout, and countless television talk-show appearances—was strategically situated between the Au Bar entrance and the dance floor. Sitting at her "usual" table, the lovely dirty-blond Roxanne was casually attired in a blue blazer, white blouse, and scrubbed jeans. She was with her boyfriend,

Jean de la Moussaye, a French count, race-car driver, and convicted fence.

The popular Roxanne and her count were involved in another Palm Beach scandal. De la Moussaye's estranged wife, Canadian newspaper heiress Francine McMahon, had accused the count of adultery. And she blamed the celebrated "Prize Pulitzer" for destroying her marriage.

On this late Friday night in Au Bar, Roxanne was providing her unique perspective on Palm Beach life and the island's publicity-conscious society to a small circle of fawning reporters looking for an angle, quote, or a soundbite.

Diagonally across the room from Roxanne, in an alcove beyond a blaring overhead speaker, another collection of journalists and television correspondents engulfed Michele Cassone, a frumpy twenty-seven-year-old waitress at a Palm Beach Italian restaurant. The nearest Michele had ever come to fame was when her family baked a popular Italian bread in the suburbs of New York and Connecticut and delivered the baked goods in trucks that bore the Cassone name. But now Michele had emerged as the "other woman" in the burgeoning scandal that involved an Easter-weekend allegation of rape behind the oceanfront walls of the three million-dollar Kennedy compound on Palm Beach.

As champagne splashed from her glass, Michele regaled the eager press, recalling her visit to the Kennedy mansion at the very hour Patricia Bowman was allegedly being raped on the estate's backyard lawn. Omitting no details, Michele told how she was necking with twenty-three-year-old Patrick Kennedy in his room when his father, Senator Ted Kennedy, suddenly appeared at the door in a long shirt without his pants and sporting a "weird look" on his face. For several hours, Michele lovingly repeated her entire story for any newspaper, wire service, or television correspondent with a notebook or micro-phone. Standing nearby, and also monitoring her performance, was Michele's friend and roommate, Gaynor Gwynne. The gangly blond Gwynne bears a striking resemblance to her famous father, Fred Gwynne, the popular stage actor and television star best known as Herman Munster in "The Munsters" and Office Muldoon in "Car 54, Where Are You?"

In an odd way, the patron who seemed the most interested in Michele and the other goings-on in Au Bar was a tall salt-and-pepper haired man who was the most conservatively dressed person in the room. This eagle-eyed spectator was Mark Schnapp, a Miami lawyer who had been retained by William Kennedy Smith, the grandson of "Bootlegger" Joe

Kennedy and a nephew of late president John F. Kennedy. Smith, a thirty-year-old medical student, had been accused of raping Patricia Bowman at the Kennedy mansion a week earlier, on March 29, Good Friday. Because their star-crossed encounter began at Au Bar, Schnapp was in the nightspot to "inspect" the club where they had met.

Standing beneath a thumping speaker a few feet from where Michele was "holding court," Schnapp looked bewildered by the whirling activity about him. A former high-ranking prosecutor, he was accustomed to less raucous evenings, discussing legal strategy with other attorneys or sipping beers with FBI agents at Tobacco Road, a funky low-key blues bar in Miami. He had never been to Au Bar. To Schnapp, a cautious and earnest lawyer with a controlled lifestyle, the flamboyant scene at Au Bar must have appeared as bizarre as the goings-on in the Wookie Bar of *Star Wars*.

As he watched the extraordinary spectacle, an exotic woman in a tight blue designer dress started to dance nearby with an assortment of eager partners. A couple of sharp-eyed reporters who also scanned the scene noticed the sexy dancer as she suddenly pranced over to the bar and picked the astonished Schnapp out of the crowd. Before Schnapp could move, the dark-haired beauty was standing in front of him, drink in hand, searching for a new partner.

Schnapp may not have recognized his playful admirer, but she was Hyo-Sook "Suki" Sullivan, a Korean-born divorcee in another sensational Palm Beach story. (Suki's millionaire ex-husband, James Sullivan, was a once-influential political figure on the island who had fallen from grace. The FBI had accused him of masterminding the contract assassination of his second wife, partly to marry the ravenous Suki.)

Obviously, the last thing in the world Schnapp desired was to be dragged into service as an involuntary participant in the Au Bar bacchanalia. For him, the Palm Beach revelry was merely a piece of the fact picture in a legal case that had become deadly serious. He quickly squeezed a path through the crowd, finally pushing his way out of the heavy front doors.

A reporter who followed Schnapp saw him standing in the night air outside Au Bar. Instead of the loud bar noise, he could hear the sounds of water lapping against the bridge spanning the Lake Worth estuary just a few yards away. Across the waterway, he could see the evening lights dotting West Palm Beach on the mainland. Anyone standing there could not help but marvel at the whirling scene inside Au Bar and what variety of desires the club must satisfy for exclusive Palm Beach.

It is somehow symbolic that this tiny nightspot at the center of a great American scandal sits at the corner of a tract of land where modern-day Palm Beach was founded. Nearly a century earlier, Henry Morrison Flagler cleared dense jungle and erected the sprawling, light-hearted Royal Poinciana Hotel in 1893 as an exclusive, luxurious resort for the nation's rich and privileged. The Royal Poinciana was then the world's largest hotel, a six-story wooden structure that stretched from the shore as though it were a vast skyscraper laid on one side.

In 1905, Henry James, famed Anglo-American writer, stood on the great lawn of the Royal Poinciana. "To stand off and see it rear its incoherent crest above its gardens was to remember—and quite with relief—nothing but the processional outline of Windsor Castle that could appear to march with it," James wrote.

The inspiring hotel and resort was Flagler's vision, just as the Standard Oil Company had been his creation decades earlier. Flagler was the "brains" behind John D. Rockefeller, his better-known partner in Standard Oil and America's first billionaire. And from the start, Palm Beach was an instant success, with the winter seasons attracting the Vanderbilts and the Rockefellers, the Carnegies and the Mellons, the Phippses and the Drexels, the Stotesburys and the Morgans.

Soon the narrow, twelve-mile island with only a dozen settlers was transformed into America's Riviera, outshining the famous resorts of Europe at the same time this country was claiming its place as a world power. With grand Arabian Nights mansions and lavish champagne and caviar parties for hundreds of guests, Palm Beach emerged as the playground for the country's most influential industrialists and financiers, aristocrats and diplomats, politicians and inventors.

The island was a reward for the select few people who engineered America's great industrial revolution with their ingenuity, vision, and grit, driving the nation to the fore in the twentieth century. The tiny island became a private resort for Woolworth and Wanamaker, Post and Hutton, Dodge and Firestone, Kennedy and Pulitzer.

In addition to the titans of business, commerce, and banking, Palm Beach has always served royalty. The Duke and Duchess of Windsor, Russian Grand Duke Dmitri and King Zahir of Afghanistan, Countess of Lauderdale and the Duchess of Southerland, King Saud and the Maharajah of Baroda, King Hussein of Jordan, and Prince Charles and Lady Diana have enjoyed the island's splendor, as do the heads of state of virtually every European and South American country.

And the island has been home to many of America's great artists, composers, and couturiers. Irving Berlin composed music on Worth Avenue. Isadora Duncan danced at the Breakers Hotel. Florenz Ziegfeld owned a mansion on Palm Beach. Estee Lauder and Ancky Revson Johnson also live on the island. Few people know it, but the American sport shirt was created—quite by accident—on Palm Beach by Addison Mizner, the island's famed, and corpulent, mansion designer.

Like sun and sand, sin and scandal have dogged the millionaires who have graced Palm Beach society since its birth a century ago. Flagler's own enormous life serves as a paradigm for the notorious, adulterous, abusive, and wasteful conduct that has been a companion of this storied island. The founding father of Palm Beach perceived power and influence as "rights" that were earned while amassing a great fortune.

Flagler considered criticism an annoying byproduct of wealth. When he was corrupting the government of Florida in 1901 to divorce his second wife in order to marry his youthful mistress, Flagler said, "I have lived too long and have been a target too often to allow myself to be disturbed by the jealousy of others who have been less fortunate."

Since its inception, Palm Beach has served as the balmy backdrop for the nation's great affairs. Dan Shalek, who owned the island's "in" nightspot, the Patio, in the late 1940s, observed: "A man married to a beautiful girl has more chance of losing her in Palm Beach than anywhere else in the country."

Marjorie Merriweather Post, the heir to a $250 million cereal fortune, and Palm Beach resident, endured four calamitous marriages. Her three daughters made ten trips to the altar.

General Douglas MacArthur and his debutante wife, Louise Brooks Stotesbury, wrangled on Palm Beach. And when it came to ribald breakups, few divorces could match those of the Firestones and the Pulitzers.

It was Marjorie Post who once remarked, "There is more money, more champagne, more caviar, more Rolls-Royces, and, of course, more affluence in Palm Beach than all the rest of America put together." In 1986, there were no fewer than four thousand millionaires living on the island, seventeen hundred heads of corporations, over five hundred mansions and five hundred Rolls-Royces—collectively the single greatest concentration of wealth in the country. Where there once were twelve settlers, today there are 7,659 full-time residents whose ranks increase to nearly forty thousand during the winter season.

In 1952, Cleveland Amory, author of *The Last Resorts*, noted that when one arrives on Palm Beach, "You enter what amounts to an island of privilege, in many ways the most remarkable one left in this country."

For one hundred years, the island's celebrated brood has enjoyed the trappings of great wealth. And through it all, Palm Beach has remained an insular society for the "rich and famous," a tropical retreat where they are swathed in luxury and protected by an invisible shield that only money can pierce.

When Henry James traveled America in 1904 and 1905 studying the country's gentry, he stayed in cushy, quaint Newport, Rhode Island, another mecca for The Rich. It was in Newport that James was informed of a new exclusive resort that was attracting the nation's wealthiest, most influential, and most powerful people.

James ventured to Florida, which, like much of the nation, was still more frontier than civilization. For three days, from February 15 to 17, 1905, Henry James stayed at Flagler's "other" Palm Beach hotel, the Breakers, overlooking the Atlantic Ocean. On several occasions, James rode a horse-drawn railroad car that shepherded guests across the three-quarter-mile wide island from the Breakers to the Royal Poinciana.

Standing outside the Royal Poinciana—virtually on the place where Mark Schnapp tried to calm his dizzying mind in 1991 outside Au Bar— Henry James collected his thoughts on Palm Beach. James observed, "As I had gathered in advance, at Palm Beach, it had been promised...that there, as nowhere else, in America, one would find Vanity Fair in full blast."

2

The Tycoon Who Began It All: Henry Morrison Flagler

Palm Beach is a place unlike any other in the world. And only the other day it was merely sand and marsh and brush, with palms that grew from cocoanuts which drifted ashore from the wreck of an East Indian schooner. And Flagler came and saw what there was. And then he saw what there would be.

—Edwin LeFevre, travel writer, 1909

It occurred to me very strongly that someone with sufficient means ought to provide accommodations for that class of people who are not sick, but who come here to enjoy the climate, have plenty of money, but could find no satisfactory way of spending it.

—Henry Morrison Flagler, 1882

Somebody screamed "FIIIIRRRE!" and, like a newborn baby's first piercing cry, Palm Beach was born.

The panicked voice belonged to one of hundreds of black laborers whose shantytown was ablaze on the island of Palm Beach across the Lake Worth waterway. Rushing to the shoreline of the heavily shrubbed Florida mainland, they watched as fifty-foot flames engulfed their small wooden shacks in the shadow of the new Royal Poinciana Hotel. In an hour, the roaring inferno reduced their tinderbox homes to cinder and ash, leaving a great smoldering ruin near the magnificent hotel they had just completed for Henry Morrison Flagler only days before.

For the past eight months, nearly a thousand laborers drawn from the post–Civil War South—and now suddenly homeless—had struggled to build Flagler's Royal Poinciana Hotel out of the jungle and swamps of Palm Beach island. The millionaire had promised them bonuses and a great celebration if they completed his 1,750-room hotel in time for the 1894 winter season. The workers responded. Toiling through summer— the hottest, most intolerable months of the Floridian year, with temperatures topping one hundred degrees—the workers struggled to complete Flagler's vision of an exclusive island resort hotel for America's rich and powerful.

As the deadline neared, the young black workforce labored day and night. Eleven men died during the backbreaking construction, but the work never stopped, not even for their funerals.

The hotel work crews won a race against Flagler's railroad construction laborers, who were laying track and building bridges to allow trains to provide door-to-door service from America's eastern states to the Royal Poinciana. Flagler had been forging south through Florida with his money, building a railroad through thick, mosquito-infested, alligator-ridden jungle, building hotels, creating jobs and commerce as he went along.

Throughout the construction of the Royal Poinciana, Flagler, a tall, affable man with a shock of wavy gray hair and thick gray mustache, had conversed easily with his workers, presenting a concerned grandfatherly image. He paid the unskilled laborers $1.10 per hour, forty cents above the national standard of seventy cents, which seemed generous, but served more as an ironclad insurance policy taken out by a shrewd businessman to ensure that his workers would not defect. He had also pitted workers against each other in a calculated psychological game to get them to build faster. He needed the tight timetable to bring the first trainload of millionaires to Palm Beach in time for the inaugural winter season.

Flagler had a vision of transforming swampy, undeveloped Palm Beach into a private American Riviera and bringing the rest of Florida's vast frontierland into the modern era. The year was 1894. Grover Cleveland was president. Thomas Alva Edison prepared for a public demonstration of his revolutionary invention, the moving-picture camera, with film of a boxing match, a dancing girl, and a baby in a bathtub. The Republic of Hawaii was officially recognized by the United States.

The country was in a depression, politicians battled over a gold-versus-silver standard for the nation, and a violent railroad worker's strike against the giant Pullman Palace Car Company was in progress.

But there were few, if any, signs of a depression, of economic or social turmoil, on Palm Beach, a twelve-mile expanse of hot, thick jungle cooled by gentle ocean breezes off the coast of mainland Florida.

When the Royal Poinciana was completed, one obstacle remained before the doors to the grand halls and parlors of the world's greatest hotel could open. Flagler's vision of Palm Beach did not include the ramshackle, thatched-roof colony called "the Styx" where his "colored" workers and their families lived. He knew men of great money would not vacation on an island where poor, illiterate shanty blacks—the sons and daughters of African slaves freed three decades earlier—also lived. He knew they would not pay hundred-dollar-a-night hotel fees—rates unheard of at the time—in such an atmosphere.

With the grand opening of the Royal Poinciana only weeks away, Flagler announced he was throwing a special carnival for his workers, a hearty reward for their Herculean efforts in getting the world's largest hotel completed on schedule. A big top was erected on the mainland, directly across from the island, and a circus the size of Ringling Brothers was brought in. Chefs were hired to lay out huge buffets. Games were set up for the children. Everybody planned to have a gala time, courtesy of kindly Mr. Flagler.

On a warm January afternoon in 1894, the laborers and their families left the Styx for what would be the last time. They rowed west across the Lake Worth estuary. Screams of joy from the children anticipating circus clowns and trained animals and big-top excitement filled the air during the thirty-minute trip. Flagler stood on the shore of Palm Beach, waving, smiling.

As soon as the boats reached the mainland, scores of Flagler's white workers on Palm Beach converged on the Styx. They quickly collected the families' belongings, clothes, and valuables and carted them away. They then doused the town with gasoline.

At the height of the carnival, Flagler's henchmen stood at the edge of the doomed shantytown and lit a match to the first house. The gas-soaked community ignited within seconds, and the blue afternoon sky above Palm Beach filled with billowing black smoke. The incredible bonfire could be seen from fifteen miles away. The smoke wafted through the big top within minutes, and panic erupted. As five pairs of clowns did pratfalls on the stage to the gay music of the circus orchestra, the laborers tore from the circus tent, frantically heading toward the shore.

There was nothing they could do. There was not enough time to get back to the island to save their homes. Screaming, crying, clutching each other, they watched the pyrotechnics in shock and despair. But Mr. Flagler was there to lend a hand. He announced that after the terrible, "accidental" blaze erupted, his executive workers risked life and limb running into the burning Styx to save as many belongings as they could. Flagler now offered to sell his displaced laborers land where the circus had been. He said if he they built new homes there, he would pay for the town's public utilities, including a water system, post office, and, particularly after the terrible Styx tragedy, a fire department.

Unaware of his true motives or simply helpless to do anything else, the laborers accepted Flagler's "generosity." They did not know it, but in 1890, when Flagler had purchased the future site of the Royal Poinciana Hotel, he had also paid forty-five thousand dollars for several hundred acres of land opposite the island, where West Palm Beach now stands. His vision of Palm Beach had always included establishing a city on the mainland where the "help" would live. They were not the first market Flagler had cornered.

At the time of the Styx fire, Flagler was the genious partner of John D. Rockefeller in the Standard Oil Company and a leading figure in American industry. He was easily capable of using unethical practices to succeed.

Henry Morrison Flagler, the son of a poor, frugal preacher, was born in upstate New York. He left home at the age of fourteen to join a half brother in Ohio, arriving with a nickel, four pennies, and a lucky French coin he kept with him throughout his life.

Flagler took a job at the L. G. Harkness Mercantile Shop, selling food, nails, tools, and brandy by day, sleeping in a dingy back room at night. Over the next seven years, he demonstrated a true gift for business, becoming a leading salesman and a four-hundred-dollar-a-year partner in the company. At age twenty-three, he moved to the firm's flagship store in Bellevue, Ohio, and proposed to Harkness's twenty-year-old daughter, Mary. The couple married on November 9, 1853.

The Harkness firm soon branched out into the liquor business, a move that would bring Flagler into contact briefly with the man who would later change his life—a grain broker named John D. Rockefeller.

When the Civil War erupted, Flagler avoided service by paying a "second"—polite language for a replacement—to serve in his place. It was a common—if cowardly—practice for men of money at the time. Following the war, he sold his liquor interests and invested in a new speculative venture—salt. But the market collapsed and he lost $150,000. Henry Morrison Flagler—Ohio's premiere sales whiz—now found himself fifty thousand dollars in personal debt.

Almost destitute, Flagler took a menial job selling wool, often going hungry all day so he could feed his wife and baby daughter at night. In 1866, he packed up and moved his family to Cleveland—"City of Opportunity"—and renewed his acquaintance with Rockefeller, who had entered the oil business. Flagler saw the challenge and quickly began making suggestions to Rockefeller on how to maximize his profits. Soon he was a trusted—and well-paid—adviser. Flagler paid off his debts and bought into Rockefeller's company. Henry and John walked to work together each morning in Cleveland, plotting strategies to increase the Rockefeller wealth. "A friendship founded on business is better than a business founded on friendship," Flagler later said.

Flagler soon developed a vision: to create an oil monopoly by strong-arming smaller companies and forcing them out of business. He started his plan by cutting secret deals with rail companies to get reduced rates to ship his oil from landlocked refineries to larger markets and ultimately New York Harbor. There he could sell at slightly cheaper rates, undercutting the competition. This financial edge provided the leverage Flagler and Rockefeller needed to buy out smaller competitors.

After crushing the competition, all that was left to complete Flagler's vision was to establish a single company for the vast holdings in which the partners owned stock. In 1870, the Standard Oil Company was born. The act of incorporation "was a marvelous bit of brevity and a lesson for lawyers everywhere. It did not exceed 200 words," wrote David Chandler, a Flagler biographer. After several more years of tough wheeling and dealing, the team of Flagler and Rockefeller had it all: the nation's entire oil business, gathering, refining, and shipping, the most complete moneymaking machine ever constructed in American history.

By 1876, Flagler was worth $6 million—the equivalent of $120 million today. In that historic year, he made his first visit to Florida. His wife's health was deteriorating badly. She had given birth to a son, Henry Harkness, in 1870, but the delivery was difficult and she was left an invalid. Her doctors urged Flagler to take his ailing wife to Florida's warmer climate to ease Mary's crippling bronchitis. During twenty-three years of marriage, Henry Flagler and his wife had been virtually inseparable. He had been a totally devoted husband.

Even during the rigorous years when he was forging Standard Oil, Henry spent only two nights away from his wife. Now the forty-six-year-old Flagler and his forty-three-year-old wife traveled together to St. Augustine. The city had twenty-three hundred residents and was considered Florida's most modern, Flagler found the weather glorious, but the hotels were primitive and crude. Always the astute business-man, Flagler could not fail to notice that Florida land was cheap; even oceanfront property seemed inexpensive. But Florida was still a gritty, poor southern state, a sort of Wild West frontier in the Southeast. Flagler imagined what could be developed if this beauty and warmth and clear water were harnessed and packaged correctly. The intriguing notion only made him feel more detached from his daily business at Standard Oil. The couple spent two months in St. Augustine and then returned to their Fifth Avenue town house in New York.

The recuperative powers of Florida's sunshine failed to halt Mary's slide, forcing Flagler to hire a full-time nurse for his now dying wife. The nurse was Ida Alice Shourds, an attractive green-eyed redhead. A struggling actress from a poor Kansas family, Ida had attended nursing school so that she could earn a living. There was little Ida could do to ease Mary's pain. But she was there for Henry, who was starved for the affection his wife could no longer give.

As Mary lay on her deathbed in May 1881, Flagler rented a secluded thirty-two-acre, forty-room mansion named Satan's Toe in Mamaroneck, New York, on Long Island Sound as a retreat for his ailing wife. After she died, the reserved Mr. Flagler seemed to blossom. He spent weekends with Ida Alice in Manhattan and was seen frequently taking in Broadway shows, attending balls, and staying in small, private hotels with his green-eyed lover. And, with Ida playing hostess, Flagler soon began to throw huge parties at Satan's Toe.

Ida was eighteen years younger than the fifty-one-year-old Flagler. He was a spry young boy around her. Despite his happiness, the relationship created gossip. To silence the critics, Flagler married Ida Alice on June 5, 1883. Within weeks of their marriage, Ida Alice, no longer the nurse and mistress, went on huge wardrobe-buying binges in New York and continued the endless rounds of parties at Satan's Toe, with guest lists of over one hundred.

Flagler's children were bothered by Ida's spending sprees. They, and many of Flagler's friends, saw Ida as a social climber and fortune hunter, with little discernible talent. But Henry seemed oblivious. "For fourteen years, I have devoted my time exclusively to business, and now I am pleasing myself," Flagler maintained.

Flagler turned his attention to Florida real estate. He decided to return to St. Augustine for a second look, combining a honeymoon with a vacation.

"I was surprised when I got there. There had been a wonderful change," he later wrote. "Instead of depressing accommodations of the years before, I found one of the most comfortable and best kept hotels in the world and filled, too, not with consumptives, but that class of society one meets at the great watering places of Europe—men who go there to enjoy themselves and not for the benefit of their health."

He added, "It occurred to me very strongly that someone with sufficient means ought to provide accommodations for that class of people who are not sick, but who come here to enjoy the climate, have plenty of money, but could find no satisfactory way of spending it."

He started by building the 540-room, $2.5 million Ponce de León Hotel in St. Augustine, the first great concrete building in America, on five and a half acres of unproductive orange groves. The Moorish–Spanish–style hotel opened in December 1887 and proved a great success. Guests marveled at the electric lights, the plush furnishings, the great dance halls. He followed the Ponce de León with a smaller hotel, the Alcazar, and then built a large fifteen-room home, Kirkside, with a huge entertaining hall for his wife.

Ida's thirst for luxuries seemed endless, and Flagler tried to grant her every wish. She enjoyed yachting. So Flagler bought two vessels, a sloop and a schooner, to satisfy her. When that was not enough, he purchased the finest yacht of its day, a 160-foot ship, which he named *Alicia*, after his wife's middle name. With Flagler and Ida spending hundreds of thousands of dollars, Flagler found himself in a cash crunch and was forced to sell twenty-five hundred shares of Standard Oil stock to meet $375,000 in bills. The temporary cash shortfall brought a sobering realization about Ida's lavish spending.

Then an unforeseen tragedy struck. Flagler's daughter, Carrie, gave birth, but complications set in. Within weeks, both mother and daughter were dead. Flagler retreated into his world of business, shunning his wife's party planning and social whirl. But Ida Alice persisted, her social itinerary, like Flagler's Standard Oil, an unyielding force. She held parties five nights a week, presiding over the affairs in the most expensive, extravagant and "extremely revealing décolleté," according to Chandler.

As the days passed, Ida began to act strangely, bursting into unprovoked tantrums and fights with Flagler that were loud, bizarre, and usually public. Her mood swings escalated. She ranted and raved to strangers about how she was going to dump Flagler and marry her true love. When asked who this love of her life was, she replied: "the czar of Russia." The late czar of Russia, that was. She spoke to the late Russian ruler regularly, she insisted, through a recently invented spiritual medium, the Ouija board.

Her outbursts were embarrassing. At any moment, she could turn a party or dinner into an extraordinarily uncomfortable evening, throwing food and screaming about what a miserable, adulterous old man Flagler was or how he mistreated her terribly. Soon Ida's problems became other people's concern. She nearly drowned a yachtful of party guests when she refused to return the *Alicia* to shore one evening in a storm. The rough seas thrashed the *Alicia* for six hours, nearly capsizing it, before the yacht steamed back to shore.

To ease the stress and isolation of living with a madwoman, Flagler went the route of his partner and good friend, John D. Rockefeller. He took a new mistress. She was Mary Lily Kenan, twenty-four, of Kenansville, a little town in North Carolina named after her well-to-do family. Mary Lily came from American stock. Her father had been a captain in the Confederate army and his name was well known throughout the South. Born in 1867, Mary Lily was thirty-seven years younger than Flagler. She first met the sixty-one-year-old millionaire and his wife, Ida, in 1891 in Newport, and soon became a regular at Ida's parties.

Like Ida, Mary Lily saw herself as a performer, except where Ida had little talent, Mary Lily was brimming with it. A classically trained singer and pianist, Mary Lily had graduated earlier that year with top honors from St. Mary's College in Raleigh, North Carolina. She was a compassionate, well-educated young woman whose long, thick, flowing dark hair, blue eyes, and full figure hypnotized Flagler. At five-foot-one and 105 pounds, she was much shorter and slighter than he. And with a narrow waist and large bust, she was very sexy. Henry Flagler was hooked.

She made the trip to St. Augustine to be with Flagler for the first time in 1892, traveling on his private railroad car, accompanied by a Flagler niece, Louise Wise, who acted as the "beard." In the perfumed nights of St. Augustine, Flager and Mary Lily secretly began a romance. Their affair continued in New York. When Flagler and Ida returned to St. Augustine the following winter, Mary Lily was there, telling people: "I'm with Mr. Flagler." The words were magic, opening doors to exclusive homes and parties. By that time, Flagler had also expanded his view of Florida.

One afternoon he took a yacht trip south, and for the first time saw Palm Beach—a narrow twelve-mile-long coral island, laden with coconut palms, where only fifty settlers lived. Most were a collection of frontiersmen and homesteaders from southern Michigan. One was a Confederate soldier named Lang, who deserted from the cause during the Civil War. Another was Charles Moore, a fugitive wanted in Chicago. The palms were the remainder of a shipwreck of the cargo ship *La Providencia*, which had deposited twenty thousand coconuts along the island's shoreline. There were just thirty to forty tiny cottages, two stores, and a small hotel run by Captain E. N. Dimick. Stopping on the island, Flagler stood on the western shore of Palm Beach and looked across to the mainland where his sham circus would later be held. He pointed across the water and said, "In a few years there'll be a town over there as big as Jacksonville, and St. Augustine will be a way station for it."

In two short years, Flagler worked his magic. His black labor force of about a thousand men erected the majestic, six-story Royal Poinciana Hotel in a record eight months, complete with pavilion, bathhouses, and local yacht club. And his railroad crews were not far behind, charging south with two hundred miles of track from Daytona. With the Royal Poinciana preparing for its grand opening, the only obstacle to realizing Flagler's vision was the eyesore shantytown, the Styx.

By 1894, Flagler was worth in excess of $75 million. His partner John D. Rockefeller was on his way to becoming the world's first billionaire, thanks to Flagler. Years later, Rockefeller confessed before Congress that the idea for Standard Oil was Flagler's. "I wish I had the brains to think of it," he remarked. Flagler, he said, was the man with "the most imagination" he had ever known.

Imaginative, competitive, kindly, yet ruthless. That was Flagler. He put all four traits to use in devising his fiery solution to the shantytown on Palm Beach. In January he burned the Styx to the ground. The following month he opened the Royal Poinciana.

The Royal Poinciana was a breathtaking wooden structure, painted yellow and white. It could cater to 1,750 guests at one time, and its maze of corridors was so complex and intricate that if laid out straight it would stretch three miles. The Royal Poinciana was also the world's first completely electrified hotel, with its thousands of lamps powered by huge underground generators.

Flagler's great speculative venture paid off immediately. Word spread throughout the nation of his achievement, of a luxurious resort hotel unsurpassed in the world. Just two years after surveying the dense jungles of Palm Beach, Flagler's dream had become a reality: an island dedicated to the rich. In March 1896, the first train arrived on Palm Beach on a new spur from the main line, bringing passengers from the "Four Hundred," the most exalted members of American high society.

America's famous families arrived to be pampered: the Vanderbilts, the Rockefellers, and the Carnegies. Within a month's time, the Royal Poinciana's guest list read like a Who's Who of American industrialists, financiers, politicians, and artists, who—along with their wives, children, servants, mistresses—flocked to see this new, landscaped paradise called Palm Beach.

In order for guests to comprehend his vision, Flagler had specially designed rickshaws built to shuttle them around the island in comfort. The vehicles were called "Afromobiles" in tribute to the black laborers who pedaled them. During the season, the hotel staff included a chambermaid for every four rooms, a bellman in every hall, and four hundred waiters. These were the same men who had recently been burned off the island and now came back each day by boat to perform their new jobs catering to the rich and then returned at night to their homes in West Palm Beach.

"Yesterday a swamp was here, today you see the wizardry of the dollar," wrote Edwin Lefevre, a renowned travel and financial reporter:

> To make a lawn here was more difficult than it would have been to spread a sheet of solid silver on this spot, or on the golf links, where Mr. Flagler's engineers dumped thousands of carloads of earth.
>
> Lawns you have seen before, but not these curious trees and strange shrubs and polychromatic leaves; uncanny screw pines with clumps of exposed roots like writhing serpents upholding the trunk. The gaudy blossoms of the hibiscus that suggest the red lights on a Christmas tree, palms of diverse kinds... and over it all the azure splendor of the Florida sky canopying a scene of so exotic a beauty that you are not merely miles, but whole worlds away.
>
> On both sides of Lake Drive grow cocoanut palms—lithe, almost animate. You see them waving to themselves in the mirror of the lake, perennially fascinated by their beauty. Along the glaring white road, through tunnels of verdure, the noiseless wheelchair carries you, each strange tree adding impressions of a land utterly foreign. It is as if your soul were receiving mysterious little taps—Tap! Tap! Tap!—psychic hammer strokes that numb other thoughts and lull your senses into a Floridian mood.

Grand champagne-drenched drag parties became the norm in Flager's hotel. Rich and powerful men who had made the country prosper were invited to dress as famous women and show off their alter egos. And they did, wearing wigs and heavy makeup, frilly corsets and stockings under long, sequined gowns. They spared no expense for their costumes. Henry Flagler's favorite impersonation was that of Marie Antoinette. He received thunderous applause when he made his dainty, dignified entrance. The tall, stately Flagler was the star of the show.

The Washington Ball, the grandest of the drag parties, was a gaudy, lavish affair that attracted upward of a thousand guests. The ballroom of the Royal Poinciana was festooned with thousands of miniature electric lights set in scores of Chinese lanterns, the glow reflecting off the Baccarat crystal. The walls were lined with stately columns of palm leaves, ferns, and pine branches.

For this event, Flagler outdid himself, dressing, according to the *Palm Beach Daily News*, as Martha Washington, in a stunning dress "trimmed with bands of miniature silk flags and a palm leaf boutonierre." As he made his entrance, the band stopped playing, revelers stared in stunned silence at "America's first lady." With the exception of his bushy mustache and a brown lighted cigar protruding from his painted lips, Flagler looked like a stately and statuesque dowager.

After the balls ended, Flagler's specially recruited hotel whores would be waiting for his rich and powerful male guests to spirit them off to special rooms far away from their wives.

Flagler kept his own young mistress, Mary Lily Kenan, in a luxurious style that cost him several thousand dollars a week. He brought her to Palm Beach in his lavishly decorated private railroad car that featured a huge bedroom complete with four-poster bed, marble bathtub, and walk-in closet stocked with custom-made women's clothing.

He moved her into the Reef, a cottage adorned with antique furniture and china from around the world. Her own staff of about a dozen maids, servants, and cooks remained on call twenty-four hours a day. Flagler showered her with gifts of jewelry—long pearl necklaces, diamond brooches, and gold earrings. She shopped for all the latest fashions—charging everything to "Mr. Flagler's account."

But for all of the gifts, all of the clothes, all of the pampering, Mary Lily's life was not the dream existence it seemed. She learned the difficulty of being attached to a man of power and position who often had to ignore her to attend to business.

Henry's Royal Poinciana was so successful he built an "annex" in 1895 on the ocean side of the island one-quarter mile away to accommodate more guests. To his surprise, the annex eventually became the more popular Breakers Hotel because of its commanding view of the ocean, and it was enlarged time and time again. Part of the popularity developed after Flagler recruited a flamboyant business acquantance from St. Augustine, Col. Edward R. Bradley, to build an opulent casino in 1898 that would outclass the gaming halls of Monte Carlo. Soon Bradley's Beach Club, opposite the Royal Poinciana, attracted aristocracy from two continents to play roulette, hazard, and chemin de fer.

Even at the parties thrown at Flagler's hotels, Mary Lily knew she could not linger around the man she loved, for fear of causing a scandal. Young and so often alone, Mary Lily began to spend long afternoons socializing with other Palm Beach women over drinks. She drank whiskey and bourbon in increasing quantities. And like many women of the day, Mary Lily began to enjoy the fashionable practice of taking opium.

At the turn of the century, opium, morphine, and cocaine were all legal drugs—intoxicants sold over the counter to "ladies and gentlemen of class and moderation." Cocaine was such a commonly used drug that until 1909 it was a key ingredient in Coca-Cola. Mary Lily fit the description of the recreational drug user: she was young, pretty, full of life; she had every luxury she could possibly want. In return, she was a comforting figure to her beloved benefactor, as the madness that infected Flagler's wife escalated. Ida was going out of her way to make her husband's life miserable. She began threatening to kill him. Her doctors took the threats seriously and urged Flagler to sleep in another room with the door locked.

Flagler asked his close friend Dr. George Shelton to keep an eye on her behavior. One awful night at Satan's Toe, Ida began ranting about how Henry mistreated her by savagely beating and cursing her. All of this took place in front of family friends. Dr. Shelton quickly shuffled her out of the room and gave her a sedative. Everything seemed calm until Ida suddenly sprang to life with a new torrent of charges, telling of wild sex orgies she had had in the house with prominent New Yorkers and European aristocrats. Wicked sex parties in which men grappled with women, men with men and women with women; of whips and of pain.

Then she dragged the stunned physician into her bedroom and locked the door. Producing three pebbles, she told him they held magical powers that could cure paralysis and create pregnancies in women.

Dr. Shelton made a frantic appeal for two mental-health specialists to join him, and when they arrived, Ida went into a frenzy. Rushing through the house, she began smashing every bit of expensive china she could find. Maids, servants, and Henry himself dived for cover as the cursing madwoman hurled cups and dishes like discuses through the air.

"Henry, he's trying to poison me! I can't go anywhere. He's filled the house with Russian spies!" she claimed.

The tirade was the end for Flagler. He had his second wife committed to the Choate Sanitarium, in Pleasantville, New York, some forty miles from Manhattan. Flagler told friends it was the most difficult decision of his life.

The reason for Ida's madness was a mystery. One of her many fantasies pictured Flagler cavorting with various women. He skillfully had deflected suspicions about his "friend" Mary Lily. But another even more clandestine relationship was about to be revealed in divorce papers filed by an irate husband in Syracuse, New York.

Mr. C. W. Foote claimed that his wife of five years, Helen Long, had had a seven-month affair with Flagler. Flagler was so enamored of Helen that he had bought a townhouse for her at 27 East 57th Street, in Manhattan, and had given her $400,000 worth of Standard Oil stock. Helen and Henry also had sex regularly on Flagler's yacht *Alicia*. Long's husband sued Flagler, but the case was soon dropped. According to some acquaintances, Henry, who never denied the charge, paid the husband handsomely for his silence.

Just as Flagler had finished cleaning up the "Foote matter," a doctor in Mamaroneck, New York, sent word to the millionaire that his wife Ida Alice had improved enough to return home to Satan's Toe. But it became evident her time away had not cured her permanently. She began to ramble in conversation and soon begged her husband for another Ouija board. When he refused, she bribed a servant and started holding seances in her room to speak with her secret lover, the czar of Russia. Flagler wanted to put her away again, but fearing publicity, he turned his home into a private asylum, hiring a staff of psychiatrists and orderlies.

Ida threatened suicide, and all kitchen knives, forks, and sharp instruments were locked away. One afternoon she found a pair of scissors and plunged them into the chest of one of her doctors, barely missing his heart. That settled it. Ida Alice had to be committed before she killed someone or herself. Flagler had her sent to an expensive sanitarium run by renowned psychiatrist Dr. Carlos McDonald. She lived in her own private cottage on the sanitarium grounds and had her own maids.

After committing Ida again, Flagler and Mary Lily became inseparable. But the fact that she was still a mistress irked Mary Alice's family. The Kenan clan reacted by confronting Flagler, complaining that their thirty-two-year-old "single" daughter had been compromised and was now viewed as "damaged goods" that no gentleman would marry. Making matters worse, the life of a mistress was distressing Mary Lily. She began to receive inquiries from newspaper columnists asking just how friendly she and Henry Flagler were.

Feeling pressure from the growing disapproval, Flagler drew on his vast wealth and business skills to get his way. First, he boldy proposed marriage and presented Mary Lily with a long string of graduated Oriental pearls, the largest of which was the size of a robin's egg, held together with a twelve-karat diamond clasp and complemented with a diamond bracelet. The cost: $1 million.

When an excited Mary Lily told her parents of the engagement, they coldly reminded her that Flagler was still a married man and could never get a divorce, whether or not his wife was insane, because divorce was outlawed in New York, where Flagler resided. They were concerned that without the real prospect of a husband Mary Lily had no future security. Her grandmother told Mary Lily to get rid of Henry. It did not bother her that he was married, but she said that the bad publicity for the Kenan family wasn't worth it.

Flagler responded in a way many millionaires do when they are used to getting their way—with dollars. On April 3 1899, Flagler transferred $1 million in Standard Oil stock to Mary Lily to silence her family's concern about her security. And then he ordered a grand mansion built for her on Lake Worth on Palm Beach. Now, even Mary Lily's prudish father approved of the illicit love, possibly, some say, because he had orchestrated the large payoff to his daughter.

With the Kenan clan comfortably in his corner, Flagler moved forward with his plan to marry Mary Lily—a masterstroke of influence peddling that even today is heralded by Florida's legal world as a seamless blend of money, brains, and sleazy backroom deals.

At the turn of the century, divorce was not recognized in the Empire State, where Flagler wielded considerable influence but not the kind of power he enjoyed in Florida. Flagler owned railroads, hotels, huge tracts of land. Although he publicly said he hated newspapers, he understood their influence. Therefore, the shrewd businessman secretly began buying controlling interests in Florida's most powerful newspapers, intending to sway public opinion. He surreptitiously founded Palm Beach's first paper, the *Weekly Lake Worth News*—which later became the *Palm Beach Daily News*. But when asked about possible newspaper holdings, Flagler insisted, "If I had to take my choice between a den of rattlesnakes and a newspaper, I think I'd prefer the snakes."

On April 23, 1899, less than three weeks after his marriage proposal to Mary Lily, Flagler announced that he was officially changing his legal residence from New York to Florida "strictly for business." Although those business reasons were never explained, four of the state's biggest newspapers—his papers—heralded the imminent arrival of "Mr. Flagler—the state's newest No. 1 citizen!"

In Florida the only ground for divorce was adultery. A couple could not even consent to divorce for other reasons. However, on April 9, 1901, the Florida legislature convened and an odd bill had made its way to the top of the state's agenda. The law would make "incurable insanity" legitimate grounds for divorce. Only a few weeks earlier, Flagler had asked his lawyers to petition the state of New York for a medical ruling on his wife's mental competency. The court had already certified that Ida Alice was insane and incapable of taking care of herself.

The new divorce amendment sailed through both the legislature and the house in record time and landed on the desk of Governor William Jennings in three weeks. Introduced on the Senate floor on April 9, the bill passed on April 17 with little opposition and won full approval of the house two days later. On April 25, Jennings signed it into law.

Flagler and his lawyers took immediate advantage and filed papers at the courthouse that afternoon. The divorce was granted on August 14. The law was then quickly retired and never used again.

Flagler made it seem so easy. But it was his money that solved his problem. He had doled out $125,000 in bribes, including $15,000 to the governor and thousands to each politician who voted for the law. And for $20,000, he had also bribed at least one editor of a newspaper he didn't own to write favorably about the new law.

One Florida paper that Flagler didn't possess and couldn't sway was the *Tampa Herald*, which attacked the millionaire's tricky law bending, calling him a "little tin god on wheels to an army of politicians." As word of bribery spread, several politicians who had voted for the "Flagler bill" were severely criticized and eventually voted out of office.

Ida Alice Flagler never understood that she was now divorced, and she continued to live in her delusional world with thoughts of killing Henry and running off with the czar of Russia. She lived there comfortably, though. Flagler had signed over to her securities and property worth $2.3 million, which netted an annual income of

$120,000, enough for a dozen solid gold Ouija boards if she wanted them. His charity did not spring from the goodness of his heart. The divorce law required that a mentally disturbed spouse be cared for financially for the rest of her natural life.

Despite the maelstrom surrounding the new law, Flagler carried on without exhibiting the slightest concern. And, on August 24, 1901, ten days after obtaining his divorce from Ida Alice, the seventy-one-year-old industrialist married Mary Lily Kenan, his mistress of eleven years. Flagler's wedding present to his youthful thirty-four-year-old bride: a $1 million check and $2 million in registered government bonds. He also gave Lily's brother and two sisters substantial blocks of Standard Oil stock.

For the ceremony, Flagler built a private railroad through the bride's family's expansive estate in North Carolina to shuttle guests back and forth. Newspaper accounts touched off international headlines. Flagler, despite his advanced years, dressed in a Prince Albert with light trousers and beamed above his cherubic bride, who wore a gown of white chiffon over white satin, trimmed with point appliqué with a veil to match.

That winter in Palm Beach, the newlyweds entertained their friends lavishly several times a week at Whitehall, the home Flagler had built as a gift to Mary Lily. Flagler initially ordered his Royal Poinciana Hotel architects to design Whitehall in a "Cuban style," but Mary Lily wanted something grander and spent $1 million adding huge slabs of marble into the architecture. Her crowning achievements turned out to be a bathroom with a seventeen-by-eleven-foot sunken marble tub cut from a single prodigious piece of rare yellow Carrara marble.

She had no qualms about spending more of her husband's money for the sake of good taste—and the taste of good whiskey and a cocaine high. And according to the *Guinness Book of World Records*, Mary Lily never wore the same dress twice to a party at her "House of Marble," just south of the Royal Poinciana Hotel.

During opening season, Flagler and his young wife threw party after party for the rich and famous, ambassadors and dukes. The guest list included Admiral and Mrs. George Dewey, Mr. and Mrs. Frederick Vanderbilt and Mr. and Mrs. William Rockefeller.

Flagler, for all his boasting to his male friends about his lustful vigor, began to lose his stamina and his interest. He would retire early at each new party Mary Lily threw. Soon, Palm Beach regulars starting calling him the Old Man. But Flagler's mind remained sharp—he continued his master-builder vision of Florida, expanding through Miami and the

Keys—as his body wore out. His legs were weak and he often sat in a wheelchair guided by young black valets. He seldom left Whitehall, preferring to sit on the porch conducting business.

On March 15, 1913, Flagler was found sprawled on the marble floor of the large bathroom off the grand ballroom. He had been knocked down a short flight of marble steps leading to the commode. The cause of Flagler's condition was one of the bizarre modernizations Mary Lily had brought into the house, a set of electrically operated pneumatic doors that had closed with too much force. He lay critically injured for several hours before he was discovered.

Henry Morrison Flagler died five days later.

With the death of the founder of Palm Beach, the cofounder of Standard Oil, the American visionary, Mary Lily Flagler was now the richest woman in America, worth an estimated $100 million, a billionairess by today's standards. With accounts of Mary Lily's incredible wealth splashed on the front pages of most newspapers in the country, she was recognized as the nation's first independent female millionaire. Everything she did sold newspapers. When German forces sank the *Lusitania* in 1915, Mary Lily's cousin Dr. Owen Kenan was one of the lucky survivors. MILLIONAIRESS' KIN CHEATS DEATH exclaimed headlines over a file photo of a beaming Mary Lily and Dr. Kenan on the Palm Beach shore.

After Flagler's death, it wasn't long before dozens of male fortune hunters began contacting Mary Lily in hopes of rubbing up against the Flagler millions. One of them was her old college flame, Robert Worth Bingham, a lawyer and judge from Louisville, Kentucky.

Bingham's hometown newspaper recently had run a page-one picture of "Dying Millionaire" Flagler in a wheelchair on the Palm Beach boardwalk. By coincidence, Bingham's wife had been killed in a car crash just three weeks after the judge saw the front-page photo of the wounded Flagler. Mary Lily had been lonely, she told him, having nothing but money in her life. Whether Bingham actually loved Mary Lily is unknown. He did love her money, however, and he needed it fast. Bingham had met Mary Lily at a dance at the University of North Carolina in 1890, and the two had begun dating. But the Kenan family successfully pressured her to reject Bingham, saying he came from a family of intellectual snobs. Bingham later married, had two children, obtained a law degree, and successfully ran for Louisville county attorney. He later became mayor and a county judge. However, his law practice failed to bring in the kind of money he needed to pay mounting political campaign debts and other expenses. He owed a lot of people, and they were all becoming impatient.

Mary Lily's millions could wipe out his growing list of bills in an instant. Bingham, forty-nine, proposed marriage, and when forty-five-year-old Mary Lily hesitated, he enlisted friends and associates to pressure her into it.

The Kenan family knew what was going on. "She was lonely," Thomas Kenan, Mary Lily's great grandson and family historian, later recalled. "There is no question in anybody's mind that Bob Bingham plotted to get Mary Lily's money and that he wasn't going to stop until he had it. He just played on her misery and she fell for it," Kenan told Bingham biographer Marie Brenner.

The year was 1916. Mexican revolutionary Pancho Villa raided New Mexico and President Woodrow Wilson sent General John J. Pershing to capture him. The college football classic, the Rose Bowl, resumed after a gap of fourteen years. Germany sank an unarmed French steamer carrying American passengers. On the society pages, the *New York Herald* announced: MRS. FLAGLER'S ROMANCE: MRS. H. M. FLAGLER TO BE MARRIED ON NOVEMBER 12.

To silence fears he was merely a fortune hunter, Bingham waived any claim to Mary Lily's estate in a short prenuptial agreement. Quietly, however, Bingham had started reviewing his bride's various holdings, carefully poring over her impressive empire.

Mary Lily, no longer lonely, was revived by once again being the belle of the ball, on her new husband's arm. She lavished on Bingham numerous gifts, including a trunkful of one-hundred-dollar bills totaling $1 million. The same day he received the cash, Bingham breathlessly wired the money to his various debtors and instantly became financially solvent.

Bingham soon tired of his rediscovered love. He stopped paying attention to his wife and began to take long trips without her. Bingham's own children, who were known in Louisville as rampant social climbers, shunned all of the balls and parties their stepmother threw in Palm Beach.

Bingham, who just months before, during his courting, had lavished great praise on Mary Lily's Palm Beach empire of hotels and services, now seemed contemptuous of them. He continuously remarked about the superiority of Kentucky. Mary Lily was forced to host her social events alone, almost like a widow all over again.

She knew something was wrong, yet with all her millions, Mary Lily saw herself as powerless to improve her new living situation. She became depressed. She wrote in a diary, "I have been so very sad that Bob has said I should start going to a doctor. Now, I go twice a week, and he has been giving me a shot of something, a medication, and then I feel very good indeed until it wears off."

The injections were morphine and cocaine, drugs prescribed at the turn of the century for depression and for headaches. Mary Lily's husband had sent her to a physician named Dr. M. L. Ravitch, a curious character. He was a Russian-born dermatologist, known for treating syphilis as well as headaches. Judge Bingham had been seeing Dr. Ravitch himself for many years, although he never said why. Bingham paid Dr. Ravitch well to treat him and to keep quiet.

Now Dr. Ravitch had officially become Mary Lily's doctor, despite the urging of Mary Lily's family that renowned specialists might be flown in to examine the nation's richest woman or that she be taken to a first-class hospital. With his two assistants—one barely out of medical school and the other a diagnostician without a medical degree—Ravitch proclaimed that Mary Lily was suffering from "heart disease." To treat her, he recommended large doses of morphine.

Dr. Ravitch, with Bingham's consent, dismissed four of his wife's regular nurses when they complained of the increasing frequency and strength of the injections. Soon Mary Lily was a slave to her bedroom, needing to stay there so she could receive her "medication."

On June 19, 1917, Mary Lily was brought to Dr. Ravitch's office, although it is not clear at whose initiative she appeared. When she arrived, the doctor and David Davis, one of her husband's closest friends and a lawyer, were present. During the visit, which included a morphine injection, Mary Lily signed a handwritten codicil to her will, leaving Bingham $5 million. The codicil was penned on the doctor's letterhead by someone other than Mary Lily, and Mary Lily's signature was little more than a pathetic zigzag. Four and a half weeks later, Mary Lily Flagler Bingham became unconscious in a bath. Under Dr. Ravitch's "care," she died a few days later.

Her relatives said she spent her final days in great pain, suffering from demonic hallucinations and effects similar to sudden withdrawal from narcotics.

When the family attorneys unveiled Mary Lily's will, the bulk of her $150 million estate went, as expected, to her cousin, Louise Wise. When Bingham produced the secret $5 million codicil, the Kenans hired lawyers, filed lawsuits, and charged Bingham with murder. The newspapers carried haunting allegations that Mary Lily might have been slowly, methodically poisoned with drugs. Furthermore, the Kenans claimed that Mary Lily had been drugged when she signed the codicil, and possibly had been forced to affix her signature while Dr. Ravitch threatened to withhold her morphine injection until she did. A probate trial ensued in Kentucky, Bingham's home state.

Davis testified he knew nothing about what he called Ravitch's "morphine therapy" for Mary Lily. He said he could not even recall why he had been called to the doctor's office that day. Dr. Ravitch was never called to testify, nor was Bingham.

The Kenans were fighting hometown justice. They hired three private detectives who ransacked Dr. Ravitch's office and took Mary Lily's drug records. The story hit the news: RAVITCH'S DOPE RECORDS SEIZED.

Still needing more proof of foul play, the Kenans ordered Mary Lily's body exhumed. BODY SECRETLY EXHUMED AND AUTOPSY HELD trumpeted the *Louisville Courier-Journal* on September 24, 1917.

"Secretly and in the dead of night," the news article read, "the grave of Mrs. Robert Worth Bingham, at Wilmington, N.C., was opened last Tuesday. The body was exhumed and eviscerated. The vital organs were removed by unidentified physicians, said to be pathologists from Boston and New York, and then were taken away to New York."

A guard was dispatched to watch Mary Lily's grave after her remains were returned to the cemetery. Her exhumation overshadowed news of the call-up of new troops to Europe to fight the Germans in World War I.

The scandal-hungry public awaited the grand conclusion.

But seven months later the lawsuits, the murder charges, the allegations of legal chicanery, were suddenly dropped. The Kenans said "case closed." They treasured their privacy and no longer wanted to soil Mary Lily's reputation with more sensational stories about her drug dependency.

"The Kenan family prized its anonymity and nobody wanted to be in the papers in Louisville," Mary's great grandson, Thomas Kenan, said. "The family knew that if they did not pay off the judge their name would be ruined in the papers."

Biographer David Chandler has another theory: The Kenan family had obtained Mary Lily's autopsy report. They read it and then locked it away forever in their vault, making a family pledge to only describe it and never show it. Chandler believes the findings contained a startling revelation: Mary Lily Flagler Bingham had for years been afflicted with syphilis—and she had contracted the virus from Bingham himself, not during their brief marriage, but years earlier during their college affair.

The disclosure would produce a great scandal, considering that only a year earlier Mary Lily Bingham had been a respected billionairess and the widow of the visionary who had turned Palm Beach from a swampy jungle into a world-class resort.

Bingham obtained his $5 million in August. A genteel hustler—like Scarlett O'Hara in *Gone With the Wind* proclaiming, "I'll never be hungry again!"—Bingham went on a spending spree. He purchased the *Louisville Courier-Journal*, ensuring that the Bingham family would be well treated politically and socially for years to come. He is believed to have paid off Dr. Ravitch—his feel-good syphilis specialist—for his everlasting silence on the matter of his wife.

Now a multimillionaire widower with money earned by Flagler, Bingham recast himself as a progressive public figure, confidant of presidents and kings, benefactor of struggling Kentucky farmers, friend of education for oppressed blacks. Bingham, a suspected murderer and rogue, suceeded in donning to a mantle of noblesse oblige that his family and progeny, the owners of a burgeoning newspaper empire in the United States, wore proudly through the century. And he never looked back at Palm Beach.

The next time Bingham mentioned Flagler was in 1925 in his *Louisville Courier-Journal*. On March 18 of that year, Flagler's most popular hotel, the Breakers, burned to the ground. As the fire engulfed the majestic building, the West Palm Beach Municipal Band performed just down the road with a rousing version of "There'll Be a Hot Time in the Old Town Tonight."

Ironically, poor Ida Alice Flagler, Henry Flagler's mentally-disturbed second wife, had the last laugh. Although almost always in a delusionary state, she lived the longest, in great style and comfort, in a luxurious mental hospital. Possessed by her ongoing devotion to her one true love, the late czar of Russia, Ida Alice eighty-years-old, finally died peacefully in her sleep of a brain hemorrhage on July 12, 1930. At the time of her death, Ida Alice's estate, consisting mainly of Standard Oil stock, was worth $15.2 million.

3

Dancing With Fire: Isadora Duncan and Paris Singer

W hile the life was being drained from the former Mrs. Henry Flagler, the country's wealthiest widow, in March 1917, Paris Singer, one of eighteen illegitimate children fathered by Isaac Singer, the inventor of the sewing machine, made his way by train to Palm Beach. His reason for visiting this pleasure paradise was simple, and similar to that of many other men who made the trip before or after him. Singer was meeting his longtime mistress, Isadora Duncan, the world-renowned dancer, in Palm Beach, far from the glare of the public spotlight and in a sun-drenched setting fit for a star.

A few days earlier, Duncan had checked into the original Breakers Hotel after returning from an exhausting performance swing through South America and back to New York. By 1917, the Breakers Hotel, formerly Flagler's Beach Inn, had become the hotel of choice for vacationers because of its beachfront location and had expanded fourfold in size, with one employee for each of its twelve hundred guests. The hotel was abuzz with word that Duncan was vacationing on Palm Beach. One of the most widely known dancers of her day, Duncan was famous for her artistry and risqué performances. She danced barefoot in flowing translucent garments and was accompanied by classical music that had never before been used for dance.

Duncan's stay at the Breakers already was memorable. The beautiful dancer had a visceral attraction to prizefighters, or at least men with prizefighter physiques. Her ocean-liner cruise to South America only a few months before had provided a bonanza. She had boarded the *Byron* in Brooklyn, New York, with a case of champagne as a bon voyage gift and discovered to her delight that a stable of young boxers was traveling along. The fighters awakened early "to train and then swim in the big salt water swimming bath on board," she later wrote. "I trained with them in the morning and danced for them at night, so the voyage was very gay and did not seem so long."

When her first case of champagne ran out, Duncan instructed the captain to obtain more champagne at each stop along the way. Although Duncan had an international reputation for frolicking with men, her carousing on the *Byron* was so unbridled that it concerned even those used to her ways. Perhaps, they thought, her excesses were the result of a decline in popularity. Coupled with the recent death of her two children in a car accident, Isadora may have craved an unusual amount of attention and affection.

After the tour ended, Duncan stopped to relax in Havana, Cuba, but found it boring and crossed to Palm Beach. At the Breakers Hotel, she did not sit idly by waiting for Singer to arrive from New York. Even though Singer was admittedly the great love of Duncan's life—as well as her million-dollar benefactor—Duncan the Siren had her needs. She spotted a handsome physical-fitness instructor at Gus's Bath House, which was south of the Breakers, where Worth Avenue now meets the Atlantic Ocean. Duncan demanded an introduction. He was Kid McCoy, the former United States middleweight champion.

McCoy, a world-class ladies' man, had been the toast of the boxing world at the turn of the century. The term "the Real McCoy" was coined for him by a San Francisco sportswriter in 1899 when McCoy knocked out Joe Choynski. A few days before, a local boxer named Peter McCoy had succumbed to a terrific beating. The newspapers hailed Kid McCoy as "the Real McCoy."

Late in his fighting career, McCoy was suspected of taking a dive in the fifth round of a fight with Gentleman Jim Corbett. Quitting the ring, he took to the Straw Hat circuit as Kid Garvey, a character based on his own life, and played later on Broadway by Lionel Barrymore.

A handsome man with deep dimples, McCoy came to Palm Beach by way of the theater and café society. He brought his irresistible smile to the island, seeking another chance at fame and fortune—which in Palm Beach meant he was seeking a rich benefactor of his own. McCoy, whose real named was Norman Selby, would marry ten times—to eight women—and spend seven years in San Quentin prison for killing a girlfriend, the ex-wife of a Los Angeles art dealer. In 1940, McCoy was found dead in a Detroit hotel room, the victim of an overdose of sleeping pills. In one of two suicide notes, McCoy, a guard at the Ford Motor Company, apologized that he could not "endure this world's madness." His postscript read: "In my pocket you will find $17.78."

But in March 1917, in glorious Palm Beach, McCoy was a drawing card at Gus's Bath House. The Vanderbilts and Drexels and Astors all sought his instruction. It was no insult to work at Gus's. An authentic Italian count served as a towel attendant.

Duncan started to exercise with McCoy the day after they met, stretching and dancing grandly with his ever strong hands helping her float through the air. And at night, with her handsome champion now on her arm, Duncan entertained her McCoy at the Breakers Hotel. The former boxer arranged their lavish parties, inviting dozens of Palm Beach regulars eager to fawn over the famous dancer. By all accounts, the parties were rowdy affairs, catered with cases of champagne and tins of caviar. And when night turned into morning, and the bill had to be paid, the generous McCoy grabbed it, jotted down a hefty tip for the waiters and waitresses—and then charged the festivities to Singer's account.

Meanwhile Singer was heading for Palm Beach, eager to see his lover with great news of his latest gift for her, another palace where she could dance. In Paris and in London, Singer had rented great halls for Duncan. Now he had purchased an option to buy—not rent—Madison Square Garden, then on Madison Avenue and 28th Street in New York City. He had cabled ahead of his interest in the Garden, which he assumed would thrill his secret lover. He roared south on the Florida rail system forged by Flagler, unaware that his beloved Duncan was less than enthusiastic.

The volcanic dancer had the mistaken notion that poet-dramatist Percy MacKaye had persuaded Singer to buy the Garden to stage his large bals masqués. Duncan feared MacKaye would hire hundreds of actors and dancers, "recruit them from 'the Wanamaker store girls,'" and expect her, the Great Isadora Duncan, to train them. "My own school, yes! Pageants, no!" she declared.

Singer, instead of finding Duncan waiting eagerly for him, received a frosty reception that included an introduction to "my new friend, Kid McCoy." For ten years, Singer, the dashing international millionaire, and Duncan, the famous ballerina, had carried on a passionate love affair. Their relationship spanned four continents. London, Paris, and New York were at its heart. Palm Beach would be its fiery end, altering the course of Duncan's career and the landscape and skyline of the island.

Singer had met Duncan in Paris in 1909 when he called on her following a performance. At the time, Singer, the father of five children, was separated from his wife. He sent a business card backstage to the ballerina via a maid and introduced himself as a devoted fan of Duncan's work, then a daring performance that featured seminude dancing and transparent veils that stretched the limits of onstage decency.

The Great Isadora welcomed Singer in her dressing room as though they were bonded by a spiritual power. Only days before, the ballerina—nearly penniless, as usual—had visited a clairvoyant. The mentalist had predicted that Duncan soon would meet a millionaire who would rescue her from her incessant debts and fulfill all her dreams. Isadora prayed for her millionaire. When Singer's embossed business card—proclaiming P. E. Singer, architect—arrived at her stage door, Duncan announced: "My millionaire has arrived."

At six-foot-six, with curly blond hair and a cropped beard, the handsome Singer, forty-one, had impeccable manners. He bent to kiss her hand. "You don't know me," Singer began, "but I have often applauded your work."

Actually, they had met before, at the funeral of Prince de Polignac, another Duncan benefactor. The Princesse de Polignac was one of Singer's sisters. So was the Duchesse Decazes, also an early Isadora patron.

Duncan was a devout communist and a serious artiste in the strictest sense. Singer was a quintessential capitalist who decried Walt Whitman's vision of a free America as so much "rot!"

"That man couldn't earn a day's pay," Singer had exclaimed when Duncan read him her favorite poem, Whitman's "Song of the Open Road."

Duncan was always testing Singer's devotion and patience. Perhaps Singer's aristocratic upbringing gnawed at her. She goaded Singer endlessly in order to prove that his money could not control or buy her.

Paris Singer, whose father, Isaac, had died when he was eight, was raised a ward of a British court. Although his mother was French and Paris had been named after the city of his birth, the family lived in England. While still a young boy, Paris suspected his mother was mismanaging his $15 million estate. He secretly visited a judge and voiced his concern. The magistrate agreed with the child, and to protect the inheritance he made Paris a ward of the British court.

Given his wealth, young Singer became a friend of the royal family, and his sisters' marriages linked him to French nobility. With an aristocratic air of European elegance, Singer became a liberal patron of young artists and writers. Occasionally ambition seized him, and he dabbled in architectural studies. But without the need for money, he stopped short of acquiring a profession and became a celebrated romeo. But any romantic disappointment caused him to retreat to his architectural draftings and spend some of his millions on a villa, harbor improvement, or a hospital.

Singer's background, born of the fruits of capitalism, could not have been more different than the bohemian artist's life of Isadora Duncan. They did have one thing in common. Both their families had been rocked by scandals. The Duncans had their father's bank failure and their parents' divorce. Young Paris Singer was marked by a sensational lawsuit that followed his father's death. The Singer patriarch had left his entire estate to Paris and his mother, Isabella.

Isaac Singer's first wife, Catherine Haley Singer, and one of his mistresses, Mary Ann Sponsler—the mother of ten of his children—had contested the will. The litigation, although unsuccessful, laid bare the lustful and lavish life of the inventor of the sewing machine.

Singer's father had enjoyed, even by Palm Beach standards, an uninhibited life. He had married twice, maintained three mistresses, and fathered twenty-four children, eighteen out of wedlock. He lived on a grand scale. Even his carriages were custom-made rolling palaces, requiring nine horses to draw them. One even contained a lady's dressing room. Another accommodated thirty-one passengers and had a bandstand near the rear.

When Isaac Singer was in his fifties, he married Paris's mother, then an attractive twenty-one-year-old divorcée. She was demure, while Mr. Singer was, as one writer observed, "vain and contentious. He quarrelled with practically everybody who opposed him, frequently threatening bodily damage."

Paris Singer was forty when he met Duncan, then ten years younger. Within a year of their meeting, Duncan, who had had a daughter out of wedlock with the English stage designer Gordon Craig, became pregnant. She gave birth to Singer's illegitimate son, Patrick Augustus Duncan, in May 1910. Two months later, Paris Singer suffered a stroke and was sent to recuperate at the Wigwam ("my place in the country"), a villa in Devonshire, England, that was modeled after Versailles and Le Petit Trianon. Singer begged Duncan to marry him and pleaded for her to spend three months with him living as man and wife.

"How stupid for an artist to be married," she said.

But Singer persisted until the reluctant Duncan agreed. Within a few days Duncan was bored with the English regimen, which she derisively told friends revolved around eating: breakfast, lunch, tea, and dinner. And when she found her husband bedridden and protected round the clock by doctors and nurses, the tedium became too much to bear. She decided to practice and ordered a friend to send an accompanist.

The pianist arrived—someone Duncan hated. One afternoon, however, she and her pianist went for a country drive, and while returning to the Wigwam the car hit a rut. The jolt sent Duncan tumbling into her pianist's arms. "I looked at him and suddenly felt my whole being going up in flames like a pile of lighted straw. How had I not seen it before? His face was perfectly beautiful."

When the pair returned to the house, Duncan and her accompanist darted behind a "convenient" screen in the ballroom and made love for hours on the floor. From then on, they constantly sought to be alone. Soon the nurses were gossiping. Singer learned of the affair, erupted despite his stroke, and banished the pianist from his home.

"These violent passions have violent ends," Duncan later wrote. And in a brilliant bit of understatement, she then added: "The episode proved to me that I certainly was not suited to domestic life."

Their tempestuous love affair endured for years and spanned five Singer residences—his estate in Paignton, England, his villa at Cap Ferrat, a country home in Paris, and two town houses in London. Singer maintained a fifth, secret, love nest in New York City. He set up Isadora in an eight-thousand-dollar-a-month town house at 110 East 59th Street, with towering ceilings, a marble fireplace that cost twenty thousand dollars, and the first sunken tub in the United States, made of Italian marble and costing eight thousand dollars. Everyone suspected Paris would show up, but the newspaper photographers never caught a glimpse of him.

Singer had cut a secret passage—Singer's Shortcut—from his office in an adjoining building around the corner from Duncan's top-floor studio. Clad in her flowing draperies, the dancer would wait for the millionaire on the roof of her building. Singer had only to open the door cut through his office to step out into Isadora's arms, and no one ever knew—that is, until the superintendent revealed the truth after both Duncan and Singer had been dead for several years.

During his life, Duncan had used a pseudonym, Lohengrin, when referring to and writing about her secret benefactor. Later she admitted that she used the false name because she felt that if she were too explicit Singer would use his wealth to prevent publication of her memoirs.

Only weeks before the curtain was brought down on their affair, Duncan put on a tango display with a young Argentine in front of Singer that created a public spectacle in New York's most fashionable restaurant, Sherry's, on Fifth Avenue. For years Duncan had pushed Singer's devotion to its limit. She now was in the danger zone.

Singer had thrown a party to celebrate Duncan's triumphant return from South America. "To please Singer, Isadora wore an exquisite chiffon frock and diamond necklace which he had just given her," said Arnold Genthe, one of the guests.

Everything went smoothly until the dancing began. Isadora wanted to dance the tango with a young man characterized as the most famous tango dancer in the Argentine. She asked Genthe to bring over the slender dark-haired dancer.

"They proceeded to dance a tango that astonished the guests." Isadora believed the tango was meant to be a sensual and alluring dance "based on sexual desire and the right of possession." She was determined to dance it in the authentic sultry Argentine fashion. Back and forth, hips locked together, feet splaying outward in unison, Duncan and the Argentine danced as though they were alone in her boudoir.

Out of the corner of her eye, she could see Singer nervously raising his shoulders, as he did when he felt impatient or disapproving, a habit that irritated her, Genthe recalled. Singer "stood watching them, a giant of fury, until they were half through. Then he strode into the middle of the floor, took the Argentine by the scruff of the neck and slithered him out of the room.

"Isadora turned pale, and with the air of a prima donna, she called out, 'If you treat my friend like that, I won't wear your jewelry.'"

She tore the necklace from her throat and the diamonds scattered on the floor. As she swept from the room, she passed Genthe by the door and, without looking at him, whispered, "Pick them up," and was gone into the night.

Typically, their quarrel did not last long. Singer cemented their reunion with a gift. He rented the Metropolitan Opera House for November 21, 1916, so Isadora could give a free gala concert, by invitation only, for their friends. The guest list included Anna Pavlova, Otto Kahn, the Marquis de Polignac, and such public figures as Mayor John Mitchel and members of the diplomatic corps.

The *Marsellaise* was the evening's great piece. It was encored by the American anthem. When it was sounded, Duncan tore off her outer skirt to reveal herself wearing the Stars and Stripes.

After the performance, Duncan and Singer's secretary, Allan Ross MacDougall, went to Havana, Cuba, for a rest. In a few weeks Duncan grew bored and crossed over to Florida, taking rooms at the Breakers.

It was ironic that Singer's intention to buy Madison Square Garden was a last-ditch effort to control Isadora—although it resulted from a halfhearted pledge. Before Duncan left New York for Havana, she asked Singer his impression of her Metropolitan Opera performance. Singer replied: "I like half of it very much. And if you could only keep your behavior to the level of the first half and cease making these public scandals, there is nothing I wouldn't do."

"What would you get me?" Isadora asked half jokingly.

"Madison Square Garden," Singer replied.

"What are your conditions," the dancer said.

"That you always behave yourself with dignity in public," Singer said.

"I am not sure that I can meet your conditions," Duncan replied.

Despite the lure of the Garden, Duncan could not live up to Singer's "conditions." On the day he arrived at the Breakers, Duncan greeted her lover with McCoy virtually at her elbow. Singer was incensed. He dragged her out of the Breakers, ordered her bags collected, took her to the train, and they returned to New York. The following evening was their last together as a couple. At dinner in the Plaza, Duncan not only rejected his gift but evoked McCoy's image when they spoke of the Garden.

"Do you mean to tell me that you expect me to direct a school in Madison Square Garden? I suppose you want me to advertise prizefights with my dancing!"

Singer's lips quivered at the word *prizefight*. His hands shook. He got up from the table without saying a word and left the room.

"Do you realize what you have done?" someone asked Duncan.

"He'll come back," she said. "He always does."

He never did.

Singer canceled the deal at a personal loss of between $100,000 and $200,000. He broke off their relationship for good. Profoundly wounded, for the first time he refused to pay Isadora's Palm Beach hotel bills at the Breakers. Fortunately for the resourceful Isadora, she had an emerald pendant, diamond necklace, and ermine coat—all gifts from Singer— which she promptly pawned to pay her Breakers debt. With the remaining cash, she rented a home on Long Island. It was not Palm Beach, but her money would last longer this way.

Singer refused all attempts at reconciliation. They never were lovers again.

Duncan moved on to Europe. She found new loves and new benefactors. She ultimately married the Russian poet Sergei Yesenin, whose verse helped stir the revolution and who later committed suicide in 1922. Duncan died violently in 1928 when her trademark long red scarf was snared in the wire wheel spokes of a car in which she was riding and broke her neck. Her will was the first of a Soviet citizen to be probated in the United States.

Exhausted by his eight-year romance with Duncan, Singer returned to Palm Beach. He fully expected to die there. But the successor to Duncan was the spirit to build.

By 1917, the Palm Beach winter season had expanded by a month. Wealthy vacationers were growing tired of renting hotel rooms for themselves and their small army of servants. They were thinking of buying jungle property of their own on Palm Beach and erecting great Arabian Nights palaces.

No one could have predicted that a new Palm Beach was about to be born. Singer—with the aid of an eccentric rotund architect named Addison Mizner—would be the tool, transforming the enchanted island landscape for the first time since Flagler had built the Royal Poinciana Hotel. He would also serve as iron-fisted monarch over the island's warped social kingdom.

4

From Debt's Door
to High Society:
Addison and Wilson Mizner

P aris Singer, having discarded Isadora Duncan, chose to spend the rest of his days in the Royal Poinciana Hotel. Complaining of exhaustion, the sewing-machine heir wanted only to sit on the hotel porch, peacefully facing Lake Worth. He rarely spoke of the danseuse extraordinaire, but when he did, he referred to her as "Isa-bore-a Drunk-en."

As Singer sat rocking in his chair on a balmy January afternoon in 1918, a carriage pulled up in front of the hotel. Four black men were summoned hastily to help remove a stretcher from the rear. The strain of the load showed on the faces and necks of the "Negro help." Addison Mizner, all four hundred pounds of him, had arrived in Palm Beach.

Like Paris Singer, Mizner—a robust whirling dervish from New York literary circles—had also selected Palm Beach as his final destination. Suffering from necrosis, lung constrictions, heart palpitations, and a general physical breakdown, the six-foot-three blond giant had been given only a few months to live. Making matters worse, at the age of forty-five, Mizner was not only sick but dead broke. One could survive the former under the healing sun of Palm Beach. The latter was a fatal malady.

Mizner was not merely penniless; he was sixty thousand dollars in debt. In New York, his friends collected twelve thousand dollars to ship

40

him off to Florida. Mizner happily accepted their generosity, reminding them that they should be pleased to donate. "After all, it will be the last time," he said cheerfully in his sickbed.

The gregarious Mizner cut a grand figure in his day. The son of a prominent California politician, Mizner had traveled the world, acquiring a taste for Spanish décor and South American landscape. His father was a state senator who had served as envoy extraordinaire to five Central American nations. When Mizner was old enough to travel alone, his parents sent him off to China, desperately hoping to bring culture to his life and to shake him of his desire to be little more than what they called "a whimsical oaf."

Mizner, no less whimsical, returned from the Orient with several furry chow dogs, a ravenous fondness for Chinese art and food, and a conviction that silk pajamas were proper street clothes, even in San Francisco.

Mizner, like Singer, dabbled in architecture. Although he never received a proper diploma or license, he held various jobs with different architectural firms. In New York, his chatty, playful, oddball nature attracted society's fast-paced, late-night crowd. He made a name, of sorts, for himself, startling neighbors by shopping in his pajamas as he traveled about town with his two handsome chows. During the day, when he joined his crowd for lunch at Sherry's restaurant on Fifth Avenue, Mizner hitched the then-exotic dogs to a post on 44th Street. At night he often kept the town awake with raucous parties that lasted until dawn and featured the gigantic host not only doing a handstand, but also walking across his apartment upside down.

Everyone suspected Mizner's affairs attracted the riffraff from tough Hell's Kitchen on Manhattan's West Side. The opinion was well founded only to the extent that Mizner's younger brother, Wilson, a legendary American wit, was an all-around scoundrel who sometimes hung out in poolrooms and ran afoul of the law. When a New York newspaper published Addison Mizner's guest list, suspicious precinct cops found that the names of his party people were contained in the upper echelon of the Social Register.

The millionaire Singer, bored and lonely without Isadora, was delighted to meet the impoverished but colorful Addison Mizner. They spent their days sitting next to each other on the porch of the Royal Poinciana, fanning themselves, waiting for death to come while exchanging sophisticated repartee. Despite the patter, however, both were still bored.

"Mizner," Singer abruptly said, "you know I came here expecting to die, but I'm damned if I feel like it."

Mizner shrugged and turned his head slowly toward Singer.

"What are you going to do about it?" Mizner asked.

It now was Singer's turn to shrug. He sat there for a long moment and then answered a question with a question. "If you could do anything you wanted, what should you do?"

Mizner suddenly grew animated. He made a sweeping gesture that seemed to take in the Royal Poinciana, the Breakers Hotel, the Palm Beach rail station, and the island's cottages, all of which seemed to be made of wood and painted yellow. And then he declared in a booming voice: "I'll tell you what I'd do. I'd build something that wasn't made of wood. And I wouldn't paint it yellow!"

The words reverberated in Singer's mind. It reminded Singer of a time in Paris a decade earlier when, after another crushing broken romance, he channeled his energy into building a hospital for army veterans. Why not build another hospital? This time on Palm Beach for World War I soldiers returning from Europe.

The idea was like medicine for both invalids. The dashing, slender Singer, his spirits revived, took the giant-size Mizner for a walk around Palm Beach in search of a place to build his hospital. They walked south a few hundred yards and then headed east, following an "alligator path" near Joe's Alligator Farm, a trail that would later, thanks to Singer's enthusiasm, become posh Worth Avenue.

They followed the alligator path through the jungle until they reached Lake Worth. To their surprise, Singer and Mizner suddenly found an unobstructed view of the mainland. Singer looked at Mizner and announced that on this spot he would build his hospital. Mizner immediately conjured a grand facility, with towers and arches fit for America's heroic warriors and solemn enough to calm the soul of a nun.

The building began. But Mizner, the perfectionistic artist who had a hard time satisfying himself, kept making grandiose changes to the structure. In fact, he made so many changes that the building was not ready to open until the last of the returning G.I.'s were already home.

In the end, the hospital never opened, and Singer turned the building into the first private club in Palm Beach. Some skeptics came to believe it had always been Singer's intention to delay the "hospital" so that he could build the club he really wanted for his own uses. Singer named it the Everglades Club, and placed himself in charge of membership. He wanted to choose his one hundred members from the ranks of the "Golden Folks" of Palm Beach. Thanks to the allure of his famous name, the likes of the Vanderbilts and Drexels demanded admission.

The Everglades Club was a guaranteed success. Singer decreed one last fiendish regulation: No membership would last beyond the winter season. This policy made each member beholden to Singer's whims the following season when it came time to try to rejoin Palm Beach society at the Everglades. Signer's absolute power over membership afforded him sole control over who was "in" and who was "out," which in Palm Beach circles could be more important than how much money one had.

Society members waited anxiously through the summer and fall for word from Singer whether they would be permitted to return to the Everglades. By all accounts, Singer was ruthless when he made his choices. He thinned the ranks of the island's "chosen" for the slightest offenses, both real and imagined.

One woman was dropped from the Everglades roster for laughing out loud at an uneventful dinner party, while another was nearly booted for trying to intercede on the laughing woman's behalf.

The discriminatory Singer dumped others whose names had been mentioned in scandals. He conveniently overlooked his own very public battles with Isadora Duncan at the Breakers and Royal Poinciana that had ended with their eviction for drinking and fighting in the lobby.

For twenty years Singer had been a collector of colorful tiles from ruined buildings along the Mediterranean. He had stored tons of them in a warehouse in West Palm Beach, acquiring so many that their weight once broke the floor. He wanted his magnificent old glazed tiles used in the Everglades. Mizner was ecstatic at the prospect. Until then, he had only sketched buildings in Old World styles, mostly Spanish, and fantasized creating a palace in a tropical paradise.

He now was bankrolled by a millionaire with a philanthropist's cavalier sense and he was being ordered to use an extraordinary collection of antique tiles.

Mizner, who hated anything that looked new or machine made, attacked the warehouse with a flourish and used so many diverse types of tiles in the Everglades that one writer described the halls as "the most iridescent, international peacock alleys." One afternoon, a group of touring Tunisians entered the Everglades lobby, instantly assumed religious positions, and started to pray at one of the walls. The wall contained a mosaic composed of sacred tiles from a demolished Tunisian mosque. Singer had acquired several tons of holy tiles years before while cruising in his yacht off the Tunisian coast.

Mizner also attacked the tiles with a hammer—breaking them into pieces and cementing them back in place to give a time-worn look. He poured corrosive chemicals on walls and floors and ordered workmen to scrub them with steel brushes. The gold dome of the Everglades Club received two doses of destructive chemicals to give it a mellow appearance. And Mizner furniture was riddled with buckshot from a Daisy Air Rifle that was fired from an angle "the way a worm charges at a piece of furniture."

The tiles, coupled with Mizner's polyglot architectural design, prompted another scribe to call the style "Spanish-Moorish-Romanes-que-Gothic-Renaissance-Bull Market-Damn the Expense."

Mrs. Edward T. Stotesbury gushed upon seeing the completed Everglades Club, "Oh, Addie! It is beautiful! Oh, Addie! It's so beautiful."

Mrs. Stotesbury's husband was the wealthy Philadelphia financier who chaired the banking firm Drexel and Company and was a partner of the J. P. Morgan Trust Company. The Stotesburys' marriage, considered the most outstanding event of 1912, was presided over by the bishop of Washington, and President William Taft delivered the champagne toast. Both bride and groom had been married before. The new Mrs. Stotesbury, forty-seven, was the daughter of a Chicago lawyer who had practiced with Abraham Lincoln. She had been married for eleven years to Oliver E. Cromwell, a banker, club man, and yachtsman, who had died in 1909, leaving her with their three children, James, Louise, and Oliver, Jr., and a comfortable estate.

Stotesbury, sixty-three, had become a widower in 1874, a short time after his first marriage, and had two children. He began his career as a sixteen-dollar-a-week clerk and rose quickly through the ranks of the financial world. He now was worth in excess of $30 million.

A cautious banker, Stotesbury insisted that his new wife sign a prenuptial agreement disavowing any claim to his estate. As a wedding gift, Stotesbury presented to his bride, the former Lucretia "Eva" Roberts Cromwell, a pearl necklace with a large sapphire pendant worth $100,000. J. Pierpont Morgan followed Stotesbury and presented the bride with a $40,000 diamond necklace. But Stotesbury then proclaimed he had another gift for his wife. This one drew gasps. Stotesbury said he had opened a bank account in Eva's name and had deposited $4 million in it. At the time the endowment was the single largest ever given a bride in the United States.

Lucretia Stotesbury moved into the family's 147-room mansion, Whitemarsh Hall, in Philadelphia. The estate was dotted with smaller homes where the Stotesburys' eighty-odd servants lived. Whitemarsh

Hall functioned like a small town, with carpenters, chauffeurs, electricians, and blacksmiths working and living on the grounds.

When Henry Ford visited Whitemarsh Hall, he observed: "It is always a great experience to see how the rich live."

Mrs. Stotesbury was the reserved keeper of the estate who shied away from public displays—that is, until her husband had his attorneys rescind their prenuptial agreement. She blossomed and tried to break into the old-money Philadelphia social scene. Despite her husband's prominence—he even owned the Philadelphia Opera House—she was not accepted into Philadelphia society. But in Palm Beach, Mrs. E. T. Stotesbury became the leading hostess, tossing extravagant parties for hundreds of guests. Her nickname was "Queen Eva."

Any woman permitted to address her simply as Eva rose a notch in social standing. She was the island's first "grand dame" and therefore its social arbiter. Her gushing review of the Everglades Club provided Mizner with instant artistic approval.

"I simply love it. You must build for me," Queen Eva proclaimed.

Mizner was waiting to be discovered, and when Mrs. Stotesbury said she would spare no expense, Mizner grabbed his sketch pad. She said she wanted a mansion with panoramic views, a home large enough to hold twelve hundred guests at parties. Together they staked out a twenty-three-acre plot that ran the width of the island, from the Atlantic Ocean on the east to the estuary on the west. Mizner had the property cleared of jungle and in its center built a Mediterrean-style, thirty-seven-room villa for Mrs. Stotesbury, designed after a convent near Burgos, Spain.

Mizner used Singer's antique tiles on the floors and walls. Workmen installed immense fireplaces in the bathroom and the dressing rooms, and built a forty-car garage, an open-air theater, and a spacious teahouse near the lake. Mizner designed a private apartment for the Stotesburys that had lofty ceilings and grated windows that guaranteed cross-ventilation from the ocean or lake breezes.

When the project was completed, Mrs. Stotesbury decorated her thirty-seven rooms with the largest private collection of art and antiques in the country. In a large vault that doubled as a private viewing library, Mrs. Stotesbury filled a display case with the world's finest diamonds, emeralds, and pearls. Her husband, on the other hand, asked for only one vanity on the estate—a special zoo. Mizner built him that zoo and stocked it with twenty-five monkeys, twenty-five parrots, and thirteen lovebirds and parakeets.

A different kind of world would later surround the Stotesburys as their daughter entered into two scandalous marriages, one to a famous general and the other to an actor—the second boasting talk of sex orgies and pornographic films.

The Stotesburys called their villa El Mirasol. The red roof tiles were barely set when Mrs. Stotesbury, already known as "la belle de la Palm Beach," threw her maiden party, an extravaganza for three hundred guests that was more carnival than party, with "champagne flowing like water," one newspaper reported. Mrs. Stotesbury entertained lavishly and frequently. Regardless of the length of the guest list, the buffet never ran out and the unflappable hostess was never frazzled. It did not matter if she was overseeing an enormous soirée or a small birthday party for her son, Jimmy Cromwell, where his young male friends arrived in bathing trunks, full-dress shirts, and top hats.

"A nervous hostess makes an unhappy guest" was Mrs. Stotesbury's credo.

When it came to choosing her own wardrobe, Mrs. Stotesbury always came bedecked with jewelry and diamond-studded pins from her multimillion-dollar collection. A favorite was a strand of emeralds valued at one million dollars that reached to her knees, with each stone the size of a two-inch square block.

A newspaper reported that at one party she wore "a small fortune of jewels piled on her head and hands in elaborate combs, earrings, and as many rings as her frail hands could carry." Yet another glittering display left "society men rubbing their eyes [the following morning] after gazing last night at the dazzling jewels worn by Mrs. Stotesbury."

And her ostentation went beyond diamonds and pearls. At one party she wore the costliest evening wrap ever seen in Palm Beach over her jewels: a full-length gray chinchilla with a heavy double fur collar then valued at $100,000. Because her outfits were worth a small fortune, Mr. Stotesbury, no less a dapper dresser, hired armed guards to accompany her wife while she made her social rounds through the parties.

The grand Stotesbury parties were rivaled only by the gaudy costume affairs at Singer's Everglades Club. Big band stars such as Meyer Davis were brought down from the North and lodged for the season at the Everglades.

Members with an abundance of money to burn secretly tried to upstage one another by spending thousands of dollars on elaborate outfits that were made by big-city tailors and shipped to Florida. Singer's fawning minions came as gypsies and harlequins, pirates and sailors. One millionairess arrived as a red dragon while another appeared as a mah-jongg tile. At one event, Singer, the monarch of one hundred Everglades subjects, dressed as Henry VIII and his former nurse, Charlotte Bates (now Mrs. Paris Singer), came as a Venetian lady. But E. T. Stotesbury, regardless of what he wore, was always awarded first prize at the club's annual costume ball.

His first annual birthday and costume party, February 26, 1921, brought five hundred guests to El Mirasol. The following season so many people turned out for his birthday party that it was hard to determine where El Mirasol ended and Palm Beach began. Soon the costume party replaced Flagler's Washington Day Ball as the most important event on the island's social calendar.

At his eightieth birthday party in 1929, someone noticed Stotesbury, outfitted in one of his 150 costumes, standing silent at the sight of a drummer beating a snare. The frail financier stood transfixed for several alarming minutes. Stotesbury had been a drummer boy in the Civil War. Someone told the drummer to put the drumsticks in the banker's hands. Suddenly the elderly Philadelphian snapped out of his trance and proceeded to play the drum for fifteen minutes.

By his eighty-ninth and final birthday party, Stotesbury's drum solo was a tradition. He played his favorite selections: "The Girl I Left Behind Me," "Dixie," "Marching Through Georgia," and "The Battle Hymn of the Republic." The performance concluded with Stotesbury singing his favorite melody, "The Old Family Toothbrush That Hung Over the Sink."

First-time visitors and guests at El Mirasol were overwhelmed by its interior, façades, and landscaping. Mizner, as the Royal Architect of the Everglades Club and the Court of Stotesbury, was suddenly in demand.

Most Palm Beach regulars were weary of spending the two-month season in hotels with their servants, no matter the elegance. Like the Stotesburys, several had moved into "cottages" near the beaches. By 1918, vacationers were stretching the winter season in the Florida sun. They knew they were addicted to the intoxicating warmth of Palm Beach, with its lazy days and exciting nights. They knew they would return each year and were ready to invest millions of dollars in permanent homes. They demanded Mizner's touch.

All the industrialists, bank presidents, oilmen, and their wives rushed to his door, waving money and pleading with him to put his "genius" to work for them. One woman, frustrated that Mizner was not returning her calls, confronted him on the beach where he was sunbathing. She demanded to know why he had not yet designed a home for her. The burly giant rolled on his side and, using a driftwood stick, sketched a villa in the sand. "There is your design," Mizner said. "Send me a check." The woman stared at the drawing. She was thrilled.

With Mizner at the helm in the early 1920s, the island of Palm Beach was transformed for the first time since Flagler had cleared jungle for the Royal Poinciana Hotel. Real-estate brokers sold large plots of land, and Mizner then built grand Mediterranean palaces among the swaying palms.

Mizner brought his grandiose style to each mansion he built, making changes along the way. His whimsical alterations drove up the cost astronomically, but that never stopped him from making a last-minute change. "These people can't stand the sight of anything that doesn't cost a lot of money," Mizner reasoned.

Thanks to his helter-skelter style, however, Mizner sometimes lost track of his design changes. One villa was "completed" without a bathroom in its proper place. Another had a beautiful outdoor stone staircase leading to nowhere. If these structural errors had been made by anyone but Mizner, lawsuits would have been filed.

But Mizner's goofs had the opposite affect. He was the darling of Palm Beach, a half-wit genius and an authentic artiste. Any omission by Mizner was viewed as a rare faux pas. A "Mizner mistake" became a status symbol, and a home that had one was worth a little more. Several prospective homeowners offered Mizner extra cash under the table if he would build a "mistake" into their mansions.

Among his brilliant accomplishments were Casa Benedita, with its four-story octagonal tower, for John S. Phipps; Casa de Leoni, with its Venetian palazzo and a slip for a gondola, for Leonard Thomas; and the fierce citadel, Towers, for American Woolen Company president William M. Wood. Each had a timeworn look. Mizner hated anything that appeared new. To satisfy his passion for an antique look, he devised ways to make tiles appear weathered. One method was to blast the tiles with condensed milk and then rub steel wool on the surface. Mizner, who had arrived on a stretcher only a short time before, was now heralded as Palm Beach's equivalent of Stanford White and Michelangelo. He could do little wrong in Palm Beach society.

To cool his vast girth, Mizner wore his shirts open at the neck. He then dared to defy fashion standards by wearing his shirttails outside his trousers while he lumbered about Palm Beach with his faithful companion, Ethel, a small monkey, on a shoulder. Instead of being ostracized for his shabby appearance by the polished residents of Palm Beach,

Mizner's "look" was declared fashionable and the American sport shirt was born.

His prestige went beyond fashion and architecture. He dictated tastes in furniture, art, and interior decoration, and he opened businesses to capitalize on the various markets. One afternoon, Mizner announced that his brother, Wilson, was coming to Palm Beach to assist him.

In 1921, Wilson Mizner was a celebrated wit and aphorist. He was credited with several widely quoted remarks, "Be nice to people on your way up, because you'll meet them on the way down." Some even claim he coined the expression "Never Give a Sucker an Even Break."

But there was more to Wilson Mizner than his wit. Wilson Mizner was also an unmitigated huckster; a hard-drinking, drug-abusing, real-life character in Damon Runyon's New York circles. His admirers considered Wilson simultaneously a playwright and prizefight promoter, cardsharp and opium smoker, and authors such as Anita Loos and O. Henry were drawn to him.

"If you steal from one writer, it's plagiarism," Wilson Mizner advised his writer cronies. "If you steal from many, it's research."

Wilson's last attempt at creativity in New York was on the Broadway stage, but his promising career was cut short by a vicious beating. The young Wilson had stiffed a local dope ring out of cash, and to teach him a lesson, the ringleader hired thugs to break Wilson's jaw and a dozen bones in his body. To ease the pain of his injuries, Wilson stepped up his daily injections of morphine. His habit worsened. He became such an untrustworthy addict that his crooked friends would not trust him around money.

Shunned by his own band of friendly louts and cheats, Wilson Mizner suffered the ultimate shame: he had to look for an honest job. No businessman would hire him, a gangly and gaunt figure of a man obviously suffering from drug addiction. Impoverished and deathly ill, Wilson Mizner arrived in Palm Beach. His brother's standing in society could not prevent people from whispering about Wilson's appearance. Rumors quickly spread that Wilson had just been released from jail.

How did Wilson respond? He shaved his head and started inventing tales of prison life. His favorite fiction was about his Australian cellmate. One day, he said, his jailmate had received a cable from his wife. The communiqué read: "Send money. Baby and I are hungry." The Australian's reply: "Eat Baby!"

Addison imported specialists from New York to help his brother. Wilson made halfhearted attempts to quit. Nothing worked. But one afternoon, freshly buoyed by a drug injection, Wilson Mizner went for stroll in West Palm Beach. He had once said he preferred the morgue to Tiffany's, and now spotted a funeral parlor and went in. A mortician near the door was working on a particularly unpleasant-looking corpse, and he apologized for his inability to make his subject appear more attractive.

"He was a hophead," the undertaker explained. "They won't set up."

Wilson went home and replaced his morphine with scopolamine, a syrupy alkaloid plant extract used as a sedative or truth serum, and weaned himself off the opiate. He never definitively revealed whether the withdrawal was painless or difficult. To some, Wilson said he barely suffered. To others, he said he had to chew the rugs to withstand the pain.

The old Wilson Mizner returned once he was back on his feet. He started to drink small amounts of laudanum, and he enjoyed a good swindle now and then. Many playmates from New York visited Palm Beach after he was well. "They were wanted everywhere and welcome nowhere," Wilson said of his big-city friends.

Addison had put Wilson in charge of his tile factory. But Wilson could not resist embezzling money to subsidize his high-stakes gambling at the casino in Bradley's Beach Club opposite the Royal Poinciana on the intracoastal waterway.

The wily and mysterious Colonel Edward R. Bradley preferred thoroughbred horses to people, but he was foremost and always a gambler. "I'd bet on anything," Bradley once told a congressional panel.

Bradley owned stables in Kentucky, and his horses won four Kentucky Derbys during his eighty-odd years, but during the winter season he stood sober watch over his "private" club, which was considered America's Monte Carlo. The poker-faced, blue-eyed Bradley painted the Beach Club green and white to match the silks on his racehorses, which he referred to as "my children." He offered three games of chance: chemin de fer, baccarat, and roulette.

Bradley posted a menu each day at the Beach Club that contained no prices but offered the finest food in the country. Writer Cleveland Amory noted that the famous Swiss chef Conrad Schmitt first introduced green turtle soup to America in the early 1900s at the "B.C."—at the extravagant price of one dollar per portion.

Bradley also insisted his patrons wear evening attire in his plain white clapboard club that stood back from a trim expanse of lawn. The gentlemen happily responded with white tuxedos and the women gleefully donned sequined gowns with layers of their gaudiest diamonds and furs. One sign inside the Beach Club reminded: GENTLEMEN ARE REQUESTED NOT TO SMOKE IN THE BALLROOM. Another in the gambling room said: LADIES AND GENTLEMEN ARE RESPECTFULLY REQUESTED TO REFRAIN FROM LOUD TALK AND LAUGHTER.

Millions of dollars changed hands in an evening at Bradley's, with one industrialist losing $750,000 in a night. Armed guards with machine guns stood watch over the octagonal gaming room from white-trellised perches near the ceiling. Even the conservative E. T. Stotesbury got into the act. It was reported that he and Bradley had a falling out over some imagined, long-forgotten slight. They finally shook hands and made up by wagering $1 million on the turn of a card. Neither gentleman revealed who won.

The wily Bradley housed his employees in a special building called the Barracks, where they were kept under guard and never permitted, even during their leisure time, to mingle with patrons. Bradley paid his employees at the end of the season, at which time he gave them a 10 percent bonus. Despite the restrictions, most of his employees remained loyal B.C. workers for upward of forty years.

When age caught up to Bradley and he closed his casino in 1945, bootlegger Joe Kennedy commented that Palm Beach had lost "the old zipperoo." Bradley once remarked that "I don't want to be the richest man in the cemetery." In accordance with the Colonel's will, the Beach Club was torn down upon his death, the land was given to Palm Beach as a public park, and the gambling equipment was towed out to sea and sunk.

For a few fleeting months in the early 1920s, the Stotesbury mansion was eclipsed in size by Mizner's newest creation, Playa Riente (Laughing Beach), for which the jolly giant received $1,800,000 from Oklahoma oilman Joshua Cosden. Built just north of the Palm Beach Country Club, Playa Riente was Cosden's way of playing a game of social one-upmanship with the Stotesburys. Because it was situated on a beach ridge, Mizner designed a tunnel through the sandy knoll to allow a view of the ocean from the double entrance doors, which led into a grand sixty-foot-long by two-story-high hall with rib-vaulted ceiling.

Cosden, a former Baltimore streetcar conductor, was a charming chap with a delightful wife and desperate need for social standing. But he was unable to unseat the Stotesburys at the top of the Palm Beach heap. Mrs. Stotesbury thwarted the upstart oilman by having Mizner build additional wings for their mansion so that the estate could never be dwarfed again.

Her home was the center of Palm Beach society. It was, however, finally outdone in 1927 when cereal heiress Majorie Merriweather Post and her second husband, E. F. Hutton, built the incomparable 114-room Mar-a-Lago.

But for now the glorious El Mirasol—like the Stotesburys' White-marsh Hall estate in Philadelphia—was an American showplace—the palace that symbolized the opulence of the Golden Age of Palm Beach.

5

The Two Generals and the Socialite's Daughter: Douglas MacArthur, John Pershing and Louise Cromwell Brooks

El Mirasol never looked more beautiful than on Saint Valentine's Day, February 14, 1922. The sprawling Mediterranean-style villa was festooned with military bunting. Flags bearing the colors and markings of West Point and the famed Rainbow Division flew atop the Spanish red-tiled roof. The driveway and neatly kept grounds of the thirty-two-acre ocean-to-lake estate were ringed with American flags, waving in the gentle breeze.

Henriette Louise Cromwell Brooks Stotesbury, the daughter of Palm Beach grande dame Mrs. Edward T. Stotesbury, stood atop a tall stepladder rearranging decorations. She was shifting roses and ribbon, and with each alteration she leaned back on the ladder and studied her work with the intensity of an artiste. The finicky changes were so minute that only she could notice them. From her behavior, there was not a hint she was to be married in thirty minutes.

It was exactly four P.M. The groom, Brig. Gen. Douglas MacArthur, the great American "fighting" general of World War I, arrived at the mansion. MacArthur was early, as usual, and dressed in his handsome whites and ribbons. The dashing brigadier with the perfect posture looked out and saw that the two hundred guests—one hundred ninety-nine of them chosen by Mrs. Stotesbury—were already in their appointed seats on the lawn. Mrs. Stotesbury had positioned Addison Mizner, the eccentric architect of El Mirasol, and Paris Singer, the owner and president of the island's exclusive, members-only Everglades Club, in the front rows. Nearby were her industrialist and financier friends dressed in winter season white tuxedos and gowns. Mrs. Stotesbury had permitted MacArthur to invite only one friend, Clayton E. "Buck" Wheat, the West Point Academy chaplain, and the brigadier was satisfied when he spotted the chaplain talking amiably near the altar. Then MacArthur stepped into the mansion to see his bride. He was stunned to find her standing on a ladder wearing workclothes and playing with flowers.

With their wedding only minutes away, MacArthur, the stern military officer, reprimanded his bride-to-be and then lectured her on the importance of punctuality. He ordered her off the ladder and into her wedding attire. Henriette said she did not even know where to find the chiffon apricot gown and diamond necklace her mother had picked out for the occasion. The admission prompted MacArthur to erupt again. But in the face of the new tirade, Henriette only pouted. When it came to formality, Henriette Brooks—Louise as she preferred to be called—was positively cavalier. She belonged to an era of gaiety and reckless abandon. She was beautiful and rich, thanks to her mother's marriage to the country's wealthiest financier. Blessed with youthful exuberance, she was a bona fide boop-boop-be-doop girl.

By 1922, the Roaring Twenties were passionately under way, fueled by a postwar prosperity and a rebellion against Prohibition. Americans flocked to nightclubs and speakeasies with baccanalian verve. Flappers wearing tight knee-length silk dresses with frills danced with men who owned convertible cars and lived off trust funds. It was the Golden Age of Palm Beach, where Mrs. Stotesbury—Queen Eva—held sway, ruling with an iron hand in a velvet glove. And at the center of this glittering society were the grand parties for hundreds at El Mirasol.

Few women embraced the Roaring Twenties with the fervor of Queen Eva's daughter, Louise. She adored bathtub gin, hot jazz, the stock market, and everything that was new, wild, and unconventional. As a teenager, she had been the most talked-about debutante in Washington. Her coming-out party was the social event of the season. Her mother took over an expensive Washington, D.C., restaurant, Rauscher's, and converted it into a garden with cedar trees, asparagus ferns, palms, roses, and yellow lovebirds.

In 1908, Louise made the first of four trips to the altar, marrying Walter Brooks, a Baltimore socialite and contractor. The couple had two children. Their marriage ended after eleven years, with Louise's wild ways to blame. She sported short skirts, bobbed hair, and a new man on each arm. She had taken to the speakeasies and shed the restrictions of married life to play hard with the fun seekers of high society gearing up for the Roaring Twenties.

By 1919, she had booked passage on an ocean liner for "Gay Paree" to join her wealthy friends in France even before the ink had dried on her divorce papers. Writers compared her to Zelda Fitzgerald and Clara Bow, the popular gamines of the Jazz Age. William Manchester, a MacArthur biographer, wrote, "With her tousled short hair, roving eyes, and impish grin, Louise seemed forever on the prowl for the Great Gatsby."

In Europe, Louise—who appeared to be no more than twenty-five—although she was in her thirties—was soon "linked" romantically with several military officers. One was bachelor Col. John G. "Quek" Quekemeyer. Another, English admiral Sir David Beatty, was married. When his and Louise's names surfaced in the gossip columns, Sir David's very regal wife, Ethel, moved out and filed for divorce.

But the suitor who fell the hardest for the ravishing Louise was Gen. John "Black Jack" Pershing. The great American hero of World War I, Pershing now served as the United States chief of staff. The general had first met Louise in Washington, D.C., while she was still married to Walter Brooks. Pershing managed to get close to her by inviting the couple to his formal parties. In a short time he enlisted the vivacious Louise to serve as his "official" hostess at various military or political functions. Soon the newspaper columnists began to gossip that Louise and the general, a widower, were spending time together away from their "official" appearances. Several writers made scandalous remarks about the relationship, offering cutting snipes at the married Louise. When Pershing appeared with Louise in Europe, the reporters speculated that Pershing intended to take the affair public.

Pershing gave every suggestion to the "in crowd" of Paris and the writers who monitored their every move that he was in full command of the gay divorcée. Some reporters, obviously responding to Pershing's signals, speculated in print that Louise would certainly become the next Mrs. John Pershing, which was precisely what he wanted. The besotted chief of staff had been writing love letters to Louise, pouring out his heart to her. He signed each letter affectionately with his nickname, Pudgy.

Manchester wrote that Pershing hoped the four military stars on his shoulder would overcome Louise's desire for a "gold-hatted high-bouncing lover." But Louise fell for another—younger—general. In January 1922, Louise returned home, dividing her time between El Mirasol and an apartment in New York. She was only days away from heading to Palm Beach for the "season" when she received an invitation to a party in Tuxedo Park, then an exclusive resort north of New York City and about twenty miles south of the United States Military Academy. At the dinner party, she was introduced to Brigadier General Douglas MacArthur, then the forty-two-year-old superintendent of West Point.

MacArthur had become a national hero after he led the famed Rainbow Division of National Guard troops through France and into Germany in 1918. When he returned home from the war, the much-decorated MacArthur found himself hailed as the nation's greatest front-line general. The tall, distinguished officer was named the youngest superintendent ever of West Point. It was another distinguished position in a spectacular and storied career that spanned six decades and reached its peak following the World War II, when he was proclaimed "the principal architect of the victory in the Pacific."

Descended from a proud line of decorated military men, MacArthur was born to be a soldier. People who knew the young officer knew early he would be a great success. His parents would have it no other way. Particularly his overbearing and cunning mother, Mrs. Lieutenant General Arthur MacArthur, who was nicknamed Pinky. She was determined that Douglas—"my boy" as she referred to him—would one day become the nation's chief of staff.

Pinky dressed Douglas in skirts and kept his hair in long curls until he was eight to extend his childhood and increase his dependence on her. When he graduated from high school in Texas, Douglas, a sports star, was the class valedictorian and already an eloquent speaker. Despite his success and an impressive dossier of endorsements that his parents compiled for him, young MacArthur was not appointed to West Point by President Grover Cleveland in 1897 or the following year by President William McKinley. Worse still, MacArthur suffered a curved spine, a malady that would permanently bar his entrance to West Point if not corrected. Pinky devised a solution.

The family moved to Wisconsin and Pinky moved 230 miles away from Mr. MacArthur with Douglas to Milwaukee to establish residence in the congressional district of an old friend of her husband's. She also sent young Douglas to a specialist to correct his posture. Driving her son physically and mentally, Douglas straightened his spine and achieved a near-perfect score on his West Point entrance exam. Now Douglas would not be denied admission. MacArthur moved to West Point in 1899. But he did not come alone. Pinky moved with him. For the next four years, his mother stood guard over her son's window to make sure he burned the midnight oil. Her pressure kept MacArthur at the top of his class.

"He was without a doubt the handsomest cadet that ever came into the academy, six-foot tall, and slender with a fine body and dark flashing eye," another cadet commented. When those handsome features attracted young women, which they often did, Pinky feigned an illness and forced her devoted son back to her side. And when her "illness" failed to lure him away, Pinky recovered miraculously and marched over to visit with her son's suitors, telling them that "my boy" was already married—to his career. MacArthur, with few distractions, graduated first in his class in 1903.

When he returned sixteen years later to West Point—this time to serve as superintendent—Pinky, now a widow, was still at her son's side. She moved into the Academy mansion with him. People wondered how Pinky was distracted on the evening MacArthur went to Tuxedo Park and met and fell in love with a society girl who enjoyed drinking and dancing all night. Louise Brooks was positively the last woman alive that Pinky or her late husband would have chosen to be their daughter-in-law.

"Of course, the attraction is purely physical!" Pinky cried from her "sickbed." She was right. The chemistry between MacArthur and Louise was instantaneous. It was impossible to determine who was the more smitten: the sexually experienced, sophisticated flapper whose stepfather was worth $100 million or the charming, handsome officer in charge of West Point. It did not matter. By the end of the evening, they were engaged to be married.

"If he hadn't proposed the first time we met, I believe I would have done it myself," Louise later told reporters.

Word of the sudden engagement quickly reached General Pershing. He was instantly the unrequited lover and, worse, furious that Louise's choice of another man was his younger military rival. Pershing immediately telephoned Louise. He threatened her, warning that if she did not call off her plans to marry MacArthur, he would see to it that MacArthur was transferred to a remote, oppressively hot island as far away from the United States as he could be sent. Such a threat could not be accomplished easily—even by the country's chief of staff. MacArthur was in the third of a four-year assignment at West Point. But Pershing insisted he could, and would, do it. Louise, however, would not be blackmailed. Her engagement to MacArthur was announced formally in the *New York Times* on January 15, 1922.

Fifteen days later, Pershing launched his offensive. He sent a letter to MacArthur. The communiqué said Pershing had just learned that MacArthur had testified on Capitol Hill about the West Point budget without alerting the chief of staff:

> I am astonished to hear this, as evidently you neither called at this office nor on the Secretary of War during your visit. I think a proper conception of the ordinary military courtesies, to say nothing of Army regulations and customs of the Service, should have indicated to an officer of your experience and rank the propriety of making known your presence in Washington, the purpose of your visit, and to have considered with the Department the matters you proposed to bring to the attention of the Military Committee.

MacArthur responded that he had followed procedures and there must be a misunderstanding. He said he had been summoned to Congress on a few hours' notice and with "barely time to make the necessary arrangements and rail connections." Despite the short notice, MacArthur said he not only notified the Adjutant General's Office when he arrived in Washington, but had telephoned Pershing's office to find out if Pershing wanted to talk with him. He was told by an aide that the chief of staff did not.

MacArthur thought his explanation—and subsequent apology— would settle the misunderstanding. Unbeknownst to MacArthur, the vengeful Pershing was carrying out his threat to Louise. Late that afternoon, January 30, 1922, Pershing told MacArthur that he was being transferred to the Philippines.

MacArthur, the loyal soldier, accepted the assignment without protest. Louise and Pinky were furious, but each for different reasons. Louise did not want to go to the Philippines. Pinky did not care if Louise went—she just wanted her boy to remain stateside. Both were confident they would convince Pershing to rescind the transfer. Louise's stepfather, after all, was a powerful Republican contributor with political contacts reaching into the White House. Ten years earlier, the president of the United States, William Taft, had given the champagne toast at her mother's marriage to Edward Stotesbury. Pinky, meanwhile, believed that between the MacArthurs' lifelong friendship with Pershing and her considerable clout at the Pentagon, "my Douglas" would remain in the States.

Plans on Palm Beach were hastily drafted for a grand wedding at El Mirasol. Invitations were sent out. Pershing received his invitation. But he informed Mrs. Stotesbury that—unfortunately—he had a previous commitment. Mrs. Stotesbury took the excuse at face value. Pinky flatly refused to attend. The following day, newspapers across the country heralded the Valentine's Day wedding in Palm Beach as the "Marriage of Mars and Millions." Pinky moved out of the superintendent's mansion at West Point. She complained of illness and moved in with her other daughter-in-law, Mary McCalla MacArthur.

Louise, meanwhile, secretly contacted Pershing and invited him to their new home as an offer of peace. Pershing would have none of it. As MacArthur started to prepare for Manila, reporters sensed a story and traveled to West Point. Louise exploded when she heard about the chief of staff's vengeful transfer, telling a stunned press corps that Pershing had been in love with her and was vindictively banishing her and her new husband to Manila because she had chosen MacArthur over him. She told the press that Pershing "warned me if I married Douglas he would send him to an island where there was a terrible climate and where I wouldn't like it."

"Jack wanted me to marry him," she said. "I would not do that, so here I am packing my trunks...exiled by Pershing."

The tabloids rushed to Louise's side. In screaming editorials they charged that Pershing was out of control with jealously and that his power had to be reined in. The "legitimate press" ultimately joined the controversy. The *New York Times* published editorials and letters sharply critical of Pershing's actions. The chief of staff was forced to respond. And he did. In extremely undignified, unmilitary language. "It's all damn poppycock," Pershing was quoted as saying in a page 3 story in the *Times*. In the article, Pershing denied he had issued an "exile order." MacArthur, he said, was being reassigned because it was high time the brigadier had foreign service.

As for Louise's charges that he was a spurned lover, Pershing said the allegation was "without the slightest foundation and based on the idlest gossip. If I was married to all the ladies that gossips have engaged me to, I'd be a regular Brigham Young."

Taking the offensive, Pershing skillfully survived the newspaper pummeling. That summer, MacArthur and his socialite bride and her two children set sail for the Philippines, a string of islands where his father had distinguished himself years earlier and where General Douglas MacArthur would later make military history.

MacArthur actually enjoyed the assignment, seeing "once again the massive bluff of Bataan, the lean gray grimness of Corregidor...in their unchanging cocoon of tropical heat." MacArthur's father had served in the Far East before him, and during one stint, with him, a lieutenant. Both men enjoyed serving with the Filipino troops.

The newlyweds moved into number 1 Calle Victoria, an eighteenth-century villa called the House of Wall, situated on a towering 350-year-old stone wall encompassing the ancient city of Manila. Louise, the socialite flapper, tried to adjust to her new surroundings, but she could not control her urges to create excitement in the blast-furnace heat. Within months, she had herself sworn in as a Manila policewoman and arrested a man for "abusing" his horse. Occasionally, at parties she poked fun at her absent husband, gently mocking his vanity and dignity.

"Sir Galahad conducted his courtship as if he were reviewing a division of troops." To another group she revealed she had joined a cycle club but laughed at the notion of her husband cycling with her. "Heavens, can you imagine Douglas on a bicycle," she said.

Finally she started to behave like a British colonialist, treating Filipinos as inferiors and creating resentment and animosity toward her husband. Her unpleasant conduct resulted from a combination of boredom and an increasing frustration at trying to use her considerable influence to have her husband transferred back to the United States. Behind the scenes, Louise had contacted M. Manning Marcus, a former Rainbow Division veteran who had become an influential lawyer in Washington, D.C.

"I wish you would get busy and get his promotion," Louise demanded of Manning, knowing that a promotion meant a stateside reassignment.

"I don't care what it costs!" she continued. "Just go ahead and send the bill to me personally. And don't tell Douglas!"

When Marcus reported that there was nothing he could do— "MacArthur was too young now." MacArthur, unaware of his wife's role, exploded. "Too young! Why, Genghis Khan commanded the union of his clans at thirteen, and at forty-eight commanded the union, the largest army in the world. Napoleon was only twenty-six when he was the world's most celebrated military leader. Mustafa Kemal Pasha was thirty-eight when he commanded his country's armies!"

In his biography of MacArthur, *American Caesar*, Manchester wrote that MacArthur's mother wrote gushing letters of affection to Pershing, hoping to talk him into helping "my boy" with a promotion. "It was a real joy to see you on Saturday looking still so young and wonderfully handsome!" she began in one letter. "I think you will *never* grow old."

Getting to the point, she continued:

> I am presuming on long and loyal friendship for you—to open my heart in this appeal for my boy—and ask if you can't find it convenient to give him his promotion during your regime as chief of staff? You are so powerful in all Army matters that you could give him his promotion by a stroke of your pen! You have never failed me yet—and somehow I feel you will not in this request... Won't you be real good and sweet—The "Dear Old Jack" of long ago— and give my Boy his well earned promotion before you leave the Army?

She closed the letter with the type of political benediction her boy would frequently invoke: "God bless you—and crown your valuable life—by taking you to the White House. Faithfully your friend—Mary P. MacArthur."

Her shameless appeal, coupled with Louise's illicit lobbying and her stepfather's influence, paid off. Ten days before he retired as chief of staff, General Pershing promoted MacArthur to two-star general, which immediately made him overqualified for his Manila assignment. The *New York Times* heralded the promotion of the country's "youngest Major General" who "stands a splendid chance of some day becoming head of the army."

In January 1925, General MacArthur and his wife, Louise, returned to the United States, taking up residence in Louise's estate, Rainbow Hill, outside Baltimore. Their marriage experienced a new burst of romance. But the rigors of MacArthur's second gold star consumed his time. He began to withdraw into his work. He would also spend long evenings reading with annoyance about the growing pacifist movement or writing promotional leaflets or tending to the rigorous chores of military service. The general was chained to his desk. The work was tedious. It was generally a dull, bland period for a military man. Like many other officers, MacArthur viewed the Roaring Twenties as a spiritual wasteland.

Louise, however, wanted to return to society and late-night parties, the world she loved. She already had rejoined several of her old pals for foxhunts and dinner parties. The taste of the Roaring Twenties made her long for the days of youthful exuberance. She seemed to want to make up for time lost in the Philippines.

The life of a general's wife was a difficult one. Louise urged MacArthur to resign his commission and accept any of a number of lucrative jobs he was offered by her stepfather and J. P. Morgan at Drexel and Company. She knew it was futile to ask MacArthur to quit the military, considering his genuine love for the army—and his overbearing mother.

By 1927, Louise's Roaring Twenties timeclock clashed with Mac-Arthur's military schedule. She had rejoined some of her high-stepping, free-spirited friends from the past in Palm Beach and in Washington and New York. Finally, in May, Louise took her two children and moved out of Rainbow Hill and into a townhouse at 125 East 50th Street off Park Avenue in Manhattan. General MacArthur and Louise gave the false appearance that their separation was geographical and was for convenience' sake. MacArthur fell into a brooding melancholia. He cared deeply for Louise, and he had an even greater affection for her children. During the marriage, MacArthur spent more time with her youngsters than their mother did.

In September 1927, the president of the American Olympic Committee died suddenly. MacArthur, a devotee of athletics in American life, was asked to replace him. MacArthur accepted happily. But when he set sail for Holland to prepare for the 1928 games in Amsterdam, the newspapers pointed out that Mrs. Douglas MacArthur was not with him when he boarded the steamer *Roosevelt*. Within a few days, the press started to report "sightings" of General Douglas MacArthur's wife, the former Henriette Louise Cromwell Brooks. Each sighting offered a wilder account than the one of the night before. Louise was reported seen in speakeasies and driving off with young playboys. Then she spent long weekends in Westchester. During the winter months, in Palm Beach, she caroused in bars and at wild parties, each time with a different escort, sometimes not the one with whom she arrived.

When MacArthur completed his mission to Amsterdam for the president, he was ordered to return to Manila to assume command of all forces in the Philippines. "No assignment could please me more," MacArthur said. On June 18, 1929, General Douglas MacArthur set sail from Seattle for the Philippines. Louise, however, headed for Reno, Nevada, to get a divorce. According to Manchester, MacArthur received the news from her lawyers at the House on the Wall in Manila.

MacArthur said he did not care about the grounds for divorce, as long as it "did not compromise my honor." They agreed to the preposterous grounds that MacArthur had been unable to keep Louise in the lavish style to which she was accustomed. The following year, 1930, Mac-

Arthur's name surfaced as a possible candidate to replace Charles Summerall as chief of staff. But several military men spoke against him, arguing that a man who could not "hold his woman" shouldn't be chief of staff. But on August, 6, 1930, President Herbert Hoover announced his choice: Douglas MacArthur.

MacArthur was acutely aware of the "dreadful ordeal" he faced if he accepted the appointment. He hesitated—and his mother stepped in. "My mother sensed what was in my mind and cabled me to accept. She said my father would be ashamed if I showed timidity. That settled it." Prodded by Pinky, MacArthur accepted the position and was promoted to four-star general. He returned to the United States and was sworn in as chief of staff in November 1930.

His mother, of course, moved in with him—just as she had done when he was a West Point cadet and later academy superintendent. This time Pinky joined her son in his government-supplied mansion, Fort Myer's Number One, on the south side of the Potomac River. MacArthur installed an elevator and erected a sun porch for his mother. A few days after the swearing in, Pinky sat proudly next to her "boy." She lovingly ran her fingers over Douglas's four gold stars: "If only your father could see you now! You are everything he wanted you to be."

Sitting on the porch in the afternoon sun next to her son, Pinky was unaware that there was another woman in her boy's life. She was a beautiful Eurasian woman named Isabel Rosario Cooper, whom her boy kept nearby as his exotic mistress. The daughter of an Oriental woman and a Scottish man, Isabel had met MacArthur in the Philippines, and she became his mistress about five months before he accepted the chief of staff post. After he returned to the United States, MacArthur cabled his "love," Isabel, and implored her to join him. The fifty-year-old MacArthur signed the cable "Daddy." Isabel, a former Shanghai chorus girl, packed her bags and came to America. MacArthur kept her in an apartment suite in the Hotel Chastleton at 1701 16 Street, N.W., in Washington.

"I thought I had never seen anything as exquisite," said Dorothy Detzer, a Washington lobbyist. "She was wearing a lovely, obviously expensive chiffon tea gown, and she looked as if she were carved from the most delicate opaline. She had hair in braids down her back."

MacArthur kept Isabel in sexy, silky robes, gowns, and kimonos and lingerie. There were few outdoor clothes in her wardrobe. MacArthur seldom took her out. "He wanted her always there for him," according to biographer Manchester.

When Isabel tired of the Chief's tight leash, she took to the nightlife of Washington. Her conquests included George Abell, a descendant of the founder of the *Baltimore Sun*. Isabel's evening forays became frequent, and MacArthur grew angry. Finally he cut off her money and sent newspaper help-wanted advertisements to her home when she demanded cash or a government job for her brother. But the wily Isabel would not be denied. She used columnist Drew Pearson as her wedge.

At the time, MacArthur had a $1,750,000 lawsuit pending against Drew Pearson and Robert S. Allen, writers of the "Washington Merry-Go-Round," for ridiculing him. The lawsuit worried Pearson and Allen until a congressman, Ross Collins of Mississippi, told Pearson that a lovely Eurasian living in his hotel was frequently visited by the new chief of staff. Pearson raced to Isabel's apartment, where MacArthur's vengeful mistress gleefully sold Pearson several of the general's love letters.

A few days later, at a pretrial hearing, Pearson's lawyers mentioned Isabel Cooper as a potential witness. It was the first time MacArthur's lawyers had heard the name. They asked MacArthur for an explanation. He offered none. And then he secretly dispatched a trusted aide, Maj. Dwight David Eisenhower, to find the "jilted" lover. Not even the major could locate Isabel. Pearson and his brother, Leon, had her well hidden.

Rather than confront Isabel in court, MacArthur announced suddenly that he was dropping his lawsuit. There was no mention of money paid to MacArthur or a retraction offered. According to Manchester, on Christmas Eve, 1934, MacArthur gave fifteen thousand dollars to an aide, who delivered it to Pearson at the Willard Hotel. The columnist in turn gave the payoff to Isabel, who moved to the Midwest, bought a hairdressing shop, and ultimately committed suicide by taking barbiturates on June 29, 1960.

"MacArthur could have won the suit!" Adm. William D. Leahy later said, after he learned the gamy details of the story. "MacArthur was a bachelor. All he had to do was say: 'So what?'"

"But do you know why he did not?" Admiral Leahy asked. "He did not want *his mother* to learn about the Eurasian girl."

In 1935, Pinky, then eighty-four, accompanied MacArthur when he returned to the Philippines. During the cruise, her cerebral thrombosis worsened. She died in November in a suite next to her son's room in the Manila Hotel. In the spring of 1937, MacArthur married Jean Mary Faircloth, whom he had met through his mother on that final cruise.

Remembering the ostentation of his Palm Beach wedding to Louise Brooks at El Mirasol, MacArthur invited no guests and had just two witnesses in attendance. He wore a conservative brown suit; his bride, who always refered to MacArthur as "General," wore a small brown straw hat and a brown coat trimmed with a red fox collar. The bride and groom celebrated their vows with a ham-and-eggs breakfast at the Hotel Astor. They later had one child, Douglas IV.

Louise, meanwhile, traded "four stars for one." Shortly after Mac-Arthur's 1930 promotion to chief of staff, Louise married Lionel Atwill, the forty-five-year-old English-born actor, who was on his way to becoming Hollywood's quintessential "mad doctor" in films like *The Vampire Bat, Doctor X*, and *Mystery of the Wax Museum*. Atwill, like Stotesbury, had been married twice before. But he found—much to his liking—that unlike his earlier two wives, Louise was an extrovert who loved a drink and a party.

Their one true passion was sex—straight and kinky. According to author Kenneth Anger, the Atwills occasionally invited parlor maids and chauffeurs into their bedroom for group sex. But one trick Mrs. Atwill refused to accommodate was her husband's desire to bring a trained fifteen-foot python into the act. He had gotten the notion while costarring with the fearsome-looking but gentle snake in *Murders at the Zoo*.

"All women love the men they fear," Atwill once told an interviewer. "All women kiss the hand that rules them. I do not treat women in such soft fashion. Women are cat creatures. Their preference is for a soft fireside cushion, for delicate bowls of cream, for perfumed leisure and for a Master!"

Louise moved out in 1939 and returned to Washington, D.C. Although separated, Louise had not heard the last of her bizarre husband. Atwill, the gossips said, was orchestrating large orgies at their Hollywood house on d'Este Drive with famous guests including director Josef Von Sternberg and actor Victor Jory. His orgies were so well planned they were preceded by hygienic screenings of all participants to prevent veneral disease. Atwill eventually was charged with showing hardcore stag films at this home as well as staging orgies. After initially denying he had shown the films, he was later convicted of perjury and given five years' probation.

As the scandalous stories spread, Louise received hundreds of hate letters in Washington. They criticized her for rejecting MacArthur, the American military hero, in favor of "Sex Fiend" Atwill. Some urged Louise to commit suicide. At the time, 1942, MacArthur was the epitome of American resistance and determination. He had just retreated from the Philippines and taken command of the allied forces in the Pacific, vowing "I shall return" to free the islands from Japanese invaders. Eight months later, in June 1943, Louise was granted a divorce from Atwill. And although she was wealthy, Atwill gave her a large property settlement. The next year, the fifty-four-year-old Louise made a fourth, and last trip, to the altar to marry another military man, Capt. Alf Heiberg, the leader of the United States Army Band.

MacArthur, with his ubiquitous corncob pipe, "returned" to the Philippines that year and was hailed as the "principal architect of the Pacific victory." He went on to lead the American troops in the Korean War and then did battle with President Harry Truman. The president ultimately removed MacArthur from his Far Eastern post—an unpopular decision. MacArthur's storied career included an unsuccessful bid for the presidency. In 1964, the brave, brilliant, and enigmatic General MacArthur died at the age of eighty-four.

Shortly after his death, and before her death the following year, Louise Brooks confessed that the three years she had spent with the young and handsome Douglas MacArthur in the Philippines were the happiest of her life. She went on to clear up the record for reporters seeking biographical material on the general. She acknowledged that the marriage toppled precipitously soon after she and MacArthur returned in 1925 to Washington, D.C., and Palm Beach. But contrary to public opinion, she said, the problem was not her love of parties or the rigors of MacArthur's grueling army career.

"It was an interfering mother-in-law!" Louise said. "It was Pinky who eventually succeeded in disrupting our married life."

6

How to Lose Millions—
The Real-Estate Crash:
Mizner, Singer, Stotesbury,
and Company

By the winter of 1925, when General Douglas MacArthur and his
socialite wife Louise Brooks returned from "exile" in the Far East to
Palm Beach, the tropical island had undergone its first major transformation since Flagler founded the Royal Poinciana in 1894.

The gigantic oddball architect Addison Mizner had constructed several mansions of the scope of El Mirasol, the Stotesbury palace where
the general and Louise had married in 1922. Where shrub and jungle
once stood, Mizner had built Warden House for William G. Warden,
the Pittsburgh Coal Company chairman, which began as a "nice, comfortable" home but ended up with thirty-two-rooms adorned with 128
columns. Mizner had also erected Villa Flora, a twelve-thousand-
square-foot oceanside Venetian Gothic mansion for Edward Shearson,
founder of a Wall Street brokerage firm; Villa del Sarmiento for Anthony
Biddle, Jr., and his tobacco heiress wife, Mary Duke, sister of Doris;
and Casa Nana for National Tea Company founder George S. Rasmusen,
which became known for a fashionable "Mizner mistake"—a missing
staircase.

The robust Mizner also introduced two narrow, twisting, Venetian-
styled "pedestrian" streets behind Paris Singer's superexclusive Ever-

glades Club—Via Mizner and Via Parigi. The two vias formed the feet of fabulous Worth Avenue, attracting world-class retail shops and shoppers. Mizner complained he was working on a hundred jobs at once, sometimes sketching two new buildings a day. The island had blossomed to the point that he had competition. Architects Maurice Fatico and Marion Sims Wyeth were hired as rivals and were commissioned to build sprawling villas for Mrs. E. F. Hutton (Marjorie Merriweather Post), Joseph Widener, the Philadelphia capitalist and turf man, and Jessie Woolworth, daughter of the five-and-dime-store magnate.

The tropical island had such an influx of semipermanent residents that, between the mansion, the Breakers Hotel, the Royal Poinciana Hotel, and Bradley's elegant casino, the very landscape of jungled Palm Beach was gone. The Breakers Hotel alone was rebuilt on 140 oceanfront acres in 1925 following a devastating fire. Resembling a huge twin-towered Villa Medici in Rome, the Breakers was constructed with 567 rooms, 41 suites, 4 ballrooms, wood-bathed Italian Renaissance hallways, and private golf course. During Prohibition the sprawling hotel was alive with guests whose consumption of illegal spirits was unaffected by federal law. Not only did the hotel have a huge underground wine cellar and liquor supply, but the management constructed private booths in an enclosed balcony above the dining room where guests could eat and drink without detection. The hotel also provided another service for gentlemen guests—"house whores"—who were as elegantly dressed as their wives. Jim Ponce, the Breakers' historian, said, "Any good hotel at that time had them."

By the middle of the decade, Palm Beach had become a full-blown stomping ground for the rich and famous "Golden Horde" that was roaring through the twenties.

Movies stars and financiers, musical greats and industrialists, became known for their homes or winter stays on Palm Beach island. Irving Berlin and John Philip Sousa composed on Palm Beach. George Gershwin wrote "Rhapsody in Blue" on Worth Avenue. George McManus drafted his cartoon "Bringing Up Father," on Palm Beach. And Mr. and Mrs. Norman Talmadge brought show people to the island. First-run movies were premiered on Palm Beach—and some were burned right away, depending on the reaction.

John Noble, director of many of the great stars of the era, lived there. Actors in his employ included Ethel Barrymore, Lionel Barrymore, Gloria Swanson, Charlie Chaplin, Mary Pickford, and Douglas Fairbanks. Florenz Ziegfeld and his wife, Billie Burke (the future "Good Witch" in *The Wizard of Oz*), launched the spectacular "Palm Beach

Nights" on January 14, 1926, where "there were more famous persons, more wealth, more wonderful gowns, furs and jewels gathered in one audience than in any other in the whole world," one attendee recalled.

Ziegfeld, Harold Vanderbilt, and the Phippses all had "cottages," as the rich called their beachfront homes. And there was Laddie and Mary Sanford, and the Wanamakers, and, well, everyone. They all shared America's Riviera—the tropical paradise envisioned by Flagler only thirty years before.

The real-estate boom was not confined to tiny, tony Palm Beach, however. The land rush hit all of Florida. Investors gobbled up land and sold it the next day, often for double the price. There were reports of eleven-year-old schoolboys like Gray Singleton of Fort Meade swinging $100,000 deals single-handedly. Or entertainers such as E. F. Albee, the vaudeville king, shelling out $4 million for a property he had turned down for $10,000 only weeks before. And a New York cabbie who drove down a party of people who could not get railroad accommodations turned his fare and tips into a modest killing.

Along Florida's east coast, developers purchased huge tracts of land and announced that hotels and homes would soon be built. Prospective purchasers had to move quickly before the price went up, very often the next day. Even people like Colonel Jake Ruppert, owner of the New York Yankees, who hated the boom because it distracted his players during spring training, turned around and bought a beach and an island, subsequently named for him. The *Miami News* compared the stampede of the wealthy with the foot race of the original Okies into the Cherokee Strip when it was thrown open to homesteaders in 1893.

The land rush was more intoxicating than playing the stock market. For the first time, Broadway celebrities and popular sports figures were brought down by the trainload to the Sunshine State to lend glamour to the hustle of one project over another. Golfers Gene Sarazen, Bobby Jones, and Walter Hagen pitched developments with golf courses. Babe Ruth showed up at hotel openings. Gene Tunney and Jack Dempsey hawked property.

Film stars Rudolph Valentino and Gilda Gray appeared here and there for a fee. And Ben Hecht and J. P. McEvoy came to Miami to find material for W. C. Fields and instead stayed on as supersalesmen; with Hecht literally stuffing his pockets with wads of cash, people thought he was putting on pounds of fat. The boom was so enormous that developers hired press agents to boldly promote the next Venice, Nice, or Monte Carlo, which were being drained of aristocrats flocking to Florida with fists laden with lire and francs.

Since 1920, Florida's population had grown from a couple of hundred thousand to one million, with Miami, where the land rush was born, registering one hundred thousand inhabitants by itself. The city was at fever pitch, with its skyline transformed by new hotels. The July 26, 1925, edition of the *Miami News*—thick with ads—was 504 pages and weighed seven and a half pounds. As the dollars poured in, the number of banks rose from a handful to one hundred.

And the boom reached far to the north of Palm Beach. St. Petersburg, which had entered the decade with only 14,237 residents, now had six thousand licensed real-estate salesmen. The Florida boom was the first mania of the automobile age. And with hundreds of millions of dollars at stake, everyone got into the act. The rich of Palm Beach were no exception. Why stop at one fortune when another could be had just a few miles away?

Addison Mizner and his witty brother, Wilson, were slow to get in on the real-estate craze. Addison was enjoying his life as society's architect, and Wilson hated legitimate work. "You don't have to work hard to make a fortune at legitimate business, but you do have to *work continuously*," Wilson observed.

Finally, they envisioned exclusive new developments with Mizner-designed mansions and hotels on the coast at Boca Raton and Boynton Beach, to the south of Palm Beach. Mizner—evoking memories of Flagler—proclaimed that his developments would attract such wealth that they would turn Palm Beach into an island for its "help" in the same way West Palm Beach had been created to serve Palm Beach. Wilson staffed the corporation with old cronies from New York. There was the "Palm Beach socialite" who had been convicted of infanticide, a "banking chum" who had done time for manslaughter, and the couple he introduced as "Mr. and Mrs. Earl," who were two professional swindlers.

Paris Singer, meanwhile, announced that he would build a playground for the superrich on a small island about ten miles north of Palm Beach. The Singer sewing machine heir said that, after years as the monarch of his Everglades Club and Palm Beach society, he would sell the facility and use the proceeds to build Singer Island, a resort that would make Palm Beach "look like a slum."

Florida historian David Nolan wrote; "Mizner's defection from Palm Beach, the resort where he had been responsible for $50 million worth of buildings and a whole visual revolution, was compounded by the simultaneous defection of the Singer sewing heir.

"Poor Palm Beach! After three decades at the top, was it to be cast on the ash heap of history now that it was threatened by a squeeze play from the Mizners and Singer?"

Completing the Palm Beach rebellion, Eva Stotesbury's son, James Oliver Cromwell, a great playboy, declared he, too, was entering the Florida real-estate market. Trading on his stepfather's famous name in financial circles, Cromwell purchased four thousand acres of land about sixty miles south of Palm Beach in Lauderdale, which was named after a monarch, the Earl of Lauderdale. Cromwell advertised that the former king of Greece had purchased a site for a home there. He further promoted the project, called Floranda, by bringing Countess Gwendolyn of Lauderdale and her son, Lord Thirlestone, to inspect the grounds.

Mizner's Boca Raton project was a heady and immediate success once work was completed on the ornate Cloister Inn, which today is the Boca Raton Hotel and Club. Investors raced to buy sites from Mizner, plunking down tens of millions of dollars for oceanfront homes thirty miles south of Palm Beach that existed only on Mizner's elaborate drawing board. The bonanza was so quick the Mizners did not have time to purchase furniture for their offices.

When Wilson summoned a former secretary, Bess Hammon, to help, she experienced firsthand the whirlwind of a real-estate boom. According to Mizner biographer Alva Johnston, Hammon quit her routine Wall Street job, hopped a train south, and, when she arrived in Florida, was greeted at the station by Irving Berlin. The songwriter drove her from the station to Mizner Corporation headquarters, where she was greeted by one of Addison's monkeys—"Johnnie Brown, the Human Monkey," now buried under Via Mizner. Johnnie Brown jumped out of a window and wrapped its arms around Hammon's neck. Half stunned by her two unexpected welcomes, Hammon located her office, a completely bare room. She sat down on a window ledge, put her typewriter on a packing case, and starting typing contracts, stopping at midnight.

For the Boynton project, the Mizners built a broad twenty-lane mile-long highway through its midsection, called El Camino Real, or the King's Highway. Because it was short, "The Mizner Mile" had little value for traffic, but its width was vastly suggestive. Mizner said he would build a $10 million hotel along Mizner Mile that would be operated by the Ritz Carlton chain. The rest of the nine-hundred-acre "mile" would be carved into sites for Mizner estates.

"We'll get the big snobs and the little snobs will follow," Wilson Mizner philosophized.

The project had its celebrities to add glitter. In addition to Berlin, there was Elizabeth Arden, General T. Coleman Du Pont, Harold Vanderbilt, and Marie Dressler, who was Tugboat Annie on the silver screen, but in Mizner's hyperbolic world was the Duchess of Boca Raton. It also had a share of royalty: Lady Diana Manors, the duchess of Southerland, Charles Spencer Churchill, and Princess Ghika of Romania.

There were two flaws in this Mizner paradise, however. First, another highway already ran along the coast, and it separated Mizner's property from the ocean. Second, a group of Finnish immigrants had taken up residence on the beach—"our beach," as they referred to it. The Mizner renderings of million-dollar homes did not include Finnish immigrants swimming in the surf with the "big snobs."

Wilson Mizner devised the solution. In the dead of night, he had bulldozers and tractors tear up the "Finn Road." Under the illumination of road flares and automobile lights, Wilson Mizner, wearing a silk hat, white tie, and tails, directed the destruction from the top of a construction truck. A near riot resulted as Wilson stood high above the Finns, shaking his fist down at the cursing, bat-wielding immigrants. But the dozens of irate Finns were no match for the heavy equipment. The road was destroyed. With little political influence, the Finns were helpless to challenge the powerful Mizner brothers, and they simply moved on. With the Finns out of the picture, the Mizners' project took off. Part of its success was clearly due to the Du Pont name.

Only the real-estate boom could have brought two people like General Du Pont and Wilson Mizner together. Du Pont was a tireless prankster. He sometimes amused himself by pretending to be deaf and dumb. At six-foot-four, he became a familiar figure in Palm Beach, in his white knickerbockers, knee-length silk stockings, and tweed coat, from which he constantly pulled out a pack of cards to demonstrate a trick. His residence had telephones that shot streams of water from the earpiece. But he was foremost a financial whiz and a man of uncanny business acumen. As chairman of E. I. Du Pont de Nemours & Company, his name alone could attract scores of millionaires to a project.

Exaggerated claims had become the order of the day. In November 1925, *Advertising & Selling* magazine tried to warn investors: "Motion-picture scenery, trick photography, impressionistic art, distorted and unscaled maps—every twist and turn of fake advertising from the Year One appears in the Florida advertising of the unscrupulous promoters."

The Mizners were no exception. They had hired Henry Riechenbac, perhaps the greatest pipe-job artist of his day. They took great liberties in their promotions and advertising. They made grandiose claims about Du Pont's involvement in their project, prompting General Du Pont to publicly chastise them—particularly Wilson—for the wild and false promotions. Du Pont cited one advertisement that claimed "yachts could discharge directly at the lake entrance to the Mizner hotel" when there was no hotel and the largest vessel that could possibly land at the proposed site was a small skiff.

Du Pont's public rebuke of the Mizners was carried in the *New York Times* and *New York Herald Tribune*. It had the instant effect of souring investors. In fact, Du Pont's remarks carried such weight that they reverberated throughout Florida. Hardhearted bankers stopped construction as concrete was being poured. "Great" cities halted before a single inhabitant moved in. Florida, the richest country, was fresh in ruins. Many people say it was General Du Pont's warning that sent the real estate into a tailspin and ultimately a crash.

The Mizner stock, which had soared from one hundred to one thousand dollars a share on the opening day of sales, plummeted even faster. Lawsuits charging fraud were filed. During one courtroom confrontation, Wilson Mizner was asked whether he had promised a potential buyer that he could grow nuts on the property. "I said he could 'go nuts,' not 'grow nuts!'" Wilson replied. The Mizners put on a bold face until March 1927, when their Cloisters finally opened, but, as one writer said, they were fighting after the bell.

Singer's project became a monument—literally—to the crash. Construction of his grand hotel on Singer Island halted with only the seven-story skeletal frame completed. On April 17, 1927, Singer was arrested at his apartment at his Everglades Club, charged with obtaining $1,500,000 under false pretenses and making false and fraudulent promises which he never intended to carry out to investors in Palm Beach. He spent a day in jail before his friends came to the rescue posting a $20,000 surety bond. As soon as he was freed from prison, Singer took the first train north to New York. He later avoided prosecution but the wonderous metal form of his ill-fated Blue Heron Hotel stood on the horizon for years, visible from land and sea, a giant rotting steel roost for seagulls and pelicans, until it was torn down.

And Cromwell's project in Lauderdale also went under—$1 million in debt. If it were not for his proud mother, Cromwell would have spent years in embarrassing litigation. But Queen Eva would not have her name sullied by scandal. She bailed out her boy. In January 1927, Mrs. Stotesbury told the newspapers she felt responsible for the investors who had lost money because it was her "good name" that attracted them to the project in the first place. She said she would pay out $500,000 in cash and that Mrs. Hugh Dillman (the former Mrs. Horace Dodge and

Cromwell's first mother-in-law) would put up the remainder. Instead of scandal, the newspapers applauded Mrs. Stotesbury's forthrightness and generosity, and her reputation remained intact.

In a few months her family's name emerged again in the gossip columns, and not even the Stotesbury millions could contain this scandal. By September 1927, her daughter, Louise, the high-spirited flapper, and General MacArthur, the solitary soldier, had separated. MacArthur sailed off—alone—to Amsterdam to head the 1928 American Olympic Committee. Louise stayed behind and returned to her beloved Great Gatsby Palm Beach lifestyle, until she and "America's Caesar" were officially divorced.

Through it all, the Great Florida real-estate crash and the great stock-market crash, James Cromwell managed to survive quite well. He married, and divorced, two of the "richest girls in the world": Delphine Dodge and Doris Duke, the tobacco heiress. The Duke divorce was particularly messy, with the beautiful heiress rushing off to Reno for a quick divorce and charging that Cromwell was a male golddigger who married her only for her money. The Reno divorce did not prevent Cromwell from getting $7 million in cigarette money. James Cromwell went on to serve briefly as a diplomat and politician. He died in 1990, at age ninety-three.

His mother, the Mizners and Singer, however, were dealt crushing blows by the two "great" crashes.

Following the real-estate crash, Addison Mizner could barely find a commission. Not only had his sweeping, whimsical style fallen from vogue, it was fashionable to build homes in diametric opposition to the "Mizner look." Society leaders ordered homes in any style but Spanish. Young architects reversed Mizner at every point, Johnston wrote, introducing the lightest of blond woods as a contrast to the gloomy Mizner interiors. Mizner spent his final years borrowing from friends—just as he had done in New York City years before. Nearly penniless, Addison and Wilson left Florida for good and returned to their native California.

In Hollywood, which Wilson compared to "a trip through a sewer in a glass-bottom boat," he scored a final time by writing the dialogue for *One-Way Passage,* a highly successful Oscar-winning romance with William Powell released in 1932. He then joined H. K. Somborn, one of Gloria Swanson's former husbands, in opening the famed Brown Derby restaurant. In 1933, Wilson was working in Hollywood on a picture called *Merry Wives of Reno,* when he received word that Addison was dying. He wired: "Stop dying: Am trying to write a comedy!" But unlike the "fatal" illness that had brought Addison Mizner to Palm Beach in 1918, this malady was genuine. As process servers and bill collectors dogged him, the sixty-two-year-old architect, who had changed the Florida landscape, died on February 5, 1933.

Less than two months later, President Roosevelt was inaugurated, California was rocked by an earthquake, and Wilson Mizner, fifty-eight, suffered a heart attack at the Warner studio. He slipped into a coma. His friends stood around his hospital bed, telling Wilson Mizner tales. Someone remembered the time Mizner had managed Stanley Ketchel, the great middleweight fighter who went twelve rounds with Jack Johnson, the embodiment of the fighting spirit. News was telephoned to Wilson Mizner that Ketchel had been shot and killed. "Tell 'em to start counting ten over him, and he'll get up," Wilson had quipped.

Wilson rallied briefly from his coma. When he regained consciousness, he found a priest standing over his bed. He waved the clergyman away. "Why should I talk to you? I just talked to your boss."

The priest reproached him, warning that death was at hand.

"What? No two weeks' notice."

Following his death, screenwriter Anita Loos based the character Blackie Norton in the 1936 movie *San Francisco* on her old friend Wilson Mizner. The part was played by Clark Gable.

Paris Singer—the sewing heir, Isadora Duncan's "Lohengrin," and monarch of the Everglades Club—fled Palm Beach (and a phalanx of real-estate creditors) during the crash for England. He died penniless in a London hotel on June 25, 1932, at the age of sixty-six.

The greatest surprise was the toll the crashes took on the Stotesbury millions. When E. T. Stotesbury died in 1938 at age eighty-nine, the financier's estate was valued at a mere $6 million—a far cry from the anticipated $50 to $100 million.

In those Depression-era days, newspapers mocked his wife's sudden bad luck: SLUMP HITS RICH WIDOW, one headline read. There was no compassion for a Fallen Heiress forced to divest herself of an estate. Her Whitemarsh Hall, the 147-room estate in Philadelphia that left Henry Ford awestruck, was the first to be carved up and sold.

"When one gets used to 272 rooms and 80-odd servants it must be pretty hard to give them up," one story sarcastically began. "She is moving to a smaller place. She has a bit of a villa at Palm Beach that has only 30 rooms or so—just enough for light housekeeping."

The money raised from the sale of Whitemarsh Hall ran out, almost immediately, and the newspapers trumpeted another Stotesbury auction. "Can it be?" one journal asked. "Has Mrs. Edward T. Stotesbury decided to dispose of her fabulous collection of jewels?"

With the possible exception of Mrs. Anthony J. Drexel Biddle, Mrs. Stotesbury had the finest collections of "sparklers" in the U.S.A. "And unless my eyes deceive me," one story said, "some of her finest bits of what the underworld inelegantly dubs 'ice' have found their way into the famous Fifth Avenue jewelers with price tags attached to her widely recognized diamond and emerald necklaces, jewelry she wore often to her husband's society bashes."

It was true. A fire-sale liquidation. Millions of dollars in gems changed hands at bargain prices. The saddest transaction came in December 1943, at the end of the divestment. An internationally recognized Romanoff emerald necklace and diadem that Mr. Stotesbury had bought for $1 million years earlier was sold for one-third that price. The necklace, which had once belonged to a Russian empress, was the famous knee-length strand of huge square emeralds that Mrs. Stotesbury has worn at her Palm Beach soirées accompanied by armed guards.

Finally even her beloved El Mirasol—Palm Beach's first great mansion—fell victim to the money crunch. The glorious estate from which she had ruled Palm Beach society was subdivided and six parcels sold. Herbert Pulitzer, the newspaper magnate, was among the first to buy, purchasing an acre of choice beachfront property for $100,000. He and five others built smaller homes on the El Mirasol grounds before time—and exorbitant maintenance costs—caught up with the beautiful and ornate mansion. In 1971, El Mirasol itself was razed.

The great stock-market crash was cruel to many millionaires. Newspapers were filled with stories of depressed and bankrupt Wall Street executives and businessmen hurling themselves out of buildings in despair. Several of Palm Beach's best-known figures went to sleep millionaires and awoke the next morning penniless. It was common to see ladies selling furs and diamonds in hotel lobbies and gentlemen raffling off their polo ponies and yachts to the highest bidder. High-society princesses found themselves behind the sales counters of clothing shops or working as receptionists, eking out a living at less than the minimum wage.

Cobina Wright, the wife of stockbrocker William May Wright, once described her life as "all tinsel, all unreal, materialism to the nth degree." After the crash, she and her daughter donned Daniel Boone raccoon caps and formed a supper-club singing act. According to writer C. David Heymann, one newspaper roared WRIGHTS PERFORM IN FRONTIER GARB: SOCIETY IS DEAD.

But as Wilson Mizner might have said: One man's loss is another man's gain!

7

The Bootlegger and the Movie Star: Joe Kennedy and Gloria Swanson

The crash of 1929 hit hard. Fortunes were gutted, businesses wrecked, jobs lost, lives ruined. Breadlines formed all over the nation as the government attempted to feed the hungry and the homeless. The song "Brother, Can You Spare a Dime?" captured the hopelessness and the desperation of the time.

The economic blow was not as severe in Palm Beach. There were no breadlines, and people were not forced to sell apples on street corners. Many of the island's wealthy residents, however, lost millions in investments and speculative ventures. In the weeks and months following the terrible Black Tuesday of 1929, large FOR SALE signs were hammered into the ground on many of the great lawns along Ocean Boulevard and other prime streets on Palm Beach's palm-dotted waterfront. The Royal Poinciana, Flagler's first magnificent hotel, was slowly turning into a white elephant. The Breakers and other smaller hotels had become the guest houses of choice.

One self-made millionaire with financial problems was Rodman Wanamaker, the Philadelphia businessman who created the successful chain of Wanamaker department stores, and whose company still bears his name. Wanamaker owned an impressive Addison Mizner mansion overlooking the Atlantic at 1095 North Ocean Boulevard, a street known locally as "Millionaires Row."

In 1923, Mizner had constructed the sprawling, Spanish-style twenty-room mansion for Wanamaker at a cost of fifty thousand dollars. The department-store owner called his new estate, with its white stucco walls and red tile roof, La Guerida. The property included tennis courts, an underground passageway to the beach, and an Olympic-size swimming pool. In Philadelphia, where Wanamaker lived, he would boast to friends about the beauty and the peacefulness of La Guerida. He loved the tranquillity, the gentle swaying of the palms, the therapeutic coolness of the ocean breezes.

Hurt by the crash, Wanamaker now watched as his once bustling stores lost business during the Great Depression. He reorganized his cash-strapped empire. But it became clear to him that La Guerida would have to be sold. With its substantial furnishings and amenities, in a normal market the house might be expected to draw from $250,000 to $300,000. But in this new, uncertain, postcrash atmosphere, there was very little chance that any home, no matter how opulent, would command top dollar. Wanamaker put up his FOR SALE sign outside La Guerida.

An offer for the property came in the summer of 1933. It was from a young, balding, bespectacled businessman from Boston who had been driven by the property one afternoon in his open-air limousine. He walked through the grounds and then inspected the house. Inside La Guerida, the mansion was stocked with impressive dark wood furniture that had been designed by Mizner. There were six large bedrooms— four that faced the ocean—a huge kitchen, servants' quarters, and a patio overlooking the Atlantic. A few days later, the man offered $100,000 for the property.

His name was Joseph Patrick Kennedy and his offer for the Wana-maker property was accepted a few days later. As Joe Kennedy, forty-five years of age in 1933, put his signature on the contract, he was one of the few men in Palm Beach, and one of a small group of multimillionaires in the country, who could truthfully boast that his fortune had been unaffected by the crash.

Kennedy had made most of his money in the stock market, often through insider trading deals, and through his extensive bootlegging business during Prohibition. A brilliant businessman, he had predicted the crash. Once a great gambler in the stock market, Kennedy began liquidating many of his investments in the year preceding the market plunge. The market was too unstable, he told friends, when the shoeshine boys on Wall Street were handing out stock tips. "Only a fool holds out for top dollar," he warned. He had learned his business sense from his father.

Born in 1888, Joe was the son of successful Boston businessman Patrick J. Kennedy and Mary Augusta Hickey. Joe's father, affectionately known as "P.J.," had started out as a dockworker in Boston Harbor and scraped together enough money to buy a small tavern in the city's Haymarket Square. He eventually used profits from the saloon to buy two more and branch out into the liquor distribution business. As a youngster, Joe had watched his father expertly use his business skills and outgoing personality to operate his taverns and make many friends in blue-collar Boston. P.J. later used his clout to launch a successful political career as a Massachusetts state representative. He went on to be elected a state senator and Boston fire commissioner. P.J. had become a powerful man.

Young Joe Kennedy admired his father and wanted to follow in his footsteps. He believed, as his father had demonstrated, that running a moneymaking business was the key to success and power. P.J. was pleased by young Joe's drive and used his influence to help get him started. With P.J.'s connections, Joe was easily accepted into the prestigious Boston Latin preparatory school. Although he was a lackluster student with poor grades, Joe later went on to Harvard University, again with the help of his father. At the Ivy League institution, Joe continued to make poor grades. He had never applied himself in his classes. Instead, he had concentrated on sharpening his social skills. Joe wanted to meet the people who could possibly help him after graduation. His grades were of secondary concern.

Joe's college motto was "Go for it!" and when he did it was often with his father's not-so-subtle assistance. One blatant example featured the Harvard baseball team. Joe, a decent ball player, had desperately wanted to win a varsity letter in his senior year, but had not been able to play a single game during the season because he constantly had been edged out by superior talent. As the final game of the season approached, team captain Chick McLaughlin received a call from Joe Kennedy's aides, who asked to meet him in private.

At that meeting, the aides bluntly informed Chick they were aware that after he graduated, he hoped to open a movie theater in Boston and had already applied for a license. They told him that unless Joe was allowed to play and get his letter, Joe's father would see to it that McLaughlin would never get his license. On the day of the Harvard-Yale game, the coach picked the usual lineup.

But in the ninth inning with Harvard winning 4-1, McLaughlin hastily approached the coach. Would it be all right, he asked, if Kennedy was placed in the game for one play. The coach was puzzled but approved the change. Kennedy was sent to first base and made the final out of the game. He also kept the winning ball, which by tradition always went to the team captain. When McLaughlin approached him and asked for the ball, Joe refused to surrender it. "I made the putout didn't I?" Joe said.

Upon Joe's graduation in 1912, P. J. Kennedy placed him on the payroll of Boston's Columbia Trust Bank, in which he had a significant financial interest. Eighteen months later, Joe, a lowly bank examiner, told his father he wanted to be bank president. Exercising his considerable financial influence over the board and pouring on his charm, P.J. convinced the bank's board of directors to appoint Joe to the position. One of Joe's immediate policy changes at the bank was to call in loans more quickly, foreclosing on homes of families who were slow or delinquent in their mortgage payments. Columbia Trust lost its reputation as the small friendly neighborhood bank but increased its profitability.

During his rise at Columbia Trust, Joe had begun dating a young woman named Rose Elizabeth Fitzgerald, the daughter of Boston's mayor, John "Honey Fitz" Fitzgerald. Joe and Rose had been acquaintances since childhood, knowing each other from various political functions that P.J. and Honey Fitz and their families attended. Joe liked Rose, who was two years his junior, and he realized the positive political connections he could make by marrying into her family. But Honey Fitz did not believe Joe was good enough for his daughter and for a while, Kennedy was forced to correspond secretly with his girlfriend. Eventually Joe's persistence paid off, and in 1914 the two were married.

A few years later, Joe made his first trip to Palm Beach. Kennedy's friends had raved to him about Flagler's magnificent island, the grand Royal Poinciana and Breakers hotels and how they catered to men of great wealth and power. After his initial visit, Kennedy was convinced. He had fallen in love with Palm Beach. Rose already had pleasant memories of the island, having traveled there several times as a child. After the births of their first two children, Joseph Patrick Kennedy, Jr., and John Fitzgerald Kennedy, in 1915 and 1917, respectively, the young family began making yearly pilgrimages to Palm Beach to escape the harsh northeastern winters. Some of Joe's most pleasant memories were of playing with his two infant sons on the beach outside the Breakers Hotel.

Another reason Joe enjoyed Palm Beach was the discretion it provided for one of his other pleasures: enjoying the company of other women. The island regularly attracted young women from all over the country who took on menial jobs at the grand hotels in hopes of meeting wealthy men.

If Rose Kennedy knew what was going on—and most Kennedy chroniclers say she did—there was never a word about it to Joe. "It was not easy to deceive Rose Kennedy," remarked her former personal secretary Barbara Gibson. "It might perhaps be the case that Mrs. Kennedy's attitudes were shaped by the necessity of adjusting to a husband who was often away from home for long periods and was rumored to be involved with numerous other women."

It was easy for Joe to carry on his affairs even when he and Rose traveled together, because they often stayed in separate rooms, sometimes in separate hotels. In New York, Joe would check into the Waldorf Astoria while Rose stayed at the Plaza. In Paris, Joe lodged on the outskirts of the city near a golf course, while Rose would reside on the Left Bank in the heart of the city. Rose, in fact, later attributed their lasting marriage in part to their frequent separations and independent natures.

A family friend told Kennedy biographers Peter Collier and David Horowitz that Rose "knew what was happening, knew about the girls and all, but she basically liked the life she led, the money and prestige. She bought in lock, stock and barrel."

Joe Kennedy invested his savings in the stock market and often made substantial profits from insider trading information. In 1919, he entered what was to be the most profitable enterprise of his life: bootlegging. That year, the federal government had bowed to the pressures of fire-and-brimstone preachers and women's temperance groups and, passed the Eighteenth Amendment, prohibiting the sale and consumption of alcohol in the United States.

Joe realized that alcohol was a part of American life and, no matter what the government did, people would somehow find a way to have a drink. He knew that now that the big American distilleries were out of business, somebody would have to supply liquor. Kennedy realized that basically all he had to do was take "underground" the liquor-distribution operations his father had established in the Boston area. With his father's blessing, Joe Kennedy built a bootleg-liquor empire and, within two years, became one of the nation's largest suppliers of illegal spirits. He did so with the help of organized crime.

"He's one of the biggest crooks who ever lived," said Chicago mob boss Sam Giancana, who would later share one of his mistresses with President John F. Kennedy.

"I helped Joe Kennedy get rich," Frank Costello, former boss of the feared Luciano organized crime family, told author Peter Maas in 1973. Costello said he and Kennedy were partners in the bootlegging business during the Roaring Twenties. In the underworld, Joe Kennedy became known as "Bootlegger Joe."

"Bootlegger Joe" supplied the nation with liquor in two ways. He smuggled fine whiskeys and champagnes from Europe on large cargo ships. In an elaborate scheme he created to beat the system, a Kennedy ship would reach a port and be approved by inspectors to dock. However, Kennedy would not unload the cargo. With the boat officially approved to be in the United States, it would then sail to a smaller port where its unmarked crates filled with cases of liquor could be unloaded with little scrutiny.

Joe also was involved in the production of so-called bathtub gin, scotch, and rum. While illegal distilleries were more difficult to hide, payoffs to corrupt authorities assured their uninterrupted operation. The high profits from these operations transformed Joe into a millionaire at the age of thirty-two.

In the early 1920s, the motion-picture business had become one of the fastest-growing industries in the United States. Men, women, and children throughout the nation gladly parted with a few pennies every week to see the latest two-reelers by stars like Charlie Chaplin, Harold Lloyd, and Buster Keaton. Joe Kennedy, already a successful bootlegger and stock-market player, perceived the new industry as another vehicle by which to make money. He had seen Jewish immigrants like Louis B. Mayer, Sam Goldwyn, and Adolph Zukor storm Hollywood and become enormously influential there. He decided that the movie business held great opportunities for him, too.

In February 1926, during a visit to Palm Beach, Kennedy sketched out what he believed was a winning formula for successful, profitable moviemaking: low budgets, tight shooting schedules, and fast turnover from camera to movie theater. He then traveled to Hollywood and arranged to buy a failing studio called FBO Pictures. Soon Kennedy was cranking out successful westerns with cowboy star Fred Thompson and melodramas with Red Grange, the legendary "Galloping Ghost" of the University of Illinois football team. Kennedy's formula was successful indeed. It was fast, slapdash moviemaking, but very profitable.

Joe's status as movie producer grew. He became known as "the picture maker." Winter seasons in Palm Beach, Joe would hold "picture nights." For several years in a large rented house on Clark Avenue, Kennedy held special screenings of Hollywood films that had not yet been released. He invited his friends, local politicians, and society people to watch the movies in his backyard.

These picture nights were always fun. A screen and projector were set up among dozens of padded lawn chairs. At dusk, the projector was switched on and servants roamed the gathering like classy movie ushers, holding trays of champagne and hors d'oeuvres. Among Joe's frequent guests were *Time* magazine founder Henry Luce, Irish tenor Morton Downey, and New York's Catholic leader Francis Cardinal Spellman. Occasionally, if a picture was universally panned by his audience, Kennedy would burn the print immediately.

Although his studio churned out moneymaking movies, there was no question that Joe's movies were not enduring art. His production company did not have acting talent like Mary Pickford, Douglas Fairbanks, or Charlie Chaplin. And his directors were not of the stature of artists such as D. W. Griffith, Cecil B. DeMille, and Erich Von Stroheim.

Kennedy wanted to work with "big name" movie stars and directors, people who would give his productions a touch of class. He wanted to see their names shining brightly on the huge screen below the title JOSEPH P. KENNEDY PRESENTS. Among the many stars Kennedy admired was Gloria Swanson, the sultry, Chicago-born actress who had started her career doing pratfalls in Mack Sennett comedies. In the 1920s, Swanson had grown into more serious roles in pictures such as *Her Love Story*, *A Society Scandal* and *Manhandled*.

A demanding and tempestuous actress, Swanson often behaved like a tyrant on her movie sets, but the finished product was usually acclaimed by the critics and made money. She had a natural screen presence, a sensuality that stole any scene in which she played. By 1925, at the age of twenty-six, Swanson was Hollywood's top sex goddess, earning around $1 million a year.

Her marriage record was not as impressive as her box-office appeal. Swanson's first husband, whom she wed while she was a teenager, was beefy, barrel-chested actor Wallace Beery. The marriage quickly soured after Beery discovered she was pregnant and, not wanting children, fed her an abortion-inducing potion that nearly killed her.

The relationship with her second husband, Herbert Somborn, also went badly. Instead of fighting him in divorce court, which would have produced sensational headlines, Swanson agreed to pay him a $1 million settlement.

Husband number three was the handsome Marquis de la Falaise de la Coudraye, known simply as Henri. She had met him in France while filming the movie *Madame Sans Gene*. Henri came from a royal family so their marriage supplied Swanson with the title of Marquise.

As was common among many of the big stars, Gloria had formed her own production company in order to gain financial and artistic control over her films. However, the budgets of her last few movies had been substantially higher than the original projections. Her most recent film, *Sadie Thompson*, a lush adaptation of W. Somerset Maugham's *Rain*, had gone so far over budget that she had been forced to sell some prime beachfront real estate she owned in Malibu to raise cash.

One of Swanson's friends, Paramount Pictures executive Robert Kane, listened to Swanson's woes. He assured her that movies often took time to recoup their initial investment and turn a profit. If she believed, however, that tighter financial controls were needed at her company, perhaps she should speak to Joseph Kennedy, a businessman and film distributor who had a reputation in Hollywood as a budgetary tightwad. Perhaps he could give her some advice, Kane suggested. Swanson, still agonizing over the loss of what had been her favorite property in Malibu, said she would like to talk to Kennedy.

Their meeting took place in the fall of 1927, at the Hotel Barclay in New York. Swanson was impressed by the dapper, driven Kennedy. He discussed the film business as if had invented it. There was no problem for which he did not have a solution. "Everything he said was reasonable and convincing," she remembered.

In turn, Kennedy had been impressed by Swanson—particularly her great beauty. A few days after their meeting, Kennedy telephoned Swanson and made a business proposition. He offered to become her business partner and carefully monitor costs in their venture to maximize profits.

Attracted by the sheer drive of this smooth-talking, bespetacled little man from Boston, she agreed. Within a few weeks, Gloria and Joe formed Gloria Productions. Kennedy fired the business managers who had supervised her previous pictures and installed his top money men to oversee the new company's costs.

In the winter of 1928, Joe invited Gloria to Palm Beach. On the day she arrived by train from New York, a fidgety, excited Kennedy, holding a bouquet of flowers, waited on the platform. As the train slowed, Kennedy leaped on board. He pushed through Swanson's entourage, including her husband, Henri, who was busy arranging for the luggage to be carried off.

"I was standing in the doorway to our drawing room... when I saw Joe Kennedy come charging down the narrow aisle from the other end of the car like a cyclone," Swanson recalled. "He pushed me back into the drawing room, said a few excited words, and kissed me twice. Just as quickly, he released me and straightened up to his full height, and in doing so he scraped his head on an overhead rack and knocked off his spectacles. I started to laugh when he fell to his knees to retrieve them under his seat, and I laughed even harder when he stood up and I saw that the knees of his white pants were dirty and he had lipstick smeared on his face." Swanson pointed to the lipstick smear as Kennedy straightened up.

"I missed you and I wanted you to know," he told her without embarrassment.

As the group left for the Royal Poinciana Hotel by limousine, Joe Kennedy told Swanson that she was the honorary queen of Palm Beach, a compliment that would have ruffled the real queen, Eva Stotesbury. Joe had prepared all of the accommodations for Swanson personally.

"The manager of the Royal Poinciana greeted us at the door and presented me with an orchid corsage," recalled Swanson in her autobiography. "Then a parade of bellboys and a captain led all of us up to a cool, spacious suite, which in the early morning light could have passed for a florist's shop, the proprietor of which favored orchids almost above life itself."

"Everybody in Palm Beach is lining up to meet you," Kennedy said, beaming. "And, Gloria, just look at all these invitations," he continued, presenting her with a stack of handsomely embossed cards announcing a special party Mrs. Stotesbury was to give in her honor. "People will be arriving from all up and down the Eastern seaboard for it," Kennedy said.

Echoing his enthusiasm, one of Kennedy's aides chimed in, "Anybody who didn't get an invitation has just one week to leave town!"

"It left no doubt that Mrs. Stotesbury was the big fish, the unques tioned leader of Palm Beach society," Swanson recalled. When Swanson excused herself to unpack, Kennedy left with a huge grin on his face. By now he was thoroughly infatuated with Swanson's great beauty. He began to plot a way to be alone with the movie star.

Swanson's husband, Henri, was a typical romantic Frenchman—doting, attentive, clingy. In chatting with Henri, Joe learned that the Frenchman was intrigued by the sport of deep-sea fishing. It was something he had always wanted to try.

Kennedy immediately saw his opening. He generously offered Henri the use of his private yacht. Kennedy explained that he didn't fish and, in fact, had an aversion to the sport and therefore could not go himself. But a crew and a couple of top fishermen would be at Henri's disposal to help him learn the basics. The next morning, after Henri's fishing entourage sailed off from the dock, Joe proceeded to the Royal Poinciana and showed up unannounced at Swanson's room.

The star, who found Kennedy awkward yet boyishly charming—answered the door to find her new business partner dressed in white flannel trousers and an argyle sweater, resembling a Rudy Vallee knockoff.

"He just stood there staring at me a full minute or more before he entered the room and closed the door behind him," she said. Then he grabbed Swanson tightly around the waist without saying a word.

"He moved so quickly that his mouth was on mine before either of us could speak. With one hand he held the back of my head. With the other, he stroked my body and pulled at my kimono. He kept insisting in a drawn-out moan, 'No longer. No longer. Now!'" Swanson recalled. "He was like a roped horse, rough, arduous, rearing to be free. After a hasty climax, he lay beside me, stroking my hair. Apart from his guilty, passionate mutterings, he had still said nothing coherent. I said nothing at all."

Swanson, twenty-nine, tried to put the encounter with the forty-year-old Kennedy into perspective. "Since his kiss on the train, I had known this would happen. And I knew, as we lay there, it would go on. Why? I thought. We were both happily married. We were ten years apart in age.... All arguments were useless, however. I knew perfectly well that whatever adjustments or deceits must inevitably follow, the strange man beside me, more than my husband, owned me."

The Kennedy-orchestrated tryst was the beginning of a passionate and stormy two-year affair. When it began, Palm Beach was preparing for its annual Washington's Birthday Ball at the Royal Poinciana, the grand gala originated by Henry Flagler in the 1890s. The organizers, always attempting to outdo the previous year's theme, dreamed what would be the most magnificent theme of all. The theme was Babylon...Palm Beach Babylon. And this Babylon, the organizers decided, would be staged like a Cecil B. DeMille epic.

"The ball captured the Babylonian beauty of song and story when Nebuchadnezzar ruled the triple-walled city and created a kingdom whose sybaritic splendor would live in glorious memory through the centuries," reported the *Palm Beach Daily News*. The costly decorations included an altar to the goddesses Rhea and Juno that had been copied from a museum piece. It was cast in bronze with a glowing, jeweled effect and shone in a soft violet light against a silver background. Around the ballroom, red and orange temple fires burned. The fantastic Hanging Gardens of Babylon were also re-created with flowers that bloomed in "an extravagant manner." A twenty-piece orchestra played until dawn. Many of the elegantly dressed revelers still swept the dance floor with crystal champagne glasses in their hands, praying the sun would never rise.

"It was a fitting tribute to an emperor whose love of beauty was insatiable," the newspaper said. It was also a fitting high point for the hotel, which would never rise to the occasion quite as magnificently again.

In the weeks following the great Washington's Birthday Ball, Joe Kennedy visited Swanson often. Their lovemaking sessions intensified. Kennedy began to realize that if the affair were to continue, something would have to be done about Swanson's husband, who had had enough of fishing and was looking for other diversions. Kennedy devised a new scheme.

He had recently purchased a financial interest in Pathé Studios, a large movie company with several studios abroad. Kennedy approached Henri and made him a proposition. He said he desperately needed a head of operations for Pathé's Paris studio and that Henri would be ideal. He flattered the Frenchman, saying he had the intelligence and talent to take on the prestigious job, which would pay handsomely. Henri would have to sail soon, however, because the office needed immediate attention.

The unsuspecting Frenchman thanked Kennedy and told him his offer was very generous. But there was a problem. Gloria. He would be separated from her from six months to a year. Henri told Joe he loved his wife deeply. He also worried that other men would chase her once he left for Europe. Kennedy smiled and promised that he would be personally responsible for Swanson. He would make sure that she stayed away from other men. With Kennedy's personal guarantee, Henri accepted the position and sailed for France two weeks later.

With Swanson's husband out of the way, Joe began spending more time in Beverly Hills, where his black limousine would pick up Swanson at the studio and bring her to his rented home for afternoon lovemaking sessions. The couple visited Palm Beach alone several times over the next six months. Joe became so enamored with Swanson, he begged her to have an illegitimate child with him. But she wanted no part of it and privately prayed she would not become pregnant by him.

Joe's faithful wife, Rose, welcomed her husband's "business partner" with open arms whenever she came to visit his family. Rose's approval of Gloria permitted an atmosphere so cordial that Gloria was invited to accompany Rose and Joe on an ocean cruise to London. They all had separate cabins. After dining at night, Joe would spend evenings with Gloria. During the trip, Rose and Gloria became friendly enough that they went off to Paris on a shopping spree. Gloria helped Rose pick out all the latest Parisian fashions for her wardrobe.

Unlike Rose Kennedy, who was something of a miser, Gloria flaunted her wealth. She owned a stunning Hollywood mansion, a Lancia with leopard-skin upholster, a huge gold bathtub built into her solid black marble bathroom, and an amazing clothing bill. In one year, Gloria spent: $25,000 on fur coats; additional wraps, $10,000; gowns, $10,000; stockings, $9,000; lingerie, $10,000; perfume, $6,000; purses, $5,000; and hats, $5,000.

The Roaring Twenties demanded parties, and Gloria threw many posh ones for her Hollywood friends. "Oh, the parties we used to have," she recalled years later. "In those days, the public wanted us to live like kings and queens. So we did. And why not? We were in love with life. We were making more money than we ever dreamed existed and there was no reason to believe it would ever stop."

For his next film project for Swanson, Kennedy decided he would create a big-budget motion picture that would not only serve as a crowning achievement to her talents, but also as a lasting symbol of their relationship. Unlike his usual films, for this one he would spare no expense. It was a radical departure for Kennedy who, during a speech at Harvard University, discussed Swanson as a commodity. He had told the audience, "The Gloria Swanson picture that opened in Roxy's theater the other night may have rented in that theater for $50,000 for ten days. But nine months from now it will rent in Oshkosh or somewhere else for $7.50.... You are always running a race with the calendar."

For this new production, however, Joe planned to alter his surefire formula. This would be Swanson's best picture, perhaps the greatest picture of all time. He began planning a massive publicity campaign to tout what would be the masterpiece in the Joseph P. Kennedy film library.

Kennedy commissioned the notorious Erich Von Stroheim to write and direct the new production. Legendary as Hollywood's Mr. Hyde of directors, Von Stroheim, of half-Austrian, half-Hungarian extraction, came to his sets wearing riding boots, military jacket, a monocle, and brandishing a large stick, which it was rumored he occasionally used on his extras. His authoritarian costume and manner had earned him the nickname The Hun.

A few months after the deal was finalized, Von Stroheim delivered a finished script—a dark, brooding, and decadent story called *The Swamp*, which chronicled the sordid life of a virginal convent girl swept off her feet by a roguish prince and sent to live in a whorehouse run by her aunt in East Africa.

Kennedy found the story eccentric and unconventional, but he remained silent. He knew of the infamous director's reputation for ruling every aspect of his productions with an iron fist. Von Stroheim had produced some four-star epics over the years including *The Wedding March*, *The Merry Widow*, and *Greed*. He was also generally hated by studio bosses for his inability to conform. There was the "Hollywood way" and the "Von Stroheim way."

Von Stroheim also had a penchant for choreographing and filming steamy orgy scenes with his extras that could never be shown in public. Scenes of sadism and masochism. Gratuitous shots were taken of nude young starlets too frightened to protest the powerful Hun's orders to strip naked before his camera. He was also well known for presenting the studio bosses with completed films that ran much too long—from four to eight hours. Despite Von Stroheim's forbidding legend, Joe believed in him.

From the first weeks of shooting there was trouble. People at the studio said Von Stroheim was up to his old tricks, filming scenes the censors would never pass. Working on a closed set, Von Stroheim was said to have coaxed a dozen Hollywood starlets and pretty boys to writhe naked in front of him. To loosen their inhibitions, Von Stroheim charged caviar and champagne to Kennedy's account and had it laid out on banquet tables on the set. Some young extras were seen leaving the set in tattered clothes with lash marks on their backs.

Swanson had heard about the scenes, but Von Stroheim had wisely never asked her to participate in them. Concerned that the production—now retitled *Queen Kelly*—was in trouble, Swanson telephoned Joe back East, and told him of the reported excesses by Von Stroheim. Money was being wasted on footage that could never be shown. She and Kennedy had such long conversations over the production's problems, that Kennedy racked up the largest private telephone bill recorded in the nation in a single month at the time.

Swanson finally cracked during the filming of one of her scenes. In the script, a dirty, unshaven old lecher in filthy clothes was supposed to ogle Gloria and then grab her arm. As the cameras rolled, Von Stroheim yelled through his megaphone to the actor playing the lecher, "Drool on her arm!" It was too much for Swanson. She stormed off the set and, in tears, drove home to call Joe.

She told him about the scene, and a livid Kennedy promised he would fly to Hollywood in a few days to confront the maniacal director. When he arrived, Joe's meeting with Von Stroheim was brief. The director simply led him to a production room and announced that the production was rolling along splendidly. Von Stroheim pointed to a large stack of film cans containing previously shot scenes.

Kennedy investigated further and found, in fact, that the director had shot thirty hours of footage. That seemed excessive to Kennedy, even though he knew Von Stroheim sometimes shot scenes dozens of times until they were perfect. Kennedy was unprepared for what he discovered next. The thirty hours of footage, it turned out, represented only one-quarter of the shooting script! Kennedy realized if he let Von Stroheim carry on at the same rate, he might have some 120 hours of film, only ninety minutes of which would constitute the finished product. The film was already $600,000 over budget.

After viewing a few scenes, Kennedy fired Von Stroheim and ordered him off the set. In an effort to salvage the movie, he hired a new director. But after a few days it was apparent the film could not be saved, and the production was closed down. Kennedy had his first business failure. When he arrived at Swanson's home, he was near collapse. "He was making little high-pitched sounds... like those of a wounded animal whimpering in a trap," Swanson remembered.

"I've never had a failure in my life," Joe said, tears welling in his eyes.

Stunned by the experience, Joe tried to console himself by immediately starting on a new production. He quickly produced a mild mainstream comedy called *What a Widow!*, based on a script Swanson called "absolutely terrible." She had unsuccessfully begged him not to buy and produce it. *What a Widow!* was a moderate success.

But the film brought an abrupt end to the relationship. As Kennedy attempted to find a catchy title for the movie, one of his writers, Sidney Howard—a playwright who three years earlier had won a Pulitzer Prize for *They Knew What They Wanted*—yelled out "What a Widow!" Kennedy was so pleased, he immediately promised to buy Howard a Cadillac as a bonus. Several days later, Swanson's accountant asked her why Sidney Howard's new Caddy had been charged to her personal account instead of to the production company.

When she confronted Joe during dinner that evening, he "became so agitated, he choked on his food... When he regained his composure, he stood up without a word and left the room," Swanson remembered. "I waited then for the call or the note of apology I was sure would come. I imagined Joe crushed and ashamed at having behaved so childishly, and I was quite ready to forgive him... But no message arrived." It was just a few weeks before the stock market crash of 1929.

Joe, in the meantime, had phoned his attorneys and told them he wanted to sever all business ties with Swanson at once. Two days later, Swanson received, by registered mail, a legal notice returning to her the power of attorney in her business affairs that she had earlier signed over to Kennedy. As she later reviewed her financial statements over the length of their relationship, she discovered that Kennedy had charged most of her gifts to her personal account. Fur coats, jewelry, dresses, flowers, and many other wonderful presents she had thanked him for, she actually had paid for herself. It remains open to speculation whether Kennedy was merely billing her to avoid any possibility of Rose finding invoices lying around the house and had intended eventually to reimburse Swanson, or whether he was just being cheap.

Joe Kennedy never explained why he suddenly walked out of Gloria Swanson's life. The affair left Swanson bitter. Years later, a friend told Swanson that Kennedy "is still carrying a torch for you."

"Good, I hope it burns him," the actress shot back.

Ironically, a short clip from the troubled *Queen Kelly* appeared years later in the Oscar-winning 1950 motion picture *Sunset Boulevard*, a cynical look at Hollywood that starred Gloria Swanson and Erich Von Stroheim. (A few years ago, film historians pieced together what remains of *Queen Kelly* to make a ninety-minute feature hailed by critics.)

Shortly after breaking up with Swanson, Joe began dating a twenty-four-year-old brunette actress named Nancy Carroll, who resembled Gloria Swanson. Carroll was a former chorus girl who had gone on to make movies opposite leading men such as Gary Cooper and Fredric

March. She made motion-picture history in 1928 as the first actress to sing and dance in an "all-talking" picture, *Abie's Irish Rose*. Ironically, Carroll later competed with Swanson for a Best Actress Oscar at the 1929–1930 Academy Awards. Norma Shearer beat them both.)

In 1931, two years after their relationship had ended, Joe Kennedy telephoned Swanson. She had since divorced Henri and was living in London with a new husband and a new baby. Kennedy had left the movie business and had a new passion: national politics. After saying hello to Swanson, he told her, "I want you to speak to the next president of the United States—Franklin Roosevelt."

Before Joe could put FDR on the phone, a livid Gloria screamed, "How dare you!" and slammed down the receiver.

"It was so blatantly opportunistic that I was stunned," she remembered.

After his grand affair with Swanson and Kennedy's purchase of La Guerida, he began spending longer periods in Palm Beach. The house gave him a sense of belonging to the island. Rose liked her garden, long swims in the Atlantic, and strolls along the beach. Their children, nine by now—Joe Jr., Rosemary, Jack, Kathleen, Eunice, Pat, Bobby, Jean, and newborn Teddy—also enjoyed the beach.

Joe's favorite spot was the pool. Here he could relax, conduct business, refresh himself—and he usually did so in the nude. To keep nosy neighbors from getting a glimpse, he erected a white picket fence around part of the pool deck and dubbed the area the Bull Pen. Maids, servants, and secretaries would huddle around the naked Kennedy, waiting on him hand and foot as he conducted business on the telephone.

The Kennedys were now official Palm Beach residents. As the owners of 1095 North Ocean Boulevard, they were offered and accepted memberships at several private clubs, including the Seminole Club, the Everglades Club, and the Bath and Tennis Club. Nevertheless they remained outsiders.

As therapeutic as Palm Beach was, the family preferred their compound in Hyannisport, which became home base for the Kennedy dynasty. Palm Beach was good for short, refreshing retreats, but the Kennedys were cemented in Massachusetts and always would remain there. Accordingly, while cordial to Joe Kennedy and his family, Palm Beach society did not embrace them.

In December 1937, President Roosevelt appointed Kennedy ambassador to England. Kennedy was thrilled. He had lobbied for the position through his friendship with FDR's eldest son, Jimmy. Joe

Kennedy said he wanted to be the first Irishman to represent the United States in England. He and Rose sailed for London.

A year later, as World War II loomed, American citizens abroad were being warned to leave for the safer shores of the United States. Part of Kennedy's duties as ambassador was to inform Americans in Britain of the growing signs of war in Europe. One well-known American living in London was Barbara Woolworth Hutton, the niece of cereal-fortune heiress and Mar-a-Lago owner Marjorie Merriweather Post. She was a full-figured, dark-haired beauty, who had earlier renounced her American citizenship to become a Dutch citizen during one of her several short marriages.

In her London flat, as she packed for a trip back to the States, Barbara received a call from Ambassador Kennedy's office. Kennedy wanted to speak to her in person at his office. It was important. She made an appointment for the next day with Kennedy's secretary. Barbara knew Joe Kennedy and his wife quite well. They were close friends of her Aunt Marjorie and Uncle Joe, who was the ambassador to Russia. Kennedy had always been kind to her, acting almost like a father. He often related amusing stories to Barbara about Marjorie Post and the wonderful parties she hosted.

When Barbara arrived at his office for their meeting, Kennedy was not his usual jovial self. He shut the door and paced the room, his face tense. He told her how the political situation had changed and how she might have trouble getting back into the United States because she was no longer an American citizen. Luckily, he had conferred with the State Department and made arrangements for Barbara to be readmitted into America under her Dutch passport. She would have to depart as soon as possible. As Kennedy's breathless lecture continued, however, the tone of his voice suddenly lightened. He offered her a drink. When Barbara declined, he poured himself a scotch.

"As Kennedy talked on, he became more flirtatious, more direct, more threatening," according to the Barbara Hutton biography, *Poor Little Rich Girl*. "Within minutes, Kennedy was propositioning Barbara, offering to make her his mistress, chasing her around his desk." Bolting across the room, maneuvering herself out of Kennedy's grasp, Barbara escaped and rushed home, nervous and confused.

The shaken Hutton telephoned her friend Lady Diana Cooper, whose husband Alfred Duff Cooper would later become British ambassador to France, and told her about the attack. Cooper later related Barbara's story in a letter to Conrad Russell, a cousin to the duke of Bedford. "Kennedy was eager to help, but the help was to consist mainly of setting Barbara up as his mistress. I gather some pouncing accompanied these propositions. How amusing, and how little I would have thought of it! Mr. Asquith and Lord Wimbourne, to think of only two old gentlemen, both put forward more or less the same plan to me, and I thought it so flattering. While poor Barbara feels she can never look Kennedy in the face again. She is probably right and I am wrong."

The rejected Joe never mentioned the incident. When he ran into Barbara at social functions in the future it was as if nothing had happened. Perhaps he had already forgotten about it.

When war broke out and Joe and Rose returned to the United States, Joe Kennedy escalated his woman-chasing ways.

"Joe Kennedy represented the height of vulgarity. He was horny, that's all he was," recalled former *New York Post* columnist Doris Lilly in an interview with biographer C. David Heymann. Lilly said that one night after she had dinner with Kennedy, he offered to escort her back to her apartment. As they stood in the lobby, Joe made a move. "He said, 'What's that over there?' 'Where?' I said. I turned my head and he clamped his mouth over mine, kissed me. He was so disgusting."

Literary agent Marianne Strong remembered a dinner she attended at La Caravelle in New York at which Joe sat between two pretty teenage models. "It soon became clear that he was pleasuring one of them under the table. He had his hand in her panties and a hard, ugly smirk on his face. While he was doing that, he was eating dinner with his other hand."

In Palm Beach during the late 1940s, Kennedy moved a young woman named Edie into the mansion for a few months, sleeping with her just a few bedrooms away from Rose.

Slim Aarons, a society photographer for *Town & Country*, said Joe Kennedy was a master at orchestrating women in and out of 1095 Ocean Boulevard. During one period, he kept a beautiful twenty-five-year-old at the house. When Father Cavanaugh of Notre Dame came, the young girl suddenly vanished. When Cavanaugh left, she reappeared. Then Rose came for a visit and the girl was gone again. When Rose left, she came back. Arrons said, "He loved to flaunt his women in front of others. And no one was off limits, not your wife, your daughter, the girlfriends his sons brought home."

Joe sometimes asked his sons for the phone numbers of women he had seen his sons with, and who they were no longer interested in. And his sons occasionally asked him about the availability of women he was with.

"The Kennedy men passed their women around like community property, preyed off each other's dates, traded them like baseball cards," Langdon Martin, an aide to Jack Kennedy, told biographer C. David Heymann.

The Palm Beach house would gain prominence in 1960 as President Kennedy's "Winter White House."

But employees there in the 1960s began complaining about how cheap the Kennedys were. They began calling the mansion "House of the Minimum Wage."

Rose Kennedy developed an unusual habit around this time. Because the Kennedy's pool was not heated—Joe had refused to install a heating system—Rose often walked next door for a dip in socialite Mary Sanford's pool, which did have a heating unit. She customarily swam naked, often at lunchtime when Sanford entertained guests on the patio. Rather than start a fuss, Sanford laughed off the eccentricity.

In late 1961, Joe Kennedy suffered a stoke that left him speechless and unable to walk without help. The tragic murders of Jack and Bobby in 1963 and 1968 would depress and debilitate him further. He died November 18, 1969, at the age of eighty. Through the 1970s, Rose continued to use La Guerida, but as her health failed, she retired permanently to the Hyannisport compound.

The mansion at 1095 North Ocean Boulevard was transformed into a crash pad for Kennedy males and their girlfriends and an occasional holiday home for the various Kennedy children and their families.

In 1991, the home gained worldwide notoriety as the place where Joe's grandson, William Kennedy Smith, naked and drunk, allegedly raped a young woman he had picked up at a local nightclub. The alleged attack would occur just yards away from the Bull Pen, where Joe had loved to sunbathe in the nude.

8

Looking for Love in All the Wrong Places: Marjorie Merriweather Post and E. F. Hutton

The imposing front gates to the wondrous Mar-a-Lago estate were open from South Ocean Boulevard, a signal that Marjorie Merriweather Post, and her husband, E. F. Hutton, were in residence for the 1935 winter season. The newly annointed queen and king of Palm Beach society had spent virtually the past three seasons sailing around the world on their luxurious 350-foot yacht as though they were waiting for the Depression to subside. The four-masted yacht with its eight staterooms dropped anchor on the island's shore only periodically to pick up or discharge guests who joined the Huttons on their caviar-and-champagne-ladened voyages to ports as near as the Caribbean and as distant as Tahiti.

Their permanent return from a recent four-month expedition was welcome news to the island's gentry. High-stepping society longed for Marjorie Post's lavish parties and galas, which were staged at Mar-a-Lago (or "Sea to Lake") on the scale of Hollywood productions. The island's festive mood came alive when the Grande Dame and her dynamic husband illuminated their 115-room, 17.7-acre estate that ran the width of the island. The "idyllically happy" Huttons were the brightest stars in Palm Beach social circles, thanks in large measure to the sponsorship of Mrs. Edward Stotesbury, who annointed Marjorie Post as her successor. Mar-a-Lago always bustled with houseguests, whether invited by the Huttons, their daughter Nedenia (who would become the actress Dina Merrill), or by Marjorie's two daughters from a previous marriage.

In explaining her Depression-era extravaganzas, Marjorie said: "Big parties are justifiable because they give a good time to a lot of people and work to a lot more."

On one occasion, Marjorie hired Eddie Cantor to entertain for a dinner party of eighty guests, including the governor of Rome, royalty, and socialites from around the world. She ordered her extraordinary collection of gold chafing dishes and hand-blown glass to be set up in the dining room; a museum-quality replica of Rome's Chigi Palace. She gave similar dinner parties for Mary Pickford, the Ziegfelds, and Will Rogers. For larger bacchanalian affairs, Marjorie delighted in hiding in the second-floor gallery, on a small balcony high against the gold ceiling, to observe the reaction of Errol Flynn, Leslie Howard, George Bernard Shaw, and other guests as they passed through the mansion's huge cypress doors and for the first time entered the stupendous hall where centuries-old Spanish tiles lined the walls to a height of eight feet.

Her elaborate costume parties were orchestrated outdoors on her patio, which consisted of a grand mosaic constructed from polished pebbles that were shipped by the trainload to Palm Beach from the shores of Long Island. Marjorie would dress in a Louis XV gown and greet visitors on the veranda and along its crescent-shaped walkways. These arcaded paths were lined by orange blossoms and pink oleanders, adding a wondrous perfume to the giddy all-night festivities that were accompanied by a New Orleans jazz group or the big-band sound of Lester Lanin's orchestra.

Invitations to Marjorie's soirées had been coveted on Palm Beach ever since she and her Wall Street millionaire had combined their bank accounts in 1920. "I think everyone took right away to Marjorie and Ed Hutton," said Mrs. Alfred Kay, a Warden from Philadelphia with Standard Oil money. "There was no feeling about them ever being newcomers."

Together, the Huttons were one of America's wealthiest couples, and a dynamic and incomparable match. E. F. Hutton was a self-made man in the tradition of Horatio Alger. Starting out with a five-dollar-a-week mailroom job in a trust company, Hutton ultimately launched a brokerage firm that became the first to wire stock-market reports from New York, over the Rocky Mountains, to California. An exuberant, handsome sportsman with a classic profile, the fifty-seven-year-old Hutton was considered a "man's man" as well as a gentleman whom women found irresistibly attractive.

Marjorie Merriweather Post was a woman of extraordinary intelligence and distinguished good looks. With delicate fair skin and soft red hair, the attractive, spirited Marjorie would have emerged in Palm Beach society even without the dashing Hutton for a husband. In fact, Marjorie retained her regal station despite four calamitous and scandalous marriages, including the one with Hutton. She became the force that drove "society" for nearly three decades, thanks to her joie-de-vivre and $250 million fortune. And it all began with the invention of a peculiarly American food product: the "grape nut."

Marjorie's father, Charles W. Post, was a creative, ambitious man during a period of staggering inventiveness and business success at the end of the nineteenth century. Alexander Bell invented the telephone. Thomas Edison developed the phonograph. Cyrus McCormick revolutionized agriculture. Daring businessmen such as Henry Morrison Flagler, John D. Rockefeller, and Andrew Carnegie made fortunes through well-timed and skillful business acquisitions while others became millionaires by taking a chance on a new idea. It was all possible then. Entrepreneurs operated in a business environment unrestrained by labor laws, income tax, and public opinion.

The "right" product could catapult a struggling businessman into a tycoon. C. W. Post's initial "great" invention was the seed planter. It had modest success and was followed by the cultivator, a haystacker, and a furrow. A handful of new tools to his credit, Post decided to incorporate. With his money and his wife's inheritance, he opened Post Capital City Cultivators in Springfield, Illinois. Business was reasonable, but the financial worries involved in a business unnerved Post. An anxious man by nature, he began to suffer excruciating stomach pain. Doctors suspected that he suffered from an appendix ailment. His symptoms, however, were probably those of acute colitis or diverticulitis, two maladies that affected Post throughout his life. Whatever the cause, the illness forced Post to remain in bed. Without his full attention the Post Capital City Cultivators collapsed. His recuperation took months.

In 1886, when he became well enough to travel, Post and his brother, Carroll, went west to Texas in search of a fortune in real-estate development. With his remaining funds, Post purchased a "small" two hundred-acre ranch and then returned to Illinois to fetch his wife, Ella. But she had suffered a miscarriage three years earlier, became pregnant and the trip west was postponed until after Marjorie's birth in 1887. An only child, Marjorie would become both the "son" and daughter C. W. Post never had. "I was always my dad's girl," Marjorie would say nearly eighty years later.

In Texas, C. W. Post opened a woolen mill to manufacture blankets, sold steam engines to electric railway companies and, himself a meticulous dresser, invented a new type of suspenders with tiny pulleys and adjustment cords that he sold through mail order. But in his haste to expand, he launched a second land development in which he envisioned selling twenty-three-acre plots for fifteen hundred dollars. The project collapsed, however, and C. W. Post suffered another violent stomach attack that sent him to bed.

This attack was coupled with an equally debilitating depression. The melancholia was so severe that his desperate family decided Post needed special care. They borrowed funds and sent Post to the famous Dr. John Harvey Kellogg's sanatorium in Battle Creek, Michigan. At the time, Battle Creek was a small farm city near the Kalamazoo River, inhabited primarily by Seventh-Day Adventists and renowned as the country's center for health care. Dr. Kellogg, a physician, had built a reputation for curing the sick by adhering to strict tenets of the Adventists, which meant his diet excluded meat and relied heavily on nuts for protein.

Post arrived on a stretcher at the Battle Creek Sanatorium late in 1891, weighing only 140 pounds, down from 175, and unable to walk. Kellogg, who had created peanut butter, and Post were kindred spirits. Both were brilliant inventors.

Kellogg's novel diet of grainy nut patties and chunky nut cutlets were the worst possible food for Post's sensitive digestive tract. After nine months, Post's health declined to the point where death seemed inevitable. Kellogg prepared Ella Post for the worst. Even more desperate than when she arrived in Battle Creek, Ella Post removed her husband from Kellogg's clinic and brought him to a faith healer in Battle Creek named Mrs. Elizabeth K. Gregory. She calmed Post's nerves and had him eating his first proper meal in months. He felt "cured" and moved into Mrs. Gregory's boarder home to study Christian Science.

With each passing day, Post gained one pound. As his weight improved so, too, did his spirits. Finally, he sold his stake in Texas and purchased a ten-acre farm in Battle Creek to open a relaxed hostelry for the infirm as an alternative to Kellogg's rigid sanatorium. The LaVita Inn became an instant success, with guests exercising, playing games, and eating whatever food they desired, with the exception of alcohol, tea, and coffee.

Replacing those beverages, Post served up a "cereal-coffee" that he created out of roasted wheat and chicory. He called his brew Postum, and he sold it over the counter. People enjoyed the flavor and Post was on his way. By October 1896, the Postum Company had a net worth of $37,010.

Because Postum sold better during cold months, Post looked for another product that would sell the rest of the year. He discovered it in his own morning plate. For years, Post had been eating a private breakfast cereal he made for himself to accommodate his uneasy stomach. According to *Palm Beach Life* magazine, the recipe consisted of whole wheat, malted barley flour, and yeast, baked in the form of bread stocks, then rebaked slowly for twenty-four hours. The magazine added: "What emerged would then be ground up in a coffee grinder into chewy little pellets about the size of No.2 birdshot, to be eaten with milk or cream."

The small dark brown pellets tasted sweet, thanks to the dextrose, which Post called "grape sugar," that was produced during the process. Because the pellets also had a nutty flavor, he called the cereal Grape Nuts. The product was a huge success as soon as it reached the public in January 1898. Within two years, the Post company was worth millions and growing faster than any company ever had with a manufactured product.

By this time, Marjorie was thirteen, "a chubby-cheeked girl with bangs across her forehead," according to one newspaper. Despite her girlish looks, her father taught Marjorie the "manly art of boxing" when boys teased her and pushed her around. He also groomed Marjorie for a role in his company, After school, Marjorie would routinely join her father at business meetings, often sitting beside him. Later that night he would quiz her about the day's discussions.

Marjorie was devoted to her father and adored him. One evening, while discussing business with his daughter, C. W. Post imparted his philosophy on money. According to Marjorie's biographer William Wright, Post told his daughter, "Money should be kept moving. Make it work. Make it create. Make it do good, and make it help in many hundreds of ways." Then he paused. "In other words, don't be a miser and sit and count the shekels!"

Together, father and daughter planned packaging for Post products. Business boomed. C. W. Post was worth $10 million by 1903. With success came a suitable appearance. He began dressing like a dandy and sporting a white Stetson hat. He built a hotel, a small business complex, and a residential community surrounding it. C. W. Post named the thoroughfares after his daughter; "Marjorie Street" and "Marjorie Block."

Success took its toll, however, on Post's marriage. C. W. Post was a gregarious businessman with an ever widening circle of influential acquaintances. His wife, Ella, was a shy, retiring woman who preferred small gatherings where she could discuss books and music. When they moved to Washington, D.C., to open a new headquarters, the Posts separated, and soon they divorced.

C. W. Post hired Leila Young, an attractive, willowy worker at his plant, to serve as Marjorie's governess. In 1904, Post married her. Newspapers questioned his choice of a working girl. In an extraordinary public rebuttal, Post addressed a crowd at his own testimonial dinner, delivering a speech that mocked the very "society people" his Marjorie would later join and rule:

> The public generally seems to think a man of means should marry a wealthy society woman. And the so-called society paper that criticized me rather sneered at the fact that I married a new wife that was a poor girl, and earned a living as my secretary, and the fact that she ever worked seems to trouble it. I can't possibly imagine what use I would have for a society pet that would drag an old work horse around nights to social functions and make him listen to the drool about the latest kind of necktie, cut of riding pants "ye know," and all the tiresome stuff the dudes feed on.

Post, his new wife, and Marjorie moved to Greenwich, Connecticut, taking residence in a sprawling, chunky-stone and gable-roofed mansion, the Boulders, which derived its name from several huge boulders along its driveway and lawn. Within a year, Marjorie, now an attractive eighteen-year-old, met Edward Bennett Close, a young, mild-mannered, blond, blue-eyed lawyer from an established Greenwich family. "She's quite a pretty little thing—for a Mid-Westerner," one of Edward Close's relatives said of Marjorie.

On December 3, 1905, Marjorie and Edward Close married at the Grace Episcopal Church in New York City, a parish built on land originally donated by Close's great-great-grandfather. Ed Close joined his father-in-law's business for a year to learn the intricacies so that he could help Marjorie when she inherited it. Close then returned to Connecticut to learn brokerage in order handle his wife's investments and trusts.

On July 26, 1908, Marjorie gave birth to her first daughter, Adelaide. And it was her father—not her husband—who was at her bedside, holding her hand during the difficult delivery. The following year, Marjorie gave birth to a second daughter, Eleanor. Although this delivery went smoothly, Marjorie decided she needed a vacation to recuperate from back-to-back pregnancies.

In 1909, Marjorie Post made her maiden voyage to Palm Beach, spending the winter at Flagler's Royal Poinciana Hotel. For the next three years, she returned to Flagler's wondrous hotel. But in 1912 tragedy struck. Her mother died suddenly at her home in Washington, D.C.

Then two years later, in 1914, her beloved father suffered another violent stomach attack. Marjorie rushed from Palm Beach to his bedside. On March 10, C. W. Post underwent surgery for appendicitis at the Mayo Clinic, but his health continued to worsen and once again he slipped into a deep depression.

Post began to talk of suicide. His family placed him under round-the-clock surveillance and ordered weapons removed from the house. A 30-30 hunting rifle was overlooked. One afternoon, with his wife out of the house, C. W. Post put on a business suit and tie, loaded the rifle, and stretched out on his bed. He put the rifle in his mouth and pulled the trigger.

"His death left a gigantic breach in his grieving daughter's life," the writer Allene Hatch observed. "Marjorie felt the loss so deeply that for the rest of her life she would be incapable of discussing her father's death and even tried to have his suicide omitted from the biography she later commissioned."

On May 26, 1914, the *New York Times* reported: POST FORTUNE $20,000,000—*Bulk of It Bequeathed to the Cereal Man's Widow and Daughter.* The inheritance made Marjorie one of the nation's wealthiest women. Heeding her father's advice on money, Marjorie did not "sit around counting her shekels." She bought a $1 million mansion on East 92nd Street and decorated the sixty-six rooms with $175,000 Beauvais tapestries, $10,000 Rubens, and a treasure trove of antiques until the price tag exceeded $2 million. Then, to celebrate her tenth wedding anniversary, Marjorie rented the Ritz Carlton ballroom in 1915 for ten thousand dollars, or the price of Ruben's "Adoration of the Magi," which she now owned.

By contrast to her lavish spending, the mood of the country had changed. World War I was well under way. And in 1917, her husband, Ed, was commissioned a captain and sent to France to work at the

American Hospital. For the first time, Marjorie was without a man in her life. To fill her days, she devoted time to the Red Cross while Ed was overseas.

When the war finally ended, her husband returned a changed and somber man, no longer content with the life of a well-to do artistocrat and far less interested in wealth and Marjorie's "society" people. Having witnessed the brutality of war and the real-life hardships of "ordinary" people, Ed Close wanted to devote his time to helping the wounded and infirm. With Marjorie's blessing, he returned to Paris in 1919 to help run the American Hospital.

Majorie also had changed. She now embraced the Rich and had developed a capacity for making friends and collecting interesting people. And even before she divorced Ed Close, Marjorie Post had someone else in her life, a suitor who sent armloads of roses and dinner invitations.

"Mother never ended one relationship unless she had a place to perch," her daughter, Dina Merrill, later observed. Her new "perch" was E. F. Hutton, the dynamic "Beau Brummel" businessman whose expanding brokerage company had earned him a fortune that rivaled J. P. Morgan's.

By coincidence, Hutton recently had become a widower. His wife, Blanche Horton, had died in a fall from a horse, but Hutton remained vibrant and upbeat, at age forty-seven, he was at his peak. He was the sort of man who loved to tramp through the woods with a gun over his shoulder or don a tuxedo for a formal evening. He and Marjorie quickly fell in love. They married on July 20, 1920, at her East 92nd Street mansion. Hutton's brother, Franklyn, was in the wedding party. By coincidence, Franklyn Hutton also married one of the country's wealthiest women, Edna Woolworth, daughter of the dimestore founder and heiress to a $30 million fortune. But Franklyn Hutton was an unabashed philanderer. His affair with Swedish actress Monica Von Fursten was blamed for his wife's suicide on May 2, 1917, at her apartment in the Plaza Hotel in New York. The Huttons' daughter, Barbara, later became known as the "poor little rich girl," who squandered a $50 million fortune during an exorbitant life of travel and six marriages, including one to Cary Grant, the movie legend.

The Roaring Twenties were perfect for monied fun-seekers with the energy for excess. The era was made for Marjorie Post and Edward Hutton. And Palm Beach was its epitome.

By 1920, the island's facilities catered to partying. Fresh caviar was shipped in daily and, despite Prohibition, the docks were filled with deliveries of the world's finest liquor. E. F. Hutton was said to have the slickest bootlegger. Marjorie's friends, the Flo Ziegfelds, helped her stage elaborate costume charity balls. Top entertainers such as Al Jolson and bandleader Ben Bernie lent their talents. At one affair, Marjorie dressed as an exotic American Indian princess. And if the party schedule lapsed, there was always the Everglades Club and Bradley's casino.

It was a fabulous decade for the Huttons, marred only once, and early, by tragedy. In 1921, Marjorie miscarried a son while sailing on their first yacht, the *Hussar*. But in that same year, the Huttons built their first home. Hogarcito was a Spanish-style villa with a three-story tower constructed on land Hutton had bought for one hundred dollars from the Paris Singer Realty Company on Golfview Road.

Erected between the first and third greens of the Everglades golf club, the villa offered a brilliant water view of Lake Worth and the mainland. Designed by architect Marion Sims Wyeth—a rival to the king of Palm Beach mansions, Addison Mizner—Hogarcito had a red-tile roof, large inner courtyards, curved iron-grilled windows and balconies, and fabulous sunsets from the patio.

No sooner was Hogarcito completed than Marjorie referred to it as a "little home." She instructed Wyeth to enlarge it into an eight-bedroom mansion to accommodate her growing family and guest list.

As construction continued around her, Marjorie became pregnant with Nedenia and gave birth to "Deenie" on December 29, 1923. By then Hutton had been installed as chairman of the General Foods Company. Hutton and Marjorie Post had begun expanding the original Postum Company into a conglomerate that would ultimately market, among other products, Jell-O, Maxwell House Coffee, Hellmann's Mayonnaise, Bird's Eye frozen foods, Log Cabin Syrup, and Diamond Crystal Salt. Each business acquisition somehow made Hogarcito seem smaller. One afternoon, with real-estate agent Lytle Hull in tow, Marjorie crawled through snake-infested shrub and jungle where the island had an undershelving of rock. Every few yards she placed a mark, staking out a site from sea to lake. Then she returned to Wyeth's office with a grand proposal. She wanted Wyeth to build a palace that would dwarf El Mirasol, the estate owned by her friendly society rival, Eva Stotesbury.

Wyeth drew up the basic plans for Mar-a-Lago. She chose Joseph Urban, a friend of the Ziegfelds, to design the interiors. Urban had a reputation for designing remarkable sets for the Metropolitan Opera House and Ziegfeld revues. The Huttons broke ground for Mar-a-Lago in 1924. People were astonished as they passed the construction site, watching Mar-a-Lago unfold. Because of Urban's exuberance and complete lack of interest in cost, construction took three years and the price tag rose to nearly $5 million. At one point, an alarmed Hutton stormed into Wyeth's office and demanded that he return to the project to reign in his partner before Urban bankrupted the Hutton fortune.

In March 1927, Mar-a-Lago was unveiled; standing on 17.7 acres with 450 feet of beachfront, it had 115 rooms, including 42 bedrooms, 180 windows and doors, a citrus grove, a nine-hole golf course, and a private tunnel leading to the beach just north of the Bath and Tennis Club.

"I wanted a seaside cottage," Hutton cried. "Look what I got."

Hutton and Marjorie had created an estate with floor-to-ceiling doors in a two-story-high, Venetian-palace living room that offered views of the ocean to the east and the lake to the west. Marjorie adopted the "thousand wing" ceiling from the Academia in Venice for the room. Magnificent frescoes were drawn by European artisans who were flown to Palm Beach for month-long stays. Custom-made chandeliers hung in the dining room. The patio—its design taken from the Alhambra in Spain—had a large fountain and a blue overhead floodlight to ensure all-weather moonlight.

Every room, staircase, and hallway was decorated with museumlike care, with hundreds of authentic museum pieces and antiques. Each bedroom was furnished in a different style: one was Old Dutch, another Portuguese, another American. Distinctive chimneys and towers reminiscent of fairyland castles rose from the red-tile roof, evoking exotic Arabian Nights. The mansion was a monument to Marjorie Post's taste and wealth.

For Mar-a-Lago's unofficial debut in March 1927, Marjorie dressed as the princess of Baghdad. She led a harem of four hundred costumed ladies from a gala at the nearby Bath and Tennis Club along South Ocean County Boulevard to the mansion, where it seemed all of Palm Beach society partied until dawn. From then on, Mar-a-Lago was the scene of endless balls, supper dances, teas, reviews, recitals, and, in later years, square dancing. It was common for Marjorie to hire entire casts of Broadway shows to perform there or to pay for a performance of the Ringling Brothers Circus on the grounds.

Marjorie's daughter, Adelaide, married for the first time in 1927. Her choice was Tim Durant, an elegant, charming, and popular man. His interests tended toward acting and film producing. But the Hutton's "established" Durant by providing him with a seat on the New York Stock Exchange, where he traded with little scrutiny from E. F. Hutton and his wife for a couple of years. When the stock market crashed in 1929, the Huttons discovered that Durant, like many brokers on Wall Street, had engaged in unseemly insider trades and wrecklessly squandered much of Adelaide's trust fund. Within a few months, Adelaide divorced her first husband.

"The Post family was, like all families, into making big money," Durant later told biographer Wright. "They become ruthless. It spills over into their personal life. A son-in-law must produce a grandson. If this one can't do it, get rid of him and get one that can."

"But," Durant added, "Marjorie Post was a wonderful gal. She was terrific looking. I remember her once calling me into her lavish dressing room to talk about something. She was sitting there in a lacy peignoir, her light brown hair falling down her back, surrounded by all that luxury. I could have jumped her right there."

"She had a strong character, and she influenced me in many ways she never realized," said Durant, who moved to Hollywood where he became a "guy Friday" to Charlie Chaplin.

"Marjorie had courage... spirit—and many bitter disappointments."

Marjorie's twenty-year-old daughter, Eleanor, followed Adelaide with another marriage disappointment. Shortly after her coming-out party at the Ritz and her presentation at court in England in 1929, Eleanor shocked her family with her engagement to Preston Sturges, then a relatively unknown movie writer and perfume salesman. The notion of Eleanor marrying a nearly penniless bohemian like Sturges was so repulsive to Marjorie that she threatened to disown her daughter. Marjorie also thought the marriage was doomed to failure, and she enlisted Hutton to prevent the match. One afternoon, Hutton confronted Sturges and demanded to know if he could support Eleanor in the style to which she was accustomed. "I would hope in better taste," the acerbic Sturges replied.

"I told him that I had proved I could earn my living as a writer, that I had two plays then running on Broadway and that one of them alone bought in fifteen hundred dollars a week," Sturges said.

"That's pin money to her," E. F. Hutton said.

Within days of the confrontation, Sturges's fledging stage productions folded, leaving him without income. He recalled:

> The Huttons wanted us to wait for a year or two before there was any serious talk about marriage. When we insisted, they promptly decided that I was a fortune hunter, a bum, a drunkard, and every species of lowlife they could think of offhand.

They told Eleanor they would cut her off without a cent if she married me without their consent. When I wanted to marry her anyway, it knocked their fortune-hunter theory for a loop, but they were not finished with me. Mr. Hutton put detectives on my trail to try to dig up a bad reputation for me. They didn't find one, of course, but as a result of their snooping, rumors of the romance were all over the papers. Tales about heiresses, playwrights, and family threats of disinheritance made good copy, and stories continued to appear.

In a final desperate attempt, Marjorie dispatched Adelaide to prevent Eleanor from marrying Sturges, but Eleanor eloped with her unemployed beau. The struggling newlyweds settled into a Third Avenue walkup in Manhattan in 1930. Marjorie made good on her threat. She immediately instructed her attorneys to remove Eleanor from her will.

Sturges, whose mother was a close friend of famed dancer Isadora Duncan, became an overnight success with the play *Strictly Dishonorable*. With a $250,000 windfall, the playwright took his wife to Paris to live, but in less than a year they spent the proceeds from his stage success. With the money gone and Sturges rumored to be dallying with a chorus girl, Eleanor left him. She moved back to Palm Beach—and into her mother's good graces. The following afternoon, Marjorie Post contacted her attorneys, this time to restore Eleanor to her will. Sturges went on to make several famous movies, including *The Palm Beach Story*, a biting satire on the island's millionaires.

Between Marjorie and her three daughters, the Post women would marry a total of fourteen times. Eleanor alone accounted for five marriages. Marjorie contributed four, Adelaide three, and Dina Merrill two.

"Eleanor's just like me," Marjorie said later. "She always marries stinkers."

Gossip about Marjorie's own "idyllically happy" marriage began to surface at about this time. Rumors that her husband was unfaithful trailed the muscular Hutton from the pool at the B & T Club to Bradley's casino. The chatter about E. F. Hutton's infidelities increased as the Roaring Twenties drew to a close. The salacious talk reached Marjorie, but she brushed it aside as the fabrications of envious women. Fortunately for both Marjorie and Hutton, they spent much of the next three seasons on their $1 million yacht, *Hussar V*, the world's most elaborately outfitted personal vessel, with a crew of seventy-two. Before returning full time to Palm Beach for the 1935 season, the Huttons completed a four-month cruise. "Our second honeymoon," they said.

But the gossip surrounding Hutton accelerated quickly. This time the stories were alarmingly descriptive. They involved talk that the fifty-seven-year-old Hutton had indulged himself with pretty women directly under Marjorie's innocent gaze. With her suspicions finally raised, Marjorie noticed that her husband paid inordinate attention to female houseguests and housemaids. Even her daughter, Eleanor, fell victim to Hutton's lustful stare. Marjorie felt she now needed to know the truth.

Her initial sleuthing attempts appeared comical. She tied strings to many of Mar-a-Lago's forty-two bedroom doors and placed wire across the underpinnings of several beds. One morning she was forced to scamper out a window to avoid detection. Finally, on one sunny afternoon, Marjorie burst into a bedroom that adjoined her own master bedroom suite. To her dismay, she surprised her husband in bed "hard at it with a chambermaid," said biographer Wright. She was thunderstruck. Marjorie was a woman with her own healthy sexual appetite, but she was devoted to the notion of monogamous marriage. Catching Hutton "hard at it" made her realize how naïve she had been about her zestful husband.

"She would announce to him that she was going to Vichy for a few weeks," her granddaughter, Marwee, later recalled. "Hutton would tell her he could not get away that long and suggest they run down to Mar-a-Lago for a few days instead. She'd say, 'No. I'm going go Vichy.' No sooner was she out the door than he was on the phone to a lady friend."

"Or some lady friend was on the phone to him," her daughter, Dina Merrill, added. "There were a lot of women around just waiting for mother to leave town."

Despite the unpleasantness of catching Hutton in bed with a chambermaid, Marjorie Post would not allow the "incident" to destroy her marriage of fifteen years. A divorce—even an amicable one—would be extremely embarrassing. There also were children to be concerned about. And in this case, Hutton's female "distraction" was from the ranks of the hired help—and hardly a legitimate threat.

Marjorie and Hutton decided to carry on as society's "idyllically happy couple." They continued to attend the usual round of Eastertime costume balls and they continued to have houseguests at Mar-a-Lago. Among the first to visit in the wake of the "chambermaid incident" were Homer Metzger, the former Brown University football star, and his beautiful wife, Dorothy. The Metzgers had been frequent guests of the Huttons at Mar-a-Lago as well as on their yacht. In fact, Dorothy and

Homer had accompanied the Huttons on their "second honeymoon" voyage.

Dorothy Metzger was the twenty-eight-year-old blond daughter of William Y. Dear, a wealthy New Jersey printing company executive and brother of a state judge. She and Homer initially met the Huttons through her father, who was a business acquaintance of E. F. Hutton. The two couples had become friends.

To Marjorie's thorough dismay, she now caught Hutton in the throes of passion with Dorothy Metzger at Mar-a-Lago. And worse, her husband confessed that this affair had been going on for months, as far back as the "second honeymoon" cruise. While Marjorie was ashore shopping for antiques to showcase at Mar-a-Lago, Hutton and Dorothy Metzger made love in one of the yacht's eight fireplace-equipped staterooms. This time, Marjorie could not forgive or ignore Hutton's sexual interests. Dorothy's station was well above a chambermaid's. Marjorie—and Homer Metzger—planned respective divorces.

To keep scandal to a minimum, both couples agreed to keep their tawdry tale secret until final arrangements were made. While attorney's divided up property, the Huttons publicly provided few clues that there was a schism in their "royal marriage." On August 14, 1935, Marjorie's attorney, H. A. Uterhart, filed a separation notice with the court in Patchogue, Long Island, and verified for reporters that the Huttons had broken up their regal sixty-six-room townhouse on East 92nd Street.

ANOTHER HUTTON IDYLL ENDS declared a morning edition of the New York *Daily News*, referring also to the swelling list of failed marriages of Hutton's "rich" niece, Barbara.

News of the split stunned Palm Beach and New York society. Friends who previously marveled at the Huttons "second honeymoon" now wondered whether it was a final effort to iron out differences. No reason was given for the separation, which left the mistaken impression that the breakup had resulted from a simple clash of two strong and independent wills. There was not a hint that adultery was involved.

"I can only state that she and her husband have been separated for several months," Uterhart said. "There is no basis for the rumor that Mrs. Hutton has gone to Reno."

She had gone, instead, on a transatlantic cruise to flee the media and to contemplate life without the dynamic Hutton. It was not a pleasant prospect. For all of her forty-eight years, Marjorie had a man in her life. When her father died she was already married to Ed Close. And when that marriage failed, she was already virtually engaged to Hutton. As Dina said, her mother needed a perch.

The ocean liner was barely out of New York Harbor when Marjorie met Joseph E. Davies, an influential Washington lawyer, a White House insider and highly paid lobbyist for the Dominican Republic and other Latin American countries. Within days, she decided she was madly in love with Davies and would marry him. The feeling was mutual. For a man like the ambitious Davies, Marjorie's vast wealth and social connections would augment his already considerable influence. There was one obstacle to their newfound bliss. The dapper Davies was married with three grown daughters.

Marjorie cabled her lawyers, instructing them to contact Mrs. Davies in England and find out how much money she would require to end her thirty-three-year marriage. The response: $2 million cash. Attorneys apparently finalized the deal before the ocean liner docked in Southampton harbor, ninety miles south of London. *Time* magazine later explained:

> In 1935, Joseph E. Davis, distinguished lawyer and socialite, crossed the Atlantic, walked into his wife's suite in London's Claridge hotel. Mrs. Davies hurried forward affectionately to greet him, but Joe held her back with a dramatic gesture. "Emlen," he intoned to his wife of thirty-three years, "I want my freedom."
> She replied, "Why certainly, Joe."

Marjorie and her stocky, gray-haired fiancé returned to the United States, pledging to keep their engagement secret until after the divorces. On September 7, 1935, Marjorie was granted a divorce from Hutton in Patchogue Supreme Court. In a terse interlocutory decree, Marjorie graciously failed to name Dorothy Metzger as correspondent because Hutton said he planned to marry her. Instead, Marjorie claimed an unnamed young woman was to blame. It was the first time a Hutton infidelity was announced publicly.

"It was the tapping of a pair of pert French heels, belonging to an insouciant minx of 19 or 20, that crumbled away the socially and finanically powerful marriage of the Edward F. Huttons," the New York *Daily News* reported. "Her weight: 104 lbs.; height, 5 feet 1 inch; personality, petite and piquant—this was the picture painted of the budding siren who purportedly led astray the graying uncle of Countess Barbara Hutton Von Haugwitz-Reventlow.

"Society tea tables buzzed with excitement over the news," the tabloid continued, "which capped the recently announced separation of the 'idyllically married' couple. Until yesterday, everyone thought the inevitable clash of wills was at the bottom of the separation."

Because Mrs. Hutton was "far wealthier" than Hutton, there was no alimony or financial settlement asked for, the paper said. The judge then sealed the divorce papers.

With the divorce formally recorded, a new flurry of marital activity began. Within two weeks, Dorothy Metzger filed for divorce from her husky husband, charging the former football star with cruelty. Homer did not deny the charge. Instead, he had taken a "high-paying, comfortable" position with the Zonite Product Corporation, where E. F. Hutton was chairman of the board.

On October 18, the Metzgers' divorce became official, ending nine years of marriage. The next day, Hutton and Dorothy announced they would marry. HUTTON WILL WED DIVORCEE; HIRES HER EX! one headline said. The New York *Daily News* reported that the townhouse shared by Marjorie and Ed Hutton was now "dismantled" and the Metzger's charming English brick house at 317 Redmond Road in South Orange, New Jersey, "was also deserted. Only an empty swing in the backyard attested that seven-year-old Joan Metzger once played there." Neighbors told reporters the Metzgers' life appeared tranquil until a slight rift developed a year ago. But after the Metzgers "visited Hutton in Florida on the latter's magnificent yacht, the rift widened."

Rumors that Marjorie and Davies would marry also surfaced, particularly after she registered at a Washington hotel where Davies frequently stayed. The two "lovebirds" avoided the press until Marjorie finally relented. When one reporter asked about the rumors, she snapped: "Which of four of five published rumors?"

"The one about you marrying Joe Davies," the reporter replied.

"Mr. Davies is handling a tax case for me, and that is all," she barked. "One might be allowed to stay single."

On November 9, E. F. Hutton transfered the title of the *Hussar V* to Marjorie, which she promptly renamed *Sea Cloud*. Four weeks later, Hutton announced his resignation as chairman of the General Foods Corporation after twelve years because of "ill health." The truth, however, was quite different. Hutton had to step aside. Marjorie was only five days away from marrying Joseph E. Davies. Hutton was conveniently in Hot Springs, South Carolina, recovering from a severe attack of neuritis, when Marjorie married the Washington lobbyist on December 15, 1935.

Marjorie's third wedding took place at her Manhattan apartment. The eighty-person guest list of "relatives and close friends" included Mr. and Mrs. Ogden Reid, the Bernard Baruchs, the Stotesburys, the United States Attorney General Homer Cummings, and Stephen Early, the secretary to President Franklin Roosevelt. Dina Merrill appeared as her mother's bridesmaid. Reporters had been banned from the mansion, but to keep them abreast of the proceedings, a telephone system was installed to allow butlers and maids to provide a minute-by-minute description of the ceremony and reception.

The wedding cost the bride $100,000. The mansion's two ballrooms were "redecorated in pink" and the walls were hung with pink satin, according to authors George Abell and Evelyn Gordon. "Pale pink flowers costing $4,000 were dyed a deeper hue to match the bride's pink velevet gown with its ten-foot train and white fox trimming." The fact that the 150-pound, seven-tier wedding cake cost seven dollars a slice to prepare, drew sharp criticism from newspaper editorial writers eager to chatise unbridled spending during the Depression.

Forty-one days later, on January 25, 1936, E. F. Hutton and Dorothy Dear married in Walterboro, South Carolina. They announced they would take up residence in Palm Beach after their honeymoon. The revelation that the newlywed Huttons and the newlywed Davieses might meet on Palm Beach's golden shore was grist for the newspaper mill. Columnist Cholly Knickerbocker salivated:

> The season had been a bit dull and uninteresting—the same people entertaining the same people day after day and night after night. But the honeymooning Huttons and Davieses promise to change all that—so society is agog with anticipation.
>
> Ed and Dorothy are planning to spend the remainder of the Winter down at Palm beach, where Ed for a number of years, was social arbiter number one of the once-exclusive Bath and Tennis Club. One can be pardoned for wondering just what will happen with Ed and his bride and Marjorie Post Hutton Davies and her new husband in the Palm Beach colony.

On the Davieses' honeymoon cruise through the Caribbean, the newlyweds made a spectacle of their affection, nuzzling, pawing, and pecking at each other. They were so much in love that even brief periods apart disturbed them. "I would follow that pair of beautiful black eyes to the end of the world," Marjorie later said. When Joe was away, he sent telegrams to Marjorie and signed them "Wam Hilly," an acronym formed from the words *With all my heart I love lovely you.*

They shared mutual interests in politics, government, and diplomacy. Before Marjorie divorced Hutton, they each held strong positions on politics and on the country's ailing economy. Marjorie, who lauded

Roosevelt, supplied his campaign war chest with hundreds of thousands of dollars, the bulk of it contributed after she married Davies.

Following their honeymoon, the Davieses returned to Palm Beach in February 1936. They were treated to a round of elaborate and highly publicized parties thrown by Mrs. Stotesbury, who was trying to counter E. F. Hutton's anti–Joseph Davies campaign. One dance at the Bath and Tennis Club had one hundred guests, their names printed in newspapers across the country.

The newlywed Huttons also returned from their honeymoon to Palm Beach to a home they rented near the ocean. It did not take long before Hutton and Davies met at the Bath and Tennis Club. The encounter was neither violent nor ugly, as some had hoped. But it was illustrative of how "gentlemen" in "society" handled tricky situations.

Dina Merrill recalled:

As you know, we had a tunnel under [South Ocean County] road and a back entrance to the Bath and Tennis Club. Mother and I were swimming in the pool. In those days she always wore specially designed bathing suits that had high necks, long sleeves, bare midriffs, and long skirts. With this, mother also wore white gloves, a bathing cap topped by a large sun hat, and dark glasses. And lots of sun cream. This was because of her delicate skin; she was a redhead basically, and she freckled. Mother always did the backstroke very gently and held her head well out of the water, and it was my utterly fiendish delight to jump in right in front of her and splash her and get her all wet.

While we were paddling around the pool, Joe Davies came from outside of the Bath and Tennis to the edge of the pool, and my father came up from the beach side. They looked at one another, they looked at Mother, and in chorus said, "Good morning, Marjorie." She went right under the water to the bottom of the pool!

The country was vibrating that year with election excitement. And when the Palm Beach season ended, the Davieses returned to Washington, D.C., where Joe was named chairman of the Executive Advisory Commitee of the Democratic National Campaign Committee. In addition to being a friend to Roosevelt, Davies's associates included influential politicians, industrialists, and financiers, whom Marjorie found both compatible and intellectually stimulating.

On November 16, 1937, President Roosevelt commissioned Davies as ambassador to Russia. Right after the New Year, Marjorie and Davies set sail for Moscow on Marjorie's $5-million *Sea Cloud*. She had prepared well for the stay in a struggling Communist state. The *Sea Cloud* was stocked with: twenty-five store-sized freezer chests filled with meat, fish, and vegetables; two thousand pints of frozen cream; hundreds of cases of bottled water; twenty-five refrigerators; and a special electric mixer that could make mayonnaise, grind coffee, whip cream, and chop meat. And if that were not sufficient, a second vessel trailed the *Sea Cloud* with fourteen freezers, two tons of frozen foods, a masseur, and a huge assortment of fresh flowers.

Before the Davieses reached Russian soil, they graced the cover of the March 15, 1937, issue of *Time* magazine. In Moscow, they lived at the United States Embassy, called Spasso House, that paled by comparison to Mar-a-Lago. Marjorie immediately arranged dinner parties for embassy staff and dignitaries. But the grand dame of Palm Beach soon learned she could not rule these parties with the same authority she had back home. In the first week, she was briskly informed that the person she had assigned the seat next to her was not acceptable. Protocol demanded that only ranking diplomats could sit to her right.

"Of all the foolishness," she huffed. "All my life I have entertained— in New York, Washington, and Palm Beach—the most influential people in America. I know what you can do and what you cannot!" Despite her protests, she did not have her way.

There were other culture shocks. Russian women were seldom permitted to attend diplomatic functions. But when they did, Marjorie was the center of attention. One evening, a group of Russian women gathered around Marjorie, admiring her light blue evening gown and jewelry.

"What is that string of beads around your neck?" one inquired.

"Why, these are pearls," Marjorie replied.

"That is not possible," the woman responded.

"They are pearls!" Marjorie shot back.

If the Russian women were impressed by the pearls, the Russian fisherman were dumbstruck by *Sea Cloud*. And Marjorie knew how to shock her guests during dinners, telling them that the fish they were eating had been caught six months earlier. She entertained some of the world's most important figures of the day when they visited Russia. Familiar faces at her dinner tables were Charles Lindbergh, Henry Morgenthau, Cordell Hull, Sumner Welles, Steve Early, Harry Hopkins, Jesse Jones. Ranking European and Asian diplomats, dignitaries, and royalty also dined with the ambassador and his wife.

Together, the Davieses toured the seas of Finland, Sweden, Germany, and Poland as well as Russia in the *Sea Cloud*. It was perhaps Marjorie's most rewarding period as she contributed her own subtle imprint to the times.

Ambassador Davies, for his part, was overly solicitous of his Russian hosts and rarely criticized their emerging communist state. The ambassador naïvely overlooked the obvious hurdles to friendship between a democratic America and a communist Russia. Before sending documents to the State Department in Washingon, he routinely altered grim conclusions on reports that were prepared by his staff. And, when it came to Stalin's "great purges," Davies and his wife justified the murder of millions by supporting Stalin's legal right to execute "traitors" accused of plotting the overthrow of the country.

In January 1938, the State Department announced that Davies would be transferred to Brussels—a promotion on paper. Marjorie's response: "Thank God. They have a king!" When World War II broke out, Davies was recalled to Washington and named Secretary of State in charge of War Emergency Problems and Politics. He eventually wrote a stilted memoir, *Mission to Moscow*, which was made into a movie in 1943 starring Walter Huston.

Despite the success of the film, Davies's political and diplomatic role began to fade as the war years passed. With each day, however, he developed an obsessive belief that his wife was interested in other men. The imagined slights worsened as Davies became increasingly dependent on Marjorie's social status and prominence. An innocent dance appeared to be a sexual offering. Davies soon began to act out in public. One flare-up—at a war bond rally—started with Marjorie offering a kind word to Henry J. Kaiser, the industrialist, and ended with Davies issuing a snide response that was reported in the gossip pages.

Ironically, while her third marriage was deteriorating, Marjorie Post received a visit in Palm Beach from her "poor little rich girl" niece, Barbara Hutton. Barbara needed a respite from own marital woes in 1944. She was about to divorce her fourth husband, Cary Grant, the legendary movie star. Sitting forlornly at the feet of her "grand aunt" in her bedroom at Mar-a-Lago, Barbara wondered if she would ever be happily married.

"You're too impetuous," Marjorie told her niece. "You should try to patch things up with Cary."

"Maybe I just have not found the right man yet," Barbara replied.

"Nonsense!" Marjorie snapped. "You have had too many husbands. You must be doing something wrong."

"Like what?" Barbara asked.

"Have you tried rotating your hips?" Marjorie suggested. "I'm told it makes it much better for the man."

Ultimately Davies's jealous attacks on Marjorie turned violent, according to Wright. On numerous occasions, Marjorie asked her granddaughter, Marwee, to stand sentry outside a bathroom that separated Marjorie's bedroom suite from her husband's parlor until Davies was asleep. "That man is going to kill you," Marjorie's personal assistant, Margaret Voight, warned repeatedly.

To distance herself from the abusive Davies, Marjorie stepped up her usual pace of party giving in order to surround herself with people at Mar-a-Lago. And when she was away from Palm Beach, she invented excuses to stay at a rented Sutton Place apartment, saying she wanted to see her daughters and their families. The separations from Davies reminded Marjorie that life could still be enjoyed. In 1955, she decided to divorce him. When her attorneys filed papers, they discovered the ambassador had secretly placed Marjorie's coveted Washington estate, the twenty-nine-acre Tregaron, in his name. But Marjorie was desperate for the divorce and did not contest Davies's sleight-of-hand. Instead, she took satisfaction in raiding the Tregaron garden of her azaleas and building an estate twice its size.

After the divorce, Marjorie confessed she knew "Joe was an actor" within two weeks of their marriage. "He was just a fourteen-carat phony," Marwee added.

Now thrice divorced and sixty-eight-years-old, Marjorie pledged to never marry again. But, as *Time* magazine reported, Marjorie was "as well preserved as a frozen peach." She started to search for yet another "perch." Her family was incredulous. They came to believe Marjorie would try forever to fill a void created by the death of her devoted father nearly five decades earlier.

"She liked to have someone with her at all times," said John Logan, a Washingtonian who served as Marjorie's "escort" until she met Herbert May, the man who would become her fourth—and most scandalous—husband.

Marjorie met May, a former Westinghouse Corporation executive from Pittsburgh, at a Palm Beach soiree during the winter of 1957. He was a sixty-five-year-old widower with three sons and an adopted daughter. With his regal white hair and soft-spoken manner, May seemed "so nice" to Marjorie that the seventy-one-year-old heiress decided to marry him. She kept her engagement a secret because of a pledge to never marry again, but the plans for a small ceremony at

Adelaide's country home leaked to the press. When questioned by reporters, an aide to Marjorie, apparently embarrassed by May's younger age, noted that "he would be sixty-six by the wedding."

The marriage took place in June 1958 amid rumors the groom had financial troubles. "Herb May, you were one jump ahead of the sheriff until Marjorie bailed you out!" May's sister blurted out at the wedding celebration. As she had for her three previous husbands, Marjorie provided May with a multimillion-dollar trust fund.

Marjorie's family and friends took quickly to Herb because of his affable, outgoing manner. A more relaxed Marjorie Post May and her husband reopened Mar-a-Lago for the winter of 1958. May quickly put it to use with huge business luncheons for a Saudi king or two hundred industrialists. He also shared Marjorie's newfound love of square dancing and had a theater-size pavilion built to hold country music hoedowns every Thursday.

"It started promptly at 7," Betty McMahon told *Palm Beach Life* magazine.

Marjorie was always in the receiving line. Maybe one cocktail would be served at the reception, and then we'd go in to this wonderful dinner. Beautiful roast beef, mashed potatoes—everything was very simple but done well. Jell-O and cakes were served for dessert—General Foods products, of course.

The amazing thing was that you would see a completely different group of people than you saw at most Palm Beach parties. There were a couple of judges, doctors—you know, professional people. But sometimes you would see visitors like the Maharaja of Baroda.

After dinner we would all go into the ballroom. Mrs. Post hired all these pros to push us around the floor, which was fun. I wouldn't know what to do but she made it so easy. She loved people who danced. Sometimes she would dance with one of the instructors. She was so graceful, she always held her head high, like a ballerina. It was a thrill to watch her. At 10:30 or 11, they would play some good-night song. We all held hands and circled back and forth, and then said good-night to everyone. It was a very special evening.

Herb's pavilion also came in handy for a special party to honor the duke and duchess of Windsor with a screening of the movie *A King's Story*, which was based on the duke's life. Herb also convinced

Marjorie to trade her costly *Sea Cloud*—plus $1 million—for a Viscount 786 propjet owned by Rafael Trujillo, the Dominican Republic ruler. May renamed the jet *Merriweather* and then streamlined the forty-two-passenger compartment to accommodate sixteen people on comfortable divans and overstuffed swivel chairs. And it was May who urged Marjorie to build a swimming pool on Mar-a-Lago property for the first time in fifty years. But he insisted the olympic-size pool be constructed away from the mansion and on the beach, where the underground tunnel from Mar-a-Lago met the ocean.

May's desire for this swimming pool masked a startling secret he had wisely kept from Marjorie. Herb May was bisexual—and his overwhelming sexual preference was for men. Although he had fathered three children and had been married for years, May had discovered that he found men sexually attractive, according to Post biographer William Wright. During his adult life, May acted on his gay urges with increasing frequency. In fact, only a few months after his marriage to Marjorie, May complained to a male friend about her sexual desires: "My God, she wants to do it every night!"

May soon became reckless in front of Marjorie, who, at seventy-one, was suffering partial hearing loss. At a dance in Washington, May saw a handsome young man pass by. Turning to a gay friend, May exclaimed: "How do I *meet* that?"

He quickly started to use "his" new swimming pool for afternoon and late-night, all-male parties, without fear of detection by Marjorie. She was not only hard of hearing now, but she seldom ventured to the beach or into the sun because of her fair complexion. But members of the vast Mar-a-Lago staff—always the true "insiders" in a Palm Beach home— became well aware of Mr. May's sexual predilections. These "faithful" insiders guarded his secret carefully—until someone needed to use it to his advantage.

Marjorie had removed herself from the day-to-day business operations of Mar-a-Lago. Aides were now handling several important matters, including the estate's enormous supply orders. Various staffers were demanding kickbacks from stores that received the orders. But the gouging reached a point where one supermarket chain refused to do business with Mar-a-Lago.

"We expected it to some degree, but it was getting ridiculous," the store manager said.

May had warned Marjorie repeatedly to expect thievery if she relinquished control of her purse strings. He had estimated an annual sixty-thousand-dollar loss. But when he discovered the extent of the

Henry Morrison Flagler. The nineteenth-century industrialist and oil company executive who transformed a swampy jungle island into a tropical paradise for America's rich and powerful. (Henry Morrison Flagler Museum)

The Styx, home to the black laborers who built Flagler's dream hotel. When they completed their backbreaking task, Flagler burned their shantytown to the ground, forcing them off Palm Beach in 1894. (Henry Morrison Flagler Museum)

Ida Alice Shourds. Flagler's second wife had to be committed to an insane asylum when she threatened to kill Flagler; she lusted for lovemaking sessions with the late Czar of Russia. (Henry Morrison Flagler Museum)

Whitehall, a house of marble that Flagler erected as a monument for his mistress Mary Lily Kenan in 1900. The next year, he married Mary Lily after bribing Florida legislators to amend the state's restrictive divorce law. (Henry Morrison Flagler Museum)

On March 14, 1896, railroad magnate Cornelius Vanderbilt (far right), Henry Payne Whitney (third from right), and their families and friends arrived at the enormous Royal Poinciana Hotel on the first train to cross Flagler Bridge. (Henry Morrison Flagler Museum)

At the turn of the century, Isadora Duncan, the mistress of Paris Singer, the sewing machine heir, danced in costumes that were considered daring for their day. (Courtesy of the *New York Post*)

Isadora Duncan cuddles son, Patrick, her illegitimate son by Singer, in 1916. Mother and child later met separate violent deaths.

Paris Singer built the island's first and still most exclusive club, The Everglades, from which he dictated who was in and who was out of Palm Beach society. Here he lunches with socialite Mrs. Jerome Napolean Bonaparte, in 1927.

Boxing champ Kid McCoy in 1905. He was the exercise instructor at Gus' Bath House in 1917. His weekend fling with Isadora Duncan broke up her eleven-year affair with Singer.

Financier Edward T. Stotesbury and his wife, "Queen" Eva Stotesbury, in 1912, using the island's early form of transportation, the "Afromobile," named for the black laborers who pedaled it. (Courtesy of the *New York Post*)

Addison Mizner, the ailing, debt-ridden architect who traveled from New York to Palm Beach to die in 1917. Instead, his talents were discovered by High Society, for whom he designed the island's wondrous Mediterranean mansions. (Historical Society of Palm Beach County)

Addison's brother, Wilson, the opium-smoking wit and all-around conman and cardsharp, who originated the expresssion "Be nice to people on the way up, because you'll meet the same people on the way down." (Historical Society of Palm Beach County).

Colonel E.R. Bradley, 1934. He said he preferred horses to people. He built the legendary Beach Club, a private casino more opulant than the great gaming halls of Monte Carlo. (Courtesy of *New York Daily News*)

Douglas MacArthur receives the Distinguished Service medal from love rival John "Black Jack" Pershing, in 1919. Two years later, a bitter Pershing battled MacArthur for the hand of Louise Brooks, the debutante daughter of "Queen" Eva Stotesbury. MacArthur (below left, with Louise) won Louise's heart, but Pershing orchestrated his revenge by exiling MacArthur to the Philipines in 1921. (Photos courtesy of the *New York Post*)

Actor Lionel Atwill. The legendary movie villian married Louise after she divorced MacArthur. But the union soured when Atwill insisted on ménages à trois.

The fabulous Breakers Hotel burns to the ground on March 5, 1925. A thousand guests lost two million dollars in jewels and furs as a dance band cheerfully played "There'll Be a Hot Time in the Old Town Tonight." (Courtesy of the *New York Daily News*)

Joe Kennedy's mistress Gloria Swanson takes a stroll on the beach with her husband, the Marquis de la Falaise de la Coudraye, in 1925. Kennedy carried on his secret affair with the film actress by skillfully keeping the Marquis away.

Family patriarch Joe Kennedy in 1931. He had a habit of "jumping" women—a tawdry practice shared by subsequent generations of Kennedy men. He later shared women with his sons.

Senator Ted Kennedy and matriarch Rose. Teddy slipped girls into the family compound without his mother ever knowing. (Courtesy of the *New York Post*)

loss, he threatened to expose the operation to Marjorie. Within days, photographs of May—naked and with young boys—turned up at her lawyer's office. They brought the pictures to her. Marjorie was horrified. And, as importantly, she realized she was perhaps the last to know about her husband's wanderings, and just as naïve as she had been about Hutton's affairs in the 1920s and 1930s.

According to Wright, Marjorie and her lawyer took the photos to May. He denied their authenticity and claimed the pictures were doctored. Marjorie chose to ignore the truth. She was genuinely fond of May and took his side. But her hand was forced within days. Someone contacted her and said they were writing a book about people in high places who led double lives. A chapter, the "author" said, was to be devoted to her husband's homosexuality. Marjorie instructed her lawyers to buy off the writer and start divorce proceedings.

Marjorie made another vow to never marry again. This time she appeared sincere. She went so far as to legally restore her name to Marjorie Merriweather Post. However, at the age of eighty-one, Marjorie searched for another "perch." She set a tropical trap for a distinguished former secretary of the navy who was twenty years her junior. He turned down the proposal and nearly broke Marjorie's heart. But game grand dame that she was, Marjorie recovered and pursued several more men. Her family soon feared she was about to fall victim to a young gold digger. They dispatched granddaughter Marwee to save her—and their inheritance.

"Grandma," Marwee began, "I think it's wonderful you're thinking of marrying that guy. He seems like a terrific man."

Then she added: "I'm sure he'll give up his other women as soon as he marries you. . . ."

"What other women?" Marjorie replied.

"Oh, you know those ladies in Washington."

"Who?"

"Oh, Jane Bedford, Pam Pancoast, Alice . . ." said Marwee, conjuring names as she went.

The ploy worked. It shook Marjorie out of her lovestruck daze. A few weeks later, Marjorie arrived at Marwee's apartment with a necklace of yellow sapphires and amethysts with matching earrings and ring. Marwee had long desired the costly jewels. Marjorie gave them to her as a gift, claiming a husband would have cost more.

Marjorie Post died in 1973. But right up to her death she continued to seek the "right" husband.

"Grandma had a lot of doctors," Marwee recalled. "She had been crazy about one of them for years. She was really kind of in love with him. One time he's standing over her, and she's lying there—eighty-six-years-old, senile, going to die in a few months—she looks up at him and says, 'I love you, Harold. Will you marry me?' He was married, but that didn't stop her."

9

The Only Dodge That Runs on Alcohol:
Horace and Gregg Dodge

All heads turned to the entrance of Ta-boo as a white-gloved chauffeur maneuvered the wheelchair into the crowded Worth Avenue restaurant. The portly man in the chair, his eyes glassy, his speech slurred, was brought to a front table.

A white-gloved waiter marched up, but before he could offer a word of greeting, the man, in his mid-fifties, barked an order for a double scotch. The waiter nodded and did an about-face to the bar. Then the portly man's eyes closed, his head slumped down, and he began snoring lightly. A few seconds later, he awakened. "My drink!" he snapped.

When his scotch came, the man, without looking at a menu, ordered a Porterhouse steak—medium rare. Fifteen minutes and two more drinks later, the steak came and the man attacked it ravenously.

But some of the meat was not to his liking and the man began spitting small portions of his chewed mouthfuls back onto the plate. The terribly vulgar display of manners had not escaped attention. The twenty or so diners near him watched in disgust. A few complained to their waiters. Several remarked that Palm Beach was no longer what it used to be. A couple of diners who didn't recognize the man suggested he might be handicapped or disabled.

The man they were watching was Horace Elgin Dodge, Jr., heir to

121

the Dodge automobile fortune and a man who, for all his tens of millions of dollars and endless resources, seemingly had only three goals in life: to drink, eat, and chase women.

His drinking problem had become so extreme by the mid-1950s that he now often "traveled" by wheelchair. His valets wheeled him into restaurants, into the bathroom, into his bedroom. Sometimes he was so inebriated that he forgot to dress and went outside in his pajamas.

Horace Dodge, Sr., had created a company that helped forge the American automobile industry. Yet his son could seldom get behind the wheel of a car himself for fear of running off the road in a drunken stupor. In Palm Beach, Dodge had come to be known as "the only Dodge that runs on alcohol."

But Dodge—as fat, gluttonous, and usually drunk as he was—lived the way he wanted. He liked everything fast. Fast women, fast marriages, fast divorces, and fast spending. As soon as one marriage dissolved, another one started. His marriages did not stop his pursuit of other women, whom he showered with gifts in exchange for sex. Dodge was up to his fifth wife, blond ex-showgirl Gregg Sherwood Dodge, one of the island's most attractive women. Where was she? people in the restaurant wondered.

Horace Dodge, Jr., was one of a new breed of millionaires who had entered Palm Beach life in the 1930s and 1940s. These new millionaires had inherited all of their wealth from their fathers, the great industrialists, inventors, and financiers who had built America. However, the rich second-generation sons knew little about money other than how to spend it. Many did not work and led wasteful, excessive lives that got them only one thing: trouble. Horace Dodge, Jr., was among the first of this breed, and his unbelievable behavior, his life of pursuing pleasure at any cost, particularly during his last marriage, is still discussed by Palm Beach society.

Horace Dodge, Jr., was born in Niles, Michigan, in 1900, the son of blacksmith Horace Dodge and piano teacher Anna Thomson Dodge, who had emigrated to the United States from Scotland with her father in the 1880s. Horace Sr., along with his brother, John, worked as laborers in their father's blacksmith and machine shop. With overtime, they made thirty to forty dollars a week.

One day in 1901, a tall, slight man walked into the shop with a set of plans for a strange-looking engine. The man was named Henry Ford. As John and Horace listened, Ford excitedly explained how this engine, if constructed to his specifications, would run on fuel through an internal-combustion process. The engine could then be attached to a wheeled chassis. The result would be a self-propelling buggy.

Ford made the Dodges a proposition. If they built his engine, he would give them a 10 percent share of stock in his newly created Ford Motor Company. It was a purely speculative venture, Ford admitted, but what did they have to lose except a little metal and some hours of manpower? The Dodges shook hands with Ford; the engine they built for him worked, and the American automobile industry was born.

A decade later, Ford's "self-propelled buggy" was in such demand that Ford could not keep up with all of the orders. Horace and John Dodge cashed in their "speculative" 10 percent stock venture for $40 million cash and, in 1914, founded their own manufacturing concern, the Dodge Motor Company. With Ford and Dodge at the helms of their companies, Detroit was tranformed into the auto-making capital of the world.

The Dodge brothers were hard workers and hard players. With their millions they bought yachts, private railroad cars, palatial homes, and all the luxuries their families suggested. But Horace did not live long enough to enjoy most of it. He died in Detroit in December 1920 during a brief illness, leaving a $58 million fortune to Anna and a $28 million trust to Horace Jr. to be dispensed in monthly increments. Young Horace used some of his money to start a speedboat-manufacturing company. He had always liked fast things.

Meanwhile, Horace Sr.'s widow, Anna, at the urging of financial advisers, invested the majority of her fortune in tax-free municipal bonds. Anna was crushed by Horace Sr.'s death, but she regained some of her strength at the news that Horace Jr. had fallen in love and planned to be married in a few months. She prayed for grandchildren to help fill her many empty days. Horace married Lois Knowlson, a local girl from a moderately well-to-do family, in 1921. Anna was not disappointed. In the next three years, Lois gave birth to two children, Horace III and Delphine Ione.

Anna Thomson Dodge had been a wise investor since her husband's death. She was also a miser who explained to friends, who urged her to pamper herself, that she had been raised to be thrifty during her childhood in the Scottish countryside, and, despite her millions, that's the way she was. However, Anna's view of money was about to change; she would become involved with Palm Beach.

In early 1926, Anna journeyed to Italy for a short vacation. There, Dodge's widow met Hugh Dillman of Palm Beach. Dillman was a recently divorced, ex-stage actor, who, at forty-three, was six years Anna's junior. As a young actor in his twenties, Dillman's career had taken him to the Broadway stage in such hits as *The College Widow* and *The Strange Woman*. He had played opposite actresses like Ethel Barrymore and Frances Starr. He had married one of his costars, Marjorie Rambeau, in 1919, but the couple divorced four years later after she charged him with cruelty. After a flurry of stage successes, the acting competition grew too tough. Younger, more talented actors began getting the parts he once did. The money dried up and Dillman quit show business. Currently, he was living at the Alba Hotel and working as the director of the Palm Beach Society of Arts, which organized weekly classical music concerts on the island. In Italy, Anna and Hugh fell madly in love, and by the end of the trip they talked about becoming engaged. They arrived in Palm Beach three months after returning to the United States.

Dillman, like Anna, respected money and was a wise investor with what little he had. But he also enjoyed spending money. And spend it they did. First, Anna paid $4 million to Oklahoma oil magnate Joshua Cosden for Palm Beach's magnificent villa called Playa Riente (Laughing Beach), a one hundred-room marble estate built in the style of a Moorish castle. The fabulous house, on the ocean, featured a grand ballroom with a solid ebony floor; murals by the Fratelli Angeli of Florence, Italy, and a series of panels originally created for the king of Spain by the Spanish artist José Sert.

To furnish the estate, Anna and Hugh went a spending spree through Europe, purchasing such treasures as four chairs with the monogram of Marie Antionette, two large candelabras made for the palace of Versailles, and a writing table that had formerly graced the bedroom of the Grand Dutchess Marie Feodorovna, who later became the czarina of Paul I.

The couple enjoyed giving parties at Playa Riente. One party attended by two hundred guests, featured two orchestras, a champagne fountain, and twenty-five pounds of beluga caviar. As Anna understated years later: "Hugh really did show me how to enjoy my wealth." Hugh Dillman became such a key figure in Palm Beach society that he succeeded Paris Singer as one of the presidents of the Everglades Club.

As Anna Dodge's life soared in 1926, her son teetered on the edge of divorce. His wife, Lois, had flown to Paris to have lawyers prepare divorce papers. Horace Jr. would drink and become abusive, Lois had decided the marriage was over. While driving her automobile down the Champs Elysées, she struck a child. When the police arrived, she gave them her husband's name. Horace had found out about her divorce plans and flown to Paris to try to reconcile. As he stepped off the plane, the French police slapped the baffled Horace with a $20,000 judgment against him on behalf of the crippled child.

When Horace discovered the truth about the accident, he was livid. But, desperately wanting Lois to abandon her divorce plans, he never mentioned it to her. Lois wanted no part of her husband, however. When she heard Horace was on his way to her hotel, she rushed to the airport and booked a flight to New York.

Horace, more determined than ever to try to make up with Lois, followed her on the next plane. In a scene right out of a screwball comedy, Lois led him on a three-week-long intercontinental wild goose chase by plane, ocean liner, and car. He followed her from New York to Detroit to San Francisco and then on to Hawaii. To avoid reporters on his cruise to Honolulu aboard the ocean liner *Wilhelmina*, Dodge used the alias "Jack Kennedy, motion picture producer." When he finally caught up with her in Honolulu, Lois flew back to San Francisco.

When their divorce decree was finally signed, Lois was granted a settlement of $1 million. Because Horace did not have enough cash, his mother guaranteed the settlement in writing from her own personal account.

In 1928, with the ink barely dry on his divorce papers, Horace, then twenty-eight, married Muriel Dorothy Sisman, whom newspapers described as "a 25-year-old Detroit society girl." They had two children, David and Diana.

Muriel was attractive, but Horace did not like her nose, which was slightly hooked. He suggested she seek a new procedure called plastic surgery to smooth the offending bump, and she agreed. It would be done quietly, the couple decided. The daily scandal sheets that survived on gossip would not know a thing. The day of the operation approached. Muriel was wheeled into the operating room and after anesthesia was given, plastic surgeon Dr. Louis P. Berne went to work. He cracked her nose and made a small incision in it. Suddenly, Berne withdrew his hands from Muriel's nose and clutched them to his heart. Moaning softly, he dropped to the operating-room floor and was dead of a massive heart attack within one minute.

Hastily, nurses scattered from the room and found another doctor. Dr. Joseph Safian rushed in, quickly studied Berne's "blueprints," examined Muriel's partially-dismantled face, then rolled up his sleeves and successfully finished the operation.

The day after Berne's sensational death, Dr. Safian's heroic deed and

Muriel's new nose were splashed across the front pages of every paper in town.

Almost from the beginning of their marriage, Horace and Muriel fought. The tension was aggravated by Horace's drinking. Now in his mid-thirties, the Dodge auto heir had become an alcoholic. He and Muriel separated in 1934 and battled for five years in and out of court before Horace filed for divorce in 1939. He charged his wife had continously made "cruel, disparaging remarks" about him and called him "obscene" names in public. Muriel, like Lois before her, walked away with $1 million and custody of the children.

In May 1940, forty-year-old Dodge married twenty-seven-year-old Martha (Mickey) Devine. He had been seeing her for several years during his separation from Muriel. Mickey was a leggy blond showgirl who had starred in the popular Broadway variety show, *Earl Carroll's Vanities*. Their marriage lasted four years, but it seemed miraculous it had lasted even four weeks. Within one month of their union, Horace cheated again. His infidelities against Mickey began on his 150-ton yacht, *The Vanities*, named for his wife's biggest stage success.

Mike Shannon, the yacht's skipper, testified later that as the boat was docked at Manhattan's Municipal Yacht Basin on the Hudson River at 79th Street, a young woman named Sylvia Hofstadter appeared from nowhere and hopped on board.

"Mr. Dodge was already on board—completely nude except for a blue robe. After they had a few drinks, Dodge came to me and said, 'Mike, you keep watch. I want nobody on the boat,'" Shannon recalled.

Later, I spotted Mr. Dodge's wife, Mickey, on the dock and walking towards the launch. I immediately ran down to the master's stateroom. I went in and saw Mr. Dodge and Sylvia nude in bed. I said, "You had better get the hell up out of there before murder happens. Mrs. Dodge is coming!"

Mr. Dodge got excited and yelled, "Mike, get her out of here! Put her in the bilge! Throw her overboard! Do anything, but get rid of her!"

Sylvia jumped out of bed stark naked and I handed her her clothes. She put on her bloomers and slip and stockings and shoes and a light coat. She grabbed her bag in one hand and said to me, "How am I going to get out of here?"

The two then made a mad dash through a maze of rooms and the young woman climbed out a portal onto a small launch on the side of the boat.

"I didn't want to tell Mrs. Dodge about it because they had just recently been married. I didn't want to make her feel bad," Shannon said.

Horace's liaison with Sylvia Hofstadter—to whom he had secretly given a fourteen-thousand-dollar diamond ring and a sixty-six-hundred-dollar emerald ring—marked one of the few times he attempted to be discreet about his philandering. As the months passed, he dropped the façade of faithful husband and slowly began to taunt Mickey about his sexual trysts with other women. Sometimes, while in a drunken rage, he would brag cruelly about what he had actually done with the women.

The last straw for Mickey came in 1943, when Dodge told his wife about an English actress he had been seeing whenever he and Mickey visited their one-hundred-room castle outside London. Going into elaborate detail, Horace described how he sneaked the actress into the castle and made love to her in an adjacent bedroom.

"He had basically installed her as his mistress in our castle," Mickey fumed. She filed for separation in November 1943, and four months later, for divorce on the grounds of mental cruelty and adultery. In her divorce suit, Mickey named seven women she claimed Dodge had slept with and charged that there were "hundreds" of others during their four-year marriage. Horace maintained several secret "love nests" around the country, she said.

One of Horace's main girlfriends, according to Mickey, was "a little country gal from Jefferson County, Missouri," named Clara Mae Tinsley. To impress "little hillbilly" Clara, Mickey said snidely, he had bought her fourteen hundred dollars' worth of nylon stockings.

The divorce was granted and Horace once again relied on his mother for financial help: Mickey walked off with $1 million. Horace quickly married his "little hillbilly" Clara Mae, a former army nurse.

Dodge's drinking problem was embarrassingly profiled in the newspapers when, in February 1948, while in a stupor, he staggered into a London art gallery and wrote a $27,200 check for a painting he liked. When Dodge sobered up the next morning and realized what he had done, he stopped payment on the check, prompting the art gallery to sue. At the trial, Dodge was asked if he was so badly intoxicated that he had been unaware of what he was doing when he bought the painting, which he erroneously believed to be a famous work by eighteenth-century artist Sir Thomas Lawrence.

"It's a bad way to put it, but it's true," Dodge answered. He said he had thrown a huge party on his yacht, and, being the good host, had imbibed with all of his guests. "I had enough drinks to float the ship!" he admitted cheerfully.

When the case ended, British Lord Chief Justice Goddard threw the lawsuit out, but chided Dodge as "an alcoholic who on his own showing was behaving at the time of this sale as what would be described in his own country as a common drunk." In 1950, Dodge successfully fought off a lawsuit by two Manhattan gynecologists who claimed he owed him sixty thousand dollars for various services they performed on "several" of his girlfiends.

Drinking, womanizing Horace eventually found his fourth marriage going bad. His mother told him he had to straighten himself out. She begged him to give up alcohol, chasing women, and rampant spending. Horace had always tried to please his mother, so he promised her that she would soon see a new Horace.

He was right. A new Horace was about to emerge, but it wasn't the teetotaling miser that Anna had hoped for. He was about to meet Gregg Sherwood.

Gregg Sherwood was born Dora Mae Fjelstad in New York City in 1926, the daughter of a Norwegian carpenter, Mons Fjelstad, and his French wife, Helen. The family moved to Beloit, Wisconsin, where Gregg spent her childhood. In high school, Dora Mae was the most popular girl in her class and had many boyfriends. On a whim, she eloped with a high-school sweetheart, but her mother chased after the lovebirds and had the marriage annulled. Dora Mae grew tired of small-town life, where everybody knew everybody else's business, where you married the boy next door, where you earned a modest living and lived in a modest house. She wanted to move to New York City, where, if one believed the papers, fame and fortune waited around every corner.

If success would be hers, Dora Mae decided, her name had to be the first thing to go. "Dora Mae" would never do in New York. She wanted something jazzier, something with a ring to it. She started by changing "Dora" to "Gregg," after the famous shorthand course she had studied to learn secretarial skills. Gregg entered and won a local beauty pageant and went on to capture the Miss Wisconsin crown. The award afforded her the chance to travel to Atlantic City to compete in the Miss America contest in 1943. She placed fifth. Gregg moved to New York and was signed by the John Robert Powers model agency. She worked a few small jobs, but Powers told her she photographed too much like Rita Hayworth and could never make it as a Hayworth lookalike.

The only way she could succeed: dye her hair, change her hairstyle and buy a brand-new wardrobe to achieve a completely different look.

But new clothes and good hairstylists were not cheap and Gregg was nearly broke. Feeling defeated, she sulked her way back to Beloit. But one look at her hometown again was enough. She had to get out.

She struggled to save money, working days as a taxi dispatcher and nights as a wartime welder and riveter. Within six months she had scraped together two thousand dollars, enough to get her back to Manhattan and set up in an apartment. This time, she decided, nothing would stop her, she would never turn back.

"I lightened my hair a little and got a few modeling jobs. I lightened it some more and I got still more work. The lighter my hair got, the more the work came in. Is it any wonder I became a platinum blonde?" Gregg recalled.

She returned to her modeling agency and began getting steady work. Her social life also picked up. With her mother far away, Gregg was free to date whoever she pleased and date often. In New York she went out with such eligible bachelors as Joe DiMaggio and Dean Martin.

In 1948, on a weekend trip to Miami Beach courtesy of a shirt manufacturer who was smitten with her, Gregg met Walter Sherwood, a New York Yankees ticket agent. Walter made a good salary and had a lot of contacts. Gregg wasted little time. When Sherwood returned to New York, he received an Easter card in the mail from Gregg, complete with a snapshot of her in a skimpy bathing suit.

"Marilyn Monroe [didn't] look as good to me as Gregg did in that photo," he said. The fix was in. Sherwood proposed and Gregg accepted. The Yankees man showered her with gifts on their honeymoon. Fur coats, jewelry, fancy clothes—nothing was too good for Gregg. But Gregg demanded more. There was this new designer line, that new necklace. It didn't stop. Within a year the marriage crumbled. Then Gregg made the papers, but not in a way she had planned. Walter Sherwood was arrested on charges of stealing seventy thousand dollars from the Yankee ticket office. He had done so, he later admitted, to help pay the bills from Gregg's nonstop spending sprees. She had also convinced him to help finance a new home for her parents back in Beloit.

Sherwood obtained a Mexican divorce from Gregg and later painted a portrait of her as a great hunter whose prey was men. "Gregg knows how to make a man happy," he said. "She can be so convincing in telling you how great you are, that you soon share her opinion."

As Sherwood stood in disgrace, Gregg's career took off. In a few years, she landed roles in five Hollywood movies including *Naked City*, *The Iron Man*, with Rock Hudson, and *The Merry Widow*, with Lana

Turner. She appeared in Broadway shows, including *Young Man's Fancy* and *Gentlemen Prefer Blondes* and graced the cover of 144 magazines.

"She was never a leading lady but a very solid grade B or second female," said an acquaintance.

In 1951, Gregg was introduced to Palm Beach. She had just completed a television appearance in New York when a Fifth Avenue couturier asked her to model a new line at a fashion show in Palm Beach for one hundred dollars a day plus expenses.

She twirled and strutted along the runway before an appreciative audience of Palm Beach ladies, designers, and Worth Avenue boutique owners. One audience member in particular stared intently. It was fifty-one-year-old Horace Dodge, Jr., who was attending the show with his his eighty-two-year-old mother, Anna.

Dodge was quickly taken by the twenty-five-year-old Gregg. He remarked to his mother how beautiful she was. The ever lustful Dodge ran to a telephone midway through the show. He called several Worth Avenue clothing stores and told them to rush their finest, most expensive fashions over. When Gregg returned to her dressing room at the end of the show, she found mounds of boxes of expensive furs and dresses—fifty-nine thousand dollars' worth, to be exact—the price tags had been left on.

As she glowed over the gifts, Dodge walked in and asked her out. The two immediately began dating, and Dodge's courtship of Gregg made headlines as large as those devoted to two other celebrated couples of the day, Aly Khan and Rita Hayworth and Ingrid Bergman and Roberto Rossellini. One reason was that Dodge was still married to Clara Tinsley.

Gregg loved Dodge's affections—but she knew he had a lousy track record. He was already on wife number four and had a terrible drinking problem. One thing Dodge was good at, however, was spreading his wealth.

Dodge told Gregg he would do anything for her. In June 1952, he gave a party in Gregg's honor in Cannes that featured sixty pounds of caviar, twelve hundred dozen roses, hundreds of orchids imported from Paris (at fifteen dollars each), fireworks displays, and strolling musicians. He ended the festivities by proposing marriage and presenting Gregg with a $100,000, sixteen-and-a-half-carat, emerald-cut diamond engagement ring. It was a gesture Gregg made sure was fed to New York's gossip columnists. She figured that even if the proposal foundered, the publicity would not hurt her.

For his part, Dodge knew Gregg loved publicity. He said after the bash: "I hope it was an engagement party, but who knows whether she is going to like me in a week?" And the newspapers loved Gregg. She was always good for an item about what Dodge had given her this week or for an update about how the courtship was progressing.

Gregg began selling articles—written with the help of newspaper reporters—for young single women on how to hook a man. She used Dodge as an example. One article she wrote in September 1952 in the New York *Daily News* was headlined WOLVES I'VE DODGED.

She described her experiences with different types of men. The Rugged Wolf: "On one drink, screams 'Timber!' and waits to see you fall." The Athletic Wolf: "He's more than willing to forget about training... so long as he can be in bed by 9:30 P.M." The African Wolf: "Never quite sure what he's having for dinner and hopes it will be you." The Photographer Wolf: "Has a camera, phonograph, and lots of mood music, a satin dressing gown—but, honey, no film in that camera."

Gregg also made clear what these men were good for. "Wolves are far too busy making money so they can buy things like garbage disposal plants, cement factories and political districts. Of course, their money also buys the finer things in life. Finer things like mink coats, for instance."

Another article chronicled one night of drinking that ended when Dodge accused Gregg of stealing five expensive cigarette lighters from his home and threatened to have her arrested.

"He overlooked one little matter," Gregg told her public. "He had given them to me the P.M. before... He's burning up the Bell system trying to make amends and get me back. If you see an automobile magnate coming your way—dodge, girls, dodge! And I do mean dodge."

If any of this nonsense bothered Horace, he did not complain publicly. In fact, he pursued Gregg even harder. His manic courtship, his friends believed, was fueled in part by his drinking. Whenever he was out with her, he seemed to down whiskey like water. Gregg, no teetotaler herself, even worried about it. She tried to make him quit or at least cut down, but he refused. Instead, a compromise was reached. He'd drink beer instead. That lasted a year.

"He was much nicer on beer," Gregg remembered. "He'd drink just so much and then get groggy and fall off to sleep. But when he was drinking whiskey, there was no stopping him. He'd just want to keep going and he tired everybody out."

In early 1953, Dodge announced: "We will be married on Valentine's Day—if we don't kill each other first."

Murder was not the only obstacle that threatened to stop the wedding. A divorce settlement had yet to be worked out between Dodge and Clara Tinsley. Lawyers tried to hammer out a deal, but the wedding date had to be postponed a week as they haggled. In the end, Clara did as well as the other ex-Mrs. Dodges—receiving a $1 million settlement.

In Palm Beach, Gregg and Horace's big day finally arrived, a picture-perfect Friday afternoon on February 20, 1953, not a cloud in the sky, temperatures in the mid-seventies, low humidity. The ceremony took place at Playa Riente, Anna Dodge's beautiful mansion. The matriarch of the Dodge family had fought her son's plans to marry Gregg, whom she saw as just another flashy blonde trying to tap into the Dodge fortune. But when Horace told her he would marry Gregg regardless of what she thought, Anna reluctantly embraced her future daughter-in-law and offered her home for the wedding.

Several dozen reporters appeared at the event. Horace, dressed in gray cutaway and striped trousers, looked surprisingly dashing— younger than his fifty-three years. Gregg, twenty-six, was breathtaking. Her wedding dress of ballerina-length powder-blue lace was complimented by voluminous petticoats of matching taffeta and tulle. She beamed as the orchestra began to play the wedding march on the huge, carefully manicured lawn overlooking the Atlantic.

Eager photographers snapped away as the couple marched down the aisle. At least they did until Anna, not used to the attention, screamed, "How dare you do this. How can you destroy our wedding march?" She had forgotten that Gregg had invited the photographers in the first place to assure the wedding would receive maximum publicity. The chastised cameramen stopped shooting for a few minutes while the couple said their I-do's and then resumed with a round of firing flashbulbs. Gregg and Horace happily whirled around the lawn to the music of Val Ernie's society orchestra.

Anna Dodge took Gregg aside and asked her to give up show business, insisting that Horace needed her constant companionship, and Gregg agreed to the request.

The couple moved into an expansive apartment in the Colony Hotel known simply as Penthouse A, the former home of the Maharajah of Baroda. On their first night home they settled into a bed adorned by a three-hundred-dollar set of silk sheets—one pink and one blue. A few months later, they moved in with Anna at her Palm Beach estate.

Their union was a public marriage—warts and all. Gregg made sure
of that. When she became pregnant, she kept the press informed of
every kick, every moment of morning sickness. When she entered Good
Samaritan Hospital halfway through her pregnancy, she told reporters it
was to escape "constant bickering" with Horace.

A year after their marriage Gregg gave birth to John Francis Dodge. A
$2 million trust fund was established for the infant. Little John was an
adorable, blond-haired baby. His parents loved him dearly. But as the
child grew, the Dodges' domestics did their best to keep him away from
his father when he was drunk, which was often. Frequently John was
watched by babysitters as his parents made the social scene.

Dodge had not tired of giving Gregg gifts. But he detested her
spending money behind his back and then being bombarded with huge
bills at the end of the month. In 1954, she bought $200,000 in jewelry
from Harry Winston but had to return her purchases when Dodge
refused to pay the bill.

Gregg now counted among her neighbors the Astors, the Rockefellers, the Mellons, the Vanderbilts, and the Toppings. She hoped that
Playa Riente, her new $8 million address, would bring her recognition
in Palm Beach society. But she soon learned that money did not
necessarily mean instant acceptance in Palm Beach.

Bandleader Claude Kelly recalled, "In those days, because of her
background, her personality, and her early career, she felt slighted by
some of the society women and tended to lean towards entertainers for
gratification." Her friends included Zsa Zsa Gabor, Ann Miller, Lana
Turner, Jack and Bobby Kennedy, and Huntington Hartford.

Gregg and Horace were further estranged from Palm Beach society
when Anna threw them out of Playa Riente after Horace had a bitter
fight with his mother over his "allowance" of about a half million dollars
a year. But he wanted several hundred thousand more per year to pay
for the lifestyle he and Gregg had devised. Anna had rejected the
demands, telling him he would have to live by the amount stipulated by
his trust fund.

They moved back into a hotel and continued spending, accumulating
large bills. When confronted by reporters about his nagging debts,
Dodge quipped, "I just don't like bills—they're upsetting!"

To entertain, the Dodges tossed expensive parties aboard Horace's
325-foot yacht, *Delphine,* treating guests like Helen Hayes, Ethel
Merman, and Barbara Hutton to imported pheasant, caviar and
champagne.

Alcohol began playing an ever larger role in the couple's life. In

November 1955, Gregg made the papers when she insulted a Spanish guitar player back in her hometown of Beloit. Gregg had been boozing at the Corrall Restaurant, and when she got fed up with the performance of Mario Escudero, she spoke rudely to him in French. He walked over and knocked her off a bar stool.

The couple's wild, alcohol-drenched Palm Beach soirees seemed to turn guests into nasty children. As one gossip column described a party: "Gregg Dodge dropped an ice cube down Mary Howe's décolleté. Mary reciprocated with a scotch and soda to Gregg's mascara. Not long afterwards, Gregg's father took exception when a titled guest unzipped his daughter's dress playfully as they danced and [he] took a wild swing at him."

Gregg was also hell on wheels. Home for the holidays in Beloit in December 1957, she sped away at sixty miles per hour from two police officers who had stopped her for running a red light. When they caught her at her mother's home, she attacked them with a barrage of four-letter words. She slapped one of the officers twice in the face and kicked him in the shins. She was issued a summons for disorderly conduct.

One of Gregg's most embarrassing episodes occurred August 27, 1958, in Hollywood. She and Chicago columnist Irv Kupcinet had just spent the evening drinking and dancing at Romanoff's, an exclusive nightclub. As the evening drew to a close, Irv offered to drive Gregg home in her flashy Continental.

As they zoomed down Hollywood Boulevard, Kupcinet pulled out behind a slow-moving police car. It angered Gregg that the police were such slowpokes.

Leaning halfway out the window, her ample cleavage shaking, Gregg yelled, "You cops! You'd better get off the street! Go home, you're drunk!"

The police followed Gregg and Irv for several blocks, then pulled them over. "Are you the Gestapo?" Gregg screamed as Officers Larry Brown and Kenneth Bernard approached the car. "What's wrong with feeling happy? Why, you're nothing but slimy Napoleonic idiots!"

She started spitting at the two cops, pulled off one of her high heels, hurled it at them, and cursed. The officers placed her and Irv under arrest and took them to the station house. Gregg wasn't through yet. As two police matrons took her to a cell, she punched one of them in the jaw and kicked the other in the leg. "Call my husband—he's Harry Dodge, the automobile company executive," she yelled. Horace was there in a flash with two hundred seventy dollars cash bail.

Gregg had a perfect explanation for it all. "We had been to a big party and had a couple of drinks. When we passed the squad car I simply said, "Hi'ya there." She also charged that female cops pulled her by the hair and "fondled my breasts."

After a court trial in which she was found guilty of being drunk in public, Gregg was fined one hundred dollars and narrowly escaped a ninety-day jail sentence.

In the late 1950s, the Dodges' marriage began to sour. With Horace off on drinking binges and chasing other women, and Gregg spending his money and hanging out with her own friends, the pair saw less and less of each other. According to Gregg, Horace displayed a major failing. "He never had to do anything himself; he could always hire somebody. It may be easier that way, but it's certainly less fun."

It certainly wasn't any fun going out with Horace anymore. It was embarrassing when he had to be wheeled into restaurants because he was so drunk. Many of Palm Beach's eateries, in fact, had banned Dodge because of his horrid table habits.

In an incident that scandalized Palm Beach, a highly intoxicated Horace had stood up and urinated at a private club, accidentally wetting a tableful of stunned diners.

Still the couple remained married. It was not so difficult, given the vast number of properties in the Dodge empire. With their home in Palm Beach, the castle in Britain, a home near Detroit, a thirty-three-room villa in Cannes, an apartment at the Waldorf in New York, and the largest privately owned yacht in the United States, there was plenty of room for each.

Gregg was seeing less of Horace, but not less of his charge accounts. She kept on spending. In 1959, a judge ordered her to pay almost seventy thousand dollars for a diamond brooch and necklace she had taken out "on approval" from Cartier, the exclusive New York jewelry firm.

The Dodges separated in 1961. In August 1962, Horace Dodge, Jr., now sixty-two, filed for divorce. He stated that on one occasion, Gregg, thirty-six, had physically beaten him so badly that he had to seek medical attention and he feared for his life.

"She has a vicious and ungovernable temper," Dodge said in his complaint.

Gregg told reporters: "Life is too short to go on like this. Do you mean that he's afraid of me physically? I can hardly lift him off the floor."

Before the divorce papers were signed, Dodge died of a heart ailment in December 1963. He left some $14 million in unpaid bills. In his will, he mentioned Gregg only once and that was to exclude her from any inheritance. Any money left over after the bill collectors were paid would go to Horace's and Gregg's nine-year-old son, John Francis. Horace had stipulated that any money that went to his son was "in no event whatsoever" to be placed under Gregg's control.

The majority of Dodge's estate was bequeathed to his mother Anna, then ninety-three, and still healthy.

Gregg was not about to take her late husband's snub without a fight. She immediately filed a $10 million "alienation of affection" lawsuit against Anna Dodge in March 1964. Anna Dodge, Gregg said, "campaigned to disrupt" the marriage, which placed Horace under a great strain "which ultimately contributed to his early demise. . . . She threatened to and did utilize various forms of financial, economic, social, familial and personal pressure against her son. She subjected him to public ridicule and embarrassment." She also alleged that the old lady had contributed to Horace's death through her clutching, overbearing ways.

She said she was willing to settle, however. She would drop the $10 million suit if Anna would pay her $1 million, an amount she claimed Horace had promised her in a prenuptial agreement, but had not delivered.

A year later, in April 1964, Gregg claimed to win a $9 million settlement from Anna. She said, "Its the end of a long road. Now that this is over I want to go see what Florida is all about again. I want to get a sun tan."

Anna scoffed at the amount and said it was "far less." The actual amount was around $1 million.

With her new wealth, Gregg bought a Palm Beach villa formerly owned by the late Myron Taylor, United States envoy to the Vatican. She set about looking for a new man. She found him in Daniel Moran, a former New York City cop.

The dark, ruggedly handsome Moran was born in Banggheroffaly, Ireland, and had emigrated to the United States at age fourteen. He had joined the police department in 1957 and was stationed in Manhattan's rough-and-tumble Second Division. The six-foot-one black-haired, blue-eyed Irishman first met the Dodges in 1960 when Horace had hired him as a security guard for a party he was giving in New York. Moran later quit the force to work full time for Gregg, becoming her "swimming instructor and ballroom dancing partner."

In December 1964, Gregg gave a party at her sixteen-room estate to tell friends that she and Moran were engaged. She was thirty-eight, he was twenty-six. Four years later, they bought Jessica Woolworth Donohue's magnificent beach house on 1089 South Ocean Boulevard, and they renovated it with a Moroccan motif.

That same year, Moran fatally shot a burglar in their Palm Beach home. The intruder had scaled the wall and stood on the top-floor balcony in the middle of the night. Moran was awakened by the noise, grabbed a revolver he kept by his night table, and ordered the man to stop. When the burglar refused, Moran shot him twice. The burglar fell forty feet to his death in what the Palm Beach County Attorney's Office ruled was a "justifiable homicide."

Meanwhile, Gregg and Daniel Moran's bills began piling up. Their mortgage payments were habitually late. While the couple was off on a European holiday one year, creditors broke into their home and removed furniture to be sold to pay debts. A federal judge then ordered them to pay $2.8 million in unpaid bills. Next, a bank foreclosed on their Ocean Boulevard home. They could continue to live there for a while, but they no longer owned it.

Then Gregg and Moran were hit with theft charges. In New York, authorities alleged that they had stolen $375,000 from Gregg's son's trust fund and had bilked one of their creditors, a Manhattan bank, out of $75,000 by lying that they were beneficiaries of the trust, which had been established by Anna Dodge years earlier.

Drinking, depressed, and despondent over their crumbling lives, the couple had a vicious fight on August 13, 1978. Moran, high on liquor and Valium, threatened to kill his wife, her two prized Hungarian pointers, and their son, John.

"Besides being very drunk, he was crazed. His eyes were bulging and red," Gregg told authorities. "He said there was nothing more left to live for."

When she left the room for a moment, a shot rang out. "I heard the shot and spun around... I could see him fall back on the bed with blood gushing out [of his chest]," she recalled. "I didn't know what to do. I don't know what I did for a while."

When police arrived, they found not only a bloody corpse holding a .38 revolver—but tragic signs of a once rich couple living on the edge. Moran's body, sodden with alcohol, lay clad only in blue fishnet bikini underwear. The room was stifling hot—apparently the air conditioner had been turned off to save money. Dog feces and half-filled liquor glasses littered the floor.

Not far from the gruesome scene lay a beautiful cushion Gregg had

made. With great care and skill she had embroidered the words: YOU
CAN'T BE TOO RICH OR TOO THIN.

"Here was somebody used to everything, and he was living like a
pauper," commented Palm Beach Police Chief Joseph Terlizzese. The
chief also noted the number of mirrors in the bedroom. "You could tell
someone used to have a good time in that room."

Her husband gone, Gregg now had to face the theft charges in New
York by herself. In Manhattan Supreme Court, the one-time millionairess kept her head low as Manhattan Assistant District Attorney
Matthew Crossen reviewed her life in unflattering terms: "The life of
Dora Dodge Moran was characterized by deceit. Her single-minded
pursuit of unearned wealth has left a train of suffering victims extending
back thirty years," Crossen told the court in an impassioned speech,
going on to review her three marriages. There was Walter Sherwood,
embezzler. He had confessed to stealing Yankee baseball money to
satisfy Gregg's demands for money and extravagant gifts. There was
Horace Dodge, who was $14 million in debt when he died. And poor
Daniel Moran, who killed himself, as Gregg herself had speculated,
because of the couple's money problems. "The life she chose was
dedicated to the pursuit and dissolution of the wealth of others," the
prosecutor said. "She has displayed no remorse. She should go to jail for
her crimes."

In a last minute plea bargain, however, Gregg was allowed to plead
guilty to the crimes in exchange for avoiding a jail term, as long as she
paid back the stolen money.

In late August 1981, thousands of Gregg's personal items were seized
and brought to a Palm Beach liquidation house, where auctioneers
tagged every last one and put them up for sale.

When John Dodge got word of the bankruptcy sale, he was stunned to
learn that most of his personal childhood belongings were included.
They had been stolen, he insisted, when mother and Dan had gone
through their fortune. It was a sad sight as young Dodge barged his way
through the bargain hunters, retrieving several photo albums and a
mounted blue-nosed dolphin, the first fish he ever caught. "Why would
they want to sell something like that?" he asked, tears welling in his
eyes. "These things are from my childhood. They mean an awful lot to
me. Today is a very sad day," Dodge said quietly.

In the end, with the help of his lawyer and a sheriff's deputy, John
managed to stop the sale of a twelve-thousand-dollar Patek Phillipe
pocket watch, some jewelry, and other personal belongings. Many of the
250 patrons at the auction seemed stunned at some of the merchandise,

particularly Gregg's clothing collection. "I'd say her taste was a bit tacky, but what do you expect from a showgirl?" said Helen Prashma, a local resident.

John Dodge finally separated his money from his mother's clutches, but not before suing her to recover some of his belongings. Forever the loyal son, John insisted, however, "There is no fight with my mother. But I can't take her spending habits. She's too expensive for me. Too expensive for any man."

Many wondered whether John Dodge, the only son of Horace and Gregg, was wrestling with his own demons, given the excesses of his parents. The answer came in October 1981, when Dodge and his wife, Karen, were picked up and led away in handcuffs from their Palm Beach home on a warrant from Georgia. They were charged with passing a worthless check at a boutique in Savannah.

The couple also abused heroin, cocaine, and alcohol, and in 1984, Karen entered a drug treatment program. Soon after, John filed for divorce. In March 1985, John Dodge was found guilty of forging prescription slips. In September 1986, the thirty-two-year-old heir was thrown in jail, charged with trafficking Dilaudid, a liquid morphine derivative given to cancer patients. He spent more time in jail in 1988 for violating probation.

After a new marriage in 1990 to Michele Macksoud and a long, nasty, but successful custody battle for his seven-year-old son Johnny Dodge, John Dodge seems to have straightened out. He recieved a $1.1 million inheritance at age thirty-five and will come into another $1 million when he turns fifty. The day he received his inheritance check, he paid thirty-five thousand dollars to his defense lawyer in his drug trial.

Gregg, sixty-six, has survived it all. She now lives in a four-bedroom Bermuda-style home complete with pool—modest considering the splendor of her previous homes. She is immersed in the day to day bustle of Palm Beach life—luncheons with her girlfriends, benefits, dinner parties, talking about the old days. Her life has taken many turns. Yet she says she survives because of Palm Beach. "My strength and good health and the many friends who stayed with me and helped me financially have enabled me to survive all of the crises," she recently told journalist Linda Marx. "As a result, there's not a person or situation in the world I can't handle. That education has served as a valuable tool to balance my dramatic life."

Gregg also discussed the downside of the island's unique lifestyle. Her words almost seemed a eulogy to her marriage to Horace. "I know people whose lives have been torn apart if they weren't invited to every party and seated at the best table. They became alcoholics, played silly games, yearned to be with the 'right' people all the time. I learned that despite all of their money, there were very few Palm Beachers who were actually comfortable with who they were."

A lot of longtime residents are not comfortable with Gregg Dodge. "She's trash. Nobody decent will have anything to do with her," one matron huffs. Others are sympathetic. Says another Palm Beach socialite, "She has had a lot of heartache. We all love Gregg."

As for Gregg's assessment of herself: "I spit fire. I always have and I always will."

10

Terror on the Atlantic: Judge Curtis and Marjorie Chillingsworth

The year 1955 was notable in Palm Beach history. The island became the new winter home of the nation's leading polo players with the grand opening of the Palm Beach Polo Club. Major Frederic C. Collin said of his creation, "It is only fitting that Palm Beach, so long the capital of the polo crowd, should have a polo club of its own."

But as the society's patrons raved over this wonderful new addition to the island's list of imported cultures, Palm Beach was about to be thrust into the middle of the most puzzling mystery in its illustrious history: the bizarre disappearances of respected Circuit Court Judge Curtis E. Chillingsworth, Florida's most powerful jurist, and his wife, Marjorie.

Chillingsworth, fifty-eight, owned what was then the largest office building in West Palm Beach and was one of Palm Beach's richest men. His wealth had roots. The judge's ancestors had been a founding family of Palm Beach and his father had served as the first city attorney of West Palm Beach.

After three decades on the bench, Curtis Chillingsworth, with his military haircut and thick spectacles, had a reputation as a tough but fair judge who dealt harshly with criminals. He handed out long prison sentences and heavy fines. A career criminal deserving of life behind bars would get just that from Chillingsworth. A first offender would often be given a harsh lecture and a second chance.

Chillingsworth was so strict about the law that he occasionally fined himself, recalled his nephew, Charles Chillingsworth, now a prominent attorney in West Palm Beach. "One day he was speeding along Route A1A and a cop pulled him over. When the young patrolman got a look at who it was, he said, 'Look, judge, I didn't mean to stop you' and the judge said, 'No, young man. I was going too fast.' He was strictly honest about things like that."

The judge also took courtroom procedure very seriously. Unlike some of his peers who allowed the occasional joke from a defense attorney or an emotional outburst from spectators, Chillingsworth made it clear, anyone who entered his courtroom would have to conform. On one hot June day, as his courtroom sweltered in the ninety-eight-degree heat, Chillingsworth entertained a request from several attorneys before him to allow them to remove their jackets.

The judge replied, "As long as the public is not present at this hearing and as long as there are no witnesses present, I will listen to the argument of counsel without the discomfort of coats. You may take them off, gentlemen."

As the sweating lawyers gratefully stripped off their soaked jackets, they looked for Chillingsworth to do the same. He did not move. For the remainder of the two-hour hearing, Chillingsworth kept his on— and buttoned. Some formalities were never broken by the judge—no matter what.

The judge and his fifty-six-year-old wife, the former Marjorie McKinley of White Plains, New York, had been married for thirty-four years and had three daughters. Chillingsworth was now the senior judge in Florida's Fifteenth Judicial District, which covered much of southern Florida's gold coast, making him, in effect, the state's most powerful jurist.

On the evening of June 14, 1955, Chillingsworth and his wife joined a group of prominent Palm Beach lawyers, judges, and politicians for dinner at the home of James Owners, Jr., the Palm Beach tax assessor. The evening went pleasantly. At ten P.M., the Chillingsworths said their good-nights and drove home to their eight-room, gray, wood-frame cottage in the exclusive Manalapan section of Palm Beach. The house, which was nestled in the sand dunes, had a private beach and a million-dollar view of the Atlantic. The couple changed into their nightclothes and went to bed.

One thing that could always be said about Judge Chillingsworth was that he was never late for anything. Rising at six A.M. every morning, the lean, square-jawed judge had his usual breakfast of juice, eggs, and coffee with his wife and then made a punctual arrival at the courthouse at nine, beginning his courtroom sessions exactly one half hour later.

Even during the excruciatingly hot summer months when Palm Beach's population dwindled to twenty-five hundred full-time residents, the courts remained busy. There was always a full docket of speeders, drunk drivers, scofflaws, and the occasional cat burglar. So it was unusual when, on the next day, with a lengthy calendar of cases, Curtis Chillingsworth failed to appear.

His puzzled assistant dialed the judge's home expecting to hear the jurist apologize for being sick or for oversleeping. But the phone just rang repeatedly. A check with the operator showed the circuit was in working order. Never had the clerk known Chillingsworth, a man of strict punctuality and discipline, to arrive late or miss an appointment.

At the same time, two local carpenters, Frank Ebersold and Robert Force, arrived at the Chillingsworth cottage to repair a broken window frame the judge had complained about a few days earlier. Everything at the house overlooking the Atlantic appeared normal. There was a separate garage, and the workmen noticed the judge's car inside.

The carpenters knocked on the door. No answer. They peered into the small glass window on the door. They could see a beige straw rug in the foyer and a set of blue china dishes displayed on the wall. They knocked again. Silence. The workmen thought maybe the couple had gone to the beach. But the area was deserted save for a few sea gulls. They did notice a flurry of footprints in the sand that did not appear to be that old.

Something wasn't right. Ebersold returned to his truck, drove to a public phone, and called the police. Back at the courthouse, the judge had still not arrived. Fearing that maybe he had had a heart attack or some other serious medical problem, Palm Beach County Sheriff John Kirk and his deputies proceeded to the Chillingsworth home. They found the front door unlocked.

Entering and calling out the judge's name, the cops received no response. In the master bedroom, detectives found that the couples' two beds had been turned down and appeared to have been slept in. The clothes they had worn to the party were neatly folded over a dressing stand. The ventilator fans were on. But that's where all indications of the couple's ordinary routine ended. There was no sign that breakfast had been made that morning. The judge's briefcase lay untouched in the foyer.

Had the couple possibly decided to take a spur-of-the-moment vacation or driven down to Miami for a morning of shopping and sightseeing? No, the judge and his wife were much too responsible to leave town without so much as a word to anybody. And it was unlikely the formal couple would have left their beds unmade. There were no signs of robbery. All of their money, jewelry, keys, and other valuables were there, undisturbed.

Marjorie Chillingsworth's purse remained on her dresser, a sign that later alarmed her friends, who knew that she never went anywhere without it. There were two empty cocktail glasses, indicating that the couple had probably had a nightcap. But then what?

An officer yelled from the backyard. He had found something: dried blood. There were clear rusty red stains on the back steps of the cottage. Carefully following the small red blotches on the ground, police and bloodhounds traced their path to the beach and directly to the shoreline. They also saw, as the carpenters had, numerous footprints in the sand.

Again, the police theorized. Could the couple have committed double suicide, slitting their wrists and then walking into the sea to drown? That speculation ended when investigators noticed a broken floodlight the Chillingsworths had used to illuminate the beach. The bulb had been working the other night, according to neighbors. Now it lay shattered on the ground. As the day progressed, there seemed to be little doubt that the Chillingsworths had fallen victims to foul play. But who? Why? And were the Chillingsworths alive or dead? And if they had been kidnapped, why had there been no ransom demand?

The first motive cops explored was revenge. Maybe it was one of the hundreds of felons the judge had jailed. After all, Chillingsworth had served on the bench for over three decades. Obviously he had made enemies.

A Palm Beach sheriff's deputy quizzed several people including Louis Fiocchi, a landowner whom Chillingsworth had ruled against one week earlier. The judge had upheld the right of highway workers to walk through Fiocchi's property to survey some adjacent land. In court, an angry Fiocchi had warned the judge that anybody who came near his land would be hurt. But Fiocchi had an airtight alibi. So did several other possible suspects the police questioned.

Several days passed. The missing couple's three daughters came to Palm Beach to help the stalled case. One of them, Ann Chillingsworth Wright, designated a local pastor, Reverend Harry Waller, of the First Methodist Church, as the intermediary between the family and anybody who might have abducted her parents. Waller publicly announced that he was ready to talk in confidence to whoever knew the whereabouts of the judge and his wife. It was to no avail.

Reward money piled up. The City of Palm Beach and the Palm Beach County Commission offered ten thousand dollars for the return of the couple or solid information about their disappearance. The Palm Beach Bar Association increased the amount to eleven thousand dollars. Within the next five days, friends, lawmen, and philanthropists sent checks to the police to bring the total cash reward to forty-three thousand dollars.

The financial incentive brought forth several dozen new "witnesses" with "vital information." But they were disproven. A nationwide search began and every police station in the country received pictures of the missing couple to post on their bulletin boards.

A flamboyant detective on the Florida state attorney's staff, W. H. (Buddy) Gasque, announced to the world that he would crack the mystery "within three days" and said he believed the couple were temporarily abducted "to throw a scare into the judge." Three days passed and nothing happened. Despite the early flurry of calls and sightings, mostly from crackpots, the trail began to grow cold.

Cops found a witness, a man who lived in the judge's neighborhood and had been awakened around four A.M. on the day the Chillingsworths vanished. He told police his sleep was interrupted by the sound of a motor. Rubbing his eyes, the man had walked to the window and seen a small boat so close to the shoreline that at first it had appeared to be aground.

But the witness had not investigated further, preferring to return to bed. Still, for the clue-starved authorities, it was something. State lawmen ordered diving teams to search the waterfront directly in front of the Chillingsworth cottage. For two weeks, a team of scuba divers with powerful, state-of-the-art underwater flashlights combed the ocean floor like scavenger fish, looking for clues. They found some decent-size lobsters, some beautiful shells, and even ran into a small, menacing shark. But no judge and no wife.

Detectives reviewed the court files in Judge Chillingsworth's office but found no clues to move the stalled case along. What those files did not show, unfortunately, were plans by Chillingsworth to begin criminal proceedings against a fellow judge by the name of Joseph A. Peel, Jr.

Joe Peel was a Palm Beach County Court judge serving his second term on the bench. He was also a man with great ambitions. He wanted to become what he called "the king of Palm Beach," a man who would command great wealth and power on the small island. He had already taken the first steps toward his goal by working both sides of the law. Peel ran several rackets in Palm Beach County. He operated illegal betting parlors, a lucrative numbers racket, a protection service, and had an interest in a bootleg liquor operation. He also employed several mid-level mobsters.

Hoping to remain above suspicion, Judge Peel routinely signed court orders to raid his own gambling operations. But he made sure the charges against those arrested were watered down or dropped. He knew that while the raids themselves were front-page news, the eventual fates of those arrested usually did not. In addition to his judicial seat and his numerous rackets, Peel also engaged in a private law practice. It was the latter position that would bring him trouble. In 1953, the state bar learned Peel had been working both sides of a divorce case. He was sent before Judge Chillingsworth for disciplinary action. The fair-minded judge decided only to give him a public rebuke, sighting the twenty-nine-year-old Peel's "youth and inexperience of counsel."

Two years later, however, Peel found himself in trouble once again, this time in the handling of a female client's divorce. Peel had told his client she was officially divorced when in fact he had not done any work on her case and merely collected his lawyer's fee. When the woman remarried and she and her new husband attempted to adopt a child, social-services officials conducted a background check and found no record of her divorce. Thanks to Peel's unprofessional conduct, the woman was technically a bigamist.

This time Chillingsworth was furious. Around the courthouse, he vowed to see Peel disbarred and possibly jailed. Chillingsworth angrily declared Peel would never work in Florida again, except as a member of a chain gang. Peel realized the judge would not give him another break. Chillingsworth was everything Peel despised: an upstanding, law-abiding judge who had dedicated his life to protecting society.

Peel recognized that at age thirty-one he was disgraced, finished. He would never realize his dream of becoming the king of Palm Beach. His downfall would also mean the arrest of others and the collapse of his many businesses. Even if he could avoid a jail cell, he would be a marked man. Unless...

In April of 1955, Peel contacted one of his associates, Floyd "Lucky" Holzapfel, a low-level thug with a criminal record, and asked him to come to his office. The two had become friends after Holzapfel had hired Peel to handle a small-claims case for him two years earlier. The judge had quickly sized up Holzapfel and taken him into his confidence.

He had bragged to Holzapfel about the kind of power he wielded as a judge and how he often used that power to bend the law for his own unorthodox purposes. Peel told him of his plan to become king of Palm Beach. Holzapfel eventually became a partner with Peel in one of the judge's gambling operations.

When Holzapfel arrived at Peel's office, the judge was seething. "He told me a long story of difficulty with the bar association and Judge Chillingsworth," Holzapfel said. "It's the first time I'd heard the name. Peel told me, 'The judge is going to ruin me. The fact is, he is personally going to take care of me when the disbarment case comes up.'"

He then told Holzapfel that he wanted him to kill Chillingsworth. Holzapfel was at first apprehensive. But Peel told him if he refused the job, he would drag out some long-forgotten criminal charges pending against Holzapfel and make sure he went to jail. Peel had strong-armed his crooked friends before. It was a good way to keep them under his control. Holzapfel realized he had little choice in the matter and agreed to Peel's plan.

The judge promised Holzapfel ten thousand dollars for the murder and told him to get a partner to help him and await further instructions. Holzapfel went to George "Bobby" Lincoln, a brawny, mean-looking black moonshiner, who Peel occasionally used to collect his protection fees. Lincoln agreed to help Holzapfel for a small cut of the blood money. In early June, Holzapfel and Lincoln met with Peel, who told them he wanted Chillingsworth killed on June 15. Peel said the judge would be alone that evening since his wife would be out of town visiting one of her daughters. The judge also suggested they drown their victim and dispose of his body in the ocean. After all, no body, no proof.

"Our plan was to kidnap him, kill him, and make it appear as though he disappeared," Holzapfel said later. "We purchased a cabin cruiser and equipment. Peel told me, 'There must be no mistake. You must get rid of anybody who is a witness and all clues.'" When their grisly mission was completed, the pair were to call Peel and let him know by using the code words, "The motor is fixed."

It was one A.M. on that balmy June evening when the small cabin cruiser chugged toward the judge's beach. An anchor was thrown onto the sand and the boat secured.

"We arrived on the shore outside the Chillingsworth home," Holzapfel recalled in his confession. "I knocked on the door and the judge opened it. Lincoln was hiding in the bushes outside the front door. I identified the judge by asking, 'Aren't you Judge Chillingsworth?' The judge said, 'Yes, I am.' At this point I drew the pistol from under my shirt and told him it was a holdup. I asked him was there anyone else in the house and the judge said, 'Yes,' and I told him, 'Call 'em out.' That's the first time I knew Mrs. Chillingsworth would be there."

"Margie!" the judge called, and soon a small, frightened woman appeared next to him, pulling a bathrobe on over her nightgown.

"She was an accident," Holzapfel said. "We weren't going to bother her, but when they saw [us] we didn't have no choice, so we took her, too."

In an effort to calm the couple, the pair at first attempted to mask their true mission.

"What are you going to do with these people, Floyd?" Lincoln asked.

"I am going to take them and put them on a boat. We are going to have to send them off for a few days. These are the people trying to mess up Joe," Holzapfel answered.

But their real intentions soon became clear. Holzapfel grabbed a heavy cord and fashioned a noose around the judge's neck then used one-inch-wide adhesive tape to bind his hands. That done, he wrapped the tape around the judge's body to secure his arms. "Come on over here," he snapped at Mrs. Chillingsworth, binding her in the same way.

The pair marched the Chillingsworths toward the dunes. As they reached the stairs leading to the sand, Marjorie Chillingsworth let out a prolonged, bloodcurdling scream. Stunned and momentarily panicked, Holzapfel smashed her over the head with the barrel of his gun. Blood began gushing from a gaping wound. He ordered them into the boat. The foursome then began a tortuous, four-mile journey out to sea under the moonlit sky.

"We bound them," Holzapfel recalled. The judge, a veteran listener to prisoners' pleas for mercy, tried to save their lives. He looked at Lincoln and matter-of-factly offered him $200,000. "Boy, if you take care of us now, you will never have to work again," Lincoln recalled the judge saying. The pair ignored the offer.

When they had gone out about three miles, Lincoln and Holzapfel cut the motor and now all that could be heard was the continual splashing of the waves against the boat and the eerie sound of a faraway fog horn. As Lincoln guarded the judge, Holzapfel yanked Marjorie Chillingsworth up by her shoulders and began wrapping her in chains and heavy diver's weights to make sure she would sink.

Knowing his wife was about to die, the judge looked her straight in the eyes and said: "Remember I love you."

"I love you, too," Marjorie replied in a soft, whimpering voice while Floyd fastened the chains tighter and tighter around her. Then it was time.

"Floyd had the lady under his arm and he was putting her over the side of the boat. He said to me, 'Come help me,'" Lincoln testified.

As Bobby and Floyd pushed the sobbing Mrs. Chillingsworth toward the edge, the judge once again begged them to stop. But it was too late.

"I said, 'Ladies first' and pushed her in," recalled Holzapfel, who watched with Lincoln as Mrs. Chillingsworth's wriggling body thrashed in the waves.

"She went right down the first time," Lincoln remembered. Holzapfel said: "She went down with a few bubbles."

The two killers watched her body sink and disappear in the murky, choppy waters. But as they did, the judge used the few seconds of diversion to launch his own escape plan. He heaved himself up to the edge and leaped into the water, using his long legs to try to paddle away from the boat.

"The judge rolled out of the boat before Floyd got the weights on him. His hands were taped but he was swimming around," Lincoln said.

"He was such a good swimmer that even with the chains he was able to float. We tried to run him down with the boat," Holzapfel said. When that didn't work, Holzapfel ordered Lincoln: "Hit him with the shotgun!"

The somewhat stunned Lincoln was not quick enough, so Holzapfel took matters into his own hands.

"Give me that gun," he ordered.

"You gonna shoot him?" Lincoln asked.

"No, it will kick up too much of a fuss," his partner said.

"Floyd hit the judge with the stock of his gun," Lincoln said. So hard, in fact, that the gun barrel split in two.

The fifty-eight-year-old judge "still did not go down.... We came alongside him in the boat and I held him in my arms while Floyd reached out and put the anchor chain around his neck."

Holzapfel strangled the gasping judge with the rusty, barnacle-covered metal chain for what seemed like a lifetime. Then he tied the chain to a concrete block.

"He shoved him from my arms and he went down," Lincoln said.

They continued watching as the judge's head, still leaking blood, slowly sank out of sight. With the Chillingsworths dead, Holzapfel and Lincoln headed north toward Riviera Beach. But neither were good sailors, and the engine overheated several times, forcing them to stop and let it cool off. When they finally docked, a breathless Holzapfel called Peel and uttered the code words they had agreed upon.

"The motor is fixed," he said, adding, "I'm down at the dock. Bring me a shirt and pants. I got blood on these."

When Holzapfel told him of the added complication of Mrs. Chillingsworth, Peel muttered, "Oh, my God." It was the only time he ever indicated any remorse. Peel's plan seemed to have worked. With no body, few clues, and no motives, the Chillingsworth case remained a mystery.

Some four months later, as the Palm Beach "winter" season headed into full swing, the mysterious disappearances of "Curt and Marge" were all that people wanted to talk about. At cocktail parties, dinners, and gala events, revelers feasted on champagne, caviar, and the latest theories about what really happened that June night in Manalapan. Speculation about the couple's fate lasted through the season.

A year went by, and frustrated detectives began doubting they would ever solve the case. The Chillingsworth files were put into a drawer filled with files of older unsolved crimes. There was the occasional anonymous caller who offered "new" clues about what really happened. But nothing genuine turned up.

More years passed, and, as Palm Beach moved toward the sixties, residents and politicians turned their attention to a controversial new topic: the rapid development of the island, how to control and regulate expansion and keep Palm Beach from turning into Coney Island. The Chillingsworths were virtually forgotten.

In early 1960, a Florida Sheriff's Bureau investigator obtained some new information. Investigator Henry Lovern was probing the gruesome murder of a Jacksonville moonshiner who had been found floating in a swamp with a bullet in his brain. As Lovern investigated the killing, he met a shady ex-insurance agent named Jim Yenzer.

As they discussed the moonshiner murder, Yenzer mentioned the "old Chillingsworth case." He had some theories about it. Yenzer said he would not be surprised if Judge Joseph A. Peel, an ex-city judge in West Palm Beach, had been involved. Authorities remembered Joe Peel. He had made the newspapers only a year earlier. In 1959, he had been forced to resign his judgeship in a deal with Palm Beach County prosecutors. In exchange, prosecutors had agreed to drop charges that he had conspired to murder his law partner, Harold Gray. Gray had been beaten to within an inch of his life, but he had survived.

An investigation of the matter showed that shortly before the assault, Peel had taken out a fifty-thousand-dollar life-insurance policy on Gray that had included a double indemnity clause for death by violence. A thug named Floyd Holzapfel had been arrested as the man who had beaten Gray, but the charges were later dropped. The man who had sold Peel that insurance policy was Jim Yenzer. Yenzer had been arrested as an accessory, although the charges were later dropped.

Peel was also rumored to be a lecher who enjoyed posing young nude models next to the law diploma in his office and had a large collection of X-rated photos. Other than that, the soft-spoken, wavy-haired Peel seemed now to lead a quiet life with his wife and two children. But Yenzer said he had heard rumors about a connection between Peel and the Chillingsworth case. He asked his new acquaintance if the reward money was still being offered. When told it was, Yenzer offered to go undercover to investigate the Chillingsworth disappearence. He added he could use the money.

After five years, the Chillingsworth probe was on again. To start, Yenzer said he would reestablish ties with some of Peel's old cronies, including Floyd Holzapfel. Detectives discovered that Holzapfel was a fugitive, having jumped bail while awaiting sentencing on a truck high-jacking conviction. Further investigation revealed that Holzapfel was hiding in Rio and had been wiring Joe Peel for money. Peel apparently had ignored the pleas.

Investigators wanted Yenzer to speak to Peel and see if he would admit anything. On September 30, 1960, a trap was set. Yenzer met with the ex-judge at the Holiday Inn in Melbourne, Florida. As detectives listened with concealed microphones and a tape recorder from the next room, Peel suddenly turned the conversation to Holzapfel and offered his old insurance-broker friend five thousand dollars in cash to kill him. Holzapfel was a potential snitch who could land him in big trouble, Peel said, although he did not say why. Yenzer said he would consider the offer and get back to him.

That same day, police learned, Holzapfel had flown back from Rio to see his family, who lived in the West Palm Beach area. Yenzer found him and asked that he join him for a few drinks in his motel room. When Holzapfel arrived, Yenzer told him that Peel had just contracted to have him murdered.

Holzapfel was stunned by the revelation. As the liquor flowed, he and Yenzer began talking candidly. In the next room, eager detectives listened, hoping somehow the Chillingsworth case would come up.

Yenzer invited an acquaintance of Holzapfel, bailbondsman Jim Wilber, to meet them. The presence of Wilber put Holzapfel further at ease and he began to pour out the truth.

Three days later, with sixty-nine hours of tape recordings in hand, investigators had what they wanted and they arrested both Holzapfel and Peel, as well as Bobby Lincoln, for first-degree murder in the deaths of Curtis and Marjorie Chillingsworth. Holzapfel admitted on tape that he and Lincoln had killed the judge on the orders of Judge Peel, but they had never been paid for the job.

With his confession now on tape, Holzapfel knew the law had him. He agreed to plead guilty to first-degree murder and testify against Peel. No promises were made, but Holzapfel hoped his cooperation would be taken into consideration by the judge and he could avoid the death penalty. Prosecutors gave Bobby Lincoln immunity in exchange for his testimony against Peel, who they considered "the big fish" in the case.

At Peel's trial, Holzapfel described the violent murders of Chillingsworth and his wife, often speaking in a weeping and whiny voice. He admitted it had been wrong to kill two total strangers.

"People who have done what we have done should be stamped out like cockroaches," Holzapfel said. "We should not be allowed to live." His description of the watery executions of the Chillingsworths had the jurors squirming in discomfort.

In contrast, Peel, then thirty-seven, was often seen smiling, and, while he had a pale complexion from his new home in the county jail, he nonetheless appeared relaxed. On the stand he denied either "directly or indirectly" trying to persuade Holzapfel or Lincoln to kill the Chillingsworths and said he did not even know Floyd. Peel did admit, however, to conspiring to kill Holzapfel, but only, he insisted, after James Yenzer had planted the idea in his head.

The state lined up six character witnesses including the mayor and the police chief and asked them what Peel's "general reputation for truth and veracity" was. "Bad," each witness replied.

Prosecutors further damaged Peel by putting Henry Lovern, the Sheriff's Bureau investigator, on the stand to recall a statement the ex-judge had made at the time of his arrest. "They got me. They got me cold. Sometimes you win and sometimes you lose," Peel had said, according to the investigator.

Other witnesses were equally damning. Peel told Palm Beach attorney J. Frank Maynard: "Anyone who knows anything about the Chillingsworth murders don't live."

He boasted to bailbondsman Jim Wilber: "It was either that son of a bitch or me."

After a four-week trial, Circuit Judge D. C. Smith handed the case to the jury, instructing the jurors on the three possible verdicts they could render: guilty with death by electric chair; guilty with a recommendation of mercy and life in prison; or not guilty. The jury deliberated five hours. The verdict: guilty, with a recommendation of mercy. Jurors did not explain the reasons for their leniency.

Peel was sentenced to life. During his incarceration, authorities carefully investigated many of his other illegal activities, including his ties to gambling and his association with mobsters. They developed a fraud case against him, tried and convicted him.

Peel served eighteen years in jail for the Chillingsworth murders. On the day he was paroled, he was met by federal agents, who transported him to a federal prison to begin his next jail term for the fraud conviction. Numerous attempts to have his conviction overturned failed. Joe Peel was finally freed from prison in June 1982 after he was diagnosed with terminal cancer. He died nine days after gaining his freedom. "Just before he died he finally admitted that he did it," said Phil O'Connell, Jr., son of the district attorney who prosecuted the case.

Meanwhile, Floyd Holzapfel wasn't as "lucky" as his nickname suggested. His calculated plan to plead guilty, testify against Peel, and be treated leniently, failed. The judge had no sympathy for the coldblooded killer. He sentenced Holzapfel to die in the electric chair. The sentence was later commuted to life.

Holzapfel is still in prison. Now sixty-eight, the veteran prisoner has been before numerous judges, all whom have denied an early parole. In a 1991 interview, he said, "It's prejudice. Every judge, before I even get there, stacks the decks against me." Holzapfel isn't scheduled to be released until May 3, 2009. "That's a Tuesday, by the way, I looked it up. At my age, I may never get there."

Soon after going to jail, Holzapfel recanted his confession and insisted that he only confessed at the advice of Judge Peel, who promised him he would soon be out of jail and that the charges would be dropped. It was terribly stupid move, he said.

"Have you ever read Damon Runyon? He's got stories like this..." Holzapfel explained. "I wouldn't know Judge Chillingsworth if he walked into the room right now." Floyd said that if he is ever released, he plans to live with his son and daughter and help them run a campground for recreational vehicles in a southern state he declines to identify.

As for his nickname, "Lucky," Floyd Holzapfel bristles. "That name was made up by some newspaper reporter. How can I be called 'Lucky?' I'm the most unlucky man in the world. I've lost everything I've had in my life. I've lost my home...family."

Floyd's partner-in-crime, moonshiner George "Bobby" Lincoln was the only defendant to walk away free in the Chillingsworth case. He quickly vanished. In recent years, he reportedly was seen in Chicago and in Alabama, working as a Baptist preacher.

Charles Chillingsworth, a nephew of Judge Chillingsworth who now practices law in West Palm Beach, maintains that the three men responsible for his uncle's murder should have been executed and the punishment "should've been meted out quickly."

"My aunt and uncle were ordinary, decent, honest people, and Uncle Curtis was the salt of the earth as far as I was concerned," the judge's nephew said.

The Chillingsworths' remains have never been found. Their bones presumably still rest somewhere at the bottom of the Atlantic.

11

The Great Railroad Disaster: Robert Young

The sunrise over Palm Beach was brilliant on January 25, 1958. Robert R. Young, the "Daring Young Man of Wall Street," awakened at about eight A.M in his historic oceanfront mansion on North County Boulevard. Looking out from his bedroom in the twin-towered villa, the feisty "Railroader" from Texas saw the bright Florida sunshine making its way in the sky over the Atlantic. Peering to the north, he could see the Kennedy estate two mansions away.

Robert Young shaved, dressed, and then headed downstairs to the kitchen, where he made breakfast and read the newspaper. At about ten o'clock, he walked to his billiard parlor in one of the mansion's towers. An avid hunter, Young went directly to a collection of firearms. He removed a 20-gauge double-barreled, twin-triggered shotgun from the rack and sat down in a soft leather chair. Placing the butt of the shotgun on the floor and the muzzle against his head, Robert Ralph Young—the brash sixty-year-old railroad magnate and champion of the "little people"—pressed both triggers.

No one heard the fatal blast in his cavernous twenty-five-room Towers. When he failed to appear for a noon meeting in Palm Beach, members of his household were called to look for him. A short time later, his wife, Anita, a sister of Georgia O'Keeffe, the great artist, confirmed that her husband was found dead, slumped in a chair with the shotgun between his knees. "It was a suicide," Police Lieutenant Fred Mead told reporters.

As news of Young's death spread across the nation, Alfred Perlman, his successor at the New York Central Railroad, eulogized the fallen chairman. "Robert Young contributed more to the railroad industry than any other man in America." Having said that, Perlman and his counterparts at the Allegheny Company, which Young also ran, then issued a terse statement designed to distance their rail systems from his death.

"Neither the financial affairs of New York Central or Allegheny...should in any way be related to this tragedy," the executives said in a prepared press release.

Nothing could have been been further from the truth. Only four years earlier, Robert Young, the five-foot-six power broker, had successfully waged the greatest proxy battle in American history, wresting control of New York Central from those "damn bankers." Young fought for the $2,600,000,000 railroad because he envisioned a new dawn for the aging industry. A colorful throwback to another era, Young had gambled heavily on America's future—and he had lost.

Robert R. Young was born on February 14, 1897, in Canadian, Texas, in the heart of cattle country in the Texas panhandle. His grandfather, Robert Moody, was a cattleman who had founded the First National Bank of Canadian, along with Young's father, David John Young.

As a teenager, Young enjoyed the masculine life of riding and roping steers at his family's ranch. Because of his bright yellow hair and a high freckled forehead, many of his friends affectionately called him "Pumpkin Head." But it was his initials—R.R.—that earned him the nickname "Rail Road Young," as though he somehow always was destined to own a rail system.

In 1914, Young graduated first in his class from the Culver Military Academy in Indiana and won a full scholarship to the the University of Virginia. But he dropped out before his sophomore year in 1916. The only mark he earned there was the dubious distinction of having lost more money at poker and crap shooting than anybody else in his freshman class.

That same year, however, Young attended a social in nearby Charlottesville, where he met Anita Ten Eyck O'Keeffe. She was from a large Irish farming family in Wisconsin that had moved to Williamsburg, Virginia, in 1914. Anita's family, most of them women, studied art and painted. Her sister, Georgia, married Alfred Steiglitz, the famous photographer, and became the most celebrated woman artist in twentieth-century America. Anita and Robert Young fell instantly in love, and within weeks of their meeting, Young proposed. They married in April 1916.

"Get married when you are young," the Texas railroader later told a class of college students. "It will teach you to accept responsibilities. But," he added, "don't buy a house. It may anchor you to one town and one job."

True to his own counsel, Young and his new bride remained rootless until he made his first million. Shortly after their wedding, the newlyweds moved to Carney's Point, New Jersey, where the twenty-year-old Young accepted a 22.5-cent an hour job at the E. I. Du Pont de Nemours plant as a gunpowder cutter. The job entailed squeezing rifle powder into long strips that could be shipped easily for wholesale distribution.

It was about this time that Young's mother died, leaving him a fifteen-thousand-dollar inheritance. Determined to make a fortune, Young decided to gamble in the stock market. The one-time college cardsharp invested in two risky ventures. He purchased a block of stock in a new food-dehydrating firm and sold Mexican oil "short," which meant he was betting that oil prices would topple.

He should have reversed the play. The dehydration company collapsed. The Mexican oil market skyrocketed, climbing between fifty and one hundred dollars a share. Young was quickly bankrupt. "From that day on, I vowed to never go into anything until I knew every angle," Young declared.

For the next two years, Young continued to toil at the Du Pont plant in New Jersey. But he demonstrated a true gift for numbers and was eventually promoted and transferred to the Du Pont treasury department in Wilmington, Delaware. Adhering to his own advice, he rented a home rather than purchasing one. It paid off. Within two years, he hopscotched from Du Pont to Allied Chemical to the General Motors Corporation, where he accepted a one-hundred-dollar-a-week job as a statistician. The company's chief financial officer, John Jacob Raskob, soon noticed Young's ability. Raskob became so impressed that he asked Young to handle his own financial affairs when he left G.M. to preside over Al Smith's presidential campaign. During eight years with General Motors, Young rose through the ranks to become a thirty-five-thousand-dollar-a-year assistant treasurer.

But it was his vow to "know every angle" that made Young a millionaire by 1929. By his own account, Young said that since he had lost his fifteen-thousand-dollar inheritance he had invested every spare moment in studying the stock market. Obsessed with never again investing foolishly, Young said he immersed himself in investment banking reports and company annual statements until he was able to recite the net profits and capitalization of every stock listed on the New York Exchange.

By 1929, Young reportedly had earned $1 million trading in the market. And, in the months preceding the gigantic collapse, he foresaw the danger, liquidated most of his holdings, and "sold short" on the rest of his portfolio. By 1932, Robert Young was worth $3 million—in cash. And now he was looking to establish his place in a different arena—the world of high society.

Robert and Anita Young began to rent the fabulous Beechwood estate of Vincent Astor in Newport, Rhode Island. They would later purchase the 225-acre estate, Fairholme, sited on an ocean bluff only a short distance from the Breakers, the Newport palace owned by the Vanderbilt family. Young purchased Fairholme during the height of the Depression at the fire-sale price of forty thousand dollars. He and his wife, both from provincial small towns, relished being neighbors to the Vanderbilts and Drexels. Young held an extraordinary coming-out party at Beechwood in 1936 for his debutante daughter, Eleanor Jane. Even the Newport crowd considered the gala overwhelming. One newspaper reported, "The party brought 500 guests to the old rambling Victorian-style residence. A special supper room and lounge for hundreds of guests was constructed on the terrace outside, colored balloons festooned the air above while big floodlights lit up the lawns and played brilliantly on the rocks and ocean waves belows. Two well-known orchestras played dance music continually."

Ironically, the old guard of Newport normally would have shunned a "nouveaux riche" millionaire like the fiesty Young. But in the wake of the Depression, quaint Newport grew a bit shabby at the edges as the old-money folks were forced to cut back or sell out. They had to accept the new millionaire neighbors amid their fold.

A similar upheaval was experienced in Palm Beach, where several great Mizner mansions were sold by the cash-poor old guard to a new crop of millionaires. Not surprisingly, the socially ambitious Young also vacationed in Palm Beach during the winter season.

In 1932, the millionaire Texan quit General Motors and formed his own brokerage firm, Young, Kolbe and Company. The company specialized in identifying financially troubled or rundown companies and targeting these weak institutions for takeover. After Young gained control, the wily Texan took a seat at the top of the board of directors and ordered a thorough reorganization.

Such was the case with an acquisition that enabled Young to get a toehold in the railroad business. In 1933, Robert Young secretly began to amass twenty thousand shares of the Allegheny Corporation, a holding company that controlled the vast railroad empire of the Van Sweringen brothers. The Van Sweringens were once considered the strongest and most influential railroaders in the nation, but their Allegheny Corporation had fallen on hard times.

After accumulating a large stake in the company, Young was vacationing in Palm Beach when he came up with a strategy to move against the Sweringens' rail system. He took his idea to his partners in Young, Kolbe, but they were reluctant to act.

Frustrated with his own syndicate of investors, Young took his plan to a friend in Palm Beach. He was Allan Kirby, the son of the co-founder of the F. W. Woolworth store chain. At the time, Kirby was a shy, almost retiring, man who spent most of his time dealing with his family's various philanthropies. Young's persuasive appeal provided Kirby with his first opportunity to strike out in a major business investment away from his family. Kirby dove in, putting up most of the $4 million Young needed to attack Allegheny.

"To hell with them!" Kirby said of Young's hesistant partners. "Let's take it all ourselves!"

Young's years of tracking the stock market and engaging in takeovers had made him an expert in the complexities of proxy battles. With Allegheny, Young saw an opportunity to galvanize small investors in the company behind him. To win their support, he pitted himself against the eastern bankers and the stuffy financiers who controlled the railroads of America. His appeal was to grassroots stockholders and their inherent distrust in the "New York Bankers."

Enlisting public-relations specialists and experts in psychological motivation, Young presented himself as the "outsider" and "crusader" fighting the conservative eastern establishment and its old-money desire to maintain the status quo.

With the zeal of an evangelist, he linked his cause to the "little people," whom he likened to his own lovable "Aunt Jane." In fairness, Young believed that the desires of his Aunt Janes and his mission to rid the railroad of the bankers were truly the same. He even took his verbal battle to Congress, where he publicly rebuked J. P. Morgan for orchestrating rail monopolies.

"Progress stopped in 1899 in the Morgan library when railroad presidents were first brought together in noncompetitive association," Young declared.

The fiery Texan claimed that the back-room machinations of the railroad owners had "paralyzed the technological process" of the industry. He called railroads the worst-run business in America and waged a holy war against his powerful opponents.

But just as the battle neared its peak, Young suddenly suffered a nervous breakdown and was bedridden for months. No one but his wife and nurse were permitted to visit him. "Robert was so sensitive that he was either on the crest of a wave or very down in the dumps," a colleague later said. He spent most of October, November, and December of 1937 at Beechwood in Newport. Young recovered in March 1938, in time to return to the fray.

By year's end, Young had prevailed. The *New York Times* headline on April 12, 1937, told the story: YOUNG & KOLBE SLATED TO GET 'VAN' [SWERIGEN] EMPIRE; ANNOUNCEMENT DUE IN 24 HOURS; PROFIT GOES TO CHARITY. Young purchased Allegheny for $4 million. It was a bargain price. The Allegheny holding firm, through a number of interrelations, controlled seven railroads, including the Chesapeake & Ohio, Lake Erie, and Missouri Pacific.

The *New York Times* headlines during the next several months symbolized Young's aggressive, litigious, and combative nature. YOUNG IN NEW MOVE TO GAIN C & O VOTES, one headline said. Another proclaimed, FIGHT TO CONTROL C & O IS TAKEN BY YOUNG TO COURT. Still another announced, 3 COMPANIES OUST R. R. YOUNG'S FOES.

"Robert Young was beyond the profit motive," an associate later said. "He had made his fortune and entered into these fights for the sake of battle more than anything else."

Despite the headlines, *Time* magazine captured the seemingly complex nature of Robert Young. "Close up, Young neither looks nor acts like a fighting man. He is quiet and soft voiced, shows anger only by a slight tightening of his lips, a slight glint in his pale blue eyes. His body seems fragile (he stands five feet six and weights 135 pounds) and he looks more than his age. His hair, once blond, is now white. He finds his recreation in reading (Twain and Alexandre Dumas) and in writing poetry or in taking long walks."

Gentility aside, Young arrived grim faced at his first Chesapeake & Ohio board meeting. Taking the seat at the head of a long mahogony table, Young informed the directors that he was now the company's chairman. Then he left the room and addressed a press conference. "We are obligated to no one!" Young announced, sounding a warning to J. P. Morgan and the New York Bankers. "We are absolutely independent. And I intend to keep it that way!"

In a few years, Young's stern hand made the Allegheny empire profitable again. And the timing could not have been better. With the advent of World War II, the railroad business boomed. The fortunes of Allegheny and Young soared.

Despite his string of successes, Young suffered a crushing loss in 1941. Ironically the tragedy occurred in the air. On July 1, Young's twenty-two-year-old daughter, Eleanor, and her handsome boyfriend, Nicholas Embiricos, a thirty-two-year-old millionaire shipping magnate, died in a plane crash in the Long Island Sound off Rhode Island. Embiricos was piloting a four-seat light plane from Newport to New York when he crashed in heavy fog.

Embiricos was killed instantly. But Eleanor "Cookie" Young, then known as the "first glamour girl of the swing era," was found alive by Coast Guard rescuers. She was rushed to the hospital, but died without regaining consciousness. Her relationship with Embiricos had been the talk of café society in Palm Beach and Newport at the time of her death.

The grieving Young seemed to channel even more energy into his work, apparently hoping a strenuous schedule would help him overcome his loss. By 1945, Young had amassed the twelfth-largest rail system in the country, with seventy-five hundred miles of track and a business generating $39 million in annual revenue. He continued to pour profits back into the railroad system. At one point, he purchased 7,098 Pullman cars for approximately $70 million.

"Whenever Mrs. Young gets after me about getting so involved, I say, 'Do you want me hanging around the house complaining that the steak is overdone?'"

Although Young envisioned himself the champion of the Aunt Janes, his life-style was anything but moderate. A *Time* magazine story noted, "His sybaritic style of life does not sit well with his professed reform spirit."

In 1947, Robert and Anita Young finally decided to purchase—and no longer rent—a mansion in Palm Beach. They chose the fierce-looking Towers, with its unusual twin citadels. The villa, which stretches along four hundred feet of oceanfront, was built by Addison Mizner for Atwater Kent, the radio executive. Among the first guests to stay with the Youngs at their Palm Beach mansion were their good friends, the duke and duchess of Windsor, whom they had met five years earlier during a Bahamian vacation.

Young told people that he was a mystic, with powers of extrasensory perception. He said he loved to stare pensively at the Atlantic Ocean in search of inspiration for a new business maneuver and that he came up with his finest ideas while strolling the sands of Palm Beach.

A collector of sea shells, Young claimed that when he put a shell to his ear he did not hear the sound of pounding surf. "I seem to hear the roar of diesel locomotives," he said.

While combing the sands along the Atlantic, Young created an advertising slogan that eventually captured the American imagination and catapulted him to national attention. At the time Young purchased the Towers, he was serving as chairman of the Chesapeake & Ohio Railroad. It bothered him that passengers were unable to ride trains across the country without switching cars in Chicago. He perceived this inequity as the result of the boardroom machinations of Morgan and the bankers. He went on the offensive with the following claim: A HOG CAN CROSS THE COUNTRY WITHOUT CHANGING TRAINS, BUT YOU CAN'T! The slogan was followed with an advertisement that featured a cartoon showing a hog standing contentedly in the door of a boxcar on a transcontinental trip, while John Q. Public, laden with luggage, ran alongside the tracks with his family on his way to a train connnection.

In another advertisement, Young used a cuddly cat named Chessie, who was pictured sleeping comfortably on a velvet roadbed of the C & O. And breaking even farther from the Morgans and the Bankers, Young later launched a series of advertisements that exposed a black market in railroad tickets. He also criticized "sleeping cars" as obsolete "rolling tenements." And he announced a novel program in which passengers could reserve tickets by telephone and pay for them on the train.

Young, with his decidedly popular appeal, successfully positioned himself as the champion of the railroad-riding public. A rebel among railroaders, he then conjured a new moniker for his banker foes. He called them "damnbankers," who formed a "monopolistic financial clique."

"If I did not keep my guard up," he said, "those bankers would scalp me in a minute."

Young was also harsh on labor and harsher still on politicians. Commenting on the 1946 Coal Strike, Young wrote: "The public is being misled into believing that it is our labor leaders more than our politicians who are responsible for these and other layoffs. It was the politicians who, for their own enrichment, put the power to restrain trade in any one of the half dozen irresponsible hands."

His critics labeled Young a self-promoter. They tried to destroy his popularity with the little people by saying that he directed his businesses from million-dollar mansions in Palm Beach, Newport, and Manhattan. And they derisively said he was really a cavalier gambler who used card tables for desks. But one thing they could not attack was his success.

Young had transformed the Chesapeake into an effective and prosperous line. As the 1950s approached, and General MacArthur's former aide, Dwight Eisenhower, was to become President of the United States, railroads were again a dominant mode of transportation. Everything, from oil and coal, to businessmen and leisure travelers, rode America's rails. And, while some visionary businessmen touted the dawn of the jet age, Young remained snide toward the emerging airline industry. "I fly as little as possible—only when I have no important business at my destination," he sarcastically said.

In fact, he was envisioning a rail empire that would rival the great rail systems of the early part of the twentieth century that were owned by titans such as Commodore Cornelius Vanderbilt and Henry Pacific Harriman. Young dreamed of creating a transcontinental rail system, and he cast an eye on the troubled New York Central as the vehicle to realize his vision.

New York Central had 10,714 miles of track that swept through eleven states and two Canadian provinces, and its assets totaled over $2.5 billion, including some of the most valuable real estate in the world. But Central had been suffering heavy losses for years. Young secretly began to purchase shares in the system, quietly laying the foundation for the the greatest, most publicized proxy fight in American history.

As writer Dana Thomas explained in *The Plungers and the Peacocks*:

> The Central was richly embedded in American history. It was the child of Cornelius Vanderbilt, America's legendary captain of wealth, who had poured his lifeblood into its veins, pushing its growth in one historic brawl after another. The idea of snatching the New York Central possessed the mind of Young. His purchase of a home, within a stone's throw from the Vanderbilt mansion, was a deeply symbolic gesture. For years, Young sat in the shadow of the bigger, more lavish home, planning how he might move into the Vanderbilt executive suite."

In January 1954, Young emerged from the shadows of New York Central. He announced that he had a hidden interest and that it was his intention to take over the company. As he had done in the past, the brash Texan demanded that he not only be made a member of the board of directors, but that he become chairman as well.

The shocking request drew an angry response from William White, the Central president. White had worked his way up through the railroad industry since graduating from high school. He had been running Central for two years, since 1952, and he vowed to fight Young to the bitter end.

"If Bob Young is looking for a fight," White declared, "it will be bare knuckled and no punches pulled. We are not pushovers and we are not punching bags."

The jockeying for voter support was carried out with the verve of a presidential campaign. Both "candidates" enlisted supporters in the media and each recognized the newly discovered power of television to reach his "electorate."

Young used his desk as a prop. He posed behind the desk in his office in the Chrysler Building, "with a Confederate flag at his side, the epitome of the gallant rebel, wrapped in the banner of dissent against the Yankee bankers," Thomas pointed out. And in a move to win the women's vote, Young asked his friend, Lila Acheson Wallace, then the co-owner of the *Reader's Digest*, to take a place on his board of directors. "We need a woman's touch on the railroads," he said. "I think everything needs a woman's touch."

As the campaign heated up, Young supporters began to sport red-and-white buttons declaring that they were YOUNG AT HEART. The two warring railroaders purchased full-page newspaper advertisements beseeching stockholders to cast their 6,447,410 votes their way.

Both Young and White appeared for a debate on television's top-rated "Meet the Press" on NBC. Millions of Americans tuned in. The moderator, Lawrence Spivak, flipped a coin before the show to determine the order in which the two men would address the viewing audience. Young won the coin toss. But the still photographers missed the picture and asked for the toss to be repeated. Young twice more correctly guessed the toss. The camermen joked about his luck. He bristled and told them about his extrasensory perception.

White decided that, given Young's appeal to the Aunt Janes, he had to try to attract some of the small shareholders if he hoped to retain control of the New York Central. It seemed clear to him that Young's campaign for the Central mirrored his successful approach at Allegheny more than a decade earlier.

On the surface, White was correct. Young gave every appearance that he was speaking to the little people—the shareholders with whom he had been aligned. A typical Young advertisement appeared May 18, 1954, in the *New York Times*. At the top of the page appeared the word WARNING in bold one-inch type. And beneath his "warning," Young announced: "If any banker, lawyer, shipper, supplier or other person solicits your proxy for the present New York Central Board, ask him what his special interests are, or what your Company is paying for his services. Like the bankers now on your board, he, too, may be hoping to receive special favors from your railroad or from the bankers."

But behind the scenes the crafty Young was secretly meeting with the holders of the largest blocks of stock in New York Central. Two of his closest friends in Texas had acquired nearly eight hundred thousand shares. Finally, May 26, 1954, was set as the date for the Central's annual meeting—and the proxy vote.

Railroad executives and the New York State Police agreed that the site of the meeting would be the Tenth Regiment Armory on Washington Avenue in Albany. The armory seemed large enough for the anticipated throng to put their votes into ballot boxes. Just as important, the large facility could be more easily protected if there was a riot.

Tensions mounted as election day approached. The fear of a riot grew. White and his associates paid the New York Central police to guard the armory's entrances. Young asked the Albany police chief to deploy his officers to protect his supporters. More than two thousand shareholders showed up to vote. Harold Vanderbilt, a great-grandson of the Commodore, represented his family and supporters. The White management sent their proxies to the armory in a baggage car that was under heavy guard. Young's minions hired armored cars with five gun-toting guards to transport locked safes that contained their ballots. "The atmosphere was so charged with emotion" that three individuals who were designated inspectors resigned in fear.

The *New York Times* headline said: N.Y. CENTRAL VOTE CAST IN UPROAR. Reporter Robert W. Price explained, "The meeting was opened by Mr. White at noon, and for the next two hours or more the control of the session was a tenuous one." In the wildest outbreak, Mrs. Wilma Soss, a Central stockholder and president of the Federation of Women Shareholders in American Business, rushed to the dias. "There should be some discussion before the voting," Mrs. Soss screamed before she was grabbed by state police. As she was being led away by Lt. William Gallagher, she persisted, "I protest the legality of this meeting."

White pleaded for order but "crowds continually milled about the dais and stockholders speaking from the floor could scarcely be heard above the din." The only period when the hall grew quiet was when a boxed lunch of fried chicken was served during a forty-five-minute break in the early afternoon. Finally the voting began.

As Price reported in the *New York Times*, "Mr. Young, who touched off the proxy war for control of Central last February, cast his vote at 2:45 P.M. and promptly announced: 'I have cast a majority of the oustanding shares in favor of the Young board. I have cast from 700,000 to 1,000,000 proxies in our favor. It is a victory for the shareholders, employees, shippers and even the truckers.'"

The ballot counting began the next day at the Ten Eyck Hotel. Three law professors tallied the vote as more than a dozen lawyers stood at the ready to answer legal questions if any arose. It took two weeks to tabulate the votes as mail ballots poured in from around the country.

In the end, however, it was not the Aunt Janes who provided Young with his margin of victory. It was the block votes of three brokerage houses. The Wall Street firms, which represented the largest number of shares, had thrown their support virtually entirely behind Young. He had cleverly wooed the "bottom-line brokers" to welcome his approach at New York Central. Their votes provided Young with a 1.1 million margin of victory.

The New York *Daily News* proclaimed: YOUNG VICTORY FOR CONTROL OF CENTRAL MADE OFFICIAL. The story began, "Management of the $2,600,000,000 New York Central RR changed hands today with the announcement Robert R. Young had won 'The Battle of the Century.'"

That afternoon, Robert Young, accompanied by Alfred Perlman, the man he designated to be the Central's next president, strolled across Lexington Avenue to the New York Central Office Building at 11:07 A.M., June 10, 1954. They took the elevator reserved for the president to the thirty-second floor. White, in handing over the company's reins, said, "we shall see if Central stock rises...as promised...and it will be of much interest to us to ask for an accounting of promises made year after year."

Stimulated by Young's victory, New York Central common stock initally rose from twenty-three dollars to forty-nine-fifty. Young now predicted the stock would reach one hundred dollars a share and pay an eight-dollar dividend. He quickly doubled the company's dividend to two dollars a share from the conservative one-dollar dividend paid out under the White board of directors. He was so thoroughly flush with victory that in September he announced that he was considering erecting the largest privately owned office building in the world on the site of Grand Central Terminal. The plans called for a tower to rise 102 stories above 42nd Street and Vanderbilt Avenue, eclipsing the 1,250-foot Empire State Building.

But the grandiose blueprint was never completed. Young, and his New York Central, quickly ran up against the harsh reality of American life. Young could not overcome the dynamic trends that were developing in work, leisure, and living habits. Americans were moving to the suburbs and they were driving automobiles. And business followed them from the large industrial centers.

The geographical shift ironically made the truck—rather than the train—the principal instrument for delivering goods to the suburbs. And airplanes started to provide a convenient, fast, and increasingly less expensive way for people to travel.

In short, Robert Young had miscalculated the American future. A deeply rooted romantic and a throwback to another era, Young expected to revive the past glory of railroading. But, as quickly as it had risen, New York Central stock began to slide. By the end of 1956, the railroad's earnings had fallen from $6.02 a share to $1.30. An associate later said, "He had a great burden to carry since he won his proxy fight to get control of the Central."

Young had been a health fanatic, who played golf often. He never smoked or drank. He even grew his own vegetables, without the aid of synthetic fertilizers. But within months of the dip in Central stock, Young's hair began to thin and he developed stooped shoulders. The fiesty Texan appeared tired and worn.

Soon his own fortune began to erode. Pressed for cash by his dreaded bankers, Young and his wife sold three thousand shares of Allegheny preferred stock in December 1956. The sell-off undercut his primary stake in the company that controlled the Central. But it did not satisfy the bankers' demands. He was forced to liquidate most of the one hundred thousand common shares he held in Central. And because of the terrible timing, Young was relinquishing shares at extraordinarily low prices. Shares of commmon stock that he had purchaased for as much as twenty-two dollars were trading at thirteen-fifty.

Soon there were persistent rumors that Young's financial woes had reached a point where the sixty-year-old financier had to take out a $100,000 mortage on his Newport estate.

The New York Central situation became so dire that the board of directors convened a meeting at Young's Palm Beach mansion on January 20, 1958, to decide whether the company could afford to pay out another dividend. Young was unusually subdued during the meeting. Finally, the board voted for the first time in New York Central history to withhold a quarterly check from its shareholders.

Allan Kirby said the failure of the stock to rise "just broke his heart."

The following morning, one of the board directors, alarmed at Young's despondent mood, telephoned him at the Towers to make sure he was all right. He said he was, but for the next few days he somberly patrolled his mansion and its beach.

On Saturday, Janaury 25, Robert Young, the "daring young man" who had gambled on a dream, sat down for breakfast with his wife in their sunny dining room. "Anita Young noticed that her husband seemed drawn and morose," wrote Donald Rogers, a columnist for the *Herald-Tribune*. "She asked him if he had a smile for her. He had one, but it was contrived, an effort. Shortly afterward, his morning mail arrived, something that always stimulated him and, in recent months, had become the high point of his day."

Young took the mail to his bedroom, where he opened one letter from an unidentified Aunt Jane. The letter said, "Mr. Young, I loved you, and trusted in you. You betrayed me. You did not do what you said you would do. I own ten shares of Central stock, and it represents a great deal of money to me."

A short time later, Mrs. Young discovered her husband's body in the billiard parlor. After alerting the authorities, she went to the bedroom. There she found the opened Aunt Jane letter atop a pile of unopened, and unread, mail on her husband's desk.

At 11:27 A.M., the following morning, Robert Young left Palm Beach for his last ride in his famous private railroad car, number 28. His body was accompanied by his wife, Anita, who wore a black hat with a veil. Young's personal rail car was coupled to the Florida East Coast Champion for the trip north to Providence, Rhode Island, where he was buried in Newport next to his daughter, Eleanor Jane. His funeral was attended by Cornelius Moore; Henry D. Phelps; Alan Schumacher, the Wall Streeter; William Zeckendorf, the New York real-estate operator; Joseph Rouck, the president of Tiffany & Co.; William C. McMillan, Jr., president of Chesapeake Industries; and former Senator Burton K. Wheeler of Montana.

The day after the funeral, the *New York Post* reported that as Young was being buried, the value of New York Central stock had risen. The newspaper said, "The Supreme Court and the stock market have written an ironic postscript to the suicide of railroad magnate Robert R. Young.

The high court yesterday reversed a decision which had frozen $30,000,000 in Allegheny Corp. securities for two and half years and caused Young such financial embarrassment that he had been forced to start selling his New York Central Railroad holdings."

There was another irony in Young's tragic death. His suicide seemed to mark the end of the era of the Great Railroad—the industry that drove the nation. His passing foreshadowed the arrival of air travel, with planes and jets capable of reaching speeds in excess of seven hundred miles an hour.

And this new aviation technology would enable millions of fun-seekers the opportunity to quickly, and inexpensively, visit places such as Palm Beach that had been accessible exclusively to a select—and extremely wealthy—few.

The "swinging sixties" were now at hand, with a "jet set" crowd marching to a different drum. Palm Beach was destined to experience the most dramatic shift in its makeup since Flagler had burned down the Styx and forced his "help" to unchartered West Palm Beach. A real-estate and commercial transformation was imminent; and the new generation that was sweeping the nation was heading straight for this tiny, insular paradise.

12

The Insatiable Brothers: Jack, Bobby, and Teddy Kennedy

It was a thrilling moment. Several hundred spectators lined South County Road. Men, women, and children—many attired in their Sunday best—stood watching in excited anticipation. Uniformed policemen and Secret Service agents carefully monitored the gathering. Brilliant sunlight shone through the nearly cloudless sky. The temperature hovered in the low eighties. The date was November 10, 1960. Suddenly a flurry of excited voices filled the air.

"I see the car!"

"Look! Here it comes!"

"He's here! He's here!"

A sleek, polished black limo moved up the street. The excited crowd raised their arms and waved hundreds of American flags and homemade banners, turning the route into a sea of swirling colors.

WELCOME MR. PRESIDENT! WE LOVE YOU! WELCOME HOME TO PALM BEACH! the banners proclaimed.

From the window of the limo a hand waved. A famous smile beamed. JFK had arrived.

The entourage proceeded north onto North Ocean Boulevard until it reached number 1095, the twenty-room Addison Mizner–designed home Joseph P. Kennedy, patriarch of the Kennedy dynasty, had purchased in 1933. Two days earlier, the nation had elected John

Fitzgerald Kennedy thirty-fifth President of the United States. His victory had made history on several counts: At forty-three years of age, John F. Kennedy was the youngest president ever elected. In addition, he was the first Catholic ever to win the office. While Kennedy had sailed to an easy victory with 303 electoral votes to Vice President Richard M. Nixon's 219, the popular vote had been a squeaker. Kennedy had won by a minuscule margin of 0.2 percent.

The narrow victory had no effect on the celebratory mood in Palm Beach. John F. Kennedy was well known there. This time, however, he was returning to the island as the nation's leader. Newspapers had already started referring to Palm Beach as the home of Kennedy's "Winter White House."

Within minutes of his arrival at the family mansion, Kennedy was sitting on the large outdoor patio with his parents, Joe and Rose; his wife, Jackie; his brothers, Bobby and Teddy, and their wives, Ethel and Joan, and other family members. Champagne flowed as glasses were raised and toast after toast was made to the new president.

Joe Kennedy had always told his children since they had been able to walk that "Kennedys don't cry." It was his formula for success and triumph over disappointment and tragedy. Yet, at this moment, both Joe and Rose seemed a bit overwhelmed, nearly on the verge of tears. Joe's motto could not be held against him on this occasion. His looming tears were tears of joy. He then made a special toast to his son Jack and to "many wonderful years ahead in the White House." A gentle breeze blew in from the Atlantic and at the moment it seemed to the Kennedys that the world was theirs.

After champagne, Jack Kennedy put on his swimming trunks and used the special underground passageway to walk to the beach. There, under the careful scrutiny of federal agents, he frolicked in the waves, swam laps, and body surfed by himself.

The joyous mood and surrounding peace and quiet was short-lived, however. By week's end, Secret Service agents and the Palm Beach Police Department had uncovered a murder plot against the new president and his father. A local man, charging that the Kennedys had "bought" the election, had filled his automobile with dynamite. The man had planned to blow up Jack and Joe by ramming their limousine as it proceeded to Sunday Mass at St. Edward's Church. Jack Kennedy had never wanted to be surrounded by security, but he now recognized the need for it.

Fifty Secret Service agents were assigned to guard the mansion and regularly comb Palm Beach for any possible problems whenever Kennedy was in town. Still, the president often made life hard for those hired to protect him. One morning without a word to anybody, he raced to the beach, dove into the sea, and swam far out to escape his bodyguards. The frantic agents radioed to the Coast Guard, who quickly dispatched a cutter to the area to watch the president.

"Are they expecting Castro to invade Palm Beach?" Kennedy said with a laugh, as he acknowleged the boat. Ironically, Kennedy and his advisers would later approve a CIA plan to invade Cuba. The resulting Bay of Pigs attack, a complete failure, was the one true political embarrassment of JFK's administration.

Kennedy had always loved the sea and he had little fear of it. A few weeks after the election, he made headlines by swimming hundreds of yards out into the ocean despite reports that a school of sharks was in the area. Nervous bodyguards had pleaded with him to move closer to shore, but he shrugged off their warnings, assuring them that sharks did not attack presidents.

During the winter months, Kennedy traveled to his Winter White House as often as possible. Palm Beach was a special place to Jack. Some of his earliest childhood memories dated back to his times there in the mid-1920s, when he was just six or seven years old: memories of playing on the beach with Joe and Rose, and watching movies outside during Joe's special screenings. The Palm Beach mansion had also served as Jack's convalescent home from 1954 to 1955 while he recovered from back surgery.

Jack had had serious health problems since birth. He had nearly died from scarlet fever at the age of two. As a teenager and young man, he had continuously suffered from chronic back pain and fatigue. During his service as a Navy PT-boat commander during World War II, through his six years as a Massachusetts state representative and into his election in 1952 to a U.S. Senate seat, Kennedy was often in excruciating pain. The pain became so bad at times that as a senator, he sometimes was forced to use crutches to move around, setting them aside at the last moment before a public appearance.

Despite his many years of back ailments and other maladies including Addison's disease, Jack's sex life was never affected. He was a "chip off the old block," according to many friends who knew both Jack and his father. Throughout the 1940s, during his recovery from back surgery in the 1950s and into the presidency during the early 1960s, Jack kept sexually active.

In Palm Beach, his numerous flings with starlets, wives of neighbors, and local girls earned him the nickname "Mattress Jack." Like his father before him, Jack Kennedy enjoyed sunbathing nude by the pool. But whereas Joe was more modest when it came to the locations of his sexual trysts, Jack had no qualms about making love to his girlfriends by poolside or in the pool in broad daylight. As some of the women he slept with would later agree, "It was quantity, not quality with Jack." If all of the stories over the years are to be believed, then Jack Kennedy had had sex with several hundred women, before and after marriage, by the time he died at age forty-six.

The future president's sexual initiation occurred in 1935 in New York City. The seventeen-year-old Kennedy and a friend, Kirk LeMoyne "Lem" Billings, classmates at the Choate School, decided one evening it was time to "lose it." The boys, both dressed in formal evening wear, drove to Harlem in Upper Manhattan and picked up a black prostitute. She took them to a dingy tenement building and led them to a small, dimly lit room with a single bed. Jack went in first. After he and the woman had sex, the grinning Kennedy came out and pushed his nervous friend into the room for his turn.

After Jack Kennedy's first sexual encounter, he seemed to have a new girlfriend every week. At Harvard University, Jack was always seen in the company of the prettiest students from the numerous women's colleges in the area.

One of Jack Kennedy's love interests was flight attendant Susan Imhoff, whom he met in 1940. "Because of his back, he preferred making love with a girl on top. He found it more stimulating to have the girl do all the work," she recalled in an interview with author C. David Heymann. "I remember he didn't enjoy cuddling after making love, but he did like to talk and he had a wonderful sense of humor. He loved to laugh."

It gave Joe Kennedy great satisfaction to see Jack doing so well with so many women. But one exception was Danish-born Inga Arvad, a buxom blond who worked as a columnist for the *Washington Times-Journal*. Jack had met Inga in 1942 while a lieutenant working out of the Office of Naval Intelligence in Washington. He was bowled over by her magnificent Scandinavian beauty and fell in love with her. He was twenty-four and she twenty-eight. He affectionately called her Inga Binga. There were immediate problems. Inga was Protestant and twice divorced, facts that forced Jack to keep their relationship a secret from his mother, who would have been horrified to learn of Inga's background.

Then another shocker surfaced. It was a photo of Inga attending the 1936 Olympic games in Berlin. Her escort was Adolph Hitler. The question arose: Was Jack Kennedy dating a German spy?

Inga explained the photo saying she had met Hitler while working as a German correspondent for a Danish newspaper. She had covered the wedding of Hitler's friend, Hermann Goering, feared commander of Nazi Germany's air force during World War II. Her association with Hitler, she insisted, was only journalistic. She had interviewed the leaders of the Third Reich. The FBI was not convinced and started following Inga, tapping her phone and bugging her home. During the surveillance, the agency inadvertently recorded tapes of Jack Kennedy and Inga-Binga grunting and groaning during a steamy lovemaking session.

Joe Kennedy was furious. His son's future was in peril. He told Jack to give her up, and, in 1942, he did. Joe, however, knew his son was still smitten with the Danish beauty. To permanently end the affair, Joe quickly used his military connections to have Jack transferred, first to Charleston, South Carolina, and ultimately to a tour of duty in the South Pacific. Even overseas, Kennedy continued to correspond with Inga-Binga. In 1947, Inga married sixty-four-year-old cowboy movie actor Tim McCoy. Jack was depressed over the news and wrote a few last letters to her, wishing her well. He cheered himself up by believing that she really did not love her new husband.

Jack Kennedy's "mourning period" over Inga did not last long. Following the war and through 1950, his name was linked with numerous celebrities, among them Hedy Lamarr, Susan Hayward, Joan Crawford, Lana Turner, Gene Tierney, Sonja Henie, and Peggy Cummins.

When he tried unsuccessfully to seduce Joan Fontaine one evening, she told Jack that his father had once propositioned her. Kennedy said, laughing. "I only hope I'm the same way he is when I reach his age."

In 1946, Kennedy ran for and won a congressional seat in Massachusetts's Eleventh District, a seat he held for six years. At the time, Jack was said to have secretly married twice-divorced Palm Beach socialite Durie Malcolm. Jack had met thirty-year-old Durie during the previous winter season in Palm Beach. She was the daughter of Isabel and George Malcolm, who lived near the Kennedy mansion. Seen together at many island parties and benefits, the pair dated for a year before breaking up. Durie eventually married Thomas Shevlin, a wealthy lumber-company executive.

Durie's name was all but forgotten until a decade later when a privately published book, *The Blauvelt Family Genealogy*, named her as a descendant of that Dutch family. The book did not mention her marriage to Shelvin, but said that she had married John F. Kennedy in 1947. A story circulated that Joe Kennedy had intervened in his son's affairs once again, this time arranging for a quick annulment. Durie denied that she and Jack had ever wed.

One of Jack Kennedy's more disturbing traits, first exhibited by his father and years later by William Kennedy Smith, was his tendency to "jump" women—suddenly pouncing on them, refusing to take no for an answer.

In *A Woman Named Jackie*, Margaret Coit, a Pulitzer Prize–winning author, described an encounter she had with Kennedy after he drove her home following a date one evening in the early 1950s.

As they sat together, Jack suddenly lunged at her and she struggled to get free. "Don't be so grabby. This is our first date," she told him—a warning that had no effect on Kennedy. "Let me talk to you. I have standards, just like your sisters. You wouldn't want me to do anything you wouldn't want your sisters to do, would you?" Coit went on.

Kennedy said he was unconcerned with what his sisters did.

"What about your priest? What will you tell him?" Coit asked as Kennedy continued to paw her.

"Oh, he'll forgive me." He laughed. Finally, when Coit freed herself and told her frustrated date they would have plenty of time for intimacies on later evenings, Kennedy replied breathlessly, "I can't wait. I'm going to grab everything I want. You see, I haven't any time."

Once asked by a date if he jumped on every woman he met, Jack answered, "My God, no! I don't have the strength!"

The Kennedy brothers and their father sometimes traded women among themselves, swapping phone numbers of ladies they had slept with. Jack was the so-called leader of the Kennedy "swap club," often "testing the waters" of his bedmates, deciding whether the other Kennedy men would enjoy them.

In 1952, Jack Kennedy ran for the senate, defeating incumbent Henry Cabot Lodge II. Now thirty-five years old, Kennedy was considered the most eligible bachelor in Washington. He realized that soon he would have to make a commitment to marry, particularly if he wanted to advance further politically. One of the dozens of women he was dating off and on was Jacqueline Bouvier, the daughter of stockbroker Jack Bouvier. They had met while Jackie was a journalist at the *Washington*

Times-Herald. In the summer of 1953, Jack proposed to her and they were married September 12 of that year in Newport, Rhode Island.

On their honeymoon in Acapulco, it became immediately apparent to Jackie that her new husband had "wandering tendencies." When they attended a party, Jackie walked onto the terrace to find Jack surrounded by three beautiful young women, all vying for his attention. He seemed to bask in it. Soon Jack was back to his old bachelor ways, sneaking around with other women. Friends of the Kennedys said Jackie was well aware of the adultery, but remained quiet. In their first year of marriage, however, she suffered a miscarriage and some friends blamed it on her knowledge of Jack's affairs.

In 1954, Jack's back problems flared up again and specialists decided he would need intricate spinal surgery to alleviate his ongoing pain. It was a long, difficult, and dangerous operation during which Jack nearly died. Recovery was agonizingly slow. Jack was forced to remain in the hospital for two months. Finally, in December 1954, a week before Christmas, he was discharged and immediately flew to Palm Beach.

It was there, Joe and Rose had decided, that their son would recuperate. Part of the mansion was converted into a miniature hospital with a staff of doctors and nurses. In the aftermath of the operation, Jack had an open, oozing wound on his back. As he lay in the sun by poolside, attempting to forget the pain, Jack would be continuously aware of the messy wound.

In February, a new infection set in and Jack was rushed to the hospital for yet another operation in which some of his bones were grafted together. The toll on Jack's psyche was great. While he seemed to be able to bear the pain, his spirits were down. He stared straight ahead from his bed, often not realizing people were in the room. He didn't smile. He seemed terribly depressed.

Jackie became so concerned that she asked actress Grace Kelly, a Kennedy family friend, to dress up in a nurse's uniform and feed Jack. The stunning blond movie star, who had just completed Hitchcock's *To Catch a Thief*, obliged, wearing a form-fitting white dress and pinned-on cap. Lowering her voice and moving seductively, she spoon-fed the drugged and groggy Kennedy in perhaps the sexiest feeding session a patient has ever encountered. Jack didn't recognize her, however. "I must be losing it," a disappointed Kelly said as she left the room. But gradually Jack began to recover.

In 1957, Jackie gave birth to her first child, Caroline Kennedy. Fatherhood, however, did not slow Jack's appetite for sex. One of his ongoing trysts in Palm Beach was with Florence Pritchett Smith, the second wife of Earl E. T. Smith. Earl Smith, a Wall Street investor and longtime island resident, had been ambassador to Cuba under Eisenhower. Smith would later be elected mayor of Palm Beach, serving from 1971–77, and have a park opposite Palm Beach Town Hall named after him, honoring his fifty years of service to the community.

Kennedy had known Florence Smith since the mid-1940s, long before her marriage to Earl. She had been one of three women JFK was seeing while he was courting Jackie. Friends said Kennedy would probably have married Flo if he hadn't wed Jackie instead.

Jack's marriage, however, did not stop his relationship with Flo. According to FBI files, Kennedy made several trips to Cuba in 1957 and 1958 to visit her in Havana while Earl Smith served as the Cuban ambassador. After Jackie became pregnant with John Jr. in early 1960, her husband continued to see Flo regularly. Jack and Flo had easy access to each other in Palm Beach. Their homes were next to one another on North Ocean Boulevard.

On one occasion after JFK became president, he sneaked out of the Kennedy mansion, eluding Secret Service agents stationed outside. When they noticed the president was missing, the agents launched a frantic search. As the hunt intensified, the Secret Service called the Palm Beach Police Department to notify them of the disappearance. To the agents' surprise, Police Chief Homer Large said he knew exactly where to find the missing chief executive: next door at Earl Smith's home. When agents rushed across the street, they discovered Flo and Jack cuddled cozily by poolside.

"They weren't doing the Australian crawl," the police chief remarked.

"There were stories of secret interludes between Jack and Flo. Feverish encounters on the stretch of sand connecting their respective homes," added Lem Billings, Jack Kennedy's old friend.

Kennedy was so enamored of Flo that he attempted to get rid of her husband, Earl Smith, just as his father had removed Gloria Swanson's husband, Henri, years before. Jack tried to appoint Smith ambassador to Switzerland. The plan was thwarted, however.

Smith explained, "Fidel Castro objected because the U.S. and Cuba no longer maintained diplomatic relations and Switzerland represented the U.S. in Cuba. Since I had been ambassador to Cuba under Eisenhower, Castro claimed my appointment to Switzerland represented a conflict of interest. So my name was withdrawn, which was just as well because I didn't see eye-to-eye with JFK politics."

Whether Smith knew of his wife's continuing relationship with JFK is not known. Smith, however, did have an odd connection with Jackie Kennedy's parents, and it has been suggested that he was the cause of their eventual breakup. In the 1930s, Smith and his first wife, Consuelo Vanderbilt, often socialized with Jack and Janet Bouvier, and once invited them to glittery pre-Castro Havana for a vacation. When they returned, Jack Bouvier wrote a letter to his father-in-law, James Lee, lamenting that his marriage was coming apart.

Janet "believes or even knows that she's in love with Earl Smith which is a death blow in itself... All this falling in love Janet did was done under the most ideal surroundings with Smith giving her no quarter with his persistency."

Years later, Smith denied Bouvier's allegations. "I'm flattered, but I never knew Janet was supposedly in love with me. I was married at the time and very happy with my wife. Besides, I liked [Jack Bouvier]. I got along with him or thought I did. It sounds like he was just looking for someone to pin the rap on. There was never an affair, I swear."

Jack's election to the presidency in 1960 might have been a perfect opportunity for him to have slowed his extramarital activities. The newspapers had been easy on him during the election. He emerged unscathed by any public gossip. Instead, Jack used the presidency to add more notches to his belt—and at a faster pace. He remained insatiable, sometimes seeing more than a dozen women in a week. As Lem Billings explained to C. David Heymann in *A Woman Named Jackie*, the president always needed more.

"Jack could be shameless in his sexuality, he would simply pull girls' dresses up and so forth. He would corner them at White House dinner parties and ask them to step into the next room away from the noise, where they could hold a 'serious discussion.' During his forty-forth birthday party held aboard the presidential yacht, Kennedy disappeared to a lower deck for ten minutes with Hjordis Niven, wife of actor David Niven.

"No one was off-limits to Jack," explained Senator George Smathers of Florida, who once shared a Washington pied-à-terre with Kennedy. "Not your wife, your mother, your sister."

The Palm Beach mansion had a particular advantage for Jack. His bedroom, located on the ground floor facing the Atlantic Ocean, had a separate entrance from the outside. It was easy to enter and leave without being noticed by others in the house, particularly Rose Kennedy.

Jack's voracious sexual appetite had certainly intensified during his White House years. He staged private skinny-dipping parties in the White House pool for himself and two or three secretaries. To make sure he was never interrupted, a Secret Service agent would be posted outside the entrance.

Kennedy had always liked actresses and celebrities, and his term in the White House did not change that preference. Jayne Mansfield and Angie Dickinson were among his conquests. In *TV Guide*, Dickinson later admitted: "From the moment I met him, I was hooked, like everybody else. He was the sexiest politician I ever met... He was the killer type, a devastatingly handsome, charming man, the kind your mother hoped you wouldn't marry."

Stripper Blaze Starr claimed to have had sex with Kennedy for twenty minutes in a closet during a party held for Louisiana governor Earl Long. Well-known painter Mary Pinchot Meyer said she smoked marijauna and had sex with Kennedy in the White House.

Once, while Marlene Dietrich visited the White House, Kennedy cornered her in his office and pounced on her. The actress, some sixteen years older than Kennedy, managed to deflect the attack. On the way out, Kennedy asked Dietrich matter-of-factly: "Did you ever sleep with my father? He always claimed you did."

One of Jack's more controversial girlfriends was Judith Campbell Exner, a tall, black-haired, blue-eyed ex-actress whose biggest Hollywood role so far had been a fling with Frank Sinatra. Kennedy's relationship with Exner began shortly before he was elected president and lasted through the fall of 1962. Jack and Judith met whenever they could all over the country—in private homes, motels, limos, and the White House. During the Palm Beach season, Exner often stayed at the Breakers. Afternoons she would make extensive use of Jack's "private entrance" at 1095 North Ocean Boulevard.

What made the relationship so extraordinary was that Exner was seeing Chicago crime boss Sam Giancana at the same time, a fact that Kennedy knew but apparently ignored. Their relationship allowed an open pipeline between the White House and the nation's top mobsters. Kennedy had talks with underworld figures such as Miami's Meyer Lansky, although it is not known whether the mob had any influence on the president.

Another actress Kennedy became involved with, as did his brother, Bobby, was Marilyn Monroe. Jack and Marilyn met in 1957 at a party given by actor Peter Lawford, the husband of Jack's younger sister

Patricia. Their affair began two years later, shortly after Marilyn's marriage to playwright Arthur Miller fell apart and her affair with French actor Yves Montand ended. Marilyn often traveled with Kennedy aboard *Air Force One*, which was equipped with a king-size bed with satin sheets.

Marilyn also stayed with Kennedy at the Hotel Carlyle in Manhattan. She would sneak into the hotel disguised in a dark wig and sunglasses. During the affair, Peter Lawford often acted as a "beard," arranging liaisons for the two, acting as chaperone in public, deflecting Jackie Kennedy. In the book, *A Woman Named Jackie*, the author states that Lawford once snapped photos of Marilyn performing fellatio on Kennedy while JFK relaxed in a marble bathtub.

"She was crazy about Jack," Lawford said. "She devised all sorts of madcap fantasies with herself in the starring role. She would have his children. She would take Jackie's place as first lady.... It was only a lark to him."

In early 1963, Marilyn and Jack spent an intimate weekend at Bing Crosby's home in Palm Springs. A few weeks later on May 19, at a fund-raising gala at Madison Square Garden to celebrate JFK's forty-fifth birthday, Marilyn sang her now-famous, breathy rendition of "Happy Birthday, Mr. President."

Marilyn's affair with JFK was not as secret as many in his inner circle had hoped it would be. Shortly after the birthday party, Jack's brother, Robert, then U.S. attorney general, and FBI Chief J. Edgar Hoover, told the president it was likely the affair was about to compromise the presidency. They said it was possible the Mafia had secretly tape-recorded one of JFK's and Marilyn's lovemaking sessions at Peter Lawford's beach house in Santa Monica and planned to use it against Kennedy to gain influence in the White House. The threat convinced Jack to end the affair. Marilyn, however, was not as eager to give it up. She wrote Jack love letters, telephoned him, and at one point, threatened to go public. Jack dispatched Bobby to Los Angeles to meet with Marilyn and calm her down.

That rendezvous in California was more emotional than Bobby had anticipated. Marilyn wept, put her head on Bobby's shoulder, told him that she was deeply in love with Jack. Bobby told her that his brother cared for her, but as president, could no longer take the risks of seeing her. He was always traveling, had his wife and children to look after, as well as a national image to maintain. Bobby told her to stop calling the White House.

Marilyn said she understood, but still she cried on, often looking deeply into Bobby's eyes, her tearstained face revealing the sorrow of a jilted lover. Bobby fell for her. They had sex together on the second day of their meetings, in the backseat of a car outside Peter Lawford's house. Bobby had dated many women before marriage, easily keeping up with his brother, Jack. But after marrying Ethel Skakel in June 1950, he made a decision to respect the sanctity of his marriage vows. Bobby had witnessed the sex-frenzied, deceitful life-styles of his father and brothers. He wanted no part of it.

Once as brothers Jack, Bobby, and Teddy hammed it up for a photographer, Teddy kiddingly said, "Yeah! We three!"

Bobby stepped back for a moment and shook his head. "Oh no. You mean, 'You two!'"

Bobby and Marilyn's affair quickly became intense. Soon, Jack Kennedy's problem belonged to his brother. Marilyn pestered him with her telephone calls at the Department of Justice. He changed his phone number. Bobby had eased out of the relationship just like Jack had. It was another blow to Marilyn, who had recently been fired by Twentieth-Century Fox from the movie *Something's Got to Give*. Depressed and withdrawn, Marilyn began drinking heavily and popping pills. Her friends said she often appeared strung out, operating in what seemed like slow motion.

On August 4, 1962, Marilyn died in her Los Angeles home of an overdose of sleeping pills. The death was ruled an apparent suicide. *Apparent* has become the key word in recent years as numerous books, articles, and television exposés have questioned the suicide finding. One of the theories is that Jack and Bobby had Marilyn killed because she had threatened to expose her affairs with them. But most of her friends agreed that Marilyn was so depressed and abusing drugs to such a great extent that she probably took her own life.

The following year Jack Kennedy began to think about the 1964 election campaign. His win by-a-whisker over Nixon in 1960 had been too close for most Kennedy advisers. They were in agreement that the 1964 race would have to be hard fought with many more campaign stops than four years ago. Kennedy and his campaign advisers planned to hold a major strategy "bull session" in Palm Beach in late December or early January to map out their goals for the new campaign. It would seemingly be the last actual "vacation" the president would have before launching a full-scale effort to be reelected in November 1964.

But a month before the planned meeting in Palm Beach, Kennedy decided he had to visit Texas to try to head off a growing animosity he sensed between him and many of the state's political bosses. On November 22, in a ride through downtown Dallas in his open-air limousine, Kennedy was shot through the head by an assassin's bullets.

Five years after Jack Kennedy's death, Bobby was assassinated at a Los Angeles hotel as he campaigned for president.

Throughout their lives, Joe and Jack Kennedy had not always been discreet about their rampant womanizing, but somehow they were able to manage with little fallout. Bobby Kennedy's brief, but torrid affair with Marilyn Monroe had also remained fairly quiet.

Teddy Kennedy was another story. In his own philandering, Teddy seemed to magnify the boorish, loutish behavior of Kennedy men toward women. He did not have the same finesse or nonchalance as his father and brothers.

As a youngster growing up, Teddy had seen the help his brothers had received in gaining admittance to certain schools and landing good jobs. Joe Kennedy assured him he would be helped in the same way. According to John Davis, author of *The Kennedys*, "the result was a very slow-maturing personality that acknowleged few restraints and was exceedingly impatient when thwarted." It also instilled him with a sense of recklessness that would lead to several brushes with the law and would freeze his political career.

In the Kennedy tradition, Ted was pushed into going into Harvard. But he felt overwhelmed. There was too much pressure on him to succeed. He began to cheat. He sent one of his friends to take a Spanish test for him. Ted was caught and expelled.

Once again, as he had so many times in the past, Joe Kennedy came to the rescue. He convinced Harvard officials to remain silent on the cheating scandal. Teddy quietly left school and, in an impulsive, unplanned act that stunned his family, enlisted in the army. Joe was furious and screamed at Teddy, asking him if he realized that he could be sent to Korea to fight. Joe then made frantic calls to the draft board and to his friends in the federal government and was able to have Teddy's four-year stint cut in half and get him assigned to an easy European post. After two uneventful years in the service, Teddy was readmitted into Harvard, where he went on to graduate.

He then enrolled in law school at the University of Virginia in Charlottesville, after the famous law school at his alma mater had rejected him. He did not seem to have the discipline that required him to carry around thick law textbooks and spend hours in the library

Wall Street financier E.F. Hutton and his cereal heiress wife, Marjorie Merriweather Post, in 1930. They were the "idyllic" couple to Palm Beach society, until Marjorie caught Hutton making love to a Mar-a-Lago chambermaid.

Mar-a-Lago upon completion in 1927. The 117-room, sea-to-lake estate cost eight million dollars to build. In 1985, Donald Trump purchased the home, complete with Post furnishings, for seven million. Society shuddered at what Trump might do to the grand estate. (Courtesy of the *New York Post*)

The spectacular Everglades Costume Ball, in 1928, given for 300 guests on the pebbled patio of Mar-a-Lago by Mr. and Mrs. Hutton. (Courtesy of the *New York Post*)

Actress Dina Merrill. The stunning offspring of Marjorie and Hutton. She enjoyed a fairy-land existence, growing up in a household worth $100 million.

Marjorie Post introduced the Palm Beach life-style to Moscow with her third husband, Joseph Davies, the U.S. Ambassador to Russia in 1940. The couple appeared compatible until Davies grew unstable and hit Marjorie for imagined flirtations with other men. (Courtesy of the *New York Post*)

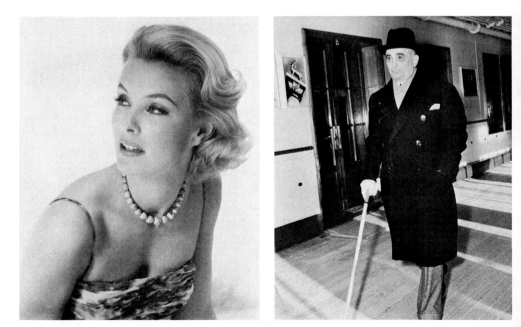

Covergirl Gregg Sherwood loved to spend money. Her second husband embezzled to support her lifestyle before she married hard-drinking Horace Dodge, Jr., heir to the automobile fortune.

Gregg and her philandering alcoholic husband, Horace, in 1963. He always had time for one more drink, and one more girl. (Courtesy of the *New York Post*)

Judge Joseph Peel did business with gangsters and racketeers to enhance his power. Peel was on his way to becoming "King of Palm Beach" until Judge Curtis Chillingsworth discovered his secrets. (Associated Press)

Judge Curtis E. Chillingworth was murdered in 1955 before he could expose the crooked Peel. His wife, Marjorie Chillingsworth, also met a horrible fate for being in the wrong place at the wrong time. (Photos courtesy of the *New York Post*)

The dapper Duke and Duchess of Windsor (left and right), frequent guests, pose in 1947 at the Palm Beach estate of their host, railroad czar Robert R. Young, and his wife, Anita. In 1958, Young went into the billiard room and killed himself with a shotgun blast to the head. Anita Young discovered the grisly corpse. Horrified and devastated, she demolished the Mizner-designed oceanfront mansion. (Associated Press)

Railroad king Robert R. Young, victorious in 1954 when he won control of the New York Central in the greatest proxy fight in American history. Young, who championed "The Little People" against the "damnbankers," strolled the sands of Palm Beach for mystical inspiration. (Courtesy of the *New York Post*)

Jack Kennedy and girlfriend Flo Pritchett, in 1944. Years later, Flo would marry future Palm Beach Mayor Earl E.T. Smith, yet still have time for poolside trysts with the President. (Courtesy of the *New York Post*)

Burt Reynolds. The one-time football star and cheerleader Mary Alice Turner were high school sweethearts in Palm Beach. Rumors swirled about the school's "Most Likely To Succeed" couple, class of '53.

Mary Alice Turner, with a 14-carat, $125,000, tear-drop shaped solitaire ring on her hand, married Russell Firestone, Jr., the tire heir, on August 1, 1961. (Courtesy of the *New York Post*)

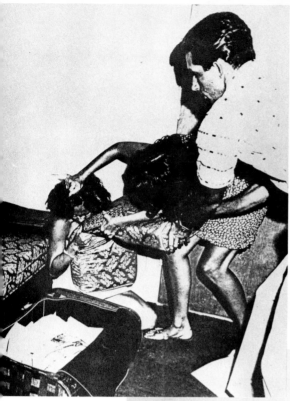

An angry Mary Alice Firestone and a private detective burst in on her husband Russell Firestone, Jr., and his secretary in his office. The secretary was not taking dictation.

Russell (below), clad only in his boxer shorts, protests the cruel invasion of his privacy.

DOG BAR

With their own water fountain on posh Worth Avenue, animals are often treated better than people on this exclusive island. (Courtesy of the authors)

Ancky Revson Johnson (left), in 1985. Once wed to cosmetics king Charles Revson, Ancky went on to marry two other men whom she divorced on the grounds they were bisexual.

Nancy "Trink" Wakeman (right) in the mid 1930s. She was the debutante daughter of Broadway producer Dwight Deere Wiman, heir to the Deere tractor empire. (Photos courtesy of the *New York Post*)

Haggard socialite "Trink" kisses her paralyzed husband, William Wakeman. A day of drinking and fighting ended on September 5, 1967, when he taunted Trink that she did not have the guts to shoot him. He was dead wrong. (Associated Press)

cramming for tests. Instead of studying to become Edward M. Kennedy, Esq., Kennedy eased into a life-style of drinking and reckless behavior that earned him the nickname Cadillac Eddie.

Cadillac Eddie, classmates recalled, chased women, drank heavily, never missed a party, and often drove around at high speeds in his Cadillac while inebriated. His late-night spins through town were well known by police who often received reports of Teddy's car "whizzing by." In the course of his law-school studies, Teddy was arrested four times for reckless driving. In one of those arrests he had been stopped while driving ninety miles per hour at night with his headlights off.

In 1958, during law-school studies, Teddy married Virginia Joan Bennett. Joan was the daughter of Henry Wiggin Bennett, a New York advertising executive. She had met Teddy at Manhattanville College in Purchase, New York, at the dedication of a gymnasium that was a gift to the school from Joe. Two years after their marriage, their first child, Kara, was born.

In 1962, Teddy was elected to the Massachusetts senate. At age thirty, he was one of the youngest state senators in U.S. history and Joan, twenty-six, was one of the youngest senate wives. Despite his shaky start in school, Ted could now say he had followed in the footsteps of his father and brothers. He had made it through Harvard. He had been successfully launched into politics. And there was another Kennedy tradition that he entered into at the same time: extramarital affairs. A wife and child in no way stopped Teddy from pursuing other women, just as Jack and Joe had. Judith Campbell Exner remembered that Teddy had made a play, albeit unsuccessful, for her around the same time she met Jack. His main weakness was blondes.

Over the next several years, he would reportedly have affairs with a dazzling assortment of beauties, including New York socialite Amanda Burden, Maggie Trudeau, the ex-wife of former Canadian prime minister Pierre Trudeau, and skiing champion Suzy Chaffee, most famous for her "Suzy Chapstick" TV commercials.

In 1967, he carried on an affair with Countess Llana Campbell, a stunning European socialite. According to the *New York Post*, the couple stayed at rented cottages on Martha's Vineyard. That same year, Ted attended a cocktail party at the Palm Beach Polo Club given by Helga Wagner, a blond twenty-five-year-old jewelry designer, former TV-commercial actress, and practicing Scientologist. Her husband, Robert Wagner, a wealthy vice president of his father's American Eastern Corporation, served as host. Despite the fact that both Helga and Ted were married, they began a prolonged "special relationship," as friends called it.

That included Helga cooking dinner for Ted alone at her New York apartment. Ted reportedly told friends that Helga was so wonderful that she was the only woman for whom he would have considered divorcing.

Kennedy women all had their own special ways of dealing with their spouses' womanizing, but Joan's was no doubt the most self-destructive. She began drinking heavily and became an alcoholic.

Following the murder of his brother Bobby in Los Angeles, Teddy also began drinking quite heavily. It was not surprising to see Ted Kennedy out on the town in Washington with a double scotch in his hand. Reporters sometimes saw him "plastered." On one memorable commercial airline flight, Kennedy, with several reporters onboard with him, became intoxicated and rambled on sadly about his dead brothers and how much they had meant to them. Bobby stuck in his mind the most, he said. "You know," he went on, his speech slurred, "they're going to shoot my ass off the way they shot Bobby."

Nobody needed to go after Ted Kennedy. He seemed to be destroying himself. In the winter of 1968, an incident involving a car wreck in Palm Beach revealed a side of Ted Kennedy that was almost a dress rehearsal for of the lack of responsibility Kennedy would show six months later in Chappaquiddick.

Teddy and Joan had rented a house in Palm Beach near the North Ocean Boulevard mansion. Well after midnight one evening, a disheveled Kennedy walked up to the staff's quarters at the mansion and began banging on the door, waking the family's chauffeur, Frank Saunders. When he opened the door, it was obvious to Saunders that Kennedy had been drinking heavily. "Car's stuck," Teddy said, his breath labored, his look dazed. "The fucking thing's stuck down the road . . . I missed the turn. Take care of it . . . and do it so nobody will spot the car."

Then Kennedy walked off. Saunders got dressed and went looking for the vehicle. When he found it a quarter-mile down the road, it was hard to believe Teddy's version of what had happened. Apparently drunk and speeding, Teddy had missed a sharp left turn, hopped a curb, and barreled through a mass of heavy shrubbery, barely missing a cement wall. Saunders called a towtruck to haul the damaged car away and tipped the servicemen well so they would not mention the incident.

The next time Saunders saw Teddy, the senator did not mention the crash, not even a word of thanks. It was as if the accident had never happened.

On July 18, 1969, the infamous Chappaquiddick incident occurred. Teddy and five males friends threw a party on the island of Chappaquiddick off Martha's Vineyard for six single young women who had worked on Bobby's presidential campaign the year before. At 11:15 P.M., Teddy left with one of the women, Mary Jo Kopechne, an attractive twenty-eight-year-old blonde who was enamored by the Kennedy name. He planned to drive her to her motel. But shortly after they left, the 1967 Oldsmobile Kennedy was driving plunged off the side of a narrow wooden bridge called Dyke Bridge, flipped, and submerged in the muddy, murky waters. Nine hours passed before Ted officially reported the accident, and there was much speculation that Kopechne might have lived had the senator acted faster.

On the morning after the Chappaquiddick incident, one of Ted's first telephone calls was to Helga Wagner. Wagner says Ted simply asked her for the number of his brother-in-law Stephen Smith who was traveling in Europe with his wife and whom Helga had planned to meet overseas. She has declined numerous offers to provide any more details.

Teddy's girl-chasing came at a time when the American press was evolving from an all-boys' club with certain rules about what was reported and taking on a more aggressive "everybody's fair game" attitude. Weekly tabloids like the *National Enquirer* and the *Midnight Globe* were springing up in supermarkets with a slant on cheap, lurid stories about American celebrities and politicians. Their reporters, with almost limitless expense accounts, hid in bushes, interviewed old lovers, and paid informants to get embarrassing information on their subjects. Teddy became a favorite of these magazines. Joan heard it all and the marriage became increasingly shaky.

After Joe Kennedy died in 1969, Teddy became the unofficial master of the house in Palm Beach. He had proprietary rights to stay there during the holidays. He also seemed to be more comfortable when his mother was not there. Still, his mother's presence did not stop him from inviting female houseguests, but it was easier to bring women to the estate when Rose was away. Since the deaths of his brothers, he had made Jack's presidential bedroom his own. It was particularly handy because of the separate entrance.

Rose Kennedy's personal secretary, Barbara Gibson, recalled how she once spotted Teddy "standing in the kitchen wearing nothing but a towel wrapped around his waist, while another one of his girlfriends who looked exactly like Joan waited for him in the former president's bedroom."

Ted tried to hide another interest from Rose: his love of fattening foods. Following the Chappaquiddick incident, Teddy had let his waistline expand, sometimes to nearly portly proportions. Drinking excessively and wolfing down high-calorie foods, Teddy sometimes ballooned forty to fifty pounds beyond his normal weight. To hide his expanding girth, Ted bought specially tailored clothes to make him appear thinner and occasionally wore a girdle during important public appearances. His efforts to hide his weight fooled some people, but he couldn't trick his mother, who had been a careful eater all her life and who considered excess weight on anybody "a mortal sin."

As Barbara Gibson remembered, "When the senator came to Palm Beach, Nellie the cook always made his favorite dessert, a chocolate roll of rich fudgy cake that was carefully rolled up with thick whipped cream. When he asked for a second helping, Rose would scold him like a little boy. His response was equally boyish. He would accept the reprimand with a blush and then after dinner slip out to the kitchen to help himself to another slice of the calorie-laden dessert. 'Don't tell Mother,' he would warn Nellie as he gobbled down his forbidden treat."

In the 1970s and 1980s, Rose Kennedy's visits to Palm Beach became less frequent. She began spending more time in Hyannisport. As a result, the Palm Beach house had started, as some neighbors put it so delicately, to "go to seed." The house staff was reduced and less money was spent for upkeep.

Teddy and Joan were divorced in 1982, two years after his failed bid for the Democratic presidential nomination. He began using Palm Beach as a base for partying and quick romancing. While the grand ocean views of La Guerida had not changed, the home itself appeared more and more like a transient hotel.

"What struck me most forcibly was how run down and shabby everything was," recalled Barbara Gibson, in her book *Life With Rose Kennedy*:

> The house itself was in bad repair, with red tiles falling off the roof and wooden window frames rotting away. Falling coconuts had cracked the glass-topped tables on the patio. Some sort of rust had attacked the stone around the pool and produced ugly stains like dried blood on the elegant pattern. Everything in sight cried out for a good coat of paint... The tennis court was covered with palm leaves and dead branches, weeds were growing up through its surface, and the net was dangling askew. The pool was empty, except for about three inches of water in the bottom, and it looked

as if someone had started to paint it and abandoned the job months ago.

Inside, Gibson recalled, things were even more depressing. Two of the bedrooms "looked like the inside of a cheap motel." The kitchen was disgusting, with the linoleum floors "covered with years of greasy dirt, buckled and crumbled. Upholstered furniture was stained and torn."

Efforts to improve and update the house made it look even worse. Heavy dark wooden furniture designed by Addison Mizner had been painted white with a flat wall paint that was already covered with dust.

"It was simply impossible to believe that this was the home of one of the richest families in the United States," Gibson said.

Residents along North Ocean Boulevard knew the house was run down. They were not surprised. The Kennedys had never really made an effort to belong. There was no doubt that the prestige of the Kennedy house had peaked in the early 1960s when Jack had ascended to the presidency. Now with Joe Kennedy dead and matriarch Rose absent, La Guerida became little more than a multimillion-dollar flophouse.

13

The Cheerleader and the Tire Baron: Mary Alice and Russell Firestone, Jr.

On February 5, 1964, a red Ferrari registered to Russell A. Firestone, Jr., the polo-playing heir to the tire-and-rubber fortune, careened out of control on Belvedere Road. The vehicle rolled onto its roof and hurtled into a ditch before grinding to a halt. Mary Alice Firestone, the multimillionaire's beautiful wife, was thrown from the passenger seat.

Arriving paramedics found Mary Alice sprawled in a culvert a few feet from her overturned Ferrari. She lay unconscious as a result of a severe blow to the head. As the paramedics administered emergency care, other rescuers rushed to the wrecked sports car to help the driver. Instead of finding her husband, the cops discovered twenty-one-year-old Michael McClain, an unemployed West Palm Beach plasterer, trapped behind the leather-lined steering wheel. He was badly shaken by the crash, but said he was otherwise unhurt.

Mary Alice and McClain were rushed to Good Samaritan Hospital. The cops charged McClain with driving a vehicle while his license was under suspension. He was then treated and released. The twenty-seven-year-old Mrs. Firestone was not as fortunate. Doctors in the emergency room listed her in poor condition and she was placed under intensive care. The near-fatal accident made news and the stories laid bare the fact that Mary Alice—the third wife of Russell Firestone, Jr.— was cruising Palm Beach without her husband.

Her recovery proved painful and difficult. But after five weeks, Mary Alice lobbied hard for her physicians to allow her to leave the hospital. On March 9, she returned to her Palm Beach home and to Russell, who was indifferent about her health. Russell—himself no "pillar of virtue"—had decided to divorce his ravishing but wayward wife. But he wanted to find a way for the divorce to cost him as few of his millions as possible, because he already was paying hefty alimony and child support to two previous wives and assorted children. His lawyers advised Russell that, under Florida divorce law, a husband did not have to pay alimony if he could prove that his spouse had committed adultery.

Armed with this information, Russell Firestone, Jr., hired a team of hardnosed lawyers and a small army of private detectives who specialized in aggressive surveillance, wiretapping, and eavesdropping techniques to catch his not-so-discreet wife "in the act." Soon Russell's undercover marauders were countered by an awakened Mary Alice, who launched offensive strikes with her own band of investigators and high-priced legal talent. The 1960s-style battle between the Firestones raged for four years. And when the fighting ended, there were bodies—dressed and undressed—all over the place.

Ironically, the marriage of Mary Alice Sullivan to Bentley-riding Russell Firestone, Jr.—grandson of Harvey Firestone, founder of the company that bares his name—was a real-life fairytale. Mary Alice Sullivan was a "local" girl who grew up on Palm Beach in the 1940s and 1950s and attended the county's public elementary and junior high schools. By the time she enrolled in Palm Beach High School, Mary Alice had blossomed into a striking young women with sexy sloecolored eyes, dimples, and a full athletic figure. She was also a warm and friendly girl who became the school's head cheerleader. Each Saturday, with the football bleachers jammed with spectators, Mary Alice Sullivan stood along the sidelines in her school sweater and short skirt with a smile that could melt the heart of the most rugged athlete. Jumping, leaping, and cartwheeling along the field, Mary Alice cheered her team onward. But she saved her wildest cheers for her boyfriend, the team's star running back, Burt "Buddy" Reynolds.

Mary Alice and Burt Reynolds were an inseparable, immensely popular couple. But like many a perfect high school pair, they were the envy of some jealous classmates, who disliked the constant attention they received. A few of those detractors spread a nasty rumor that Burt had "knocked up" his high-school sweetheart and that she had had an abortion, which was illegal at the time in the state of Florida. But the rumors and innuendo—whether true or false—had no effect on their overall popularity. When Mary Alice and Burt graduated in 1953, they were voted the Palm Beach High School students "most likely to succeed."

Reynolds immediately went on to gridiron fame at Florida State University and then turned to acting. He became one of America's macho superstars in the 1970s in films such as *Smokey and The Bandit*, and *Deliverance*, and later as the star of his own television series, *Evening Shade*.

Reynolds recently reminisced about his days in Palm Beach with Mary Alice, saying that despite their popularity in high school, they found it impossible to penetrate the Palm Beach "scene" when they were young.

"She lived in Palm Beach and that was my connection to Palm Beach," Reynolds said. "I went to the Everglades Club, but it was only to wait tables. We used to say we didn't want to go to Palm Beach parties. But honestly, nobody was inviting us, so it was easy to say that."

The rugged entertainer remains in touch with Mary Alice to this day and occasionally visits her in Palm Beach because, he said, "Mary Alice was very special in my life."

With her striking beauty and energized personality, Mary Alice Sullivan also seemed destined to have a future as bright as Burt Reynolds's. But her entry into the "real world" from high school was not as glamorous as her high-school sweetheart's. Mary Alice enrolled in Sullins College in Bristol, Virginia, and then transferred to the University of Miami, where one of her most widely reported appearances was as a contestant—she was not the winner—of the school's "Hurricane Honey of Year" crown. She majored in education and, upon her graduation in 1958, she returned to her hometown to teach the fifth grade at an elementary school she had attended.

Her return surprised many Palm Beach locals, who had envisioned Mary Alice in the spotlight of New York or Los Angeles. But they failed to realize that, unlike most college graduates who come back to their mundane hometowns, Mary Alice had returned to America's Riviera, an enchanted island where a wealthy "prince" could transform a "Cinderella" into a queen.

During the daytime, Mary Alice dutifully instructed her eleven-year-old students. In the evening she "made the scene" in Palm Beach in the early 1960s. As the ever-popular Bradley's saloon mixed the British beat of the Beatles with the Motown sound from Detroit, Mary Alice and her friends chatted about marriage and how if they were to marry, it should be to someone wealthy.

As one longtime Palm Beach observer cynically noted, Palm Beach women often "look at love as a matter of business. Money is first," he said, "last, and always."

With that sentiment perhaps in mind, a friend of Mary Alice's coaxed her into accepting a blind date at expensive La Petite Marmite restaurant on Worth Avenue. Her date was Russell A. Firestone, Jr., the boyishly handsome heir with a $16 million trust fund, a monthly income of $50,000, a small fleet of Rolls-Royces and Bentleys, and several horse farms and oil wells.

Mary Alice found the thirty-four-year-old Firestone attentive, affable, and charming. Russell, by all accounts, fell instantly in love with his luscious twenty-four-year-old schoolteacher date. Falling in love quickly was something Russell had done at least twice before. Russell Firestone—like many second and third generation Palm Beach heirs—was the type of man who enjoyed an opulent, casual life filled with idle time, thanks to the hard work and brilliant enterprise of his grandfather. But his trust-fund bankroll had made Russell a bit cavalier when it came to matters of the heart and marriage.

"Russell was not very sharp," his former lawyer, William Pruitt, said. "And he could be taken in easily—especially by women."

Shortly after dinner, the smitten Firestone stunned Mary Alice Sullivan with a proposal of marriage and, before she could refuse, regaled her with stories about the life she would lead as Mrs. Russell Firestone, Jr. There were his homes in New York, Dallas, and Illinois, and his championship horses that cost no less than twenty thousand dollars a month to feed and board.

He told her about his country club memberships and that he was widely known along Florida's Gold Coast as the captain of the national open championship Circle F polo team, which made its home at Boca Raton's Royal Plum Polo Grounds. And if that were not enough, when he was not riding ponies, Russell said he was racing his own thoroughbreds at the nearby Hialeah and Gulfstream racetracks as well as at other tracks around the country. Mary Alice was overwhelmed and hooked.

The following morning, Firestone purchased an engagement ring; a fourteen-carat teardrop-shaped diamond solitaire that cost $125,000, approximately ten times Mary Alice's annual salary. But there was one obstacle to their newfound joy. Firestone was still married to his second wife, Linda Langley, the woman with whom he had three children. He had told Mary Alice that he was trying to divorce Linda, but that squabbles over alimony and child support were dragging out the proceedings. It ultimately took nine more months and several million dollars before he reached a divorce settlement with Linda.

Seven weeks after the divorce, on August 1, 1961, Mary Alice and Russell Firestone, Jr., married at the Riverside Church in New York City. They lunched at "21" on West 52nd Street. and then embarked on a six-month around-the-world honeymoon. The couple returned to Palm Beach shortly after the New Year in January 1962.

By now, Russell had a nickname for his bride; he called her Silky after the colored silk fabric that adorned his thoroughbred racehorses. Everywhere they went, Russell proudly introduced Mary Alice to his friends, whether they were attending a social ball or a private dinner party at an opulent oceanfront mansion. For her part, Mary Alice slipped easily into the role of the wife of one of America's wealthiest men. She immersed herself in the luxurious Palm Beach life-style of beauty salons, exercise classes, and shopping sprees along expensive Worth Avenue. And when the facials and Armani clothes could not hide a perceived flaw in her face or figure, Mary Alice, like many Palm Beach women, made a visit to a top cosmetic surgeon; one of the expensive physical sculptors who try to keep the island's ladies forever young and beautiful.

By her own accounting, Mary Alice's lavish life required fifteen thousand dollars per month to maintain: six to nine thousand for clothes "if you don't count the furs." Another thirty-five hundred was needed for a press-clipping service to monitor times when she, Russell, or friends Lilly Pulitizer, Brownie McLean, Mary Sanford, and Trink Wakeman were mentioned in the newspapers. An equal amount was spent on gifts and various sundries for her mother. And when those bills were paid, she still needed three thousand dollars in "funny money" just "to play with" or bet on horses.

In the spring, she learned she was pregnant. And as the months passed and her figure became matronly, Russell seemed to spend longer periods away from home traveling "on business." When he was in Palm Beach, he tended to stay on the polo fields rather than being attentive to his pregnant wife. By the time their son, Mark, was born in January 1963, the initial spark in their seventeen-month-old marriage had been extinguished.

"Russell would go around from racetrack to racetrack, driving a

Bentley, a Rolls, or in his thirty-five-thousand-dollar plane," William Pruitt later recalled. "And in no way did it stop him from playing around."

In fact, the birth of their son seemed to heighten Mary Alice's sense of isolation and confinement. Increasingly lonely, she began to invest her time at the Hialeah and Gulfstream racetracks, where the Firestone family kept private boxes. To the "railbirds" along the quarter-mile, finish-line stretch, the beautiful dark-haired Mrs. Firestone became a familiar attractive face and a respected handicapper. But afternoons at the track could not adequately fill her time or satisfy her emotional needs.

Mary Alice Firestone, one of America's wealthiest women, began to drive aimlessly around Palm Beach and West Palm Beach. Soon she began cruising the area's high-school playgrounds in search of male companionship. One muscular nineteen-year-old recalled meeting Mary Alice while playing touch football with his younger brother. She pulled alongside them in her Ferrari and interrupted their game, making small talk. Then she asked the nineteen-year-old teen to come with her for a ride. For hours, the young man cruised along the intercoastal waterway with Mary Alice, unaware that his chaffeur was heiress to the Firestone fortune. He later joked that the closest he had ever come to a Firestone before that was in a tire shop.

Mary Alice's young "friend" insisted that he and Mary Alice never engaged in sex that afternoon or during any of the subsequent times they were together for drinks in a bar. Generally Mary Alice talked about her lonely life and their dates ended with little more than a friendly kiss. After a few weeks, she stopped calling, apparently because she had found a slightly older man to keep her afternoons occupied.

During the final months of her pregnancy, Mary Alice expressed concern that her cheerleader figure might be lost forever to mother-hood. After her son's birth, she told her friends she felt she had lost her shape. They advised her to hire a fitness trainer and masseuse, and recommended John Timmins from Fort Lauderdale. Handsome, dark-haired Timmins was a six-foot-three-inch muscleman who weighed a proportionate 220 pounds. He was a personal trainer who made housecalls. Mary Alice did not have to leave her home to work out.

One afternoon, while Mary Alice was exercising with Timmins, Russell returned home unexpectedly from a business meeting. He surprised his wife and trainer by the pool. Mary Alice, wearing only a towel, and Timmins appeared to be in the middle of foreplay.

"Timmins testified later that they were just playing around and that he never put it in," said Joseph Farish, the famous Palm Beach divorce lawyer who represented Mary Alice. "Timmins denied it all and said it hurt his career. He sued everyone who suggested otherwise because he had nine kids and a wife who was a singer in a nightclub with a three-piece band. He even sued the *Palm Beach Post,* and when no one would take his case he defended himself, but never won a thing."

Despite Timmins's and Mary Alice's protests that Russell had mistaken an innocent scene, Russell increased his travel time away for business and for the polo-playing field. When news of the Ferrari car crash involving Mary Alice and the young plasterer McClain reached him, Firestone seemed ambivalent about whether his wife lived or died.

Just four weeks after Mary Alice was released from the hospital, she went into a bathroom in their Palm Beach home, took a razor blade from the cabinet, and walked into the room where Russell was sitting. Right in front of her multimillionaire husband, she began to slash her wrists. Russell did not move. She made seven more cuts along her wrists and forearms. Russell still did "absolutely nothing" to stop her from taking her life, she later charged.

"After all," one lawyer later observed, "this was now about money!"

Within days of Mary Alice's suicide attempt, Firestone retained the prestigious law firm of Fisher, Prior and Schulle to discuss divorce strategy. His wife, meanwhile, continued to act in a very self-destructive way. With gashes still wrapped in gauze bandages, Mary Alice Firestone began to sleep indiscriminately with an assortment of strange men, apparently in a desperate search for affection, court papers charged. In short order she had a string of one- and two-night stands. One investigator later swore in court she had a young man in her home for seventy-two hours only three days after she had stood in front of her husband slashing her arms.

"So many men said they slept with Mary Alice at that time that I think I'm the only man in Palm Beach who didn't," Dick Hurley, a veteran Palm Beachite, ruefully recalled. "There was something very sad about it all." At the same time, Mary Alice began to drive to Jacksonville for weekends or jet to the nearby Grand Bahamas where the West End hotels and casinos had become the in get-aways for Palm Beach regulars. On July 12, 1964, two months after slashing herself, Mary Alice went for the weekend to Jacksonville, the Florida city that is home to the Gator Bowl and the annual football game between the Florida Gators and the rival Georgia Bulldogs. The clash attracts more than seventy thousand fans and tens of thousands more for a three-day bash affectionately known as the world's largest outdoor cocktail party. Every hotel and motel manager has been hardened to the sounds of raucous partying.

Mary Alice, her friend Jack Hodge, and another couple rented rooms at the Thunderbird Motel and Spa, a popular lodge with three pools and a huge bar. "The Thunderbird was a place Mary Alice and her friends liked to party," Pruitt recalled. When Jack Rubin, the Thunderbird's manager, heard a commotion in Mary Alice's room at two P.M. he called the police.

The first cop to arrive knocked on the door of room 9. When the door opened, Mary Alice's companion, Jack Hodge, spotted the officer. Hodge grabbed a telephone and swung it at the officer's head, knocking off his hat. As Mary Alice watched from a corner of the room, the officer grabbed his powerfully built, two-hundred-pound attacker and wrestled him to the floor.

With the cop on the floor, a second couple who were in the room with Mary Alice and Hodge seized the opportunity to flee. Suddenly Hodge broke free of the officer's grasp. He picked up a whiskey bottle and smashed it against a table, transforming the bottleneck into a jagged knife. The officer pulled out his service revolver.

"Don't kill him, don't hurt him!" Mary Alice screamed at the lawman. "He's got a family and two lovely children!"

The officer feared Mary Alice might join the fray to help Hodge. "I was doing fairly well handling him up to that point," the cop later said. "My shirt was torn, my buttons were off. But at least I was hanging on.

"You know a lot of times we have trouble with the women more than we do with the men," he continued. "I kept looking back thinking that she might possibly jump me from behind. It distracted me to a certain extent because I kept looking around and that hindered me somewhat in making the arrest."

As other cops arrived to back him up, Mary Alice continued to yell at the officers that they should not hurt Hodge. "He's got children, leave him alone," she screamed.

The officer tried to handcuff Mary Alice, but she struggled. "I took hold of her arm and told her: 'Lady, it's time to quit or I will treat you like a man.'"

She stopped wriggling. At headquarters, the police vouchered fifty thousand dollars in jewelry they found in Mary Alice's handbag, which she had taken because she originally planned to go to the Bahamas that weekend. She was charged with disorderly conduct, posted bail, and was released. Instead of returning to Palm Beach after her ill-fated afternoon, Mary Alice rejoined Hodge, who had also posted bail. They spent the rest of the weekend at the Golden Sands Hotel.

A few weeks later, she made a trip to the Grand Bahamas, staying at the elegant Yucatan Hotel, which was known for its beautiful beach and casino. "She would frequently go there on her own," said Attorney Pruitt. One night, he added, she was picked up by the chief operating officer of a large American corporation. When she awakened the following morning in his bed with the executive beside her, he ordered breakfast and then summoned his lawyer to the suite to conduct some business. As Mary Alice clutched a bedsheet over her body, the executive gave a list of commands to his counsel, who sat at the foot of the bed taking notes.

"We subpoenaed that attorney later to testify for Russell," Pruitt recalled. "He was figuratively and literally a 'lay' witness."

With rumors abounding about Mary Alice's sexual escapades, Russell's hired investigators planted recording devices in her home and started to track her movements twenty-four hours a day, keeping detailed minute-by-minute accounts of where, and with whom, she stayed. Considering the amount of money Russell could save if Mary Alice were caught in bed with a man, the hard-charging detectives— cameras in hand—smashed through the wooden front door of her home at 2:35 A.M. on August 3 and crashed into her bedroom, only to find her screaming in fear and very much alone.

"She saw two white males, one of them with a camera and taking pictures," the Palm Beach police report began. "Both doors leading to the bedrooms from the stairs had been broken into, with the locks broken off. She said they said they were private detectives chasing a prowler in the house. The complainant wanted to call the police, but was told by one of the white males not to call them until they got back. Both men left, and never returned. The nurse said [both women present] were frightened and were afraid to use the telephone to call the police. The nurse came to the station to make notification."

She thought she recognized one of the intruders as Russell's lead investigator.

By now, Mary Alice's lawyers were working on their own strategy. They countered Russell's application for a divorce by charging him with abandonment. Then they decided the most effective way to halt his divorce action—at least temporarily—was to have Mary Alice declared "mentally incompetent," which would automatically prevent her from being deposed by Russell's attorneys. They presented medical testimony in court about her recent suicide attempt and her nearly-fatal head wounds from the car crash.

On November 2, 1964, Mary Alice was determined to have "suicidal propensities and emotional instabilities," and was declared "mentally incompetent." Her brother, Charles Turner, was named her guardian. Ten days later, she filed a maintenance lawsuit against Russell, declaring that his net worth was $10 million and that the feed bill for his string of polo ponies alone came to two thousand dollars a month.

Russell countered that same day. His detectives broke into Mary Alice's home and kidnapped their fifteen-month-old son, Mark. From then on, Russell permitted his estranged wife to visit their son only between the hours of four and six P.M.—and only under the watchful eyes of Russell's armed guards.

On November 20, Russell ordered Mary Alice out of the $1 million house he rented at 757 Island Road and into a smaller, leased dwelling at 236 Pendleton Avenue. The prospect did not please her. The events of the past weeks were dizzying. She had been declared incompetent, was without her son, and faced an embarrassing, unavoidable move to cheaper quarters. Mary Alice Firestone temporarily fled Palm Beach— for the Grand Bahamas.

Over Thanksgiving weekend, Mary Alice, a guest at the Yucatan Hotel, joined some of its staff for a party in a wing of the complex where the employees live and where guests seldom travel. There were about forty people in an employee apartment. Mary Alice was picked up quickly by a busboy, John "Stubby" Buster. He led her out of the room and down a hallway to an efficiency apartment that was stocked with whiskey and used primarily by staffers for casual sex.

"I was thinking of nothing but going to bed," the former motorcycle and real estate salesman testified. "I didn't know her last name and I didn't know who she was. It did not make any difference to me. It was just another girl at the party I was trying to put the make on and I did."

Mary Alice's lawyer, Joe Farish, put Buster through an extraordinary and detailed cross-examination, demanding to know if the busboy had discovered any peculiarities about Mrs. Firestone's anatomy.

In addition to cosmetic surgery, Mary Alice was born with a deformed right hand that was missing fingers, a defect she skillfully hid. She also had unusually small feet.

"How about her feet? Did her feet have any scars on them?"

"I don't know. I did not get down to look."

"Well, how about her hands?" Did her hands have any scars on them?"

"Nothing unusual that I noticed."

"Ordinary hands?" Farish asked.

"Yes. I do not go checking a girl out completely before I put the make on her," Buster shot back.

Buster said he and Mary Alice had intercourse twice, but he admitted forlornly that he had not satisfied her. Buster said he walked out of the efficiency apartment before Mary Alice, leaving her behind buttoning her clothes. He returned to the party, alone.

After a year of marital estrangement and legal maneuvering, it was clear that Mary Alice was losing the Battle of the Firestones. The year 1964 was almost over. Russell's attorneys and investigators had gathered enough incriminating evidence to make an overwhelming case proving adultery. The argument that Mary Alice was "incompetent" and unable to stand trial seemed the only thing that spared her certain defeat. But the extra time created by that legal maneuver started to pay handsome dividends. Mary Alice's husband became careless about his own sexual dalliances. And his estranged wife and her investigators were at the ready to eavesdrop, peer through a window, or break down a door to record the action.

"Each side was surveilling the other with all types of tactics and procedures," said Attorney Farish:

> I recall one instance where we knew that Russell had placed some sort of eavesdropping equipment in the Pendleton Avenue home, trying to obtain evidence against Mary Alice. In those days electronic technology was just beginning and any type of microphones had to be powered by batteries, which would wear out and have to be replaced. Also any tapes that would activate had to be replaced. We found out where the batteries were located. I put one of my detectives on surveillance. Fortunately Russell's man came there to replace the batteries and pick up the tape—and a big fight ensued and we caught him!

Mary Alice's investigators then learned from informants that Firestone was visiting the home of his ex-wife, Linda, and that he often spent the night with her there. The private detectives trailed Linda to her home in Fort Lauderdale, Florida, which was located on a quiet street on a canal behind Pier 66. One of Farish's detectives slipped into the house and "concealed a mike in one of the drapes," Farish later reported. "We obtained some real good evidence."

But Farish's detectives were not the only spies interested in Russell Firestone's whereabouts at night. There was another woman besides Mary Alice who had an interest in Russell's fidelity. She was his secretary, Joyce Jane Simms. They were having a torrid office affair during the spring of 1965. Russell was taking his secretary on business trips to Miami and North Carolina and Texas. He even used the annual Firestone Country Club Golf Classic, a prestigious PGA tournament, as an excuse to spend a weekend with his secretary in Ohio.

"Russell would sleep most every night at my apartment," Simms later said. And the next morning he would leave early to return to his own home "before the maid woke up so she would think he had been there all night."

Then one night, his secretary became suspicious that Firestone was cheating on her:

> We had dinner and I wasn't feeling too well, so instead of going to my apartment as he usually does he said that he was going home. And so I thought, well, this doesn't sound right because he usually goes with me.
>
> So, I followed him and he went to [his ex-wife, Linda's] apartment. He got out and went inside the apartment, so I called her apartment and asked to speak to him because this was very upsetting to me to find out that he would do me that way, after we had been so close.
>
> She said: "He is not there." She said, "There is a party going on next door. He's probably there." But I know he wasn't there because that was a teenage party and he certainly wouldn't have been there.
>
> I sat outside the house from that time, about ten o'clock until six-thirty the next morning. His car was there the whole time.

Mary Alice's investigators eventually developed their suspicions about Joyce and Russell. On June 4, 1965, they decided to pay a surprise visit to Firestone's office at 907 Harvey Building in West Palm Beach. Armed with cameras and accompanied by Mary Alice, they barged through the door like trained commandos.

With cameras flashing, they stunned the half-naked couple. Russell was caught in his shorts. Simms was in her bra and slip. They had been sleeping on a cot. Mary Alice went straight for Simms, punching, scratching, and kicking the scantily clad secretary. Investigators had to break up the catfight, but not before they recorded the tussle.

"The surveillance became so hot and heavy on the part of both sides," Farish recalled, that Judge James Knott issued an order halting surveillance by everyone involved in the case. Farish later took two depositions from Joyce Simms. Simms denied having sex with Firestone during her initial sworn interview. She returned a second time, repentant and prepared to tell the truth:

> I want it known that I do care as much about [Russell] as I ever did and I am not giving this deposition to hurt him or to see that he loses his child or anything.
>
> I am just doing it because the last deposition I gave, I did not tell the truth. And I am sorry that I didn't, but I was trying to protect him. But I was coached and told what to say by his attorneys before I even came here.
>
> I was told not to say anything that would hurt Russell. Excuse me, your honor. Am I allowed to use bad language?
>
> Russell's lawyer is a very abrupt and awful-talking person, and he told me: "No matter what you do at that deposition, don't admit any fucking!" It is a nasty word and I hate to use it, but that is the very word he used. And that is just the way he talks. He has no respect for a lady at all.

Joyce went on to acknowledge that Firestone had underwritten the cost of her Mustang automobile, but she quickly complained the expense was paltry when compared to the gifts he showered on another woman—the millionaire-husband-hunting society gossip columnist, Myrna O'Dell, for example.

O'Dell was an Ann-Margret look-alike who had worked as a gossip writer for the *Miami News*. In the early 1960s, she and her friends were regulars at Miami's "millionaire parties," where the beautiful young women of Miami met rich and eligible bachelors. Two of her friends, in fact, found their husbands at the "millionaire" soirees. Their good fortune, however, only made Myrna wonder if she would ever find a seven-figure man. She turned to a fortune-teller for the answer. The soothsayer predicted Myrna would find both fortune and fame before she turned thirty-two. Myrna turned the forecast into a self-fulfilling prophecy.

She quit bustling Miami to write a society column at the *Palm Beach Post-Times*. The move to a newspaper with a smaller circulation than that of the *Miami News* put her geographically in the middle of more than four thousand millionaires, seventeen hundred corporate executives, over five hundred mansions and five hundred Rolls-Royces.

On September 18, 1965, columnist O'Dell gossiped about the Firestones:

> They call her Silky Sullivan, after a racehorse which not only lost, but ran last in a race several years ago. This Silky is a former schoolteacher who doesn't intend to lose since her stakes are a lot higher. Silky's recently hired attorney Melvin Belli, the man who once defended [Jack Ruby], the man who supposedly shot [Lee Harvey Oswald], the man who supposedly shot President Kennedy.
>
> "Mr. Belli went to Cleveland to take a deposition of my husband's trust fund," Silky giggled. "I think that's interesting—to see what's behind all those Firestone millions. Probably a dollar and a half."
>
> Good looking Mary Alice's brother, Charles Turner, 26, is her guardian. "You see, I'm incompetent. Legally incompetent," Mary Alice says, adding that she has been followed for two years. "It's horrible. I don't even trust the phone I'm on. Private detectives have broken into my house in the middle of the night and terrified my child, my child's nursemaid, and me."
>
> Russell says nothing about what's happened or who's following whom, except that he's sorry his wife wants to try her case in the newspapers... well, I always said there must be better material for a column than the details of a divorce but after all, it is a quiet summer in Palm Beach and most people are getting their jollies talking about the Firestones.
>
> Both of them are living in comparatively small homes in Palm Beach, only a few blocks from each other—both say they haven't been "out" in a year or more. (That's with a member of the opposite sex). Both are probably sick of it all by now.

If O'Dell wanted to get the attention of the estranged multimillionaire heir to the Firestone fortune, it worked. She met Firestone a short time later at a charity function. Photographs appeared in her newspaper of them posing at cocktail parties. A comparison of a caption beneath an early photo and a later caption revealed their emerging relationship. The first caption said:

"The fourth estate—*Palm Beach-Times* Society Editor, Myrna O'Dell, covered the Griffis party honoring Fulton Sheen. Here she chats with Palm Beach sportsman Russell Firestone, Jr."

The later picture, however, reported: "The news—Fourth Estater

Myrna O'Dell was escorted to the Trosby auction by rubber industry scion Russell Firestone."

In December 1965, Joseph Farish returned to court to have Mary Alice declared competent, in order for the divorce proceedings to resume.

The following summer 1966, Farish's men flushed Firestone and Myrna out of an apartment he had rented for them under the alias R. E. Hall on 2525 Sunset Drive on La Gorce Island in Miami Beach. Farish had Myrna arrested under Florida law on charges of "fornication, adultery, and lewd and lascivious behavior." The charges were later dropped, but not before a flurry of headlines detailed the latest development in the Firestone divorce.

In late 1967, attorneys presented their evidence before Judge Knott. Each side presented bundles of documents and sworn testimony that chronicled both parties' sexual escapades. By now the expense of the legal skirmish was more than one million dollars. At the last moment, Farish had Mary Alice declare that she was prepared to stay married to Russell to protect him from falling victim to greedy women.

On December 16, 1967, more than four years after the spark died in the Firestone marriage, Judge Knott issued a Solomon-like decision, criticizing both sides in granting a divorce.

"According to certain testimony in behalf of Russell Firestone, Mary Alice's extramarital escapades were bizarre and of an amatory nature which would have made Dr. Sigmund Freud's hair curl." the judge said. Russell Firestone fared little better. Other testimony reported Russell "bounding from one bed partner to another with the erotic zest of a satyr." However, the judge added that he was inclined to discount much of the testimony as unreliable.

The judge then declared.

> Mary Alice strongly resists her husband's claim for divorce; she urges that her marriage be preserved in order to protect guileless womankind from [Russell's] roving marriage tendencies. As phrased by her counsel, he should not be allowed to "hop from wife to wife while leaving a child here and there along the way." It might be argued with equal plausibility that the present marriage should be preserved for defendant's own protection from predatory females whose amorous instincts seemingly are instantly aroused to fever pitch by the charm of his wealth. It might readily be contended also that others, in the spirit of the day, have equal rights to share in the economic fruits of the more abundant life provided by defendant's marriage proclivities.

It is abundantly clear that neither of the parties has shown the least susceptibility to domestication and the marriage should be dissolved.

Mary Alice was awarded three thousand dollars monthly in alimony, custody of their son, Mark, and $750 child-support payments.

On May 20, 1968, Russell Firestone married Myrna O'Dell. They had a son and within six years were divorced. Myrna's settlement provided her with their homes in La Gorce Island and Kentucky, several country-club memberships, including Russell's card for the Bath and Tennis Club in Palm Beach, and his family box at Hialeah for the 1974 season.

She also arranged for a cost-of-living alimony clause that—regardless of the economy—could never fall below sixty thousand dollars a year. And there was another unique stipulation— if Russell remarried, any future divorce benefits could not exceed Myrna's. If they did, Firestone had to pay $100,000 to Myrna for the privilege.

"Russell was a nice enough fella," Farish said. "But he was like a pussycat, and maybe a few cards short. Actually, he was kinda pitiful, just watching his polo horses run. Then he'd zero in on these women. And these women would just clean his plow!"

Within six months of Myrna's divorce, Mary Alice won a new settlement of her own from her former tire heir husband. This one guaranteed her a thirty-thousand-dollar-a-year income for the rest of her life regardless of whether Russell was alive or dead. It also increased her son's support to $1,150 a month and guaranteed that two-thousand shares of Firestone stock would be held in trust for the then eleven-year-old Mark until he turned twenty-one years of age. None of it seemed to faze Russell Firestone. He married wife number five shortly after divorcing Myrna.

The thirty-seven-year-old Mary Alice fell in love with John Asher, a Kentucky mining company owner. They married on December 2, 1974. It was also Asher's second marriage. His first wife, Mabel "Tootsie" Asher, a twenty-eight-year-old beautician, was murdered on February 22, 1972, when she turned the ignition in her Cadillac and several sticks of dynamite exploded under the chassis. At the time of her death, Tootsie was involved in an extremely nasty year-long divorce battle with her husband, whom she had accused of intentionally depleting the assets of their J&T Coal Companies to minimize her share in a divorce. Tootsie's death remains an unsolved mystery.

Mary Alice and John Asher lived relatively anonymous lives together, dividing their time between Palm Beach and an estate in Middleboro, Kentucky, not far from the place where Asher founded his strip mining and underground coalworks thirty years earlier. Mary Alice was so rarely seen on Palm Beach that many people believed she had stopped spending time there.

Her anonymity ended on July 11, 1985, at 12:17 A.M., when she called police, complaining she was groggy, dazed and afraid she had suffered a seizure. She greeted the medics on the lawn of her $2 million home at 8 South Trail. She allowed them to take her inside. They found more than they expected: a pound of cocaine; ten ounces of marijuana, some of it stashed in the refrigerator and in Mason jars; bottles of amphetamines and barbituates; three scales; a cocaine sifter; pipes for smoking marijuana; three-foot marijuana plants, some hanging to dry on a closet door; twenty-three Polaroid pictures of marijuana being grown, and a copy of the "hippie magazine" *High Times*.

"After being read her Miranda rights, Mary Alice Asher stated that the cocaine in the house belonged to her husband, John, and that before he left the house he told her emphatically to not let anyone into his bathroom, where we found 24.7 grams of cocaine in an ashtray," a police investigator reported. The police also said several ounces of the cocaine was found in her son Mark's room.

Eventually Mary Alice confessed that she had a drug problem and pleaded guilty to seven drug-related charges. The court sentenced Mary Alice to five years probation. Then the charges against Mark were dropped, primarily because, on the day the drugs were found, he was in Kentucky getting married. Finally, prosecutors acknowledged they could not prove that the drugs belonged to the sixty-two-year-old Asher. In the end, all three defendants walked out of court grateful for the outcome. The cops, however, were not satisfied.

"It's a disappointment," said Palm Beach police Sergeant Robert Price, the lead investigator. "Those drugs obviously belonged to somebody."

Mary Alice withdrew from the spotlight along with her husband, John Asher, settling into a less public life on South Trail in Palm Beach. Her ex-husband, however, fell in love twice more after he and Myrna O'Dell parted. The polo-playing heir to the Firestone tire fortune currently resides in Dallas, Texas... with his sixth wife.

14

Ancky Panky: Ancky Revson and Ben Johnson

The plumpish dowager walks slowly east along Worth Avenue, the island's most opulent street. She wears a flowing, roomy blue cotton dress, a Carmen Miranda-style turban on her head. Her pace is slow, but steady. Occasionally she stops in front of one of the many pricy clothing stores along the pristine street and gazes at the displays. By her manner, she has obviously walked down this block many times before. In years past, however, it had always been on the arm of a handsome, tanned, and younger man.

Her name is Ancky Johnson. Now in her late seventies or early eighties, depending on whom you believe, Ancky, in her own small way, is a Palm Beach legend.

Despite her quiet, dignified lifestyle now, Ancky managed to find herself unwittingly in the center of two sensational Palm Beach divorce cases that between them produced testimony lurid enough to make the top of the evening newscast and the front page.

In her last two marriages—there have been five—Ancky's name has been mentioned along with bisexuality, sadomasochism, faked impotence, and alcoholism. Intimate details of her sex life have been bared. There is little that Palm Beach does not know about Ancky Johnson.

She was once married to one of the world's richest men and commanded great respect as an important New York socialite. Now, with a string of divorces behind her, she lives alone in a large mansion along South Ocean Boulevard. Her clothing, the furnishings in her home, the artwork she collects, the flowers in her garden—are all perfectly placed. Unfortunately, Ancky has one serious flaw: she is unable to pick the right man.

It seems to have started so well. Ancky was born Johanna Katrina de Knecht in Amsterdam, Holland, around 1910. Her parents wanted her to have a full, culture-filled education and so they sent her to schools in France, Germany, and England. After leaving school, Ancky moved to Paris and met and married French army officer Jean Eric de Bazire. He was killed in a land-mine explosion at the start of World War II.

With the German war machine grinding toward France, Ancky knew she had to leave. She had worked successfully as a coiffure model for some of Paris's brightest stylists, and many of them had spoken of New York City as a place where young, talented models could have great careers. Ancky packed her bags and set sail for New York in 1939, and it wasn't long before the slender, long-legged beauty landed a modeling job at Saks Fifth Avenue. During one fateful runway show, she caught the eye of makeup king Charles Revson.

Revson was the lanky, Boston-born businessman who created the hugely successful Revlon Cosmetics firm. Revson had started his career selling nail polish to beauty salons in New York City. He saw how popular these polishes were with women, from the fashion-conscious socialite to the housewife with six kids. Revson, along with his brother, Joe, and chemist Charles Lachman, set up a small shop in suburban New Rochelle, New York, and started manufacturing ten different types of polish. The trio bottled their concoctions in a twenty-five-dollar-a-month factory on West Forty-fourth Street in the bustling Times Square district.

Soon the partners branched out, making lipsticks, powders, eye-liners, cold creams, and any other beautifying products they could imagine—and they all became millionaires within five years. Revson was thirty-two in 1939, which for that time was considered quite old to still be single, especially for a well-to-do gentleman.

As he stood in the Saks showroom, his eyes scrutinized Anky's buxom body and wavy blond hair while she paraded back and forth modeling a new hairdo. After the show, Revson approached her. His refined, Bostonian speech contrasted with her thick, sometimes nearly unin-telligible Dutch accent. Still, Revson asked her for a date.

Much later, Revson—always consumed with his cosmetics line—

would remember only one thing about their first meeting. "The first time I saw her she had the wrong shade of lipstick," Revson recalled.

Ancky changed her shade of lipstick; the couple fell in love and were married a year later on October 26, 1940. They purchased a mansion in Westchester and within six years Ancky gave birth to two sons. Each day Revson commuted into Manhattan in a limo painted "ultra-violet," the color of one of his famous nail polishes.

A workaholic, Revson never seemed to have enough time for Ancky, at least by her count. She wanted him to spend more time with her and the children. After all, Ancky reasoned, her spouse had plenty of money, so why shouldn't he relax and enjoy it? But that was not Revson's nature. In the late 1950s, the Revlon empire was threatened by the infamous quiz show fiascos. It was revealed that the immensely popular "$64,000 Question" and "$64,000 Challenge" TV programs were fixed, allegedly by their advertisers. Revlon sponsored both shows. Now Revson was away from home more than ever, as he tried to repair the public-relations damage that had been done. He also had to fight off a lawsuit filed by his brother, Martin, who claimed he had been cheated out of a large block of Revlon stock.

Ancky had had it. She filed for divorce in April 1960 and was awarded the couple's mansion in the quiet waterfront town of Rye, New York, $7 million in cash, and custody of the two boys, John Charles and Charles Haskell, Jr.

"Charles did not want a divorce," she said. "The trouble was it was always work, work, work. It was no good. He always gave 100 percent to the business and he was always a difficult man."

After the divorce, Ancky married a baron, but the union—little is known about it—lasted less than a year. Looking more glamorous than ever, Ancky, now about fifty, began to travel. One of those forays brought her to Palm Beach.

On a fateful evening in 1964, Ben Johnson, a handsome male model, walked into the darkly elegant bar of the Palm Beach's Colony Hotel, ordered a drink, and changed Ancky's life forever. He may have looked suave and he may have seemed like just another young Palm Beach playboy living the good life with a family inheritance, but nothing could have been further from the truth. The twenty-nine-year-old Johnson had little more than twenty dollars in his pocket and the clothes on his back.

"To marry rich, you dine where the rich dine, you drink where the rich drink, and you sleep where the rich sleep," he once said. So it was not surprising that he struck up a conversation with Ancky Revson. The pair began a whirlwind romance. It was a relationship that puzzled Ben's closest friends, who knew that Johnson was bisexual. And like a lot of men of that era, he guarded his gay lifestyle, knowing that its exposure, particularly in a conservative state like Florida, could ruin him. Was he finally about to marry and "go straight," and with a woman some twenty-five years older? Did Ancky know about his sexual preferences?

Nobody seemed to know, but regardless, she liked his looks, his manners and the way he paid attention to her. The pair were soon jetting off to Monte Carlo on Ancky's money. They married two years later in 1966 and lived in Ancky's spacious midtown apartment in New York before moving to Palm Beach for good in 1973.

For eight years, it appeared that the marriage was a great success. Ancky and Ben lived in their large mansion on South Ocean Boulevard, appearing as a vibrant, happy couple on the social scene. Whatever doubts Ben's close friends had, they were fading fast. Then the shenanigans began.

Ben was hauled into jail for allegedly propositioning three Florida police officers. Ancky didn't believe a word of it and quickly posted bond for his release. The charges were later dropped. Meanwhile, Ancky longed for a new family. With her children grown, she wanted more kids. Alas she was way beyond the point of being fertile. So the couple adopted two children whom they named Alexandra and Douglas Johnson.

Ben's fast and loose modeling days were far behind him. He decided to enter Palm Beach's booming real-estate business, and with his handsome good looks and resonant baritone voice, he found he was a born salesman. He eventually sold some of the island's most exclusive waterfront properties, including the stunning El Salano mansion to John Lennon and Yoko Ono.

Still, after Ben's business began to grow, Ancky started complaining to Ben about his lifestyle. He was spending too much of her money, he was staying out so late, he wasn't spending enough time with her. Just where was he going so many nights by himself?

Ancky kept herself quite busy though, overseeing many of Palm Beach's charitable organizations and social events. Meanwhile, Ben continued his late night trips out, and in 1984, he moved out of their home at Ancky's insistence. It was a trial separation. Ben took up in a less affluent residence on Washington Road in West Palm Beach on the less prestigious mainland. Ancky didn't know it, but a major sex scandal involving her estranged husband was about to explode.

In June 1985, the police were called to Ben's house in response to a report of an armed robbery. As they arrived, the cops drew their service revolvers, expecting to confront a gunman. They found no guns, but were surprised by what did confront them. Johnson, they discovered upon arrival, was sitting naked on the steps with his arms handcuffed behind his back, moaning in pain. Inside, officers found a quantity of cocaine, a whip, leather wristbands, and a man named Paul Elrod.

Elrod's version of what had happened went like this: Johnson had picked him up at a bar by promising some great coke. But once there, Elrod said, the promised coke party turned into an S&M extravaganza. Johnson stripped naked and started parading around wearing nothing but a blonde wig and metal clips on his nipples.

Elrod said Ben asked him to handcuff him in the bedroom and tried to seduce him. Elrod refused, punched him, and would not remove the handcuffs. Johnson then ran through a second-floor glass door and leaped from a balcony, fracturing his arm, according to the police.

With the Johnson scandal on the news, Ancky was furious and confronted her husband. According to Ancky, Johnson admitted he had bisexual leanings and confessed to numerous affairs with both men and women during their marriage.

Ancky charged that Johnson was a fraud attempting to "fleece me for as much money as he possibly can...

"He was a bisexual who had an affinity for sadomasochistic practices," she sniffed. Ancky also said Ben was a rampant boozer and drug user, smoking marijuana in the house against her wishes.

Ancky added that Ben had depleted her fortune with his "horrible" gambling habits, reducing her bank account from $7 million to between $3 million and $4 million. She also complained that Ben had not kept her in the style to which she was accustomed. Only one of the four cars that Ben bought during their marriage was a Rolls-Royce. Why, her neighbors must think of her as, as...as poor white trash!

Ancky continued her complaints about Ben. She said his extravagant spending and mounting debts had forced her to cut her own living expenses from twenty-eight thousand dollars a month to fifty-two hundred dollars a month. She even had to sell off some of her personal stocks and jewelry to make ends meet.

Despite her complaints, Ben wanted money. His real-estate business was in a slump and he was nearly broke. He filed a petition for temporary alimony in Palm Beach Circuit Court and was awarded four hundred dollars a week for expenses. Among the expenses Johnson had claimed in his court papers were a monthly seven hundred fifty dollars for taxis and limousines, seven hundred for food, and four hundred for clothes.

Ancky was furious and charged that Ben's business was fine. He had simply stopped working just to get more cash from her.

Some of Ancky's friends said she was truly mad at Ben—but not because of all the money he was demanding. No, Ancky was mad because in court papers, Ben had listed her age as seventy-five. "I think she was more angry about that than about any of the other allegations," a friend said.

Ancky herself volunteered: "I'm not seventy-five. I'm sixty-six!"

During the 1985 divorce trial, Ben admitted being bisexual, but said Ancky had known about it from the start. "I told her I was bisexual and she said, 'You can change that.' I said, 'I don't think you can change that.'"

But on the stand, Ancky bristled: "Mr. Johnson was very male, macho male, when I met him. He always told me about all the girls he was going out with. I would not marry a bisexual—it's ridiculous. I had two teenage sons. I was certainly not going to bring a homosexual into my home."

Ancky said she had been all too gullible at Ben's excuses for his behavior in the past, particularly when he tried to explain why he had solicited the three police officers.

"He told me he was helping an old bag lady who was being harassed by the police and that's why they threw him in jail. He told me so many lies over the years that I believed everything he told me."

Nonsense, Ben replied. "I told her what it was—lewd and lascivious behavior. She acted like she didn't want to believe it."

Ben denied Ancky's allegations that he'd wrecklessly spent her money. In fact, if anybody had taught him bad habits, it was Ancky herself. "I had never been to a casino until I met Mrs. Johnson. We would gamble every afternoon, every night in Monte Carlo, the Bahamas. We went to Moscow, Berlin, stayed at Claridge's in London, visited Madrid. We never got to Asia," he told the court. Ben added that Ancky had refused to allow him to get a real nine-to-five job.

"She repeatedly told me she'd been married to a workaholic for twenty years and she refused to be married to another one," Johnson testified.

Ancky said Johnson had left a lot to be desired in the area of sex. She testified in court that she hadn't made love with Ben for a decade. In 1975, she said, "He conveniently became impotent. We never had sex anymore."

Ben charged that Ancky had turned their children against him by showing them the sensational newspaper articles chronicling his bisexual lifestyle.

After all of the Johnsons' problems had been bared, Palm Beach residents eagerly awaited the verdict. Circuit Judge Maurice Hall didn't disappoint them. He granted the divorce and said that Ancky owed Ben nothing—no alimony, no property "because of the husband's repeated wrongdoing and adulterous wrongdoing."

Hall added: "The court further finds that the wife has more than adequately and reasonably contributed to the husband's well-being during the course of the marriage." Ben's talent, the judge said, was his ability to "squander money away."

A jubilant Ancky proclaimed: "I won all the way! I don't have to pay him anything—not one red cent. I had offered him a very good settlement. He didn't take it. Now he gets nothing!"

As far as another marriage, Ancky said, "From now on I'll say, 'I will! I will!' But not, 'I do! I do!'"

During their bitter divorce, Ben had countercharged that Ancky had taken up with a New York boutique owner named Tommy DeMaio for the last five years of their marriage. Exactly who Ancky had seen or what indiscretions she had indulged in during her marriage to Johnson—if any—were unclear. But the man Ben had named was soon to become another milestone in Ancky's life.

Just six months after her divorce from Ben in December 1985, the seventyish heiress married again. Groom number five was Gaetano "Tommy" DeMaio, a flamboyant forty-nine-year-old businessman and owner of a pricy clothing boutique in New York's Sheraton Centre. He invested in Broadway shows and had backed the successful productions of *The Elephant Man* and *Dracula*. He went by the nickname of Tommy Tomato.

Tommy Tomato certainly did not have anywhere near the $5.6 million that Ancky was worth. In a prenuptial agreement, the couple agreed that each would keep their own properties. Ancky also agreed to pay Tommy $128,000 to solve his longstanding tax problems and a fifteen-hundred-dollars-a-month allowance for his "personal expenses and entertainment."

As in her past marriage, Ancky was taken by the fact that Tommy paid so much attention to her. It was all so romantic. The two were wed in a quick ceremony in Las Vegas in 1986. They were a bizarre-looking couple—she with her Carmen Miranda–like face and turban and he with boyish blond hair and Elvis sideburns.

In less than two years, however, Ancky's fifth marriage seemed doomed. She and Tommy Tomato fought all the time and seemed to have nothing in common. Tommy complained that Ancky had become a tightwad. On February 3, 1988, Ancky's friends in Palm Beach watched as Tommy Tomato went on the nationally televised "Phil Donohue Show" and began blasting his wife. "She was tight, to put it mildly," Tommy said. "When we entertained, she asked if I bought the liquor. She said she was not running a charity house for my friends." He said that soon after their marriage, while on vacation in Monte Carlo, "she threw a bottle of vodka at me because I ordered a dollar-seventy-five cheese sandwich."

Within a month, Ancky filed for divorce. "I couldn't believe it when I found out I'd married another bisexual!" she raged. "I just got rid of one bisexual and found myself married to another one. I made a mistake. I admit it and I want to get out of it."

In her divorce suit, Ancky continued. "He told me he used to be gay but had gone straight since dating me. But then he continued to see men after our marriage."

Furthermore, she said, Tomato had "violent propensities" and said it had been him, not her, who had hurled the vodka bottle in Monte Carlo. Tommy's statements on "Donahue" were all false, causing her to worry and suffer "mental anguish, humiliation, chagrin, sadness, depression... and creating medical conditions as a result of the stress."

Tommy promised he would fight. "It's gonna be bigger and dirtier than her last one, because she hasn't lived up to her commitments," he said about the impending divorce. "I got the name 'Tommy Tomato' because I was soft and easy for picking. But now I'm green and hard."

" She's cheap," he insisted. "I spent thirty thousand dollars in dinners and she never bought one."

Ancky's friends did not have too much sympathy for her. After all, hadn't they told her about DeMaio? Only four years before she had met him he had been involved with another wealthy dowager some twenty-four years his senior, Bobo Rockefeller, a former Miss Lithuania who had been briefly married to Winthrop Rockefeller. In the end, when their divorce was finalized in February 1989, Tommy walked out of court with a check for fifty thousand dollars which he immediately had to surrender to the Internal Revenue Service for a late bill.

With five husbands down and no prospects in sight, Ancky lashed out. "You have to date homosexuals because there aren't any real men left to date in Palm Beach!"

She did, however, become friendly with Ben again. They did not remarry and did not move in together, but the reacquaintance seemed to reinvigorate Ancky. Johnson later moved to Detroit to take a real-estate job there.

Now in her late seventies or early eighties Ancky sits by herself in her gorgeous mansion at 190 South Ocean Boulevard. Her health is reasonably good considering her age, a fact she will readily admit when she answers the telephone. She has a touch of sadness in her voice.

Not that the octogenarian Baroness Johanna Ancky Von Boythan Revson Johnson DeMaio should be counted out. In Palm Beach, marriage is often compared to last year's fashion. When it's out of date, move on.

15

"You Wouldn't Dare Shoot Me. You Haven't the Guts!": Trink and William Wakeman

The voices coming from the elegant Spanish-style villa at 120 El Brillo Way were loud and angry. The battle between socialite Nancy "Trink" Wakeman and her husband, William Wakeman, had been going on all day. And now it was nearing a dramatic climax on this warm evening of September 5, 1967.

Trink had accused her spouse of fooling around with another woman. He denied it. He was angry because earlier at the club she had pushed him fully dressed into the pool. As the fighting raged on, the battling Wakemans paused for a moment, poured themselves two more stiff cocktails, and then continued. The words got nastier as the infusion of alcohol took hold.

Suddenly Trink opened a bureau drawer and retrieved her husband's .22 revolver, a weapon he kept around the house in case of robbers.

"If you lay a hand on me, I'll shoot you!" Trink bellowed. Wakeman, his eyes filled with rage, didn't flinch. "You wouldn't dare shoot me, you haven't got the guts!" he taunted.

But he was wrong. Trink had a steady finger on the trigger, which she pulled quickly. A single shot ripped through Bill Wakeman's back. He collapsed face first to the floor, his blood spilling over the white bedroom carpet. As Bill lay moaning and writhing, Trink called for

214

help. When the police and an ambulance arrived, a patrolman knelt beside Wakeman and asked him what had happened.

"Posie shot me," he said in a whisper, evoking his private nickname for Trink.

There are two views of the shooting of former Florida Republican State Committee chairman William Wakeman by his wife, Nancy Deere Wiman Carter Wakeman. One holds that Nancy, who is known by her friends as Trink, got away with the shooting. The other contends that William Wakeman should have known his wife was prone to outrageous melodramatic theatrics, coming from the famous family she did.

To young Nancy Deere Wiman, born into a fabulously wealthy family in 1918, much of the world was a stage. Trink's father, Dwight Deere Wiman, was one of Broadway's biggest producers. Since seeing his first show in Chicago at the age of nine, Wiman had been stagestruck. He wanted to be the behind-the-scenes impresario whose name would be above the title. He had the drive and certainly the money to pursue his dream. Wiman's grandfather was John Deere, who invented the first steel plow in 1835. The new-fangled gadget revolutionized the farming industry and had made Deere a multimillionaire.

Dwight Deere Wiman produced such shows as *The Road To Rome* in 1927, *Little Show* in 1929, and *On Borrowed Time* in 1938. His 1932 production of *The Gay Divorce* introduced Cole Porter's "Night and Day" to the world, and he brought Kurt Weill's *Street Theme* and Clifford Odets's *The Big Knife* to the stage.

Nancy was the second of four daughters, born to Wiman and his wife, Dorothea. Trink grew up in affluent Greenwich, Connecticut, and was educated at four finishing schools. She often visited her father's productions, chatting with the actors and playwrights, enjoying a privilege few could. She appeared in a few shows including *Stars in Your Eyes*, in which she played a chorus girl. Trink became further immersed in the theatrical world when, in 1943 at the age of twenty-five, she married twenty-five-year-old William Carter, a dashing actor just breaking into the movies. The couple moved to Hollywood, living in a hillside home "where we can see the lights of Long Beach and even Catalina on a clear day."

Bill's movie career took off. He appeared with Humphrey Bogart in *Sahara* and in the Technicolor musical *I've Always Loved You*.

Carter told a reporter early in his career, "They plan to make an Alan Ladd of me—one of those side-talking, quick-on-the-trigger guys. Sure,

I'm looking forward to it, but I'd rather do an Errol Flynn. You know, ride horseback in costume and down ten guys at a time with one sabre or maybe swim the Atlantic Ocean successfully."

Life was wonderful. "On Sundays," Carter said, "we play baseball. John Garfield and the Epstein brothers and Gene Kelly are usually there. We often play touch football with the local kids. It's a great life." Nancy gave birth to two children, Dwight and Katherine.

In his earlier days, Bill had been a World War II flying ace and a champion swimmer who had worked in *Billy Rose's Aquacade* and other water shows along the Florida coast. He loved Palm Beach, and when his Hollywood career fizzled, the family moved there. Trink inherited $2 million when her father died in 1951.

In the mid-1950s, the marriage began falling apart. Bill charged that in March 1958, when he returned from a two-week skiing trip in Switzerland and Italy, he found himself locked out of his homes.

He said that Trink had packed his bags and that his cars, bank accounts and children were all in his wife's possession. "But I still like being married," he complained.

Bill moved to New York where he took a job as host of a posh East Side club, The Night Owl. There he struck up a "friendship" with jazz singer Helen Merrill, who was billed as "the champagne blonde who popped her cork."

Trink kept a close watch on her estranged husband's movements and quietly set a trap. In October 1958, as he relaxed with Helen in her Bronx apartment, there was a violent hammering at the door.

Carter said that Trink, her sister, and five burly "apes" burst through the door, grabbed him, and began ripping off his clothes while a photographer took pictures in an effort to obtain incriminating evidence for a divorce. The men punched him in the stomach and kidneys numerous times, he said, before they fled the apartment and escaped in several waiting taxicabs.

Trink admitted to society gossip columnist Cholly Knickerbocker that she had indeed broken into the apartment to get "satisfaction." She said she found Bill and Helen "not fully clothed in the living room," but denied attacking him.

"This is beyond me—it's too much. I am embarrassed and upset for Helen," Bill shot back. "Helen and I are good friends and I'm very fond of her, but we are just business associates, that's all. My wife has just gone too far now."

A few days later, Trink charged Bill with "adultery and intolerable cruelty" in a divorce petition. She said Carter had cheated on her with "Jane Doe and others."

In November 1960, Trink was granted a divorce, which included a $290,000 settlement for Carter. She was awarded custody of Dwight, seventeen, and Catherine, thirteen. If the idea of marriage had in any way soured for Trink it was not apparent.

Shortly after her divorce, Trink, forty-two, wed strikingly handsome William Wakeman. The thirty-six-year-old Wakeman was a former male model who had made money as an oil wildcatter in Ohio. He was not a multimillionaire like Trink, but he had a talent for knowing where to find big money, particularly in politics. Wakeman chaired the Florida State Republican Committee and was one of Arizona Senator Barry Goldwater's biggest supporters during Goldwater's 1964 presidential campaign.

Palm Beach society knew him as the area's most innovative GOP fund-raiser thanks to affairs he chaired, like "Dinner With Ike."

When Goldwater—whose slogan was "In your heart you know he's right"—lost to Lyndon Johnson in November 1964, Wakeman's hopes of working in the White House were dashed. He went on to serve as chairman of the Florida Republican Finance Committee, but retired from politics in 1966 at the age of forty-two.

Bill never made it quite as big as he would have liked. However, there was one thing that both he and Trink did magnificently: throw parties. In the mid-1960s, they were known for tossing great wingdings at 120 El Brillo Way. Only a handful of others like Marjorie Merriweather Post and Brownie McLean could rival their bashes.

It was not surprising. With an eighteen-hundred-square-foot game room, an enormous bar, and several indoor fountains, the Wakemans' place was more like a party palace than a home. Back then, if you failed to be invited to Trink's gatherings, you were not considered a real player on the island.

Just as they were great party throwers, the Wakemans were also grand brawlers, having their fair share of marital problems. A rumor had it that Bill had taken on a mistress and that Trink was furious. On September 5, 1967, the pot boiled over. All day, Trink and Bill had bickered about Bill's alleged indiscretions.

When tempers exploded that night, and shots rang out, the police acted swiftly. Within twenty-four hours, Trink Wakeman was charged with aggravated assault and culpable negligence, but she was quickly freed on a thousand dollars bond and rushed to the hospital to see her husband.

Anybody who comes so close to losing his life could be expected to want his attacker prosecuted. As a groggy Wakeman lay in the intensive care unit at Good Samaritan Hospital, many of his friends savored the thought of Trink spending the rest of her previously privileged life behind bars. Wakeman had lost a lot of blood, so the police were not immediately able to interview him. But they were sure that when he could speak, he would give them further damning evidence against Nancy Wakeman.

The next day, surgeons at Good Samaritan had good news and bad news. Happily, they reported, Wakeman would recover. But sadly, he would probably never walk again. The single bullet had lodged in his spinal cord three inches above the waist near the aorta. Vital nerve connections controlling the use of the legs had been severed. The prognosis: Wakeman was to be a paraplegic, bound to a wheelchair for the remainder of his days.

Trink's trigger finger had shattered his life. When representatives from the Palm Beach County District Attorney's Office appeared at his hospital bed that night, they expected Wakeman to swear out a criminal complaint.

Much to their surprise, Wakeman did not. He saw the whole thing as a terrible, tragic accident, he said. He didn't blame Trink and he would not testify against her in court. Even if called to the stand, he would invoke the Fifth Amendment, he insisted.

In a statement to police, Trink said: "Bill hit me several times so I went and got a gun and told him to leave me alone or I would shoot. At that point, he turned away and I shot him in the back."

While Bill refused to testify against Trink, her lawyer, Joe Farish, unveiled a strategy in which he charged that Wakeman was a violent man who had badly beaten Trink just prior to the shooting. In fact, Farish told the court, Wakeman was about to attack his wife when the gun went off. The lawyer added he had also ripped an earring from his wife's earlobe.

Wakeman was wheeled into the courtroom on January 15 to testify. The prosecution knew he would prove no help in the case, but the sight of a man in a wheelchair might aid the state.

"I have sort of fragmentary recollections of being shot," Wakeman testified. He remembered that the .22 slug had instantly paralyzed him and that Trink had gone into hysterics, but that was about it. As promised, he took the Fifth in response to all other questions about Trink's actions.

Farish, advancing his abusive-husband argument, called a private investigator to the stand who identified three color photos he said he had taken of Trink three hours after the shooting. The photos showed Trink with abrasions on her forehead and left cheek and a sizable laceration on her lower earlobe as if an earring had been forcibly jerked from her pierced ear. Another witness, Donna Humes, testified that the day after the shooting, Mrs. Wakeman had bad bruises on her right hand and thigh and appeared to be in a great deal of pain.

But under cross-examination, Humes also testified that prior to the shooting Mrs. Wakeman was "highly intoxicated." Humes's testimony suggested another theory for Trink's condition: that she had injured herself, possibly falling over in a drunken stupor.

Trink's first husband, Bill Carter, testified as a character witness. "Trink couldn't do it. She's the greatest. Our children love and adore her."

Despite her character witnesses and the lack of cooperation by her husband, a six-man jury found Trink guilty of aggravated assault. She was sentenced to five years probation.

Life proved frustrating for William Wakeman. Instead of the envy he once used to experience as one of Palm Beach's most handsome men, he became an object of pity from friends and strangers alike as they watched him being wheeled around in his chair. Even the simplest of functions, like going to the bathroom, was now a complex procedure that required the aid of a nurse or domestic.

Wakeman obsessively began to consult neurologists from around the world. Someone must have the surgical skills to give him back his legs, he argued. But the answer was always the same. Yes, we can operate, but it's extremely dangerous and there's almost no possibility the procedure will work anyway.

William Wakeman eventually decided that undergoing a risky operation was better than having to be cared for for the rest of his life. He made arrangements to have the delicate spinal operation performed at the Hospital for Crippled Children in Newark, New Jersey. The surgery was to be performed by the world-famous heart surgeon Dr. Michael DeBakey.

On April 2, 1969, after several hours in the operating room, Wakeman was taken back to his hospital bed. A few minutes later, his heart gave out. His wife was by his side as he expired.

"He took a gamble, but his heart wasn't up to it," said his stepson, Dwight Carter.

A month after her husband was buried, Trink was brought into court for alleged violations of her probation. Neighbors complained of loud parties at Trink's house, and the sweet scent of marijuana seemed to waft through the neighborhood during these bashes. Trink was purportedly seen drinking in a Miami bar. Criminal Court Judge Russell McIntosh read her the riot act. Probation means no parties; you can't attend them or throw them, he sharply reminded her.

And what about these marijuana complaints, the judge wanted to know. Marijuana? The only thing being burned in the Wakeman house, Trink insisted, was incense. McIntosh concluded that there could be no more burning of incense or any other substance that even remotely smelled like cannabis. McIntosh also ordered her to perform twenty hours of community service a week. The court said from now on a probation officer would make surprise visits to her home.

There was one more break ahead for Trink. In March 1970, the Florida Court of Appeals reversed the 1968 jury decision that found her guilty of aggravated assault. The court said a statement Trink had made to police about the shooting was inadmissible as evidence. With the court's reversal, her sentence and probation conditions were immediately dropped and Trink was a completely free woman.

Trink would next marry Winthrop (Winnie) Gardiner, Jr., a Palm Beach society sportsman and onetime owner of Gardiner's Island, a gorgeous 3,300-acre retreat off the coast of eastern Long Island. It had been granted to the Gardiner family in 1639 by the English Crown, and was later popularly linked with Captain Kidd's buried treasure.

Gardiner had been married five times before his union with Trink. He previously was wed to ice skating star, Sonja Henie. That marriage ended when Gardiner charged that Heine's mother was ruling the union and that he and Sonja "had only had two weeks alone together during their marriage."

In the late seventies, Trink and Winnie began fighting and eventually, in 1980, he sued her for divorce and asked for alimony. The lawsuit turned out to be moot. Gardiner died of cancer October 16 at age sixty-seven.

Trink, seventy-four, still lives in Palm Beach and although no longer a party giver, she mingles in the island's social circles. She never speaks about the shooting.

Bill Carter, Trink's first husband and the man who rushed to her defense as a character witness, is also still there. A year after his divorce from Trink, Bill had married twenty-seven-year-old screen actress Elaine Stewart, an auburn-haired beauty who had vamped Kirk Douglas in *The Bad and the Beautiful* and played Anne Boleyn in *Young Bess*.

Elaine—who, on occasion, dyed her hair blond—was nearly as famous for her offscreen publicity stunts as she was for her movie roles. A few years before her marriage to Carter, she had gone on a one-woman crusade against foreign screen sex kittens.

"What's the matter with our own girls?" Elaine pouted. "There are hundreds of girls around Hollywood who have just as much beauty, talent, and chest expansion as those foreign dolls. The producers don't have to go looking all over the world for actresses; they can find them two blocks from the studios.

"Those foreign girls like Brigitte Bardot and Sophia Loren and Gina Lollobrigida have nothing to offer but chest expansion. Well, we've got girls who can match them inch for inch, and they've got talent, too! Marilyn Monroe can stack up to any of them, and she's a good comedienne, too, not to mention Jane Russell."

Perhaps Elaine was too modest to mention herself in the lineup of Hollywood stars, but she attempted to prove her theory by posing for a series of bathing suit shots prominently displaying her bust.

Her marriage to Carter did not last long. In 1963, Stewart sued for divorce. She testified that he was "given to violent rages and terrible temper tantrums," and said he had struck her and several times had tried to choke her. She also charged that Carter refused to get a job.

"He said, 'What do you want me to do—get a job like an ordinary person? I am above and beyond that.'" Carter did not contest the divorce. The former actor is now in his late seventies, but looks much younger. Bill Carter now spends many afternoons lunching at Palm Beach's popular Safari and Polo Club, reminiscing with pals about the old days, chatting about the latest goings-on in his longtime home.

Sipping his scotch slowly, the slender, silver-haired Carter appears relaxed. He smiles whenever he speaks of Trink. There is good reason.

"I'm the only one of Trink's husbands to survive," he says.

16

When Harry
Stuck It to Leona:
Leona and Harry Helmsley

The 1973 Thanksgiving holiday passed without so much as a hint of scandal or trouble. It was making life uncomfortably dull for Palm Beach regulars. After all, in Palm Beach, there is little else people prefer to talk about than who is getting divorced, who's sleeping with whom, or whose financial empire is about to fall to ruins. The scarcity of gossip forced the local gentry to muddle through *their* endless rounds of charity balls and cocktail parties chatting about such mundane matters as Watergate and the tenth anniversary of the assassination of John Kennedy, whom Palm Beachites consider *their* president.

The gossip ennui was even affecting the cops. They assuredly were disappointed at the lack of law-enforcement activity that traditionally accompanies the first major rush of vacationers for the winter. No doubt they prayed for real police work to erase the feeling, if only temporarily, that they were little more than high-priced baby-sitters for the rich and their mansions. Only weeks before, the pristine streets and manicured estates of Palm Beach were deserted. Now they bustled with millionaires arriving from the North with their children and domestics, hangers-on and partygoers in tow.

Saturday, November 24, was no different. The Palm Beach police—the only cops in America to wear brown uniforms that look as though they just came pressed from the dry cleaners—spent most of the day sitting aimlessly behind the wheels of their blue-and-white cruisers. They listened to the sound of Michelin tires rolling along the islands' smooth roadways. Occasionally the evening's monotony was cheerfully interrupted by a weaving Mercedes Benz or Jaguar that negotiated more S-curves than Ocean Boulevard had, and therefore had to be stopped.

The evening silence finally broke at 1:03 A.M. A 911 emergency call came into the dispatchers in the lobby of police headquarters. For the record, it was now Sunday morning, November 25. The male caller said there had been a stabbing, a crime so rare in Palm Beach that it occurs only once a year. The man gave the address as 44 Cocoanut Row, apartment A514. Two people were bleeding, one badly, he said.

Patrolmen S. R. Scott and William Cypher were the first to respond to the Palm Beach Towers, a white, horseshoe-shaped complex sitting on the intercoastal waterway and facing West Palm Beach on the mainland. They arrived within minutes and were met in the garden courtyard by Sam Geraci, the Towers' assistant manager. Geraci was waiting anxiously for the cops, not only because he was worried about the victims' wounds, but because he wanted the officers to be aware of other equally important concerns.

Geraci ushered them into a waiting elevator and quickly explained that this "crime" had not occurred in just any apartment in the cavernous three-hundred-unit complex. The stabbing, Geraci said breathlessly, had taken place in the penthouse owned by his billionaire boss, Harry Helmsley. And, he nervously added, Helmsley and Helmsley's new wife, Leona, were the victims! The importance of Geraci's words were not lost on the cops. They, like much of Palm Beach, knew about the aura surrounding the powerful real-estate czar from New York City.

As the cops completed their ride to the Towers' top floor, an ashen-faced Harry, his six-foot-three frame filling the entranceway, met them at the door. He was clad in blood-spattered pajamas, and he winced as he clutched his right forearm in pain. The cops could not see beyond Harry because the penthouse was pitch black.

Standing in the hallway light, Harry hurriedly gave the cops a sketch of what had happened: He and Leona had been asleep when they were startled by an intruder who stood menacingly above them. Harry had fought off the intruder. During the fray, he had been slashed across the arm, and Leona was more seriously injured. Helmsley said the attacker had plunged a knife into her chest and then fled. The billionaire said he had tried to summon help, but could not because the phone lines and electric power had been cut.

Officer Scott yelled into the darkness to Leona. He did not want to rush in and risk damaging any evidence. There was no answer. As the policeman stood at the doorway, the superintendent arrived. He made his way to the fuse box in the kitchen, where he found the switches. They were in the *off* position. He suggested they were moved to one side with a single push of a hand.

With the electric power restored, Officer Scott peered into the apartment. In the master bedroom, Leona lay across the mattress, moaning and breathing heavily. A large circular bloodstain covered her chest. Sections of the cotton-fitted bedspread and sheets were also a dark crimson. "The bedroom was splattered with blood," Officer Scott wrote in case file C. 7105. Cables to separate telephones—one on a night table, the other in the master bathroom—also had been severed.

The Helmsleys told Officer Cypher that they had gone to sleep about 11:15 P.M. Harry said he "was awakened by the noises of his wife," after she was startled by the thief. "I saw a dark shape of a figure leaning over her," Harry said. The intruder tried to cover Leona's mouth and nose with his hand, but Leona screamed. That, said Harry, was when he sprang into action.

The then spry billionaire "pushed away" the burglar and then "went after" the figure in the dark. "I struck out at this person—[Leona] did too. I was able to knock the burglar down at the door of the bedroom, near the television."

While the intruder was on the floor, Leona came rushing up to help her Harry. But the burglar—although outmanned—got off the floor. Cypher reported that "it was here that Mr. Helmsley believes that both he and his wife were "stabbed." Harry was slashed on his arm. Leona was stabbed hard in the chest.

Despite his wound, Harry initially seemed unaware that Leona was wounded and chased the intruder down the hall until he heard "his wife cry out for help that she had been stabbed." Turning his attention to Leona, he allowed the intruder to escape. Harry recalled seeing a flash of light as though the door had been opened and closed.

Frantic about his wife, Harry raced around the penthouse searching for a telephone. He grabbed the phone on the night table by the bed, but it was not working. Hanging up the receiver, the lanky billionaire rushed into the master bathroom, where there was a wall phone. But this one also was out of order. Realizing the phone lines in the bedroom had been slashed, Helmsley ran into the living room, where he grabbed an in-house telephone. He heard a dial tone. He contacted the Towers' switchboard operator and asked her to call the cops.

While everyone waited for the ambulance, the police asked the Helmsleys whether they could provide a description of their attacker. Both of them said they did not get a perfect look at the intruder in the dark. But they both agreed the attacker appeared to be a black woman, with a silver streak in her hair. And the Helmsleys said she was wearing a gas mask with large fish-eyed goggles.

Within minutes, the Helmsleys were rushed to Good Samaritan Hospital. Leona was placed in intensive care with a serious wound near her heart. Harry's cuts required thirteen stitches to close, but he was otherwise unhurt.

With the Helmsleys safely in the hospital, crime-scene specialists arrived to inspect the Helmsley penthouse for evidence. Several initial observations, however, raised more questions than they answered. There were no signs of forced entry into the apartment. And when an officer examined the front door he found that it had two locks, each of which required a separate key to open.

Detective M. Forman personally inspected the severed telephone cables. They had been crudely cut with a pliers rather than a knife. And the investigators wondered why the lines in the bedroom were the ones that were cut, rather than the cables in the living room, which were closer to the front door.

The officers stepped down the narrow hallway leading to the bedroom. They noticed a bulky golf bag along the corridor. The cops wondered how Helmsley, his wife, and a knife-wielding burglar struggled and ran down the hall in the dark without someone knocking over the cumbersome bag. The police found a second golf bag. This one was in the master bathroom. It was untouched—even though Helmsley went racing into the unlit bathroom in search of a working telephone.

In the bedroom, the police found an empty World War II canister of paralyzing gas near a nightstand. There were also several hundred metal tacks spread along the floor. The tacks apparently were poured in a semicircle around the king-size bed.

The only plausible reason for the burglar to sprinkle tacks around the bed was to prevent the Helmsleys from getting out of bed while their apartment was being robbed. If they were awakened, they presumably would step on a tack, injure their bare feet, and cry out, thereby alerting the burglar that they were awake.

But Harry and Leona had not sustained any injury to their feet during their battle with the burglar. And, more important, the floor of the Helmsleys' bedroom was not carpeted. It was tiled! Why would an intruder risk awakening his victims with the *tick-tick-tick* sound of hundreds of metal tacks striking a tiled floor?

These curiosities were the first to surround the "stabbing" in apartment A518 in the Palm Beach Towers. Detectives are taught that when there is a stabbing in a home, they should explore primary theories. The first theory is that a burglar—perhaps someone who knew the victims—broke in, found the owners at home, panicked, and attacked them. The second possibility, which occurs with equal frequency, is that a dispute between husband and wife turned violent.

The cops could not predict which turn this case was going to take. They launched an investigation to find the gas-masked female intruder with the silver streak in her hair whom the Helmsleys described. But after one hour at the "crime scene," it was apparent that the Helmsleys may have had a violent battle that nearly ended in murder. And they had hastily created a crime scene and concocted a wild story about a "gas-masked intruder" to cover up the truth; that Harry had stabbed Leona! The detectives were interested in the Helmsleys' brief, seventeen-month-old marriage.

Before Leona Mindy Rosenthal met Harry Brackman Helmsley, she was an ambitious twice-divorced mother from Brooklyn's Coney Island section, who wanted to recast herself as American royalty. She lied about her upbringing as the daughter of a Polish immigrant clothier and had changed her name from Rosenthal to Roberts. In order to climb the New York social ladder, Leona Roberts entered the tough real-estate game, angling for a chance to meet a king.

By all accounts, Leona was an exceptionally attractive woman, blessed with full lips and a fuller figure. She exercised regularly and her figure remained shapely well into her middle years. She also took special care to enhance her most appealing features. She wore rich colored lipstick to exaggerate her mouth and she always chose dresses with plunging necklines to show off her ample bosom.

Leona was also extremely shrewd. According to Helmsley biographer Ransdell Pierson, author of *The Queen of Mean*, Leona studied Harry Helmsley for years and chose her moment carefully before approaching him. She learned that, next to real estate, Harry's only other passion was dancing. But dancing was an avocation Helmsley rarely had the opportunity to enjoy.

Helmsley's wife, Eve, was a Mormon who tended to shun the glitzy parties associated with Harry's real-estate world. Eve Helmsley preferred the sanctity of the church and the quiet surroundings of her suburban ranch home in Briarcliff Manor over Harry's fast-paced world of business and finance. On rare occasions, Eve Helmsley dutifully performed her role as wife to a real-estate corporate executive and accompanied Harry to an important function. But that was not the case on April 16, 1969, when Harry attended the industry's annual Realty Foundation of New York dinner at the Waldorf-Astoria Hotel. Leona Roberts seized her opportunity.

As soon as Leona noticed Helmsley alone across the ballroom floor, she dumped her dining companions. Without so much as a word, Leona got up from her seat and marched across the room to Helmsley. "There goes the Leona ship. It's sailing," one of her jilted tablemates remarked.

She walked up to Helmsley, introduced herself, and quickly asked Harry for a dance. Helmsley accepted, almost gleefully. As they danced to the sounds of the Mark Towers Orchestra, Harry could not help but notice Leona's heaving bosom. She had carefully chosen her well-preserved Ceil Chapman gown for the occasion, the one with the most revealing neckline.

Although Harry Helmsley had a staid manner, he actually had the stamina of men half his age. When his wife permitted, Harry remained on the dance floor until the last song was played, well past midnight.

Not surprisingly, Leona kept Helmsley whirling for hours. By the final waltz at 1:30 A.M., Leona Roberts had not only met Harry Helmsley, but she now had a job with Helmsley Spear, Inc., complete with her own office and a secretary. And before she converted her first building into a cooperative for her new boss, Leona Roberts and Harry Helmsley were having a torrid affair. According to Pierson, the couple dined by day in French restaurants, such as Georges Rey. After lunch, they would retire to Helmsley's office for midday lovemaking sessions. One employee said he actually walked in on the seminaked couple as they were passionately intertwined across Helmsley's majestic desk.

In the evenings, their adulterous liaison shifted indoors to the Gallery House at 77 West 55th Street, where Leona had moved into a modest penthouse. The apartment was decorated in a casual style, with bohemian curtains of blue and green glass beads separating the dining room from the living room and white and blue Chinese rugs scattered on buffed hardwood floors. The illicit affair lasted for months before an unrepentant Harry Helmsley revealed his secret life with Leona to his faithful wife. Eve Helmsley promptly divorced Harry in the fall of 1971, after thirty-seven years of marriage.

The divorce, however, was not a guarantee that Helmsley would marry again. To help him make up his mind, the impatient Leona devised a scheme to "trick" her reluctant Harry into a proposal. With the help of her sister, Leona fabricated a romance between herself and a mysterious suitor from Georgia. For several months, Leona's sister sent boxes of flowers from her home in Atlanta to Leona's apartment in New York. Each bouquet was accompanied by a passionate note of undying love and affection from Leona's devoted "suitor." Finally Leona's beau purchased a diamond engagement ring and proposed marriage. Leona showed the ring to Harry and said that her suitor had given her ten days to answer.

Although the ring, like the romantic suitor, was a fake, Harry Helmsley—man of great business acumen, king of the dealmakers—fell for the ploy. He even mentioned his dilemma to Eve, saying that he had seen "the letter and the diamond."

"I have only ten days to decide," the worried billionaire said. His ex-wife Eve was incredulous. She told a close friend: "Can you believe this man believes this hogwash!"

Rather than risk losing the fifty-one-year-old Leona, the sixty-two-year-old billionaire rushed to her side and proposed marriage. The ceremony took place on April 8, 1972, in their penthouse in the Park Lane Hotel. The couple then repaired to the Pierre Hotel for a small ballroom reception. Shortly after their marriage, Harry Helmsley coincidentally announced his plans to convert the Palm Beach Towers into condominiums. At the time, apartment conversion was a novel business concept. And because it was a relatively untested process Helmsley decided to mix business with pleasure during Thanksgiving 1973 and visit Palm Beach. The trip offered him an opportunity to enjoy the sun and yet be available in case problems arose during the course of convincing tenants to purchase their rental apartments.

It was somehow fitting that Helmsley, a great real-estate developer, owned the Towers, which stands on the site of Henry Morrison Flagler's original Royal Poinciana Hotel. The Towers, which was built as a hotel in 1957, also adjoins Flagler's Whitehall mansion, the grand marble home Flagler built in 1901 for Mary Lily Kenan, his mistress and third wife. The complex also abuts the Royal Poinciana Plaza, a strip of small, expensive stores that, nineteen years later, would become world famous, thanks to a nightclub called Au Bar and the carousing of Senator Ted Kennedy and his nephew William Kennedy Smith. When Helmsley converted the Towers into condominiums in 1972, he was putting his own imprint on Palm Beach.

With parcels of buildable sites at a minimum, Helmsley's conversion was a novel way for a new generation of pleasure seekers and investors to partake in another Florida real-estate boom. In just a few years, several condominium complexes were built on Palm Beach, especially along the ocean a few miles south of Mar-a-Lago. Some Palm Beach residents dubbed the stretch of condo towers "Hebrew Hills" because the units were purchased primarily by second-generation American Jews who took to Palm Beach the same way an earlier wave of American Jews had flocked to Miami Beach in the 1950s.

In 1973, Helmsley had accurately predicted that the process of transforming rental apartments into tenant-owned "homes" would sweep the nation. The tall, silver-haired billionaire developer from the Big Apple was the man behind the vision. He perceived conversion as a vehicle to reap enormous profits with only a minimum investment. He had previously found other low-risk techniques to finance acquisitions of skyscrapers and hotels, such as the Empire State Building, the jewel of Manhattan's skyline, and the Plaza, the stately hotel at the southeast corner of Central Park.

But Helmsley had another reason for venturing aggressively into the condominium conversion business in New York and in Palm Beach. His new bride, Leona, fancied herself the undisputed queen of conversion. By 1973, Leona Helmsley had made a name for herself by successfully converting prime rental apartment buildings in Manhattan, such as the Park Cinq near the Plaza on Fifth Avenue. Her desire to turn New York City's luxury rental market into a sea of privately owned apartments was legend in real-estate circles.

And so was her compulsion to "do whatever it takes" to reach that end, including using terror tactics to coerce reluctant tenants, often elderly and frail, to join the plan. Pierson reported that Leona once chose the sacred evening of Passover to harass a Jewish family who did not want to buy. Leona had been pestering Penny and Leon Kachurin for months, threatening to barge in on them and show their home to prospective buyers at any time, day or night, without warning. On that Passover evening, the Kachurins and thirteen of their children and grandchildren were gathered around the dining-room table celebrating the holiday.

Suddenly, their seder was interrupted by a pounding at their door. It was Leona. "We want to show the apartment!" she bellowed.

A startled Penny Kachurin shouted back, "You want to see my apartment, make an appointment."

After several harrowing minutes, Leona marched off. But she had ruined the family's holiday.

When Leona married Helmsley, he was a business titan who prided himself on making instinctual decisions, without needing the approval of others. He also was a vigorous man who traveled in his own circle of friends. But once Leona married her Harry, his new bride quickly began to cut him off from his friends.

By the time they arrived in Palm Beach for Thanksgiving, 1973, Leona was smothering Helmsley with affection and, at the same time, restricting his movements unless she was consulted and gave her approval. The once vibrant and independent billionaire was being increasingly controlled by Leona. A number of Harry's friends complained to him that they could not get around Leona to speak with him alone.

Leona even "pushed aside" Helmsley's partner, Larry Wein, the tycoon credited with making Helmsley a billionaire. Wein was the brilliant tax attorney who created a complex acquisitions formula that enabled Helmsley to make huge real-estate deals with minimum tax liability. Wein's formula—now standard practice—was used by Helmsley and himself in the purchase of the Empire State Building and the Graybar Building that adjoins Grand Central Station. But Leona roundly criticized Wein and his wife and drove them away from "her Harry."

Instead of rebuking his wife, Harry patiently contained his annoyance and frustration. He remained, at Leona's insistence, with her by the pool—listening to her ideas about how to expand "their" empire. Acquaintances said Harry finally began to resent Leona's undisguised meddling in his real-estate empire.

And worse still, Leona abused his friends in public, speaking "down to them like 'Who are they to talk to me and Harry,'" an insider said. "These were extremely influential and powerful people in his circle of business and social contacts." Harry was being humiliated by her increasingly imperious manner.

During the 1973 Thanksgiving week in Palm Beach, the Helmsleys spent their afternoons swimming laps in the Towers' rooftop pool or barbecuing on their 120-foot-long wraparound deck overlooking Lake

Worth. At one end of the deck, Harry had an authentic captain's wheel that he proudly showed off to guests.

In the evenings, the Helmsleys also were seen dining and dancing at that season's popular nightspots and restaurants, such as Ta-boo. In New York, the then sixty-four-year-old Helmsley and his fifty-three-year-old bride always danced till closing time, staring into each other's eyes like lovestruck teenagers. But that was not the case the night Leona's blood gushed all over the couple's king-size bed in Palm Beach.

Rumors abound that they had had a public row at a dinner party. The story says Leona verbally abused a former governor of Florida when he talked to her husband. The rumors, however, remain just that. But the fact that a knife—rather than a handgun—was used that November night in the Helmsley's Palm Beach penthouse raised the most interesting question of all.

Police investigators know that burglars rarely, if ever, use knives when they commit household break-ins. Knives are considered extremely unreliable and risky weapons. If a potential victim resists and puts up a struggle, a knife involves close physical contact and requires a great deal of strength to plunge into a body. Their violent use in a home is generally the result of a crime of passion, often between the homeowners.

Guns, on the other hand, are the weapons of choice for criminals. They provide a safe distance and are extremely impersonal. They also require only a simple trigger squeeze to dispatch a victim.

The police launched a thorough search of the Towers for the knife. They checked the hallways and stairwells, from roof to the basement. They also combed the grounds, but no knife was found.

But the officers did locate a pair of cutting pliers in a small tool kit in the bathroom off the Helmsleys' bedroom. Detective Forman inspected the cut phone and cable lines and noticed they were "compressed slightly" as if they had been jiggled back and forth until breaking rather than severed cleanly with a knife. The officers believed the pliers could have made the cut.

At five A.M., nearly four hours after Harry and Leona were taken together to the hospital, Harry Helmsley returned to his penthouse. The cops were eager to ask more questions. Harry remained close to his original account. But this time he added new details that pointed toward a specific suspect.

Harry now said that he had a better look at the burglar than he originally thought. The burglar's hair, he said, was "reddish or reddish blond." Furthermore, the intruder was attired in a "white dress, like a maid wears." In fact, Harry Helmsley said, this burglar was a black woman who "reminded him of a maid that recently worked for him." He said her name was Chi Chi.

Harry said Chi Chi had abruptly quit his employ about a month before. And, he told detectives, she had left an angry and rambling note behind. Harry could not remember the details of the letter. He had read it and thrown it into the garbage. But he said Chi Chi was definitely angry with them. Perhaps she was the burglar, seeking revenge.

In many ways, Harry Helmsley had provided the police with an "airtight" case—a maid and a motive. But they wanted to speak with Leona, to see if her memory had cleared, before they did anything else. She was still in serious condition with an inch-and-a-half stab wound. The knife had punctured her left breast and had missed her heart by just inches. Her physicians said she remained too badly wounded to answer questions.

At 11:02 A.M., a security guard at the Towers reported finding a knife with an eight-inch blade on the property. Richard Michaud, a member of the Palm Beach Merchant Police, a private security patrol hired by the Towers and other apartment complexes, said he had found the weapon near an eight-foot seawall off a footpath just fourteen feet south of the Towers property line. Michaud suggested the burglar perhaps had dropped it there while escaping.

Gazing up from the path, the detectives discovered the knife could have been thrown there from the Helmsley balcony. Also this knife was not just a petty thief's switchblade or serrated knife. Rather, it was a black-handled carving knife manufactured by Sabatier, the top-line French cutlery manufacturer. It cost about fifty dollars. Several investigators went to the Helmsley kitchen to check the utensils. They found a drawer filled with Sabatier knives that matched the one found on the path.

Adding this new evidence to an already unusual list of information, the detectives were asked to believe the following scenario: a gas-masked female intruder—armed only with a box of tacks—slipped through heavy condominium security, opened a double-locked door without using force and then borrowed a knife from a kitchen drawer to cut phone lines and rob the apartment. All this while the Helmsleys were asleep.

Detective Forman and Officer Cypher returned to Good Samaritan's surgical intensive care unit at one P.M. to reinterview Leona. Leona, with tubes in her nose and intravenous lines feeding into her veins, said her recollection now was much clearer. She even thought she knew her assailant.

"I woke up screaming and heard the [burglar] saying 'all right I'm going, leave me alone.' She was black, wearing a kind of mask, a 'World War Gas Mask' with big eyes."

Despite the burglar's fish-eyed mask, Leona volunteered that the attacker looked like "someone who worked for [me]." The cops wanted to know to whom she was referring. But Leona said she was faint, "tired and sleepy and could not continue."

As soon as the two men left Leona's bedside, Harry hired private bodyguards and posted them round the clock outside his wife's hospital-room door. The first security guard to stand watch for Leona was Richard Michaud. The once-eager-to-please Michaud now firmly told investigators Mrs. Helmsley would be willing to speak to them "as the occasion arose."

After talking to the witness-turned-bodyguard, cops decided to look for Chi Chi, the alleged vengeance-seeking ex-maid. They found her living on North Jay Street in nearby Lake Worth. Detective Forman and Detective Woods confronted the woman Harry Helmsley wanted them to see as the prime suspect. She was hardly the portrait of a burglar who could not be restrained by the two Helmsleys.

Mrs. Helene "Chi Chi" Kennedy was a plump, sixty-one-year-old woman. She weighed 145 pounds and stood just five-foot-three—a full twelve inches shorter than the towering Harry Helmsley. Mrs. Kennedy invited the police into her modest home and answered their questions for an hour.

She explained that she had worked for the Helmsleys for ten months from December 1972 to October 1973. She said she had been planning to retire when she overheard the Helmsleys saying they were unhappy with her. She admitted leaving a note, but she said it was a harmless good-bye note that simply explained her departure. It was not, as Harry had insisted, a rambling message filled with threats.

And did she have an alibi?

"Detroit," Mrs. Kennedy answered matter-of-factly.

Mrs. Kennedy said she and her husband, Patrick, had flown there in early November and spent most of the month in Detroit trying to sell some property she owned.

The couple also bought a used pickup truck, which they had driven home to Lake Worth. She then handed police a stack of real-estate and motor-vehicle records that proved her statements. She said she and her husband had completed the fifteen-hundred-mile trip at about ten P.M. Saturday, a few hours before the Helmsleys had been attacked.

Mrs. Kennedy had never left the house that night. She was exhausted from two days of driving. Her husband, she said, visited the nearby Blue Marlin, said hello to friends, had a quick beer, and came back within fifteen minutes. That, too, she said, could be verified.

There was one more thing to clear up. The Kennedys had left their home in charge of a friend, Steve Birch, who they said had been out when they arrived home, but later showed up drunk at eleven P.M. and went to bed. Patrick Kennedy and Steve Birch had once done maintenance work on the Helmsleys' patio. The detective' antennae went up for a moment. Then they learned that the Kennedys' friend, Steve Birch, was a white man. Both Harry and Leona Helmsley had described the suspect as a black woman.

The cops thanked Chi Chi, crossed her name off their list of potential suspects, and prepared to leave. But first the officers asked Chi Chi if she knew anything that might help the investigation. Chi Chi Kennedy said yes.

She said Leona Helmsley had a drinking problem! How severe the problem was, Mrs. Kennedy did not explain. For years, Leona was known to have enjoyed a couple of Absolut vodkas with friends. But Mrs. Kennedy was the first person to publicly suggest it was more than occasional cocktails.

And then Mrs. Kennedy said something only a person living behind the Helmsleys' closed doors could know. She said Leona and Harry argued often. She explained that the Helmsleys, although virtual newlyweds, had not been on pleasant terms. In fact, the former maid told police the Helmsley arguments sometimes became extremely intense shouting matches.

Did Harry and Leona ever come to blows? the cops asked. If they did, it wasn't in front of her, Mrs. Kennedy replied. The officers left Mrs. Kennedy's home and never returned. They drove back to the Towers, where they were met by Hank Boettcher, the building maintenance supervisor at the Palm Beach Towers and a former New York City police officer.

Boettcher also volunteered his doubts about the Helmsleys' story. He spoke with Detective Forman at the Helmsleys' fifth-floor penthouse. Without even being asked for his opinion, he said the Helmsleys were covering up what really happened. Boettcher insisted only Mr. and Mrs. Helmsley were in the apartment that night.

"It just did not look right," Boettcher said. "There were too many little things that didn't add up. If I was going to burglarize a place I wouldn't go to all that trouble. I'd just hit and run."

"There were some problems between them. She's a piranha," the ex-cop and former Helmsley employee said. "It would be unlike Harry, but everybody has their point of stress."

The cops didn't need Mr. Boettcher's unofficial sleuthing; they had theories of their own. And they found it nearly impossible to believe that an unarmed, gas-masked burglar had invaded the Helmsley penthouse, with only a can of tacks to sprinkle around their bed for defense.

Further interviews with the Towers' security force and a thorough scrutiny of the guest log at the condo entrance turned up absolutely no evidence of a wild-eyed, weirdly dressed black woman sneaking in or out.

One thing is certain: No one close to the Helmsleys believed their fantastic tale, including Leona's late son, Jay Panzirer. He had a theory about how Leona came to be the dominant, overbearing force in the Helmsley dynasty.

"Jay said that Harry stabbed her and that Leona always held it over him and used it to gain power over him," said Jay's widow, Mimi Panzirer. "He thought Harry stabbed her and he said it to a number of people."

"[Jay's opinion] was no secret," she continued. "Jay was very open about it when it came up at parties or dinner. Jay talked about it by the pool, at dinner parties whenever the subject came up. He was always saying Harry stabbed Leona.

"Jay was his mother's son and knew her as well as anyone," Mimi continued. "He used to say living with Leona would drive anyone over the edge.

"Let's face it! Where does someone get a 1940 gas mask in downtown Palm Beach? Do you call Khadafy and ask for a leftover? It was not even a good lie."

But the private detective hired by the Helmsleys to find the burglar stood by their account. "I know the police thought the Helmsleys made it up," said Jack Harwood, one of Palm Beach County's best-known private investigators. "But there is no question that there was a burglar. None. Using tacks was an old burglar's trick and the knife was found far enough away that only Joe Namath could have tossed it there. Anybody who thinks the Helmsleys had a fight and put tacks around their bed and staged it themselves is crazy."

Then who was the burglar?

"Someone who used to work for them. I know who, but I couldn't prove it," Harwood said. He declined repeatedly to identify his suspect.

During the entire 1973 winter season in Palm Beach, however, Detective Forman checked out every person who worked for the Helmsleys and ran down every license plate spotted near the Towers the night of the stabbing. The cops went so far as to ask law-enforcement agencies from Palm Beach to Virginia Beach whether they had any cases with similarities to the strange events surrounding apartment A518. It was all to no avail.

Safely back in New York, Leona's stock began to rise in the Helmsley empire. Suddenly she emerged as a real player in her husband's business. She was on her way to becoming the queen she dreamed of years before in Coney Island. And the real story behind the stab wound a few inches from her heart was the billion-dollar insurance policy that guaranteed she would never, ever be stopped.

On February 13, 1974, less than three months after the stabbing, Detective Forman reviewed the entire case file with prosecutor Joseph Tringali from the Palm Beach County State Attorney's Office. They determined that unless he suddenly confessed to the crime they were at a loss to prove that Harry stabbed Leona. Even the police laboratory tests of the weapon and the other evidence proved inconclusive.

In a final notation to the file, Detective Forman wrote: "Any charge based on an internal or personal conflict between husband [and] wife would not be entertained or pursued" unless Leona or Harry told the real story.

Harry's secret was safely buried in Palm Beach.

In 1986, the Helmsleys were charged with evading millions of dollars in taxes and faced four years in jail, thanks primarily to Leona's imperious belief that "only the little people pay taxes."

Before they stood trial, Leona—and the Helmsleys' high-priced lawyers—scored yet another victory for the hotel queen. With Leona's blessing, a federal court judge declared Harry incompetent and too feeble to stand trial. The judge ruled that he was unable to participate in his own defense or manage his affairs.

In a single decision, the judge accomplished what Leona had not so secretly strived for during her entire life with Harry: she was made titular head of Harry Helmsley's $8 billion empire.

Following a highly publicized summer trial that was closely watched by the "little people," Leona Helmsley was convicted on August 30, 1989, of underpaying federal income taxes by $1.2 million. She was sentenced to a four-year prison term. Expressing no remorse, Leona posted $25 million bail and hired Alan Dershowitz, the attorney who had earned national attention for successfully defending another unlikable millionaire, Claus Von Bulow, an accused murderer. Dershowitz filed several appeals, scoring only minor victories.

Finally the U.S. Supreme Court refused to hear the case, sending Leona before Manhattan Federal Court Judge Thomas P. Griesa. Dershowitz argued that sending Leona to prison would be tantamount to a death sentence for her and her husband. He maintained she could better serve the public by performing community service. Judge Griesa was unmoved and suggested clearly to Dershowitz that Leona should prepare for imprisonment.

In March 1992, Leona appeared again before Griesa, pleading that her beloved and ailing eighty-three-year-old husband could not live without her care. But Griesa upheld her original four-year term and set April 15—tax deadline day—as the date for Leona's surrender to federal prison officials.

Hit hard by the judge's ruling, Leona left the imposing courthouse in a daze and was escorted by Dershowitz and Romolo Imundi, the United States marshal for the Southern District. Fighting her way through a crush of reporters, television correspondents, and hundreds of photographers and cameras, Leona's legs gave out on the bottom steps, as she neared her waiting limousine. Only Marshal Imundi's firm hand kept Leona Helmsley from falling to the pavement. She was taken to New York Hospital and admitted into intensive care as a precaution. Physicians said Leona suffered from high blood pressure and an arrhythmic heart beat.

The following Saturday, she left her room in the cardiac care unit at 10:45 A.M. and was released from New York Hospital. She had not suffered a heart attack.

On Tuesday, April 14, 1992, her attorneys announced that Leona had received death threats from the Aryan Brotherhood, a neo-Nazi organization, claiming she would be killed in prison. The lawyers also said Helmsley would be willing to donate several skyscrapers and hotels to house the homeless if she were not imprisoned. The judge declined the offer.

Later that night, Leona Helmsley boarded her private Boeing 727 jet in New York and flew to Louisville, Kentucky, avoiding the press awaiting her arrival at Lexington airport near the Federal Medical Center. Accompanied by her niece, Frances Becker; her doctor, R. A.

Rees Pritchet, and bodyguard Edward Brady, Leona was driven eighty miles east in a limousine to the barbed-wire gate of the federal compound.

At precisely 4:15 A.M. on tax day, Wednesday, April 15, 1992, Leona Helmsley, the hotel queen who vowed that none of her guests would ever be treated like a number, surrendered to prison matrons at the eighty-five-bed facility and officially became number 15113-054.

"She was carrying only an overnight bag with the few items she was allowed to bring inside, including shoes, underclothing, and a coat," a Helmsley public-relations aide said.

Later that night, Harry turned out the lights on his Empire State Building and his gold-leafed Helmsley Palace, a glittering illuminated showpiece that straddles Park Avenue near 46th Street. The lights and beacons were dimmed "as a symbolic gesture," a spokesman said.

In May 1992, Leona Helmsley was transferred to a minimum-security penitentiary in Danbury, Connecticut, about sixty miles from her Dunellen Hall estate, and one hundred miles from the Helmsley Palace, where she once was proclaimed "queen." In September Leona was ousted as sole ruler of her Palace, but employees say Leona continues to run the rest of the $8 billion empire by telephone—from the federal prison in Danbury.

17

Naked in Babylon: Brownie McLean and Larry Flynt

T he 1970s spelled troubling times for Palm Beach as development and "progress" continued to change the face of the island. Wonderful old Mizner mansions that had fallen into irreversible disrepair were razed. The Breakers Hotel announced it was demolishing its lovely three-story shingled "cottages" next door to make way for four modern apartment complexes. The new structure would have little of the charm of the old one, but it would be able to accommodate more people and contain more amenities.

At the same time, the historic Shorwinds Hotel, designed by Frank Lloyd Wright, was leveled to make way for condominiums. And the glorious Paramount Theatre, once the home of star-studded movie premieres, was razed. In its place developers built a shopping center. As the new projects went forward, builders showed no hesitation in chopping down historic trees, many of them rare one-of-a-kind specimens. This became such a problem that the town hastily passed an ordinance that threatened heavy fines and jail time for indiscriminate tree cutters.

One of the most jarring incidents of this period, however, was not the introduction of a new project, but of a new resident. His name was Larry Flynt. In some ways, Flynt had the business acumen of other wealthy residents of Palm Beach. He was a self-made millionaire, a publisher whose company brought in higher profits year after year. But Larry Flynt's success was not the right kind for Palm Beach. He was the publisher of *Hustler,* a pornographic men's magazine.

Even worse, Flynt's arrival on the island in 1976 came about through popular socialite and island darling Mildred "Brownie" McLean. Brownie rented her magnificent Addison Mizner–designed estate, El Salano, at 720 South Ocean Boulevard, to the self-styled king of sleaze. It was bad enough that the outspoken, 250-pound Flynt was going to live there. But islanders soon discovered the porn czar had outrageous plans in mind for Brownie's genteel property.

In 1976, Jimmy Carter was in the White House, disco music was at its peak, and *Hustler,* the raunchy Columbus, Ohio–based sex magazine, was pushing the limits of what mass-market adult magazines could do. One infamous issue featured nude women amputees. In another, elderly women showed off their bodies, wrinkles and all. These weren't tasteful, airbrushed nudes such as those in *Playboy. Hustler's* photos always gave the reader full-color, gynecological views of its models.

As the red-haired, green-eyed publisher explained proudly: "Good taste is taboo with *Hustler.* Where *Playboy* might tiptoe around bad taste, we go marching through in combat boots." He added that *Hustler's* motto was: "The magazine nobody quotes."

So it was quite a shock when the *Palm Beach Post* ran a front-page story in June of 1976 revealing that Brownie McLean, one of the grande dames of Palm Beach society, had quietly rented her estate to Flynt. El Salano remains one of Addison Mizner's most striking architectural feats. Built in 1919, it combined medieval, Mediterranean, Spanish, and Italian designs. It features two swimming pools, seven bedrooms, five servant's rooms and 150 feet of beachfront property.

Brownie leased the property to Flynt for two years. With her seemingly thoughtless move, she had taken the first step in turning South Ocean Boulevard into Florida's version of 42nd Street. Renting the property to Flynt might have been expected of a second- or third-generation family member or an unsuitable newcomer, but Brownie McLean?

The fifty-three-year-old, blond-haired Brownie was the widow of Colorado mining millionaire John R. "Jock" McLean. His family had once owned the *Washington Post* and the world-famous Hope Diamond.

When they married in 1951, Jock had offered Brownie the legendary jewel as a wedding gift. But she had turned down the priceless gem because it had brought misery and death to whoever possessed it. "I get bad vibrations from it. My skin is crawling right now just talking about it," she once told a reporter.

Jock and Brownie had been the social darlings of Palm Beach for years. Brownie was a master party giver and organizer, putting her heart and soul into the growing number of charity balls Palm Beach held each year.

It all seemed so easy for Brownie, but then she was used to being in the spotlight. Originally from Virginia, Brownie had been orphaned at age twelve when her parents were killed in an accident. "I had wanted to be a lawyer," she said, "but when I lost my parents, I figured I couldn't make it. . . . My family was wiped out and I had to be realistic."

Six years later, at the age of eighteen, she set out for New York determined to be an actress, enrolled in acting school, and rented an apartment with a girlfriend on Manhattan's Sutton Place. She took a job as a cigarette girl at the Versailles nightclub.

"In those days every schoolgirl wanted to be a Powers and Conover model," she explained, "so I decided to give it a try." She was signed with Conover and became one of the most photographed fashion models of the 1940s, her most remembered ads produced for Lucky Strike cigarettes and Jantzen bathing suits.

In 1946, she married millionaire George Schrafft, a playboy race-car driver and speedboat racer and the man who brought her to Palm Beach. Two years later, Brownie gave birth to a baby girl and begged George to abandon his dangerous sports for the sake of their new infant. He wouldn't, the marriage soured, and the couple divorced a year later.

Brownie made a big impression on Jock McLean, who proposed to her a few months after they had met at a Palm Beach social function. Anybody who thought Brownie was going to be just another bored young housewife sitting around her husband's estate spending money was wrong. She threw herself into the Palm Beach scene with a vengeance—giving parties, organizing charity events, getting the wives of her rich neighbors involved. She soon became a staple on the cover of the *Palm Beach Daily News*, the society daily nicknamed "the Shiny Sheet" because it is published on high-quality paper.

To the elite, Brownie was special. She had once said about herself, "I'm a combination of homeloving and partyloving." Everybody remembered her novel and refreshing platform when she decided to run for mayor against Earl E. T. Smith in 1971. She had promised champagne would be served at Palm Beach Town Council meetings and pledged fresh flowers would be brought into the city jail each day to cheer up the prisoners.

In July 1975, Jock died of cancer at age fifty-nine. The grieving Brownie left the house, traveling around the world with her French poodle, Maximilian. Mansions such as El Salano needed constant attention. Just like most other Palm Beach estates, even a few months of neglect could prove harmful. With Brownie absent, El Salano took on a kind of *Sunset Boulevard* look of faded elegance. Brownie knew in order to keep the mansion from becoming a white elephant, she would have to rent it or sell it.

But to Larry Flynt? So what if this thirty-two-year-old "publisher" was a self-made millionaire with a beautiful wife? So what if he could afford it?

Flynt had come to Palm Beach from a completely different galaxy. Born in the ultraconservative Kentucky county of Magoffin, Flynt was very familiar with the fire-and-brimstone preachers who regularly traveled through his middle-American community espousing the credo that "sexuality equals sin." He was impressed by the slick salesmanship of these traveling, circus-tent preachers who often blew through town.

Flynt told friends he would either become an evangelist or a gynecologist. He was bored in Magoffin. To escape his hometown where "the biggest industry was jury duty," he lied about his age to join the armed forces and served in both the army and navy. A civilian again in the mid-1960s, Flynt embraced the salesmanship of a traveling preacher, but not his message. He opened a go-go-dancing strip joint near Columbus, Ohio.

The place proved so successful that he expanded the venture in various cities across the state. He called them Hustler Clubs. Flynt began a club newsletter that eventually turned into *Hustler* magazine. His mission was to deliver a sexually explicit, controversial magazine with extremely graphic photos, cartoons such as "Chester the Molester," and articles Middle America would find grossly offensive—and to make money. His gamble paid off. By the mid-1970s, the five-times-married Flynt collected $30 million a year from his porn businesses.

Could Flynt live in Palm Beach quietly and without fanfare, Palm Beach society wondered after the initial shock of his arrival had worn off. It got the answer to its question as soon as the new issue of *Hustler* appeared.

Inside was an eight-page pictorial of "Torrid Tina." The near-telescopic, spread-eagle shots of the big-breasted Tina were sleazy enough. But the tropical settings she posed against looked familiar. Why, it was the McLean estate! Larry Flynt had turned El Salano, which once had hosted Palm Beach's brightest parties, into a porno photo studio.

The McLean home as well as a dozen other Palm Beach estates that Flynt declined to name were the perfect settings in which to photograph his nude, oiled-up models. On any given day, a half-dozen of his girls would be sitting at poolside completely nude.

"In most of our girl features," Flynt explained with a boyish grin, "you see nice suntans but no bikini marks. The girls live at the house and get their suntans there, and we let them lie out in the sun a week before photographing them."

He also admitted, somewhat proudly, that he had no intentions of trying to make an entrance into Palm Beach society. "I'm not here because I'm looking to get accepted by a group of pompous, unimportant people. The last thing I want to do is change my image. You know these people are so conservative down here that they gag on a gnat and swallow an alligator."

Soon, rumors circulated that kinky sex orgies were being held nightly at the estate. The promiscuous young models, the rumors went, were having sex with nearly every man—or woman—who walked into the place. Flynt and his associates vehemently denied that the mansion was being used for anything more than a legitimate business operation.

One of the angriest residents was then Mayor Earl E. T. Smith. "I think something like that in the middle of Palm Beach is the kind of thing we don't want to happen. This is not a hippie town," Smith rumbled. But he ackowledged sadly, "As far as I know there are no laws against taking pictures of naked women."

The mayor remembered El Salano in its heyday. He recalled a major party of Brownie's that had taken place there in 1972. Some six hundred Palm Beach society figures had gathered to honor Betty Betz McMahon, general chairman of the St. Mary's Hospital Benefit and the wife of Canadian industrialist Frank McMahon.. Men in tuxedos and their wives in breathtaking, sequined evening gowns had sipped Dom Perignon champagne and danced through the night. Most of the isle's biggest names had been there, including Douglas Fairbanks, Jr., Joseph and Estee Lauder, Nicholas Du Pont and his wife, and the von Furstenbergs. Yes, it had been a glorious evening in Palm Beach's social history for Addison Mizner's beautiful El Salano.

Smith may have had another reason for appearing so indignant. Prominent Palm Beach residents began to march into his office with copies of *Hustler* in brown paper bags and slamming them down on his desk.

At Palm Beach's top magazine store, Main Street News, a clerk explained, "People got curious when [Flynt] rented the place. We sold an enormous amount of *Hustlers*. Every little old lady in town bought it."

Smith asked all newsstands in town to stop carrying *Hustler* and they complied. Flynt instantly labeled the mayor a "twerp," but then tipped his hat to him. While *Hustler's* sales in Palm Beach ended, he said, sales in neighboring West Palm Beach had increased tenfold thanks to Smith's "indignation."

"I can't be intimidated," Flynt said. "It's my world and everybody else lives in it. I have nothing in common with the Earl E. T. Smiths of the world, but there are a lot of them. The Earl E. T. Smiths of the world always play into my hands."

Anyway, Flynt reasoned, Smith, the former U.S. ambassador to Cuba, was something of a hypocrite with his conservative, holier-than-thou comments. To begin with, the seventy-three-year-old mayor had a lovely new thirty-nine-year-old wife whom he enjoyed showing off in public. Smith, Flynt noted, also had a horrendous driving record in Palm Beach. He was always being stopped by the police. And just how important was Smith's position, anyway, Flynt wanted to know. Hadn't it averaged out that Smith, in his mayoral campaign, had paid more than six dollars a vote to get elected to a position that had no real power and no salary?

Smith and Flynt could argue as much as they wished, but Brownie eventually became the critics' main target. Just how had Flynt rented her house? According to Brownie, she had been flimflammed.

"I was in London and there were several people bidding on the house. I told my lawyer to take the best one," the red-faced society matron explained in a statement.

Her lawyer, John Hope, said the highest bidder turned out to be the "H & F Realty Company" of Columbus, Ohio. He said he didn't find out until after the lease was signed that H & F stood for "Hustler and Flynt." An apologetic Brownie sent her regrets to her angry friends, but there was little else she could do. "I am sorry it is happening the way it is....Some people seem to get excited about it," she said in a memorable understatement.

She said she had been traveling a great deal since her husband had died a year earlier. The house was too big for her to live in by herself and with her memories. She had not paid enough attention to the matter. Brownie also argued that if Flynt had not rented her home, he would have found another.

For some, Brownie suddenly became the wronged woman. A widow in mourning who had been taken advantage of. But Brownie seemed to be talking from both sides of her mouth. While apologizing to her neighbors, she gave a more sobering statement to the *New York Times,* telling a reporter she had no real regrets.

"I'm delighted with the money," she said. "I got exactly what I was asking [$120,000] and if it wasn't me [Flynt had chosen to rent from], it would be someone else. So far as I know, they're doing nothing wrong. I imagine they're skinny-dipping in the pool a lot, but it's walled... it's as private as a bathroom and no one would expect you to take a bath with your clothes on."

Pausing for a moment, she added: "If you scratched around, you'd find a lot more provocative situations here." That may have been a gross understatement.

The town started looking into legal ways of ejecting Flynt. Had he violated any laws? It did not seem so. A clause in the rental lease prohibited any commercial photography on the estate, but that was a potential court battle that could take years to resolve.

A year later, in July 1977, as Palm Beach vs. the Porno King raged on, Flynt suddenly announced he was leaving Florida and moving his graphic photo sessions to Los Angeles. "New York and Los Angeles are more or less the flesh centers of the world," he said in explaining his decision.

All in all, how did Flynt rate Palm Beach?

"We've done a lot better job of staying out of other persons' ways than they have in staying out of ours. I never was invited to any of their parties, but I never missed any of it either. I doubt if they'll miss me."

Then Flynt added a chilling thought. "Maybe if they ever get the Post estate, Mar-a-Lago, untangled, I could come back and buy it."

Brownie moved back into the mansion a few months later and assured her bruised Palm Beach neighbors that El Salano had survived the Flynt fiasco.

"I'm amazingly pleased and surprised to see the house is in very good condition," she reported. She said that except for a pay telephone Flynt had installed in a foyer, the house was exactly the way she had left it.

Much to everybody's relief, Flynt never made good on his threat to move back to Palm Beach. His life would change forever a year later while he was being tried on obscenity charges in Georgia. A deranged gunman shot Flynt in the stomach, and the bullet hit his spinal cord. Doctors informed him he would be a wheelchair-bound paraplegic the remainder of his life. Soon thereafter he became a born-again Christian, aligning with evangelist Ruth Carter Stapleton, the sister of former President Jimmy Carter.

Flynt still maintains ownership of *Hustler.* And as long as he does, some Palm Beach residents fear, the possibility always exists that Larry Flynt will someday return.

Leona and Harry Helmsley. As soon as she married "her Harry," she restricted his movements, abused his associates and kept his friends away. In frustration, Harry erupted and allegedly stabbed her near the heart in 1973, Leona's son and police investigators believe. (Courtesy of the *New York Post*)

Hustler publisher Larry Flynt rented a landmark South Ocean Boulevard estate from cash-poor socialite Mildred "Brownie" McLean and transformed the mansion into a porno palace. (Associated Press)

John Lennon and Yoko Ono with actor Peter Boyle. The reclusive ex-Beatle hoped for a conventional evening on the town. But when the photographers descended, he blamed Boyle and they nearly came to blows. (Courtesy of the *New York Post*)

Brownie McLean, in the mid 1970s. She refused the cursed Hope Diamond as a wedding gift, but had no trouble turning her home over to "riffraff" such as Flynt and John Lennon. (Courtesy of the *New York Post*)

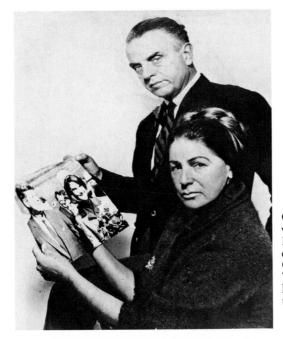

George de Mohrenschildt and his wife. Once an "uncle" to Jacqueline Bouvier Kennedy, the Russian-born college professor became Lee Harvey Oswald's closest friend. He was a "suicide" victim in 1977, hours before he was to talk to Kennedy Assassination investigators. (Associated Press)

David Kennedy, the troubled middle son of Senator Robert Kennedy. At the age of twelve and alone in a hotel room, he watched his father's murder on television in 1968. Endless nights of drugs, alcohol, and women could not erase that haunting image. In 1984, he was a drug fatality at the Brazilian Court hotel.

John and Patricia Kluge. The wife of America's richest man seemed the perfect choice to host a 1985 charity ball graced by the presence of Princess Diana and Prince Charles—until it was learned she had an X-rated past. (Courtesy of the *New York Post*)

Longtime Palm Beach resident Estee Lauder near her oceanfront mansion. Despite the cosmetics queen's prestige around the world, she experienced the cruelty of anti-Semitism at the Everglades Club.

Donald Trump, the King of Mar-a-Lago, declared war on his ex-wife Ivana and on Palm Beach society. He was blocked from sub-dividing the estate and building eight smaller mansions on the 17.7-acre spread in 1992. (Courtesy of the *New York Post*)

Wherever Donald's girlfriend, Marla Maples, goes, Donald is never far behind. "The Donald" even keeps a picture of Marla in a handsome silver frame next to his bed at Mar-a-Lago.

The new and improved Ivana. A fresh face. A new book. Sequins. But she prefers plastic ice buckets while serving guests at the mansion. (Courtesy of the *New York Post*)

Teenage Roxanne Pulitzer in 1967. Even in high school in rural Cassadaga, New York, Roxanne took center stage on the cheerleading squad. (Courtesy of the *New York Post*)

Roxanne Pulitzer stands between Kleenex heir James Kimberly and his wife, Jacqueline. Kimberly later learned that his wife was sleeping with Roxanne and her husband, Peter Pulitzer. (Courtesy of the *New York Post*)

Roxanne Pulitzer knowingly glances at her husband, Peter Pulitzer, as the publishing heir testifies during their sensational divorce trial.

James and Suki Sullivan. Born in a rough Boston neighborhood, James dreamed of becoming an influential millionaire with a gorgeous wife. He achieved both in Palm Beach. But did he commit murder to remain there?

The Kennedy mystique engulfed Brooke Shields. The teen beauty was smitten with eighteen-year-old William Kennedy Smith at a 1980 fundraising party for his Uncle Teddy's unsuccessful presidential campaign. (Courtesy of the *New York Post*)

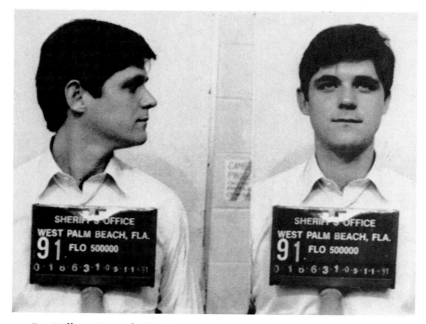

Dr. William Kennedy Smith, rape suspect, in April, 1991. The grandson of Joe Kennedy is arrested in a third-generation Kennedy scandal. (Courtesy of the *New York Post*)

Patricia Bowman. The young mother's evening at Au Bar and the Kennedy mansion ended with her accusing Smith of rape. At his December 1991 trial, she sobbed that she wanted to prevent Smith from attacking any more women.

The verdict in the William Kennedy Smith rape case was reached in seventy-seven minutes on December 11, 1991. The jury found Smith not guilty.

Count Jean de la Moussaye with his wife, Francine McMahon, heiress to a Canadian newspaper empire. McMahon claimed Roxanne Pulitzer broke up her marriage. But on the day she divorced the Count, McMahon marched down the courthouse hallway and married for a second time.

18

Rock 'n' Roll in Paradise: John Lennon and Yoko Ono

Brownie McLean's reputation as one of the grandes dames of Palm Beach had been tarnished by the Larry Flynt fiasco. But Brownie had had good reason to allow Flynt to occupy her beautiful home.

With the aging El Salano costing her in excess of $100,000 in maintenance and property taxes a year, the reputation of her tenant was less important than his ability to pay the rent. After Flynt's departure, Brownie moved back into El Salano temporarily. But she decided she no longer wanted to live there. With the death of her husband, Jock, the house evoked too many memories. So Brownie brought her next surprise to Palm Beach. John Lennon, ex-Beatle and one of the kings of rock 'n' roll.

In the 1960s, Lennon sang "Baby, You're a Rich Man." Back then he probably could not have imagined himself as one of the suntanned residents of Palm Beach. Now in 1980, more than a quarter century after the Beatles took America by storm, the thirty-nine-year-old Lennon paid $725,000 cash to buy one of the fabled pieces of real estate along South Ocean Boulevard. With its seven bedrooms, five servant rooms, nine baths, four fireplaces, ballroom, and two pools, the airy Mediterranean-style estate did not seem like the kind of place where Lennon would feel comfortable. The eccentric rock star had hated pretense and conformity. He had once screamed out to America's youth: "You say you want a revolution!"

But it was a new age. The Beatles were history. The country had lived through disco and punk rock. Paul McCartney's solo albums continued to be runaway hits while Lennon's recording career had floundered. Moreover, Lennon really loved New York. Living in the Dakota on Central Park West where *Rosemary's Baby* was filmed, the ex-Beatle preferred the anonymity of Manhattan.

But people can be seduced by visions, and within a few weeks of seeing El Salano, Lennon made a decision. Palm Beach would become the site of his dream retirement home, a place where he could spend his golden years in sunshine and comfort.

When the news spread, there was instant concern. Never before had a musician of such worldwide notoriety, let alone a rock 'n' roll star, lived in Palm Beach. Many of the big bands of the 1940s had visited Palm Beach, and the great Irish tenor Morton Downey had a long history with the island. But John Lennon?

Lennon had first come to Palm Beach in March 1979 when he rented Brownie's home for two months. New York's brutal winter was nearly over, but freezing temperatures still battered the city.

Yoko Ono, credited by many rock fans with breaking up the Beatles, decided she and John needed a respite. She asked their staff to find a spacious, private rental on the ocean in southern Florida. Palm Beach was the immediate choice for someone of Lennon's stature. Their staff sought out the perfect home. El Salano seemed to be it. The mansion was on the ocean, had plenty of privacy, and was a little weather-beaten—run down, actually—so if there was any damage done it could be repaired. A contract was signed, forty thousand dollars for two months. The man responsible for renting Brownie's mansion was real-estate dealer Ben Johnson, the husband of socialite Ancky Johnson. Lennon then invited his estranged son, Julian, sixteen, who lived in Britain, and three Japanese nieces of Yoko's to join him and Yoko and their four-year-old son, Sean.

John's nerves would quickly become frazzled. He had not seen his older son in twelve years. Julian had been born just as the Beatles became major stars. Then, in 1966, John met Japanese artist Yoko Ono and within two years began an affair with her. Julian had lived with his mother ever since. Julian also had never met his Japanese-American half-brother, Sean, and John seemed worried that they wouldn't get along.

John had confided his concern about the Palm Beach reunion to his aide, Frederic Seaman. "During the early years when the Beatles were making it big, I led a real bachelor's life—even after Cynthia and I were married," Lennon said. "I mean, I knew I had a wife and small kid at home, but I didn't want the responsibility. It's like Julian is a semi-orphan. It just boggles my mind that I have this sixteen-year-old kid now. He's into Rush, Led Zeppelin, and all these weird bands, and you know, I sometimes ask myself, 'Who is this stranger?' I have no idea what he's thinking or feeling or what he really thinks about me. I don't know any of his friends. I have no idea if he has any girlfriends. I don't even know if I should assume he's into girls."

When John and Yoko arrived at Palm Beach International Airport in early March, he was instantly impressed by the sunshine and clear blue skies. It had been months since he had been able to walk outside in just a light cotton shirt and the warm air made him feel good. Fifteen minutes later, the couple's limousine pulled into the driveway of 720 South Ocean Boulevard. John spent a half hour getting acquainted with his new quarters.

As Lennon walked though the mansion's twenty-five large, airy rooms, he tried to picture exactly how it had been some six decades earlier, brand new, at the height of the Roaring Twenties with flappers, bootleg liquor, and Al Jolson's music. The impressive oak floor, twenty-five-foot-high vaulted ceilings, and valuable antique furniture were the caring works of craftsmen long gone. He stood in the ballroom and knew that grand parties had taken place there. He was now the latest piece of history for this great dinosaur of a home.

Wearing cutoff jeans and T-shirts, the barefoot Beatle would stroll around El Salano with his guitar, strumming riffs, jotting down notes for new songs. There were no penguin-suited butlers, no frilly-dressed maids, just a similarly attired staff at his beck and call. Lennon felt at home. Still, he had not come in contact with Palm Beach society.

John's angst over Julian was well-founded. When the pale-white teenager arrived, father and son stared awkwardly at one another. The gangly teen, who had barely reached his father's thigh in height when John had last seen him, was now a beanpole nearly as tall as his dad. Everyone around father and son noticed their close resemblance.

John's staff tried to make small talk to break the ice. Finally Lennon put his arm around Julian's shoulders, gave him a hug, and offered to show him around "my new digs." Catching up on the lost years seemed so difficult. Lennon found his attention span growing short as Julian described his childhood and memories of seeing his father on the news. The conversation was stilted.

A day into their vacation, John and Julian finally discovered the one link they had to share: music. Julian also played the guitar. In one poignant moment, the pair sat in the living room one evening, quietly strumming together. They played a few duets and traded riffs and ideas. Laughter and music soon filled the room and the awkwardness that had been present seemed to vanish, at least temporarily. Some of Lennon's staff who heard the musical give and take wondered then if someday Lennon and his son would produce an album together. There was no doubt that by the end of the retreat, Julian seemed to have picked up some of Lennon's verve. When Julian later released his debut album, *Valotte*, his songs and vocals sounded eerily like John's.

Julian and Sean hit it off right away. Sean had many toys and games and urged his half-brother to play with him every morning after breakfast. Julian was only too happy to oblige. He seemed to relate to Sean more easily than to John. But the two half-brothers and their father eventually all bonded together in Palm Beach. Some of the family's brightest moments were spent at poolside, where John, Julian, and Sean would race into the pool together and splash each other furiously. As the two-month vacation drew to a close, Lennon took a solitary walk around the property one night. He was happy and at peace.

Both John and Yoko agreed they had enjoyed Brownie McLean's home. "I'd like to own a piece of Palm Beach," John told friends when he returned to New York. In late 1979, they asked Brownie's real-estate representatives if the place was for sale. Brownie had no idea what Lennon had in store for El Salano. For all anybody knew, Lennon could be the wrong choice to take over her beloved home. But with so many memories there and with the mounting upkeep, Brownie decided it was time to part with the old Mizner mansion. She agreed to sell the house.

Before John and Yoko could make a bid, however, Yoko had to have the house tested. Not by engineers. Not by termite inspectors. Not by surveyors. By a psychic.

It was a habit she had gotten into before purchasing any real estate. The routine went like this: a Lennon aide would go to the property in question and take dozens of Polaroid photos of the interiors and exteriors. The bathrooms and broom closets were as important as bedrooms and kitchen.

One of Yoko's psychics would then go into a trance, touch the photos to feel out the karma of the house. Was it a friendly house? Was it haunted by spirits? Did negative vibrations exist that would make it a bad place to live? Did she and John and Sean have the right spiritual makeup for the place? These questions had to be answered before any deal could be made.

It was a practice John detested. "John frowned upon Yoko's habit... He often complained that this was a foolish way to go about buying real estate," explained Frederic Seaman in his memoir about the couple.

He described one of Yoko's real-estate psychics, Marlene Weiner, this way: "She was a good-natured, tremendously obese woman who required a constant supply of chocolate brownies and other treats to fuel her enormous bulk. Marlene would place her hands over the photos, taking in the house's 'vibe.'" She would then inform Yoko of her feeling about the place. Deals had been made or broken this way for the Lennons.

Regardless of John's distaste for psychics, he let "Mother" have her way as he always did. He crossed his fingers and hoped that the "crystal-ballers" would okay El Salano. Luckily the estate passed Yoko's tests, and she and John purchased it in January 1980.

In February the couple flew down to celebrate Yoko's forty-seventh birthday. Fireworks were about to fly. Lennon had not yet gone out on the town in Palm Beach and was reluctant to do so for fear of overzealous fans. While El Salano's previous tenant, Larry Flynt, basked in the spotlight and encouraged publicity, Lennon hated it.

To Lennon, one of the great things about New York was that he could walk along city streets and nobody would recognize him and even if he was recognized, New Yorkers would not neccessarily approach him for an autograph. In a concentrated area of rich people like Palm Beach, everybody knew everybody else's business, and reporters and paparazzi were always on the lookout for celebrities. Every sip of alcohol, every grimace, every inflection could mean a hyped-up, sensation-fueled page-one story in the tabloids about drunkenness, infidelity, and raucous behavior. To add to that problem, the *National Enquirer* was just a half-hour drive away in nearby Lantana. That tabloid loved to print Beatles stories.

Against his better judgment, Lennon agreed to "test the waters" of his new vacation home, by going to dinner along Worth Avenue. Two of his houseguests, actor Peter Boyle and his wife, Lorraine, wanted to take the Lennons out. They insisted that the fancy French bistro, La Petite Marmite, was the only place to go. Lennon dressed for the occasion in white pants, black jacket, white shirt, dark tie, and a straw hat. Certainly not outrageous for Palm Beach, where Lilly Pulitzer's psyche-delic paisley sports coats had once been the rage.

Dinner went fine until local photographers spotted the foursome, raced up, and began to take pictures while firing questions at Lennon.

The cameramens' nonstop strobe flashes lit the place up like a disco. In moments everybody in the place was staring at John. Somebody started to hum "Yellow Submarine." Lennon was furious. He knew that within twenty-four hours the entire world would know that he and Yoko were in town.

The two couples finished dinner hastily and returned immediately to the house. Lennon was glaring at Boyle.

In his book *The Last Days of John Lennon*, Frederic Seaman recalled the explosion. Lennon screamed at the startled actor, "Always dragging us to second-rate, trendy eateries so you can get your picture taken with us, Peter? Don't you think it's a bit lame-brained?"

"What the fuck do you mean, 'lame-brained'?" Boyle, never one to mince words, snapped back.

"Well, Peter, I just mean dumb. Don't you think it might be just a little bit stupid?" Lennon continued.

"Don't you call me stupid," Boyle raged. "Who the fuck do you think you are, calling me names? You dumb scumbag! I'll tear your fuckin' head off!"

However, a few days later Lennon agreed to go out once more.

This time the foursome chose to brunch at the Breakers, the famous resort hotel on the Atlantic. Entering the stately white structure, Lennon was impressed. Its long corridors were adorned with marble statues, elegant furniture from a bygone era, and stunning fresco ceilings painted by Italian masters, and the Breakers exuded a grand elegance and charm. The hotel's many dining areas—some overlooking the ocean and the golf course—offer four-star dining and dancing and host most of Palm Beach's annual charity functions.

On this night, Lennon wore a straw hat and aged leather jacket. The maître d' refused to seat the party, saying neither man had a necktie and that tielessness was strictly forbidden. Boyle, remembering the fiasco at La Petite Marmite, quickly pulled the maître d' aside and waved several bills in front of him. He discreetly pointed to Lennon. The no-tie rule was dropped and the two couples were shuttled off to the room's best table. Still, word spread quickly that a Beatle was dining there. People peeked at Lennon as nonchalantly as possible. Boyle braced for another scene, but brunch went by uneventfully and the foursome escaped the Breakers without incident.

Seaman says Lennon had mixed feelings about Palm Beach. "John was very impressed by the wealthy atmosphere" and "squeaky clean" streets, but he also complained about the preponderance of well-dressed, clean-cut, and tanned men and women.

Seaman wrote, "It was just a bit too wholesome for John's taste. He said that a 'little sleaze' might give the place some much-needed 'color,' and he wondered what would happen if a bizarre-looking punk with spiky green or purple hair were to suddenly appear in the midst of this civilized Palm Beach scene."

It wasn't always that civilized. Sometimes gum-snapping teenyboppers, spoiled siblings of the rich, would spot Lennon's bright red Cadillac and give chase.

No matter, John grew more and more fond of El Salano. The place was conducive to writing and composing. Maybe it would inspire him to write songs that were as great as those he had written with Paul McCartney. He liked the peaceful, gentle feeling there, heightened by the soothing ocean breezes from the nearby Atlantic.

He enjoyed the fact that he had his choice of pools—the afternoon pool on the west side of the house and the morning pool on the east side, so named for when the sunshine hit them. His favorite room was the grand salon, the forty-by-twenty-seven-foot wing with a glorious hand-painted cypress ceiling and Palladian windows that offered a view of the Atlantic, And he enjoyed the monstrous bathtubs, where two people could easily bathe in comfort.

But the deepest tie was that El Salano had become the place where he had awkwardly attempted to make peace with his son, Julian. His memories of their short time together connected him spiritually to El Salano forever.

John and Yoko began renovations. There was going to be an area called "John's Bar," featuring a sleek black granite pub where cocktails could be served. Yoko wanted some of the original wooden detailing, which had been painted over the years, to be restored to its former glory. A new flower garden was planted.

The "old guard" of Palm Beach seemed to accept the ex-Beatle. Several longtime residents privately remarked how John and Yoko's arrival in Palm Beach had been amazingly uneventful. They were quiet, kept to themselves, and caused no problems. They were good neighbors.

As Lennon left the house in March 1980, he lamented about facing the cold, bitter weather in New York. But there was work to be done on his "comeback" album, the one that eventually would be released as *Double Fantasy.* As he left, Lennon told friends that he already savored returning the next season.

He never made it. On December 8, 1980, John Lennon was shot dead outside the Dakota by an obsessed fan, Mark David Chapman, as he returned from a recording session. News of the assassination echoed around the world within minutes. Radio stations in every country began playing nonstop Beatles tunes and Lennon's solo music and offered tributes. The legendary Beatles reunion, which had been talked about for a decade, was now just a dream. John Lennon, rock 'n' roll legend and advocate of peace and nonviolence, was gone, murdered by a maniac.

In New York City, hundreds of young people flocked to the Dakota, cutting off the traffic flow along Central Park West. Standing arm in arm and holding lighted candles in the chilly December weather, they sang Lennon's signature pieces "Imagine" and "Give Peace a Chance." Their choruses were mixed with the sobs and quiet prayers of fans overcome by grief. TV crews flew in from all over the world to film the scene.

Aside from the warmer climate, the scene wasn't much different in Palm Beach. More than a hundred fans lined up outside 720 South Ocean Boulevard, quietly singing John's songs. Their choruses were gently enhanced by the sound of the nearby surf. Because there are strict no parking rules along most of South Ocean Boulevard—rules enacted by the town council to keep tourists from gawking at the mansions—many of the fans had to walk several miles to get to Lennon's home. They laid flowers at the entrance and flashed peace signs to rubbernecking motorists.

Palm Beach police, normally strict about quashing any impromptu public gathering in town, instead just watched. Several of the officers, young enough to be fans themselves, had tears in their eyes. The great dream of El Salano and how it would be there for John in his twilight years was now over.

The house sat empty for months. Yoko decided to continue the renovations she and John had started. Hiring top designers and craftsmen, Ono went about restoring the home's appearance to the glory it had displayed under Mizner and Vanderbilt. She did so under the watchful eyes of the Palm Beach Landmarks Preservation Commission, which is so strict that residents jokingly complain it monitors the changing of light bulbs.

In June 1984, with $3 million in renovations completed—more than triple the price the Lennons paid for the house—Yoko put it up for sale. The asking price was $8 million. Yoko had certainly done a magnificent job, but the price was too steep. In two months, only six potential buyers came to see El Salano, and the suspicion was that most of them had feigned interest only to get a peek at the place where John Lennon had slept.

A year later, Yoko slashed the price to $4.5 million. Still no buyer. Finally, in 1986, Massachusetts developer Howard Fafard offered a bid of $3.5 million for the property and Yoko accepted, suffering a substantial loss.

Ironically, while most of Palm Beach's old guard could not name a Beatles song or tell you much about John Lennon, they do readily praise Yoko for renewing the badly neglected El Salano, returning a landmark house to its former splendor. Many mansions, neglected over the years, had had to be torn down.

Yoko seldom speaks about her days with John at El Salano. The few public statements she has made bring her near to tears. In 1987, Yoko returned to Palm Beach to sell a collection of her late husband's doodles and drawings at the Frankel Gallery on Worth Avenue. It was a mob scene. Reporters from around the world asked Yoko for her thoughts about Lennon and how she felt about returning to the place where they planned to someday move for good.

Looking somewhat uncomfortable, Yoko paused and lowered her head. As she did John's voice could be heard over the gallery's stereo system singing, "Just Like Starting Over."

"We had so many happy times here," she began. "It was a place that John and I spent very happy days with our son, Sean. I have very good memories...It's really too painful for me to talk about."

John Lennon has been dead for twelve years now. There are few memories of him left in Palm Beach. Whenever a new Lennon book comes out, the disc jockeys in the Sunshine State always hype it by identifying Lennon as "a former Palm Beach resident."

But is that really true? Can John Lennon really be considered a part of Palm Beach? As it turns out, El Salano stands today as a living tribute to Lennon's memory.

"John really loved this house. That's why I wanted to restore it in his memory. I wanted to make sure this house wasn't demolished," Yoko said later. "Eventually he would have wanted to live here all year round."

Restoration expert Ray Johnson, who once remodeled actress Judy Holliday's apartment and who led Ono's restoration project, said the house is forever dedicated to John's memory, no matter who owns it.

"The house is a tribute to John because he loved Palm Beach and when they acquired the house, they planned that it would be done this way. So in a very large sense it was sort of done as a memorial for him."

There is another reason why Palm Beach will always have a piece of Lennon's spirit: His music. Every December 8, a few flowers are laid in front of 720 South Ocean Boulevard by the slain Beatle's Palm Beach fans. They are usually white and red roses. Next to them, fans leave handwritten copies of Lennon's lyrics: "Give Peace a Chance," "Instant Karma," "Watching the Wheels." They also leave drawings of Lennon. One showed a smiling Lennon sitting on the beach with Sean, watching the waves as the sun shone above.

The fans apparently never intend to forget Lennon's brief but poignant flirtation with their island. A note pinned to a white rose in front El Salano one year read simply: "You'll always be a part of us here, John."

19

The Man Behind
Lee Harvey Oswald:
George de Mohrenschildt

At 3:45 P.M. on March 29, 1977, three patrol cars from the Palm Beach Sheriff's Department raced south along South Ocean Boulevard. Motorists pulled over to the side of the picturesque road to allow the vehicles, their sirens screaming and emergency lights flashing, to pass. Five minutes earlier, the lawmen had received a frantic telephone call from a maid at 1780 South Ocean Boulevard, the home of Mrs. Charles E. (Nancy) Tilton III, located in the Manalapan section. A houseguest had been killed in one of the upstairs rooms. Blood was splattered all over the floor and walls.

Murder rarely occurred in Palm Beach, and it was even rarer in Manalapan. The last homicide had been the murder of Charles and Marjorie Chillingsworth, some twenty-two years earlier.

As the sheriff's vehicles turned into the curved, pebbled driveway at number 1780 and pulled up to the three-story, green-and-brown New England–style home along the Intercoastal Waterway, four people ran from the front door to meet them. There were two uniformed maids, a chauffeur, and a thirty-three-year-old woman named Alexandra de Mohrenschildt.

As tears streamed down her face, de Mohrenschildt told the law-enforcement officers that she had found her sixty-five-year-old father, George, dead in the second-floor drawing room. She and her father

257

were staying as guests of Mrs. Tilton, her second cousin. Three of the
sheriff's deputies hurried into the house and vaulted up the stairs two
steps at a time. When they reached the drawing room, the lawmen
realized the maid's description of the scene had not been exaggerated.
Finely sprayed blood covered parts of the floor and one wall. In a
polished wooden chair next to a desk sat a man dressed in long pants and
a white cotton shirt. His head was slumped forward and his arms
dangled at his sides. Small pieces of brain matter were evident on the
man's clothing. Blood dripped onto his lap from his mouth; nearby on
the floor lay a twenty-gauge double-barreled shotgun.

One of the deputies crouched to examine the body. He noticed a
large hole at the back of the man's skull, apparently an exit wound from a
bullet. As is common in law enforcement, the deputy reported his
initial impression to his fellow officers. Judging from the positions of the
body and the shotgun, and from the direction of the spray of blood, it
appeared that George de Mohrenschildt had placed the barrel of the
shotgun into his mouth and pulled the trigger. There was a "99 percent
certainty" that de Mohrenschildt had committed suicide. It seemed like
a reasonable assessment. The officers believed the Palm Beach Coroner's Office would agree.

A few hours later, that "99 percent certainty" evaporated when police
discovered George de Mohrenschildt's identity as well as the identity of
the person who had attempted to visit him only two hours before his
death. De Mohrenschildt, a Russian-born college professor from Dallas,
Texas, had been one of the few close friends of Lee Harvey Oswald, the
accused assassin of President John F. Kennedy. In the weeks prior to his
death, de Mohrenschildt had been considered a "crucial witness" in an
inquest by the U.S. House Select Committee on Assassinations on
whether to reopen a federal investigation into Kennedy's murder on
November 22, 1963, in Dallas. Only a few weeks earlier, he had spoken
with a reporter, telling him he had had "prior knowledge" of Oswald's
plan to kill President Kennedy and, in fact, had advised him on how to
carry it out.

As a result, the assassinations committee had assigned one of its
investigators to travel to Palm Beach to interview de Mohrenschildt. But
a few hours after the official had attempted to make contact, the witness
was dead. De Mohrenschildt was now another name on a growing list of
more than one hundred potential witnesses in the Kennedy assassination who had died or disappeared, some under questionable circumstances, before they could be interviewed.

Teams of investigators from federal, state, and local law-enforcement agencies converged on Palm Beach to try to learn the truth about George de Mohrenschildt's death. Had he really committed suicide or had he been silenced by a hired killer? What part, if any, had he played in the assassination of President Kennedy? And what about the rumors that de Mohrenschildt had had a bizarre connection to Jackie Kennedy, years before she married the man who would be president. The answers turned out to be as compelling as best-selling espionage fiction.

De Mohrenschildt was born in the Ukrainian village of Mozur in 1911, the son of a minor nobleman in the czarist regime. In the turmoil following the Communist revolution in 1917, his family fled to Poland because, de Mohrenschildt said, "my father was exceedingly strongly anti-Communist, almost fanatically so."

In 1931, George de Mohrenschildt enrolled in a Polish Army cavalry academy and, after graduating, moved on to Belgium and studied international commerce at the University of Liege. Despite his intelligence and a natural ability to learn languages—he now spoke five fluently—de Mohrenschildt was unable to find work in his field. He decided to move to the United States and room with one of his brothers, who had emigrated earlier and lived in an apartment at 750 Park Avenue in New York City.

Arriving in Manhattan in 1938, de Mohrenschildt failed to find a job in international commerce, but he landed a well-paying position as a perfume salesman. That same year, while on a vacation in the waterfront village of Bellport, Long Island, de Mohrenschildt met a young couple named John and Janet Bouvier and their nine-year-old daughter Jacqueline, who would one day wed John F. Kennedy. The Bouviers coincidentally lived in the building next to de Mohrenschildt at 740 Park Avenue and maintained a summer home in Southhampton on Long Island. Because both the Bouviers and de Mohrenschildt had traveled extensively and had an excellent command of world affairs and issues, they quickly became good friends. Indeed, they became such good friends that young Jacqueline referred to the heavily accented de Mohrenschildt as "Uncle George."

De Mohrenschildt also began to date John Bouvier's sister, Michelle. At the same time this new friendship was being bonded, John and Janet Bouvier's marriage began to fall apart. Their friends were not surprised. The Bouviers had had trial separations in the past, often due to John's womanizing and heavy drinking. This time, however, Janet said she wanted to end the marriage. As John moved out, de Mohrenschildt, who had recently broken up with Michelle Bouvier, became Janet's "shoulder to lean on." In 1940, Janet sued John for divorce on the grounds of adultery.

Even before the divorce was finalized, de Mohrenschildt had fallen deeply in love with Janet Bouvier. He had quietly proposed marriage several times, but in each instance the young divorcée said no.

"He took Janet out during the time she was divorcing Jackie's father. George was very much a potential stepfather to Jackie. He wanted to marry Janet, but Janet wanted a very rich man," said John David, a Kennedy biographer and first cousin of Jackie.

Instead, Janet married Hugh Auchincloss, a wealthy stockbroker, two years later. With his prospects with Janet Bouvier now dashed, de Mohrenschildt, dejected and lonely, began chasing women. His vacations became "hunting expeditions" for young, pretty, rich blondes.

On one of these "expeditions" in 1943, de Mohrenschildt flew to Palm Beach, a place he had been told by friends was America's tropical paradise for the rich, and a destination overrun with well-to-do women. As soon as de Mohrenschildt arrived on the island, he knew his friends had been right. In his first week there, he met Dorothy Pierson, the daughter of a prominent real-estate developer and stepdaughter of an Italian count. They married a few months later. Dorothy was the sister of Nancy Tilton, owner of the home in which de Mohrenschildt would eventually die.

De Mohrenschildt's stay in Palm Beach was short lived. Within a year's time, in 1944, he was accepted at the University of Texas in Dallas where he obtained a master's degree in petroleum geology and engineering. His new degree helped him enter the volatile world of Texas oil. He applied for and was granted United States citizenship.

Over the next decade, de Mohrenschildt worked for several oil companies as a petroleum engineer, a position that would take him several times around the world. His personal life became as frantic as his travel schedule. Divorcing his first wife, de Mohrenschildt married twice more, with both unions ending in divorce. In 1959, he married his fourth wife, Jeannie, a Russian woman, who had emigrated to America in the 1940s. Jeannie became a successful women's dress and sportswear designer. The couple settled in Dallas.

Aside from its bustling oil trade, Dallas was home to a community of about fifty Russian immigrants who had formed a social clique and often met together. It was through this group that de Mohrenschildt encountered twenty-three-year-old Lee Harvey Oswald, a New Orleans native, and his Russian wife, Marina, in 1962. Oswald enthralled de Mohrenschildt with stories of modern-day Russia, where he had just spent the past two and a half years.

Oswald, an ex-marine, had a shadowy past. After an honorable discharge from the marines in 1959, he had defected to Russia, renounced his U.S. citizenship, and married Soviet pharmacist Marina Nicholaevna. Then, in a move government officials have never fully explained, Oswald returned to America with his new bride. He was given a government loan of $435 to help reestablish himself.

De Mohrenschildt became a surrogate father to both Lee Oswald and Marina, acting as their counselor and confident. In April 1963, de Mohrenschildt and Jeannie moved to Port-au-Prince, Haiti, where they attempted to promote an oil exploration deal with then-President François Duvalier. They remained in Haiti for a year, missing the Kennedy assassination on November 22 and the subsequent murder of Oswald by Dallas strip-club owner Jack Ruby. When they returned to Dallas, however, de Mohrenschildt and his wife were immediately summoned by the Warren Commission, which had been informed by federal investigators that they had been Oswald's close friends.

De Mohrenschildt led the commission through his biography all the way up to Dallas and his friendship with Lee and Marina. He said both Oswalds often confided in him, particularly Marina, who would discuss the sex problems she was having with Lee.

De Mohrenschildt said, "It was strange for me to hear about a young girl like that speak so boldly about sex. I was shocked by it, you know— even though I was twice as old as she. She said her husband doesn't satisfy her."

He added that Lee Oswald occasionally beat Marina. "We saw her with a black eye once," he told the assassination committee. He had even helped Marina leave Lee for a short while to escape her husband's brutality.

While de Mohrenschildt's testimony about the Oswalds' sex life and marital difficulties was titillating, his account shed no light on Kennedy's murder. De Mohrenschildt, and his wife, who also testified, said they were not sure why Oswald would have killed Kennedy.

De Mohrenschildt told the commission, "In my opinion, if Lee Oswald did kill the president, this might be the reason for it: That he was insanely jealous of an extraordinarily successful man, who was young, attractive, had a beautiful wife, had all the money in the world and was a world figure. And poor Oswald was just the opposite. He had nothing. He had a bitchy wife, had no money, was a miserable failure in everything he did."

The Warren Commission found in its final report that indeed de Mohrenschildt and Oswald had been close friends and de Mohrenschildt had been the only person in the small group of Dallas Russians for whom Oswald had any respect.

Still, the commission concluded: "Neither the FBI, CIA, nor any witness contacted by the commission had provided any information linking the de Mohrenschildts to subversive or extremist organizations. Nor has there been any evidence linking them in any way to the assassination of President Kennedy."

In 1969, de Mohrenschildt accepted a professorship at Bishop College in Dallas teaching French and Russian. It was a low-profile position that suited de Mohrenschildt, and few at the school knew of his ties with the late Oswald. For the next seven years, de Mohrenschildt lived in near obscurity. The small, insulated world at Bishop College was light years away from the globetrotting lifestyle he had as a geologist and ladies' man in the 1940s and 1950s.

It was over the next few years that de Mohrenschildt's world started to unravel and the specter of the JFK assassination began to haunt him. He seemed jumpy and became agitated without provocation. He began telling his wife that he was positive he was under twenty-four-hour surveillance. He was not sure who was watching him, but he guessed it was either agents from the CIA, FBI, or KGB. He insisted that his house and telephone had been bugged.

At his wife Jeannie's urging, de Mohrenschildt met with a psychiatrist who diagnosed his mental state as "psychotic depression." On November 9, 1976, he agreed to commit himself to the psychiatric ward of Parkland Memorial Hospital in Dallas for therapy, including shock treatment. Coincidentally, Parkland was the hospital where President Kennedy had been pronounced dead following his fateful ride through Dealey Plaza.

De Mohrenschildt was released December 30. His apparent mental problems had proved too much for Jeannie, however, and she left him a month later. In mid-February 1977, de Mohrenschildt was visited at Bishop College by a Dutch journalist, Wilhelm Oltmans, who asked to speak with him about John Kennedy's assassination. Oltmans, a respected investigative journalist, had a reputation for digging around older stories with unanswered questions. He had been researching the Kennedy murder for a decade. Meeting in the college library, the two men discussed Kennedy's untimely death for several hours. Oltmans apparently heard much more than the Warren Commission had been told when de Mohrenschildt had testified before it in 1964. The two men agreed to meet again.

On March 1, de Mohrenschildt was granted a three-day leave of absence from Bishop after telling the college's administrators that he needed to make an emergency trip to New Orleans to see his daughter. It was a lie. De Mohrenschildt flew instead to Holland with Oltmans, where the journalist planned to conduct a series of in-depth interviews surrounding his friendship with Oswald. It seemed a long way to go just to talk, but de Mohrenschildt had insisted. He told Oltmans he refused to discuss the case in the United States because he "no longer felt safe" there.

After they arrived in Holland, the two men drove to Brussels, where they planned to stay in a hotel for several days. It would be here, de Mohrenschildt had promised, that he would unravel the "mystery" behind Kennedy's death. But a few hours after they reached Brussels, de Mohrenschildt vanished. Oltmans combed the city and had a posse of friends search for the wayward de Mohrenschildt. The search proved futile. De Mohrenschildt reappeared ten days later in New York City, but refused to say what had happened to him in Europe.

Meanwhile, Oltmans had contacted the House Select Committee on Assassinations in Washington. He had "vital information" about de Mohrenschildt's role in the Kennedy case. Oltmans declared, "He said to me, 'How do you think the media would react if I came out and said that I feel responsible for Oswald's behavior.'"

The journalist also reported that de Mohrenschildt told him he had helped Oswald plan a possible assassination of Kennedy. He said, "De Mohrenschildt thought Kennedy was a symbol of a degenerating, decadent, phony America. He discussed the assassination from A to Z with Lee Harvey Oswald. De Mohrenschildt advised Oswald if he was interested in it—how to do it." Oltmans did not elaborate.

A coroner's inquest into the death of George de Mohrenschildt was convened in Palm Beach County Court on April 4, 1977. A six-member jury was selected to hear evidence. Some of it suggested that de Mohrenschildt had not killed himself. Alexandra de Mohrenschildt insisted that her father had "absolutely no" fear of speaking with federal investigators about the Kennedy assassination, despite earlier reports that he had been "terrified" of cooperating with the government.

Anna Viisola, one of the housemaids, also testified at the inquest. She said she had spoken with de Mohrenschildt a few minutes before his death and he had shown no outward signs that anything was wrong.

One piece of evidence—definitely the strangest in the case—was an audiotape recording of de Mohrenschildt's death. The owner of the house, Nancy Tilton, was a soap-opera fanatic, and when she went out she often asked one of her maids to record episodes of her favorite soaps with a small cassette tape recorder. In the midafternoon of March 29, 1977, a maid activated Mrs. Tilton's tape recorder to pick up the NBC-TV program, "The Doctors," from two to three. The maid placed it next to the loudspeaker of a television in a bedroom next to the drawing room where de Mohrenschildt sat.

When the tape was played back by investigators, the sound of footsteps could be heard followed by a loud explosion. Then about fifteen minutes passed as the tape continued to pick up all the soap's dramatics. Next, the loud, high-pitched screams of Alexandra de Mohrenschildt can be heard as she found her father's body. And finally, Alexandra's desperate calls to the servants for help.

The tape recording shed little light on de Mohrenschildt's bizarre end other than to establish the exact time it occurred. But the lingering question concerned light footsteps heard on the tape just before the gunshot. Did they belong to de Mohrenschildt—or possibly to his killer? The jury heard from Palm Beach coroner Gabino Cuevas, who had performed the autopsy on de Mohrenschildt. Cuevas testified: "All evidence to me indicates a self-inflicted gunshot wound. He could have easily used either the thumb or the index finger to press the trigger."

Police evidence showed that the weapon involved, a twenty-gauge, double-barreled shotgun, belonged to Mrs. Tilton. She kept it in her house for protection and stored it in a second-floor closet. This discovery lent credence to the suicide theory because if a killer had sneaked into the house, he would have been unlikely to know about the gun.

On April 5, 1977, a jury of four men and two women ruled unanimously that George de Mohrenschildt had committed suicide. Despite the ruling, Rep. Richard Preyer, chairman of the Senate committee probing the Kennedy murder, said he was still troubled by de Mohrenschildt's death and hinted that the case should not be closed.

"In thirteen years since John F. Kennedy's death," Preyer declared, "so many witnesses involved in this case have come to such mysterious ends that you don't take anything for granted."

Four months later, on August 30, 1977, the "closed" case landed on the front page again as journalist Wilhelm Oltmans released new information about his conversations with de Mohrenschildt. Appearing on NBC-TV's "Today," Oltmans said he believed de Mohrenschildt had been murdered. De Mohrenschildt, Oltmans said, had told him he and Oswald had been employed by anti-Castro forces and several Texas oilmen, including billionaire H. L. Hunt, to assassinate Kennedy. De Mohrenschildt further stated he was "very, very much involved."

Oltmans also said that he had evidence pointing to a suspect in the de Mohrenschildt "murder" and wanted to meet personally with President Jimmy Carter to discuss his findings. The state attorney for Palm Beach County, David Bludworth, called Oltmans's statements "outrageous" and said, "There's no question in my mind that de Mohrenschildt committed suicide." H. L. Hunt's family denied the allegations.

Oltmans never got his presidential meeting and faded into obscurity. He was labeled a "publicity psychopath" in the *Palm Beach Post* and discredited for inconsistencies in his remarks about de Mohrenschildt.

The case did not die down, however. In July 1978, an explosive new angle emerged and this time it had nothing to do with Oltmans. Several memos about de Mohrenschildt from the secret files of the Central Intelligence Agency were declassified and released to the public following a journalist's Freedom of Information request. The undated memos showed that de Mohrenschildt had been less than candid when he had described his background to the Warren Commission back in 1964. The memos also revealed that de Mohrenschildt had once been a CIA agent.

One of the memos, written by then-CIA deputy director Richard Helms, said de Mohrenschildt had applied for a job with the CIA's forerunner in 1942 but was rejected "because he was allegedly a Nazi espionage agent." Helms also stated that de Mohrenschildt had taken a 1957 trip to Yugoslavia and provided the CIA with "foreign intelligence which was promptly disseminated to other federal agencies in ten separate reports." Another memo indicated that de Mohrenschildt had furnished lengthy reports to the CIA on his 1958 trips through Mexico and Panama. And an unsigned memo described him as a "dubious character" with Communist leanings.

When asked about de Mohrenschildt's time with the CIA, the agency refused all comment. The new revelation bolstered one of the theories of conspiracy students that the CIA had murdered Kennedy because the agency feared he would limit its power and no longer back its plans for actions like the Bay of Pigs invasion.

As the years passed, inquiries into the life of George de Mohrenschildt seemed to generate many more questions than answers.

Did George de Mohrenschildt die by his own hand? Officially, yes. But for conspiracy theorists, the cause of death remains unsolved. Nancy and Charles Tilton, the owners of the house where the mysterious death occurred, have refused to discuss the case. Nancy, described as a shy and private person, told friends that it was an incident that could have happened anywhere, and she "prayed for the publicity to go away." It did—for a while.

In December 1991, *JFK*, a big-budget, all-star film about the Kennedy assassination directed by Oliver Stone, generated intense controversy. It suggested that several United States government agencies might have been involved in a conspiracy to murder the president. De Mohrenschildt is one of the names mentioned briefly during the course of the movie.

The antigovernment publicity caused by the film compelled numerous federal agencies, including the FBI and CIA, to publicly denounce *JFK* as "misleading fiction." The CIA, so silent in 1977, denied that it had any connection to the death of President Kennedy. The publicity also prompted senators on Capitol Hill to promise the eventual release of thousands of pages of classified documents on the assassination.

Perhaps buried somewhere in these stacks of documents will be clues as to de Mohrenschildt's true relationship to Oswald, just what his alleged ties to the CIA and the KGB were, and what connections, if any, he had in the planning and carrying out of the murder of John F. Kennedy. And perhaps we will learn the conclusive story behind the terrible, violent act on a sunny afternoon in Dallas, and one that occurred fourteen years later on another sunny afternoon on South Ocean Boulevard in Palm Beach.

20

A Tragic Life, a Heartless Death: David Kennedy

It was April 1984, and the Kennedy clan had flocked from all over the Northeast to Palm Beach for what they called a "traditional Easter weekend." In the warm Florida sunshine, they would pay tribute to Rose Kennedy, the family's forever ailing matriarch, then in her mid-nineties. Former president John Kennedy's two children, Caroline and John Jr., already had arrived at the family's $3 million oceanfront estate nestled behind the tall groomed hedges at 1095 North Ocean Boulevard. Numerous cousins and in-laws had also come for the celebration. The spacious six-bedroom villa was packed.

But there was no place for David Kennedy, the third son of Senator Robert Kennedy. There was seldom room for David, who had become the wayward, troubled member of the clan.

To make the weekend easier for everyone, the family told David that because of the "overflow" of guests, they had arranged for him to stay in a one-bedroom suite at the Brazilian Court Hotel in a quiet residential section of Palm Beach, just four blocks from the ocean. The hotel, which has an air of "shabby elegance," consists of a series of unassuming white stucco buildings that surround two courtyards containing stately bronze fountains. The Brazilian Court has a reputation for discreetly pampering the rich and famous. That was one of the main reasons the Kennedys chose the hotel as an alternative home for their extra family and friends, but it was not the only reason.

Their arrangement for David had an added bonus: they would not have to pay for the suite that often was reserved for months at a time for $250 a night. In the hotel business, what the Kennedys arranged for David was referred to as being "comped," a term given a complimentary room. It also kept David out of Rose Kennedy's view, except for short, controlled daytime visits. Not that the twenty-eight-year-old Kennedy objected. The four-star suite along with twenty-four-hour room service provided the kind of privacy Kennedy actually coveted, shielding him from the vigilant and often scornful eyes of his relatives.

David Kennedy visited the compound every day and struggled to play the perfect grandson. Putting on a Brooks Brothers dress shirt and a Burberry sports jacket, David would sit on the porch next to the wheelchair-bound Rose and make small talk. The gesture was appreciated by his family.

But at night, the other David Kennedy emerged: The well-to-do night crawler cruised the bars, the restaurants, and the nightclubs in and around the island's palm-tree-lined Royal Poinciana Way, looking for women and searching for drugs. His quest was not unlike that of many of the other bored, restless, and privileged young rich on the balmy island retreat.

At the conclusion of each evening, David retreated to room 107 at the Brazilian Court to satisfy his many habits, both legal and illicit. If he was lucky—and he often was—a beautiful woman would be at his side. Picking up girls was really no problem for a Kennedy, especially for David, who had already had a two-year affair with Australian actress Rachel Ward. And if the night went extraordinarily well, David was graced by both a beautiful woman and a plentiful supply of high-grade heroin or cocaine. The night after Easter Sunday proved no different.

David had dined with forty-one-year-old Marion Niemann, a German fashion model whom he met on the circuit one evening. The starry-eyed couple sat at a candlelit table at Chuck and Harold's, an informal, open-air dinner spot near the Breakers Hotel where well-dressed, deeply tanned Palm Beach residents often started their evening rounds of bar hopping with a casual meal and a bottle of champagne or cocktails. On this evening, David felt particularly expansive. He kept the waitresses busy refilling his drink orders. In just over an hour, he downed six or seven vodkas. But he barely touched his food. The effect of the alcohol had David and Marion feeling romantic in the warm breezy night air.

The couple chatted intimately. After a short while, they both agreed it was time to retire for the evening.

Back in David's room, the statuesque beauty and the young Kennedy kissed passionately on the hotel's couch and spoke in romantic whispers. But before the festivities could become more intimate, Kennedy gently broke away. He casually shifted his attention to a somewhat more pressing need.

Without hesitation, David Kennedy produced a small glassine envelope, and in full view of Marion, he skillfully poured its powdery contents—cocaine—onto the table in thin white lines. Tightly rolling a twenty-dollar bill into a thin green straw, he placed one end in his nostril and quickly sniffed several lines.

Kennedy paused for a moment. He then snorted more and waited for the euphoric rush to surge through him. But the goodtime feeling he craved—and usually got—did not come. Instead, the son of Robert F. Kennedy turned maudlin, almost forgetting that a beautiful woman was stretched out a few feet away. David's mood swing surprised Marion. She moved toward him offering consolation. But Kennedy, sobbing, his eyes and face red and wet, raised a finger and pointed to the TV set. In a quivering voice David Kennedy tried to explain.

"I cannot forget when I saw my father die on television," he said. "I have never been able to find peace inside. Ever since then, I've been full of pain."

Marion fully understood. Tears came to her eyes as well. She took him in her arms and cuddled him on the bed. She lovingly suggested he needed help. Marion was unaware that David had undergone several expensive "cures" to ease his mental anguish. But nothing had eased his pain. Not the needles filled with heroin or the endless supply of coke, not the gorgeous women or the pulsating disco nightlife. Nor could he find help at the world's top drug rehabilitation centers.

David wasn't the only one who was unhappy with himself. His family and closest friends had grown weary of his drinking and his drug-enhanced exploits. They called him undisciplined. The Kennedy family had provided David with the finest opportunities. They helped him gain admission to Harvard, but he dropped out. When he expressed a desire to be a journalist, they obtained a coveted editorship for him at *The Atlantic*, but he quickly lost interest.

The family understood that Bobby's murder had affected him deeply. But the death had moved them too. They felt that David should have long ago gotten on with his life. But what David had experienced on that unforgettable day in 1968 was seared into his soul so deeply that he couldn't overcome it.

On June 5, 1968, David, then a lanky, happy-go-lucky twelve-year-old, sat alone on the floor in a darkened Los Angeles hotel room watching television. Just hours before, his dad, Robert F. Kennedy, Jr., had swept California with an impressive victory in the state's Democratic presidential primary. That day's victory virtually guaranteed that he would be the party's nominee.

The bond between father and son had been forever sealed earlier that day on the California seashore. David, not a strong swimmer, had waded into the surf when a dangerous, sucking undertow pulled him under and began dragging him into the Pacific. Bobby Kennedy saw his panic-stricken son bobbing in the surf and raced into the choppy waters, pulling him to safety.

The senator, himself a third son, had always gone out of his way to show special attention to David. He took him to work and on trips. During the family's trademark football games, Bobby made sure David was thrown passes. He always remembered to give David extra hugs even when the boy should have been scolded. Bobby Kennedy knew that middle children often were lost in the shuffle and sometimes felt neglected even when they were not.

It was with this overwhelming love for his father that David watched Robert F. Kennedy on TV, as he jubilantly accepted the Democratic victory in the lobby of the Ambassador Hotel, just a few stories beneath him. As his father stepped off the podium and walked toward a group of reporters for an impromptu press conference, David's heart was uplifted. He knew he would be seeing his father any moment now in his room. But suddenly the TV camera that was trained on his father jerked up and down. A flash of people raced across the screen while panicked voices blared through the set's tinny speaker. A shaken announcer said, "The senator has been shot!" and at that moment the camera zoomed in on David's father. He now was lying on his back on the floor, his eyes staring up into space. A pool of blood began to grow around his father's head.

Amid the panic and confusion, the Kennedy clan and its associates rushed to help the mortally wounded candidate. Everyone forgot twelve-year-old David. For the next six hours, David Kennedy, mesmerized by the terrifying madness on the television screen, watched again and again and again as the networks continuously replayed the bloody assassination of his father—sometimes in slow motion. He heard perhaps one hundred times that his father—with a bullet in his brain— had been assassinated.

David's mother, Ethel, was downstairs with her husband during the speech and had witnessed his shooting. She frantically tried to help save her husband's life, as decathlon champion Rafer Johnson and football great Roosevelt Grier restrained gunman Sirhan Sirhan. Only moments earlier, Ethel had planned to join Bobby in David's room. But now she accompanied her mortally wounded husband to Good Samaritan Hospital, where she was met by her sister-in-law Jacqueline Kennedy.

The widow of John Kennedy was so stunned at the news that a similar tragedy had struck her husband's brother that she had taken sedatives to calm her nerves. Meanwhile, Ethel tried to explain the inexplicable events at the Ambassador Hotel.

Several hours passed before she realized she had not gone to see David. Ethel Kennedy had believed mistakenly that her son had slept through the evening's tragedy. She asked family friends, astronaut John Glenn and Nicole Salinger, wife of John Kennedy's former White House press spokesman, Pierre Salinger, to visit David's room. Nicole found David, ashen-faced, in front of the flickering blue-and-white TV screen. She called his name, but he did not answer. He continued to stare blankly at the monitor.

Glenn gently lifted the youngster from the bed and said, "Son, we'll take you out of here. You'll be all right." David broke down and cried.

A few days later, David wrote: "There will be no more football with daddy, no more swimming with him, no more riding and no more camping. But he was the best father there ever was. I would rather have him for a father for the length of time I did than any other father in a million years."

From that day on, David became a rebel without a cause, a troubled, tortured soul who battled his family with a caustic tongue. And, throughout his life, he also attempted to fight off an unstoppable army of inner demons with heroin, cocaine, and painkillers.

David Kennedy's ongoing problems with substance abuse were not unlike those of other third-generation Kennedys. Born into money and raised during a period of loosening sexuality and drug experimentation, several of the younger Kennedys engaged in often reckless behavior.

In 1970, sixteen-year-old Robert Kennedy, Jr., was arrested in Hyannisport along with his cousin Robert Sargent Shriver III, also sixteen, for marijuana possession. Thirteen years later, at the age of twenty-nine, Bobby Jr. sought help to beat a thousand-dollar-a-week heroin habit that often took him to the same seedy haunts in Harlem where David had gone. In August 1983, he was found sitting in the lavatory of an airplane in Rapid City, South Dakota, babbling incoherently for help during what was believed to be a heroin overdose.

In 1980, Pat Kennedy Lawford's son Christopher was arrested in Aspen when he tried to coerce a pharmacist into dispensing the prescription painkiller Darvon. That same year, Lawford was using heroin and was arrested making a heroin buy outside a bar in a seedy section of Boston.

In the summer of 1973, Joseph P. Kennedy II, David's older brother, borrowed a friend's Jeep and went joyriding on Nantucket with six passengers crammed into the vehicle. Among them were David, David's girlfriend Pam Kelley, and four other young women. As he cut across a highway, Joe failed to notice an oncoming station wagon. When he swerved at the last second to avoid a collision, the Jeep flipped over and rolled several times, scattering bodies everywhere. David suffered a fractured vertebrae and Pam's legs were permanently paralyzed. Joe was convicted of negligent driving, fined one hundred dollars, and had his driver's license suspended for six months.

During his hospital stay, David was prescribed heavy doses of morphine to ease his back pain. Some family friends theorize that it was the morphine that sparked his experimentation with and eventual addiction to hard drugs.

And now, fifteen years later, here was David in Palm Beach, slipping into his grandmother's master bathroom and stealing Demerol capsules from the medicine cabinet. Later that Easter weekend, security guards turned David away at the Kennedy compound entrance because he was stoned on drugs and alcohol.

On April 25, 1984, David was scheduled to leave Palm Beach. He packed his bags at the Brazilian Court. But before he checked out, he prepared a last-minute fix, combining Rose Kennedy's Demerol with cocaine and Mellaril, an antipsychotic tranquilizer that had been prescribed for him during his most recent rehabilitation treatment.

Kennedy unhitched his belt, lowered his trousers, and pushed down his underpants. He injected the mixture directly into his groin. The effect was almost instantaneous. David Kennedy collapsed face forward, landing between twin beds. His jaw struck a wooden table leg as his body hit the floor. The impact split open the inside of his lip.

When he failed to arrive at Boston's Logan Airport hours later, Ethel Kennedy became concerned and sensed that something was terribly wrong. She telephoned the Kennedy compound in Palm Beach and asked if anybody there had seen her son. But nobody had. Caroline raced to the hotel and went to room 107. She told police she noticed a DO NOT DISTURB sign on the doorknob, knocked for several minutes and repeatedly called out her cousin's name. She said she then left the Brazilian Court virtually unnoticed, without entering David's room.

Forty-five minutes later, the hotel received a phone call from a woman identifying herself as "Mrs. Kennedy from Boston." She said her son had apparently missed a flight out of Palm Beach International Airport. She said she was concerned and asked a concierge to check his room.

Vincent Moschiano and hotel operator Betty Barnett found Kennedy. He had been dead for several hours. The hotel's public-relations man, Gerry Beebe, called Mrs. Kennedy back. "I'm sorry," he told David's mother. "We have had to call the paramedics."

Ethel Kennedy replied, "He's dead, isn't he?" and put down the phone.

A short time later, Caroline Kennedy and her cousin Sydney Lawford returned to the Brazilian Court. A Palm Beach police officer told them that David had been found. He reluctantly admitted that David was dead. For some inexplicable reason, Caroline, twenty-seven, her younger brother, John F. Kennedy Jr., twenty-four, and David's older brother, Joseph, thirty-two, were given the difficult task of identifying the body.

David's death was yet another public tragedy for the Kennedy family. Since the days of the family patriarch, bootlegger Joseph Kennedy, and his shady affairs, the Kennedys had developed a public-relations machine to polish their image. But many of David Kennedy's escapades were so bizarre and public that the well-oiled machine could not control the stories that David was a spoiled, drug-addicted figure.

It was never more evident that David was out of control than in 1979, five years before his suicide. At the age of twenty-four, David went to New York City's bustling Grand Central Terminal and panhandled commuters for money to buy drugs. With him was his favorite cousin, Christopher Lawford, son of the actor Peter Lawford.

On other occasions, David routinely drove the family's tan BMW sport coupe into Harlem, where some whites only go after dark to buy narcotics. He had made the trip often and was such a familiar face in his flashy car that local pushers had given him the street nickname White James.

Most affluent drug users would avoid cruising an inner-city street searching for a pusher to make an illicit curbside deal. Ghetto drug deals can lead to robberies and murders. And undercover police are often assigned to these areas to make narcotics arrests. In a place like Palm Beach, drug arrests are rare and treated with discretion. But in New York, rich and poor, famous and obscure run the risk of being jailed—and becoming grist for the media. For David Kennedy, any such risk had ceased to be frightening long ago.

On September 5, 1979, White James drove his BMW up to the Shelton Plaza Hotel, at 300 W. 116th Street. The Shelton was a seedy transient hotel, a place where small amounts of narcotics were sold.

On this warm, late summer night, David was feeling ill. Earlier in the day, he had suffered another attack of endocarditis, a tightening of the heart valves widely associated with drug addiction. In fact, Kennedy had been scheduled to return to Boston to receive hospital care for his worsening heart affliction. Faced with the prospect of spending weeks in the controlled, sterile hospital environment, David decided he needed to take a final trip to his familiar Harlem drug haunts.

Kennedy walked into the hotel lobby and toward the bulletproof cashier's cage, where a faded photograph of his uncle, John F. Kennedy, hung on the wall. As he made his buy, a wide-eyed black man stormed up, demanded all his cash, and then blocked David from leaving. "You get out of here! Don't come in here, you honky!" the enraged man bellowed. Then he punched David in the face repeatedly. A woman watching the brutal beating called police. Cops responded within minutes. But when they began to ask questions, the street-smart locals said nothing. Kennedy was too stoned too keep quiet.

"I should have just said it was no big deal and walked off," David said later. "But I was so out of it that I walked up to the cop in charge and started acting suspicious and said I didn't want to get involved. Naturally I was arrested and the next day the news was all over the papers. David fucks up again." The officers impounded his car. Inside the glove compartment, they discovered a prescription for two hundred tablets of Percodan, a powerful painkiller.

At the Harlem police precinct, David told detectives that he had been a victim of a crime and not a criminal. He explained that he had accidently ventured into Harlem, where two men approached his car. He foolishly followed them into the Hotel Shelton, where he was assaulted. The seasoned New York police listened to Kennedy's contrived tale. If not for his family name, the third son of Robert Kennedy would have been dismissed as just another misguided white junkie lost on the streets of Harlem. His arrest made front-page news.

Stephen Smith, the family member known for softening media

coverage of Kennedy scandals, portrayed David as a courageous young man battling heart disease, albeit an ailment he admitted was drug related.

When David entered the hospital, his family seemed almost unsympathetic. The only person close to David to visit him, in fact, was Rachel Ward. One of her visits was memorable. She and David retreated to his room, blocked the door, and made love.

"Rachel wanted to get an apartment with me and settle down, but I knew I was too fucked up," David would later recall. "I was back on smack. She had no idea what I was up to. I don't know what she thought of those little marks on my arms when I was naked. I guess she thought they were some odd Kennedy rash."

Shortly after the beautiful actress left him at the hospital, he met another patient in the corridor. She was terminally ill, dying of cancer. He arranged for a chilled bottle of champagne to be sent to the young woman's room, where he joined her for a drink. The two patients sipped the champagne from hospital-issue plastic cups. Then they climbed onto the bed and made love.

After he was released from the hospital, David reluctantly agreed to go into a drug rehabilitation program in Sacramento, California, where he had to abide by three rules. "I had to jog every day. I wasn't allowed to say, 'Fuck off and die!' anymore. And no drugs. If I broke any of these rules, it would cost me another month, and every month I was there cost me twenty thousand dollars of my own money."

David referred to the program as "therapy by humiliation," according to Kennedy biographers Peter Collier and David Horowitz. During his stay, none of his family visited him and David became increasingly bitter toward his relatives. He had previously blamed himself for his shattered family relationships, but now he began to blame them.

"I felt they should have done something earlier. My mother, although in a sense she wasn't really competent, but even more Teddy, Steve Smith, and the rest of the group, who were always figuring out ways to keep Joe, Bobby, and Chris from having to pay the piper, but who just let me go. When they finally did do something, it seemed like it was more to keep me from o.d.'ing in the street and causing a problem for Teddy's campaign, than anything else."

On one occasion, one of David's girlfriends, Nancy Narleski, contacted his older brother, Joe, because she feared David was deathly ill. Upon hearing the news, an irritated Joe yelled at the caller that, "Everything is under control. There's a lot of things you don't understand. This is the big leagues, so butt out. Just forget that David Kennedy exists!"

When David's body was found in room 107, police also discovered 1.3 grams of "Snow White pure" cocaine. The lab technicians said the powder was an extremely potent 70 percent pure.

Forensic experts arrived within minutes of the discovery of David's body. They found traces of the drug around the edges of the toilet bowl, which led to the suspicion that Caroline Kennedy in fact had entered the room before police had arrived and that she had attempted to sanitize David's death.

It turned out that the "wonderful accommodations" David's family had made for him at the Brazilian Court had afforded him with an extraordinary convenience that wasn't on the room-service menu. Two of the hotel's bellhops, Peter Marchant and David Dorr, were charged with selling him the cocaine that he used in the lethal injection. Both men later pleaded guilty to lesser charges and received suspended sentences. Ironically Marchant had once received a glowing recommendation from Ethel Kennedy to work at the exclusive Hyannisport Club.

Detectives cordoned off the hallway with yellow police tape and slapped a CRIME SCENE sign on the door of room 107. They dusted the bronze doorknob and the cheery white and green furniture for fingerprints. And they drew a chalk mark around David's corpse on the pastel rug. They took dozens of pictures of his body, the syringe, and other drug paraphernalia. As they went about their grim business, the only semblance of normalcy and beauty were the palm trees gently swaying outside the window.

The dozens of lawmen were an odd sight amidst the guests in their smartly creased summer clothes. Finally, David's body was placed in a black mortuary bag that was then zipped up and carried out past a gallery of gawkers and newsmen. Authorities drove him along Australian Avenue, toward the ocean, and into the heart of Palm Beach. The ambulance then turned left onto South County Road in front of the police station. David's remains made a final trip past the resort's shopping center and past many of the exclusive restaurants and nightclubs that had filled his evenings with women, booze, and narcotics.

The Kennedy spokespeople issued an undetailed, simplistic account of David's "tragedy." But the press demanded more information and hounded the Palm Beach police and State Attorney's Office. Meanwhile, the young Kennedy's body was transported to McLean, Virginia, where the Kennedy clan maintains a suburban Washington, D.C., estate. The family flew in from around the nation to pay their respects to the first of the new breed of Kennedys to die tragically.

His passing came at a time when Senator Ted Kennedy, still battle scarred from his involvement in the Chappaquiddick scandal, was making a run for president. He quickly assumed the role of Kennedy family patriarch and took charge of the funeral arrangements. The somber Catholic mass and burial drew various factions of the far-reaching Kennedy family, and the great gathering of Kennedys was reported on the front page of virtually every newspaper in the country.

With painful awareness, David had once said, "From an objective point of view, I found it rather interesting that the only time anybody ever gave a damn was when I was fucked up."

21

Shocking the Royals: Prince Charles, Princess Di, and Patricia and John Kluge

In early September of 1985, the island was abuzz about the most important pending social event of the Palm Beach season and, possibly, of the decade. Prince Charles and Princess Diana were jetting in from London for a visit and would be the star attraction of a large benefit ball for the prince's favorite charity, the United World Colleges Fund.

As the social set saw it, the gala event at the Breakers on November 12 would raise money for a good cause, but more important, it would allow the island's movers and shakers to meet and be photographed with the handsome Prince of Wales and his then storybook princess, Diana. With an admittance price of five thousand dollars per person, the cost of meeting royalty would not be cheap, but at least it was tax deductible.

To lend another touch of elegance to the affair, the Palm Beach Social Committee wanted to choose the right person to host the event. She had to have beauty, style, grace, poise, and above all, be rich enough to set the proper tone. Patricia Maureen Kluge seemed to be the perfect choice. She definitely had the looks. Part British and part Iraqi, Patricia had thick brunette hair, high cheekbones, and a long shapely figure that gave her an exotic appearance. Her charity credentials were impressive. She sat on the national board of directors of Ford's Theatre in Washington and served as a trustee on the board of the National Association for the Advancement of Colored People.

And Patricia Kluge had possessed another credential. She was married to America's wealthiest man, John Kluge, the self-made businessmen who had single-handedly created the Metromedia TV-radio-cellular phone empire. He was worth about $5 billion. The Kluges had only recently come to Palm Beach, having quietly rented a villa at the exclusive Palm Beach Polo and Country Club.

The social committee agreed the charity ball would integrate the Kluges into the island's social scene in a grand way. How wonderful the photograph would look on the front page of the Shiny Sheet. The nation's richest woman greeting Britain's royal couple in the most magnificent setting in the United States. At the request of industrialist and philanthropist Armand Hammer, a driving force behind the United Colleges charity project, Patricia Kluge agreed to take on the title of general chairwoman and hostess of the ball. Mrs. Kluge told reporters her main responsibility was to "set the mood" of the event and help publicize the worthy cause.

The event was about to receive plenty of publicity, but for reasons that had nothing to do with colleges or charities. In planning its coverage of the royal couple's upcoming visit to the United States, one of Britain's gritty Fleet Street tabloids, the *London Star*, discovered an interesting fact about the wife of the richest man in the United States. Patricia Maureen Kluge had, a decade earlier, starred in a series of soft-core porno movies, modeled nude in a raunchy sex magazine, penned an explicit sex advice column, and engaged in lesbian and group sex.

On September 23, the *Star* splashed the news across the front page as if the world had ended. DI'S PORN QUEEN HOSTESS—SEXY SECRET OF A TYCOON'S WIFE, the headline screamed. Suddenly explicit nude photos of Patricia Kluge appeared in the London papers, giving the topless page 3 models some competition. The prospect of Charles and Di trading pleasantries with an ex-porn queen had editors salivating. Buckingham Palace was surrounded by reporters. A spokesman for the royal family would only sniff a terse "no comment," the usual reply when the family faced yet another scandal cooked up by the racy London newspapers.

In the United Kingdom, Brits took the news with the usual good-natured chuckle. After all, who could get too serious about these things? But on Henry Morrison Flagler's sand-swept island the racy revelation was a completely different story.

Members of the charity-ball committee wondered how Patricia Kluge had managed to keep her secret and why John Kluge had even married her with that kind of past. How should the matter be handled? Should it be simply ignored or should Pat Kluge be forced to resign? As the committee searched for answers, reporters from around the world scrambled to piece together Patricia's scandalous past.

She was born Patricia Maureen Rose in 1949, the daughter of British businessman Edmund Rose and half-Scottish, half-Iraqi beauty Sylvia Arbuthnott. Raised in Baghdad when Iraq was still under British rule, young Patricia watched as the country's revolutionary nationalists made life increasingly uncomfortable for "outsiders." In the early 1960s Patricia's parents divorced, and in 1965 she and her mother moved to London. The precocious, long-haired brunette beauty was instantly subject to culture shock. It was the height of Mod London—Carnaby Street, free love, the Beatles, the Dave Clark Five. Twiggy was about to become the anorexic sex symbol to be emulated by women around the world.

If there ever was a time when Britain was the hip, tuned-in place to be—this was it. The almond-eyed Patricia observed it all, but remained the conservative, shy woman she had been raised to be in repressed Iraq, where native women not only hid their bodies in long heavy gowns, but concealed their faces.

As the ultra-cool, ultra-groovy period reached its crescendo in 1969, Pat finished high school and tried to decide what to do with her life. The transition from Iraq to Great Britain had not been easy. Pat and her mother had shared a one-bedroom flat in a depressed part of London. They made do with what little money her mother earned from a part-time sales job. It was certainly a far cry from the exotic, lavish splendors and royal lifestyle they had enjoyed in Iraq.

Pat remembered, "When you lead a colonial life, you really live in . . . Shangri-La, an ideal world of uniforms and tea garden parties and balls and men who looked so gorgeous."

She worked for a short time in a shipping office, then decided to enroll in a local secretarial school. It didn't last. "I walked into that class and I saw pale, sallow faces and I thought to myself, 'I am not like them, nor will I ever be like them.' So I walked out of that class and never walked back again," she recalled. "It was appalling, absolutely appalling. . . I remember deciding there and then that whatever happens to me in life, I will always depend on me."

So, at age nineteen she took a job as a belly dancer at the Labyrinth nightclub in London's Soho district. Patricia was an instant hit and became a favorite with the club's patrons. Her paycheck and the tips she made were enough to give her the sense of financial freedom and independence she so desperately wanted, even though her place of employment was not the classiest of venues.

"The Labyrinth was one of those places where the girls danced and the men put money in whatever they were wearing," recalled one of Patricia's old friends, Toni Marks.

One night a bearded, shaggy-haired man decked out in the definition of Mod with bell-bottom trousers, a collarless jacket, and love beads entered and sat down in front of the stage. It didn't take long for Patricia Rose to notice that she was being scrutinized intensely by the man.

After the show, he introduced himself as Russell Gay. She had heard the name. He was the publisher of the racy *Knave* magazine. With its blend of full-frontal nude pictorials and lurid sex advice columns, *Knave* was Britain's most explicit and popular mens' magazine. Although he looked young, at age fifty-two, Gay was just old enough to be Patricia's grandfather.

Gay became many things to nineteen-year-old Pat. He was the father she had lost when her parents divorced. He was the wealthy and powerful businessman who knew rich and famous people. He was Mr. Confident, knowing what he wanted and never looking back. And he looked straight into Pat's eyes as he talked. In a week's time, Pat and Russell Gay were dating. He showered her with flowers and gifts and, most important, attention.

She fell in love with Gay and immediately began to change her image to suit his wishes. She threw away her long, unfashionable dresses, exchanging them for the miniest of miniskirts. She updated her hairstyle. The "happening" couple were out and about at London's "grooviest" nightspots almost every evening.

The new Patricia Rose had arrived. They married in 1970, and Gay launched a new career for his young bride. He had decided Patricia should pose for his magazine, *Knave,* her lovely naked body out there for Britain's working class to see. A series of provocative full-frontal nude photos of Patricia were taken. One of her first pictorials was titled: "Patricia Rose: The Newest Sex Game."

Russell then gave his wife a sex-advice column to write. It was an instant hit. The letters poured in from the fans who had admired Pat's previous picture spreads. Wrote one fan, "Both my wife and myself are great admirers... There you were being caressed on a bed showing your sensational shaven body..."

Patricia dived into her new career with a passion. Photographer

George Harrison Marks—who publishes the British S&M magazine *Kane*, and who was best man at Pat and Russell's wedding—said: "Patricia was outrageous in *Knave*. She had a tremendous following. She was the forerunner of them all. The raunchier her full frontal pictures the better, as far as she was concerned. She was sensual and always wore extremely revealing clothes. When the see-through era was in, she would walk into restaurants almost naked."

Many of her photos were part of "how-to" pictorials, in which she posed in positions suggested in the *Kama Sutra*. Her column regularly critiqued the bedroom quirks of different nationalities.

"She loved the porn business," Marks recalled. "She was a total, total exhibitionist. Her poses for *Knave* were so explicit that I had a terrible row with Russell Gay about it when they came to dinner. I said, 'How can you put your wife in these pictures?' They showed the lot." Marks also said Pat dabbled in kinky sexual behavior and had once made love to his ex-wife, Toni.

Luckily for Pat, she had not appeared in any hard-core photos in which actual penetration was shown. But her soft-core pictures left little to the imagination. She also produced a series of erotic audiotapes featuring titles like *Nymphomania* and *The Education of Mandy*. And she was said to have been the opening act one year at the Danish Sex Fair in Odense, performing a striptease on stage.

She and her husband also liked to throw wild parties. Dancer Gess Whitfield told writer Sharon Churcher of *Penthouse* magazine: "[Pat] would loosen anybody up. Instead of kissing you [hello], she'd grab your dick… There was never a total gang-bang at these parties. It would be people disappearing upstairs for a quickie… I made love to Pat a couple of times… it was like [in] a foursome."

Whitfield remembered that once, while seated next to Pat at a dinner party, she "suddenly took a tit out, put it in prawn cocktail sauce, and said, 'Go on! Lick it off!'"

Years later, Pat explained her risqué behavior this way:

> Russell had a very strong personality and I did it because I fell in love with the man. He was everything I was brought up not to get involved with. [But] just consider the situation. Here was a girl brought up with a certain set of values, in a strict Catholic family where everything was proper and your whole future was laid out for you.
>
> And suddenly circumstances change. But your family still wants you to be that person even though it no longer seems very natural.

I just felt they can't possibly be right. There must be another world out there, one that I can call reality. Russell thought I was so beautiful. Can you imagine how mesmerizing that was to a simple nineteen-year-old? Eventually we parted because it was a question of my sanity.

When she and Gay divorced in 1976, twenty-seven-year-old Patricia gave up all of her old haunts and many of her old friends. She never looked back and offered no apologies for her behavior. "I was very young, very much in love, and very naïve, and I'm not ashamed of it. It was very amusing, I have to say," she later reflected.

While she was no longer married to him, a part of Russell had remained with Pat—his business sense. She had often helped him in the marketing of *Knave* and other ventures. While she no longer wanted any part of the adult-magazine trade, she was eager to apply her business knowledge to a new venture. She went on to form a small film company that distributed low-budget movies in foreign countries.

In the late 1970s, Patricia, while visiting New York, attended a show-business fund-raiser. One of the many people she was introduced to that night was John Werner Kluge. At five-foot-nine, the long and lean Patricia towered a full four inches over Kluge. But it did not seem to matter. Pat and John hit it off immediately. She was extremely impressed by Kluge. Here was a very wealthy, self-made man who seemed modest, almost shy.

John Kluge was shy in many ways, but business was not one of them. He had built a multibillion-dollar media empire to become one of the world's richest men.

Born in Chelmnitz, Germany, in 1914, Kluge came to America with his parents eight years later, settling in Detroit. Kluge excelled in school and when he reached college age won a scholarship to Columbia University. He studied economics by day and received very high marks, but at night he swapped his books for a deck of cards and ran all-night campus poker games.

"I loved to gamble in those days," Kluge told *Forbes* magazine. "The dean called me into his office and said, 'We just don't understand. You're up gambling half the night.' So I said, 'You will never catch me gambling again. But I never said I wouldn't play. I had a book all ready and if there was a knock at the door, I had to fold my cards."

When Kluge graduated in 1937, he had a savings account of seven thousand dollars from four years of poker winnings. Poker aside, Kluge had impressed many people at the university. Author Clarence Lovejoy wrote in one of his books about young Kluge: "[He] can't be president of the United States because of his birth, but he won't stop far short of it."

After serving with U.S. Army Intelligence during World War II, Kluge began to build the foundations of his career. In 1946, with the money he had saved, he purchased a small AM radio station with the ironic call letters, WGAY, in Silver Spring, Maryland. It made money and within two years he had bought another station. As Kluge ran his businesses, he sharpened his managerial skills, learning how to maximize profits by controlling cash flow and finding ways of obtaining tax breaks through investing.

In 1959, Kluge had a chance meeting with an old friend on a street in Washington, D.C. The friend told him about two television stations for sale in New York and Washington. Kluge studied both properties, researched the television market in both cities, and arranged financing to buy the stations, which he ran under the name of the Metropolitan Broadcasting Company. Over the next decade, Kluge acquired five more stations—the maximum then allowed by law.

Instead of transforming his TV stations into a national network to compete against NBC, CBS, and ABC, Kluge ran them as independents. While this meant no prestigious network shows, Kluge's stations proved highly profitable with their combination of old movies, reruns of popular network TV series, and syndicated programs. He changed the name of his company to Metromedia.

By the mid-1970s under Kluge's dynamic leadership, Metromedia entered into a fledgling business some Wall Street investors criticized at the time as being highly risky: the cellular-phone and beeper industry, which has since become one of the fastest growing businesses in America. Metromedia stock rose from $4.50 per share in 1974 to nearly $500 a share by the early 1980s. Kluge sold his TV empire in 1984 for $2 billion to media magnate Rupert Murdoch, who used it to create the Fox Network.

Kluge provided a clue about his business savvy in an interview with *USA Today.* "The thing I like is not the score, it's the game, seeking new challenges. The score means nothing. What means something is what you're going to do tomorrow." In another interview, he said that, just like his nights at the poker table at Columbia, there had been a gambling aspect to his success. "Luck plays a large part," he said.

While Kluge's empire thrived, his personal life did not. He had divorced his first wife and was having marital problems with his second. A conservative and intensely private man, Kluge had successfully shielded much of his personal life from the public, including the details and circumstances of his unhappy marriages.

As Patricia Maureen Rose Gay conversed with Kluge for the first time at the New York party, she found him a refreshing change from the boisterous and exhibitionistic characters she had left behind in London. Likewise, Kluge found Patricia charming, beautiful, and easy to talk to.

As Pat recalled, "I was absolutely enthralled with his mind. But he was married and I was engaged."

Several months later, Kluge divorced his second wife and, as he had so many times in his businesses, decided to take a gamble. He flew to London and made a dramatic offer of marriage to Pat, who was living with her fiancé, Kenneth Newton, a psychiatrist. At first she said no. Kluge, however, would not go away. For three months he pleaded with her by telephone, in notes, and in person to drop her betrothed and marry him.

His persistence paid off. Patricia finally agreed to marry him, and John Kluge presented his new love with a 20.5-carat diamond engagement ring. They were wed in New York's majestic St. Patrick's Cathedral on Fifth Avenue on May 23, 1981. Two weeks earlier, Kluge had agreed to convert to Catholicism to satisfy his bride's religious requirements.

Photographer George Harrison Marks did not seem surprised by Kluge's actions. "Men are putty in Pat's hands," he said.

Patricia and John Kluge lived in a large triplex penthouse on top of the Metromedia office on East 67th Street, complete with an indoor waterfall. Weekends and vacations were spent in their waterfront home in Westchester County's Premium Point and at a ten-thousand-acre horse farm near Charlottesville, Virginia. Patricia, who had had a childless marriage with Gay, wanted children by her new husband, but Kluge had undergone a vasectomy sometime before. Although he went to several specialists, Kluge was told the process could not be reversed. The couple decided to adopt and soon had a three-month-old boy, christened John W. Kluge, Jr. Kluge's friend, Frank Sinatra, agreed to be the infant's godfather.

Pat certainly enjoyed her newly acquired wealth, playing interior decorator in her new homes, going on extended spending sprees at New York's finest boutiques, and traveling. But she always liked to downplay her lifestyle, coyly telling reporters, "I'm just a little housewife in Virginia, minding my own business, doing my bit for the world."

Friends say Patricia taught Kluge how to enjoy his fortune, making him dress more stylishly and spend more freely. Gone was the man who sometimes left his overcoat in his limousine so he wouldn't have to tip the coatcheck girl at a restaurant.

Patricia had told her closest friends about her porno past and her husband was aware of those earlier years although not in such graphic detail as the papers eventually described them. Before the Palm Beach scandal broke, Pat had always given acquaintances and reporters a sanitized version of her past, saying only that she had been "a writer," not that her most extensive writing job had been solving sex problems in *Knave*.

As more and more information about Pat Kluge's past emerged, the members of the charity-ball committee began to squirm. They met at the Breakers over shrimp salad and iced tea to try to decide what action to take. If Pat stayed on as hostess, the entire event could be overshadowed by her past. Her presence could be terribly embarrassing for Charles and Di. They might even have to cancel. If the ball was to be saved, the committee agreed, Patricia Kluge would have to go. But how would she be told?

Meanwhile, Pat Kluge attempted to contact some of her society "sisters" for advice and counsel on the publicity nightmare. But nobody would take her calls. A few days later, Pat made the announcement that, regretfully, she would be unable to host the event. She and her husband, she said, would be "traveling abroad" on the night of the party.

"Mrs. Kluge is no longer chairman of the event," socialite Maggie Shearer announced solemnly. "I like her and I hate to see things going on that would not please her. But now it's over and I would hope we can move onto more positive aspects of the party. I just heard that Joan Collins is coming down...and that should be fun. Going on about Mrs. Kluge is just beating a dead horse, don't you think?"

Remarked socialite Mary Sanford, "I was told that they asked her to resign. Why they asked her in the first place, I don't know. I was horrified. She must have known it was going to come out. It certainly was embarrassing for the crown prince of England."

Publicly, John Kluge remained quiet about the scandal, but privately he was livid. It was not so much that Pat's secret was out, but rather all of the attention it was getting and the manner in which his name was being dragged into the newspaper. He hated the cheap, tawdry headlines. It was one reason he had never written an autobiography. Kluge told *USA Today*, "Some...I've read...well, I wouldn't want to...let's just say it strikes me that there is little left unexpressed."

On the other hand, Patricia Kluge did not mince words. "This was the best thing that could have happened. First, you have to be secure in yourself to be able to come out of a thing like that well. And then I suddenly realized how many friends I had."

The black-tie charity ball in Palm Beach came off without a hitch. More than four hundred people attended the event in one of the chandeliered ballrooms of the Breakers. The prince and princess shook everybody's hands and posed for pictures. About $2 million was raised. Nobody seemed to miss Patricia Kluge—or at least nobody said they did at the time.

But a few weeks after the ball, Patricia received a letter on handsomely embossed Buckingham Palace stationery. In a handwritten note, Prince Charles told her he had not understood what all the fuss had been about. Furthermore, he and Diana were disappointed not to have met her and hoped to in the near future. When Patricia visited London a few months later, she met the royal couple and they became friends. With this gesture, it was as if Charles and Diana had subtly thumbed their noses at Palm Beach.

Meanwhile, John Kluge's fortune continued to grow, so much so that some people joked he could probably buy the island of Palm Beach and do away with all those people who had been so mean to his wife. Named in 1989 by *Fortune* magazine as America's wealthiest man—estimated to be worth $5.5 billion—he was three times as wealthy as media tycoons Ted Turner and Rupert Murdoch and real-estate moguls Harry and Leona Helmsley. Looking at it another way, Kluge would be able to send a five-hundred-dollar check to each of New York City's eight million residents and still have over a billion dollars left for himself.

But while Kluge's business empire continued to blossom, his marriage did not. He and Patricia separated, for reasons neither has talked about in public. On April 22, 1990, the Kluges announced they were divorcing. It was done quietly and ever so discreetly. In divorce court papers, the reason for the separation was listed simply as "irreconcilable differences." A statement released jointly by the couple read, "They have resolved all matters amicably and wish each other well."

Prior to the marriage the couple signed a complex, minutely detailed prenuptial agreement. Donald and Ivana Trump might have had a more publicized prenup, but the Kluges definitely had the biggest—a document that was some two-and-a-half-inches thick—making it lengthier than most phonebooks. Pat's share of the settlement was one of the two mansions on the couple's Virginia estate and the yearly interest on $1 billion. The interest works out to approximately $1.6 million— per week.

Patricia and her ex-husband remain "friendly," but what was the ultimate reason for their divorce? Liz Smith, one of the nation's most influencial gossip columnists, had one theory. "The bottom line, friends say, is he's a city guy, she's a country girl."

But the more widely held theory is that the Palm Beach debacle was the snowball that started the avalanche. A friend of the couple said, "The exposé about her past could have been the big problem. It could have strained the marriage."

Some place the blame squarely on John Kluge, saying he should never have allowed his wife to participate in the benefit. Another friend of the couple said, "He knew all about [her past] but it was he who decided to get her involved in the royal visit. To put her on public display like that was pure idiocy."

After the divorce, forty-one-year-old Patricia Kluge wasted no time in finding herself another man. Just a few weeks after the separation was publicly announced, a limousine was seen cruising Patricia's estate. It belonged to sixty-year-old Virginia governor Douglas Wilder, one of the country's foremost black leaders. The two had met at a party several months earlier. Soon they were seen horseback riding together and taking drives in the Virginia countryside. In mid-1991, Wilder briefly flirted with the idea of running for president in the 1992 election. A few months later, however, he dropped out of the race and ended his relationship with Pat.

Still, the momentary possibility that Patricia Kluge would be the nation's first lady had not escaped the editorial offices of the trashy supermarket tabloids. PORN QUEEN HEADED FOR THE WHITE HOUSE, one scandal sheet cheerfully announced.

22

Not in Our Club!
Estee Lauder, Sammy Davis,
Jr., and a U.S. Senator

I never want to join a club that would have me as a member," the late comedian Groucho Marx once quipped. Groucho wouldn't have to worry in Palm Beach. No country club would have accepted him as a member. With one exception, Jews need not apply for membership at the country clubs here.

Nor do blacks. Nor do other minorities.

Today, as the nation continues its slow but determined efforts to wipe out anti-Semitism and racism, Palm Beach seems to unashamedly bask in it. Not only at its private clubs, but in its government. For years, town fathers forced all domestics working in Palm Beach, mainly nonwhites, to carry specially issued I.D. cards whenever they came to the island.

So segregated is Palm Beach that some residents have joked that signs should be posted at the intercoastal bridges leading to Palm Beach that read: WHITE ANGLO-SAXON PROTESTANTS ONLY—ALL OTHERS SCRAM!

The two most blatant examples of organized discrimination in Palm Beach are the policies of the Everglades Club and the Bath and Tennis Club. Both ban all Jews and blacks from membership and even from entering the club as guests. The Everglades Club, at 356 Worth Avenue, is the island's oldest club, with about fourteen hundred members. Inside and out, it exudes tropical elegance.

Built in 1918 by Paris Singer, heir to the Singer sewing machine fortune, the club remains a throwback to the turn of the century. With its stained wooden detailing, antique Spanish furniture, and huge potted trees throughout, the Everglades is the picture of elegance. Its huge dining room has a roof that rolls back to allow diners to watch the constellations on clear nights. Nearby is an eighteen-hole golf course. The initiation fee is fifteen thousand dollars, and annual dues are fifteen hundred dollars.

In the bylaws of the Everglades Club, the membership clause reads: "Membership in the Club is restricted to persons who, amongst other qualifications, are of good moral character, financially responsible, twenty-one years of age or older and possessed of a background, personality and interests which are compatible with other members."

In recent years, some members have been severely chastised and sometimes suspended for bringing Jewish friends to the club. In 1979, socialite and *New York Post* gardening columnist C. Z. Guest found out how serious the club was about its ban when she brought two prominent Jewish women to lunch—one of them cosmetics queen Estee Lauder, who lives in Palm Beach. Guest was promptly suspended for a short time.

While both Lauder and Guest have declined to discuss the matter, a spokesman for Guest said, "You couldn't print what she said to the president of the club. She thinks all the members are a bunch of jerks."

Last year, an Everglades member wanted to show her friend, a Jewish woman, the club, and the two went to lunch. Luckily for the member, her guest had blond hair and none of the stereotypical Jewish traits the club's management might look for. All went well until it came to paying the check.

"I pulled out my credit card and was about to summon the waiter," the guest recalled, "when my friend screamed, 'Oh my God, No! Put it away! If they see that card with your Jewish name on it, I'll be in terrible trouble. Please! Put it away!' I couldn't believe it! It seemed incredible it was such a big deal. It was as if the Gestapo were watching us."

The discrimination is defended—on the record—by prominent residents. In a series of investigative articles about the clubs, the *Miami Herald* and the *Palm Beach Post* printed some startling admissions.

Everglades member Benjamin Oehlert, Jr., a former U.S. ambassador to Pakistan and ex-Palm Beach Town Council member, was one of those who defended the no-Jews rule: "If there is such a rule, what's wrong with it?" he asked. "It wouldn't be a private club if anybody could be brought into it."

Mortimer Howell Cobb, a retired navy captain and *Titanic* survivor, was more candid. "The public be damned in these matters. What business is it to anybody? I don't give a good goddamn what the guests think of the clubs!"

Of Jews and blacks, he added, "I'm not going to have them sitting in the dining room if I can help it."

Cobb did admit, however, that the discrimination rule could cause inconveniences, because he was unable to invite some of his bridge partners.

The late Wall Street financier Otto Kahn once amused some of his Palm Beach friends by asking them if they knew the definition of the word *kike*.

"A kike," Kahn said, "is a Jewish gentleman who has just left the room."

A rumor that has circulated for many years around the Everglades is that its founder, Paris Singer, himself was partly Jewish. "If he were applying for membership today, there's no way the club would let him in," says a member.

The Jews finally hit back at the Everglades and other clubs in 1965. They built their own club on the north end of town and named it the Palm Beach Country Club. And just to show it wasn't as uptight as the other clubs, it promptly recruited a Christian member. Additionally, it topped the Everglades' initiation fee by twenty thousand dollars.

The founding of the "Jewish club" allowed members of the other clubs to say, "See. Now they have their own place." It only seemed to make the discrimination lines more clear.

No one is immune. Neither children nor senators. In 1980, recalled Michael Burrows, a Jew and prominent developer, his teenage son was kicked out of the Bath and Tennis Club as he had lunch with another boy who was a member. "It was a fightening experience for them," he said.

The late New York senator Jacob Javits remembered an ugly incident in the 1960s at the now-defunct LaCoquille Club, as he played tennis with a member there. As the two left the court, the senator's host was told that Javits had to leave and could never return.

"I played tennis pretty well and I was dressed in the proper white tennis outfit," recalled Javits, a devout Jew. "It was really very insulting for my host."

Soon after men's fashion designer John Weitz joined the Beach Club in 1979, he received a shock. Another member walked up to him and called him a kike. Weitz resigned and, in fact, began coming to Palm Beach less and less.

The clubs aren't the only ones that discriminate. A prestigious women's club, the Junior Assembly of Palm Beach—which sponsors by-invitation-only dances and etiquette classes for youngsters—seems to have a problem with Jews. In 1987, a group of Jewish parents charged that twenty established Jewish families had been turned down by the Junior Assembly while non-Jewish newcomers were welcome.

"This is definitely discrimination," said Louise Shure of Palm Beach's small but feisty Anti-Defamation League.

Why has it all been tolerated? One major reason might be apathy. "For a lot of Jews, as long as people aren't being shot in the street, they're content to let it go on," explained Max Fiterman, a board member of the Palm Beach Country Club.

One couple in an odd situation is Alfred Lasher, Jr., and his wife, Jeanne, who hold memberships in a half dozen private clubs. However, the couple can't go to all of their clubs together because he is Jewish. Lasher says: "It doesn't bother her and it doesn't bother me. If I'm not welcome in her clubs, I don't go."

The question arises, who would want to belong to a club that would keep out his friends? Some members of the clubs that discriminate protest that they truly believe in equal rights and do not like the segregationist rules their clubs enforce. However, they say, to protest could mean expulsion. And club membership in Palm Beach, like it or not, is a powerful status symbol.

Some major changes have occurred in recent years. Oilman Nathan Appleman has been instrumental in getting many of the charity balls traditionally held at the discriminatory clubs to change locations. In the last decade, more than a dozen prominent groups have been persuaded to stay away, including the Palm Beach Bar Association, Princeton University, Good Samaritan Hospital, and the Palm Beach Civic Association.

"It's their right to discriminate, but it's our right not to patronize," said an official at the Bar Association.

In January 1992, the Anti-Defamation League received a lot of attention when it protested the appearance of the Dutchess of York, Sarah Ferguson, at a charity ball at the Everglades. Fergy's flimsy excuse was that it was okay because the ball had not been organized by the Everglades, it was only being held there.

Because few, if any, blacks live on Palm Beach—and several prominent citizens surveyed could not name one—the issue of blacks at the clubs is not as prominent as the Jewish issue.

But occasionally the color issue does surface. One night, when entertainer Sammy Davis, Jr., was in town, Jim Kimberly, heir to the Kimberly-Clark tissue fortune, invited him to dinner at the Everglades Club. But as they entered, Kimberly was pulled aside by a club manager and told that Davis would not be allowed in. Kimberly realized immediately that Davis was a double threat to the club's discriminatory guest code. Not only was Davis black, but he was Jewish. Kimberly quickly guided him to a limousine and proceeded to another restaurant. Over dinner, they laughed at the incident.

One local physician, Dr. Harold Spear, who is a member of the Bath and Tennis Club, told the *Miami Herald*, "At the hospital where I work, the black doctors are intellectually fine and wonderful people, but they aren't able to handle the cosmopolitan aspects of circulating in society."

When Henry Flagler used fire in 1894 to rid his newly created paradise of black people, he set in motion a pattern of discrimination that lasted for decades. Blacks who could afford the steep prices were routinely denied the opportunity to buy real estate in Palm Beach. Property was suddenly "off the market" when an inquiry was made by a black. Those discriminatory policies are no longer in effect, at least from the real-estate broker's end. It is an unwritten rule among Palm Beach's old guard that anyone selling his house will not sell it to a black family, even if it means taking a loss. The point is almost moot, however. Very few blacks look for real estate on the prohibitively expensive island.

Some say that within five years the nation's worsening economic climate will force clubs to loosen their membership criteria. Others believe that with the year-by-year erosion of the so-called old guard, hipper, more tolerant Palm Beach millionaires will force their clubs to become politically and morally correct.

"This situation in Palm Beach does not exist anyplace else in the United States," adds millionaire businessman and philanthropist Nathan Appleman.

Another resident, Richard Rampell, whose four-year-old son was excluded from a pal's birthday party at the Everglades because of his religion, raged: "These clubs perpetuate this kind of bigotry. I think the guest policies are positively reprehensible. In anyplace else in America, this would be a reason for shame."

Longtime Palm Beach resident Dick Hurley added: "They don't want Jews, they don't want blacks. These people don't have careers and don't want to change. Their bigotry is all they have going for them."

"In this day and age, it is very disheartening to know that these rules still exist," said Max Fisher, a Jewish oilman listed in *Forbes* magazine as one of the four hundred richest men in America. Fisher, ironically, would find himself in the forefront of another raging controversy when his daughter, Mary, admitted she had the AIDS virus and made a stirring speech at the Republican Convention in August 1992 pleading for the government to provide more funding for AIDS research.

Oddly, there is no discrimination against women, as long as they are ethnically "suitable." The Everglades Club has many women members, but they are all white and Anglo-Saxon Protestant.

For many years, discrimination was not limited to the clubs. The government of Palm Beach also maintained a highly suspect law for forty-five years, until it was struck down recently. In 1940, the town board enacted a rule that all workers in Palm Beach had to be fingerprinted, photographed, and issued identification cards by the police. This list included domestics, nightclub workers, hotel workers, delivery people, restaurant help, liquor vendors, salespeople, gardeners, janitors, caddies, and newsboys older than seventeen. White-collar workers were not included.

For forty-three years, the system continued, with over 125,000 cards being issued. The Palm Beach police knew who was coming and going from their island. Police had the right to stop employees and demand to see I.D. The occasional upstart who hadn't bothered getting a card or had refused to do so could be fined or jailed.

Then, in 1983, the town's practice was thrust into the spotlight in cases involving two would-be workers, Rochelle Vana and Ignatius Wallace. In April, after moving to West Palm Beach from Indiana, Rochelle Vana landed a twelve-thousand-dollar-a-year job as a waitress at the Sailfish Club on North Lake Trail. She was told she would have to fill out some forms over at police headquarters.

But as Vana looked over the forms and the fingerprinting ink was readied, she burst into tears. The humiliating process reminded her of her husband Rosti's bleak life in Czechoslovakia. He had fled the then Communist-controlled country in the 1950s for a better life in America.

"This is America, not Russia," Vana cried to the officer before running out.

At about the same time, a black man named Ignatius Wallace had just gotton a job delivering ice at the Breakers Hotel. At the police station, he was told the card would cost him a registration fee of four dollars. "I did not have the money. I had been out of work for so long and there was no one I could borrow it from," he recalled. Besides, he said, "it reminded me of conditions in South Africa," where blacks were required to carry a "pass card" at all times.

Both refused to comply and left their jobs. Their plights came to the attention of the American Civil Liberties Union, which offered to represent them in court. Soon Palm Beach was facing a lawsuit charging that its I.D. law was discriminatory and unconstitutional. Battle lines were drawn and statistics released.

Over the years, it was revealed, more than 125,000 cards had been issued. It seemed that one of Palm Beach's oldest residents had been Big Brother. The town called the cards "a matter of vital security for our residents." Opponents said Palm Beach's policy was racist, discriminatory law that created a two-class system.

Ironically, said some, the I.D. law seemed aimed at West Palm Beach, the heavily black neighbor of Palm Beach that Henry Flagler had built as "a city for all of my workers to live in."

The debate raged for two years as both sides prepared for a showdown in court. Until then the publicity had been pretty much limited to Florida. That changed rapidly in June 1985 when controversial cartoonist Garry Trudeau took on the issue in his nationally syndicated "Doonesbury" strip. The comics were devastating. In one, a Palm Beach dowager breaks the news to a friend that her worker is in trouble with the law:

> "I'm dreadfully sorry, dear, your Mr. Royce didn't have an I.D., so he was detained."
>
> "You mean arrested? For being an undocumented black man?"
>
> "Ordinarily, dear, it's a good system. In fact, our employees all love it. It gives them a sense of security, of belonging. The cards make them feel like members of our big Palm Beach family."
>
> "Are they?"
>
> "Don't be silly, dear. It's just something they can show their friends."

The satire wasn't strong enough for the town to voluntarily stop its practice. The ID cards remained.

In December 1985, a two-day hearing took place. Police officials testified that island residents and businesses lost up to $5 million a year in thefts and robberies and without that law the crime rate would increase. Besides, they said, the I.D. cards had helped them catch two killers over the years as well as break up a couple of burglary rings.

Opponents countered that Palm Beach was actually practicing apartheid. They noted that workers who didn't get I.D. cards within forty-eight hours were hounded by police who threatened to arrest them. And why was there a two-tier system where white-collar workers didn't have to carry the cards?

Finally, in December 1985, after more than two years of legal wrangling, U.S. District Judge Norman Roettger ruled the I.D. requirement unconstitutional. The judge made two points. He said the law had impeded the free flow of commerce by placing restrictions on employment. And, he added, it was "intimidating to those who do not want to reveal former incarceration, residence in a mental institution, covert cohabitation, illegitimacy, or race."

Reaction was mixed. "I wore black today," said Palm Beach Town Council member Nancy Douthit. "I think it's a black day in the history of our country."

Added Town Council president Paul Ilyinsky, a grand-nephew of the Russian czar Nicholas, "It represented a certain protective screen, a barrier. In this outrageous age we live in, that meant a lot to our people. It has been a nice feature of living in a town like Palm Beach."

Workers, however, rejoiced, saying the whole system had made them feel like thugs. Rochelle Vana, the woman who'd started it all, remarked: "When I did this, I really just thought the Palm Beach Town Council would just hold a meeting or something and decide they'd get rid of the law because it was stupid. For an employer to do it, that's one thing. They can ask for fingerprints and whatever. But don't make it a law."

The Town of Palm Beach was smarting from the defeat. What to do? The possibility of a voluntary I.D. system was raised, although it was determined to be too expensive and probably wouldn't stop the kinds of people it was intended to keep out.

Palm Beach leaders thought carefully. A few years later, in April 1989, the town sprang back with a brand-new idea: surveillance cameras on the bridges. According to the plan, Palm Beach police would place video cameras on the three bridges leading to the island and record every car, truck, bicycle, and pedestrian heading to the island. Officers would then be able to review hours of videotape taken before and after any serious crime.

At town meetings, residents heatedly debated the issue. Some who had angrily defended I.D. cards for employees just a few years back were now livid at the suggestion that they would be videotaped along with common criminals while driving back to their homes.

And did the town want to provide Garry Trudeau with more devastating material? "This situation might work against us in our public image," said resident Phillip Radlauer. "We've been taking a terrible beating as an elitist community."

But dozens of other residents said the cameras were a must. They pointed to the case of a woman from nearby Lake Worth who had been murdered and her body dumped in the road next to the Bath and Tennis Club. Cameras might have identified the killers and their car.

The *New York Times* entered the fray. The newspaper suggested that if Palm Beach placed cameras on one end of the drawbridges, the residents of West Palm Beach should put customs agents on the other end to pat down Palm Beachers coming into their community.

Two months after the debates, the Town Council dropped its proposed plan, ironically just after a plea from Police Chief Joseph Terlizzese, who only a few years before had fought hard to have the I.D. card system. Terlizzese had told the town fathers he doubted the cameras would produce pictures of sufficient clarity to identify drivers.

"And we can't continue to build fortresses and barriers around ourselves," he said. "Next thing you know we'll be building machine-gun nests."

With I.D. cards gone, with the camera proposal dead, Palm Beach residents are searching for new security measures. Violent crime is going up in neighboring West Palm Beach. In recent years the police have had to deal with race riots in its heavily black neighborhoods.

During the last round of racial unrest in the summer of 1991, another "plan" made its way around the island in the form of a joke: "Hey, if the natives get too restless over there, there's only one thing to do. Pull up the bridges."

Another longstanding joke in Palm Beach gibes that residents treat their pets better than they do nonwhites and Jews. It is humor mixed with reality. Several dog owners send their pets for baths and haircuts in chauffeur-driven limousines. In the 1970s, one white French poodle could be seen alone in the back seat of a sleek black Rolls-Royce as it was driven to the beauty parlor.

Along Worth Avenue there are no water fountains for humans. But a small, tiled "dog bar" is a welcome oasis for dogs in need of a drink of water.

On November 5, 1965, two poodles were "wed" in a ceremony at the Poodle Boutique in Palm Beach. The groom was Muggins Carvey, the bride, Petite Brabham. The *Palm Beach Daily News* highlighted the wedding in an article. "Petite was attired in a dual-length ivory satin gown trimmed with Alençon lace. Her long veil of French illusion fell to her turquoise-tinted toenails from the crown of seed pearls attached to her topknot." Muggins wore a white collar, black bow tie, and white hat. While the newspaper did not describe the honeymoon, it was understood the pets could enter any club of their choice.

23

No Trump:
Donald, Ivana, and Marla

The names of both the late E. F. Hutton and Marjorie Merriweather Post made page-one news in the mid-1980s, and the circumstances were hardly flattering. On May 2, 1985, E. F. Hutton, one of the nation's largest brokerage firms, pleaded guilty to two thousand federal charges involving the illegal manipulation of its checking accounts. The Wall Street firm agreed to pay $2 million in fines and return as much as $8 million to banks it had defrauded.

Eight months later, another story broke that a few of Marjorie Post's friends were certain had her rolling over in her grave. MAR-A-LAGO'S BARGAIN PRICE TAG ROCKS COMMUNITY declared the front page of the *Palm Beach Daily News* on January 5, 1986. Mar-a-Lago, one of the nation's most famous private homes and crown jewel of Palm Beach's estates, had been sold for the bargain price of $5 million.

Many island residents, however, were more concerned about the new owner. Donald Trump, the sometimes arrogant, publicity-driven New York City real-estate developer and owner of Atlantic City casinos, now held the keys to Mar-a-Lago. Trump had plenty of money—he estimated his fortune at $500 million—but to some he seemed to have little class. With boundless energy for self-promotion and willingness to speak on almost any topic without a public-relations team at his side, Trump often was accused of being crude and tactless.

He had shocked the art world with his blunt assessment of Van Gogh's masterpiece *Irises*, which he had been given the opportunity to buy.

"What would I do with *Irises*? Hang it up on a wall? Some janitor might walk away with it. Charge people to look at it? You know what *Irises* is? It's a piece of canvas with some paint on it."

Whether Trump could appreciate Marjorie Merriweather Post's majestic estate that reached from the Atlantic shore to Lake Worth remained to be seen. But then Mar-a-Lago had not been appreciated for quite some time. During the final years of her life in the early 1970s, Marjorie Post—heir to the C. W. Post cereal fortune—began planning for the future of Mar-a-Lago. She was aware that nobody in her family could afford to maintain the 118-room mansion after her death, but she did not want her home torn down like so many of the other great estates in Palm Beach. She decided to will her palace to the federal government to be used as a residence where monarchs and other visiting dignitaries from foreign countries could be entertained during the winter months. The U.S. government would certainly like to own Mar-a-Lago, she thought.

When Post died in 1973 at the age of eighty-six, her estate, known as the Marjorie Post Foundation, announced that Mar-a-Lago would now become a national treasure to be enjoyed by the nation's leaders and visiting rulers of the world. President Richard Nixon journeyed to Palm Beach and extolled the splendors of Marjorie Post's magnificent gift to her country.

After the initial hoopla, however, the government found several drawbacks to owning Mar-a-Lago. The mansion was located under the flight path of nearby Palm Beach International Airport, making it an unsuitable residence for world leaders because of the possibility of crashing planes. Then there was the cost. Upkeep, maintenance, and staffing of Mar-a-Lago costs in excess of $1 million a year.

The government retained the property until 1980, when the considerable expense forced the Department of the Interior to return the deed to the Post Foundation. The transfer occurred one year after the home had been placed on the National Register of Historic Places. Post's executors, not wanting to pay a large tax maintenance bill for the year, immediately sought $25 million for it, a price many considered low. Robin Leach, who had filmed his TV show, "Lifestyles of the Rich and Famous," at Mar-a-Lago several times, said he thought the home was worth at least $35 million. Leach added, "And if you tried to build it today, you would have to at least double that figure when you added in the cost of land and furnishings. Quite frankly, you couldn't do it."

The offering caused an initial flurry of interest. The island's real-estate dealers bet among themselves as to which brokerage firm would land a sale on Mar-a-Lago. But two years later there was still no sale. The price was reduced to $20 million. Mar-a-Lago was becoming known, even among its greatest admirers, as "the house that everybody loves but nobody wants" and, with its seventeen-acre spread, "the biggest white elephant in the world."

In 1982, while vacationing in Palm Beach, Trump toured the property at 1100 South Ocean Boulevard and offered $15 million. The bid was considered a lowball offer and rejected by the Post Foundation. Two years later, after several other prospective buyers failed to offer an acceptable price, the Post estate announced that it would sell the property to Houston developer Cerf Stanford Ross for $14.3 million. A contract was signed. Ross said he would subdivide the seventeen-acre property and build "historically appropriate" condominiums around the main house. His plan ignited considerable outrage in the community. Some town leaders criticized the Post Foundation for being insensitive to the history of the grand property. It was a moot debate. Twelve months later, Ross, unable to come up with financing for the project, defaulted, and Mar-a-Lago went back on the market.

Real-estate brokers now speculated that the property would sell for $10 million, maybe less. In late 1985, Trump made a new bid of $5 million for Mar-a-Lago—one third the amount he offered three years earlier. This time the offer was accepted. Donald Trump was the new owner. He paid an additional $2 million for an adjoining piece of beachfront. Amazingly, the total price tag of $7 million was still $1 million less than what Marjorie Post had paid to build it in 1926!

How had he struck such a deal? "Negotiation is an art and I have a gift for it," he answered in his usual cocky manner.

Nobody seemed to know exactly what his plans were, but the Palm Beach library had numerous requests for material on Trump that week. Everybody wanted to discover what he was all about. In over two decades, Donald Trump had acquired a number of substantial properties, including the Plaza Hotel, Trump Tower, three Atlantic City casinos, the Grand Hyatt Hotel, and several condominium buildings. Until 1992, he owned an airline, the Trump Shuttle.

Donald John Trump was born in 1946 in Jamaica Estates, Queens, an affluent section of New York City. He was the third of five children of Fred and Mary Trump. His father, a man of Swedish Protestant background, is a successful real-estate developer, having established himself during the Depression by building single-family homes and numerous rent-controlled and rent-stablized apartment buildings throughout Brooklyn and Queens.

As a youngster, Donald was "a pretty rough fellow," recalled his father, who sent his son to the New York Military Academy in Cornwall in upstate New York to straighten him out. Donald excelled at the academy, refocusing his youthful energies on school projects. He was elected captain of the baseball team as well as the student regiment. Recalled Col. Theodore Tobias, his coach, "He was a real leader. He was even a good enough first baseman that the White Sox sent a scout to look at him."

Trump next attended the prestigious Wharton School of Finance at the University of Pennsylvania. He specialized in real estate, but found many of his classes boring because they emphasized single-family homes rather than large-scale projects. While at Wharton, Trump learned more about the real-estate business, and, upon graduation, he joined his father's Trump Organization.

One of his first "major deals" was completed in 1976 when, against his father's wishes, he worked out a fifty-fifty arrangement with the Hyatt Corporation to acquire the rundown Commodore Hotel on Forty-second Street. He simultaneously negotiated a then-unheard-of forty-year tax abatement from New York City, which wanted to invigorate the shabby, depressed location. He then rebuilt the old hotel into the beautiful Grand Hyatt Hotel.

In 1979, he went into another fifty-fifty partnership with the Equitable Life Assurance Society to build Trump Tower, a gleaming residential and commercial skyscraper next to the exclusive Tiffany & Company on Fifth Avenue, in an area containing Manhattan's most expensive stores. The tower, which cost $200 million to construct, opened in 1982 and attracted such residents as Johnny Carson, Sophia Loren, and David Merrick and such retail shops as Charles Jourdan and Aspery's of London.

A year later, Trump erected a luxury condominium tower, Trump Plaza, on East 61st Street. In New Jersey, he opened what would be his first of three gambling casinos in Atlantic City. His father, using Donald's own hype, raved that "everything Donald touches turns to gold."

The young developer was also quite a ladies' man. "I met a lot of beautiful young single women and I went out almost every night," Trump recalled. "But many of them couldn't carry on a normal conversation. Many of them were phonies."

In 1976, while visiting Montreal for the summer Olympics, Trump met his future wife, Ivana Zelnickova, a blond ex-skier and fashion model. Ivana's entry into Canada from her native Czechoslovakia was the stuff from which melodramatic movies are made.

Born in 1949 in the industrial Czech town of Gottwaldov, Ivana moved to Prague as a teenager to attend Charles University with a major in physical education. She also took acting lessons and appeared in a few low-budget movies. In Prague, Ivana fell in love with a young, dark-haired skier named George Syrovatka. When Syrovatka moved to Canada to pursue his skiing career in 1971, Ivana wanted to follow but had trouble obtaining a passport. Syrovatka arranged for Ivana to marry his friend Alfred Winklmayr, an Austrian resident, whose nationality would assure Ivana the right to travel outside her country.

Shortly after the marriage of convenience in November 1971, Ivana packed her bags, flew to Montreal, moved in with her lover, and divorced Winklmayr. A few years later, the relationship broke up, and Syrovatka ran off with one of Ivana's girlfriends.

As Trump and Ivana began dating, the developer soon realized she "wasn't someone you dated casually," and ten months later they were married in Manhattan. The ceremony was performed by Dr. Norman Vincent Peale, whom Donald had credited with some of his success through Peale's teachings of "the power of positive thinking."

When Donald bought Mar-a-Lago, he estimated his worth at close to a half billion dollars. He also indicated he would spare no expense on the property.

"Mrs. Post had a kind of style that was unique," Trump said soon after his purchase. "She was highly intelligent and extremely graceful. I think every bit of that aura should be preserved...I cherish it, and we are going to take very good care of it."

Trump changed very little. He began to restore portions of the home that had been neglected. All of the original furnishings remained in their original places. The landscaping was not changed. The most radical addition to the estate was a sixty-four-by-thirty-foot swimming pool that was approved for construction by national and local architectural commissions. The elegantly tiled pool fit in with the character of the house. Trump's work on Mar-a-Lago prompted the Palm Beach Tax Assessor's Office to value the house at $11.5 million. Trump successfully sued, and the property was reassessed at $7 million, saving the developer more than $80,000 a year in taxes.

Inside Mar-a-Lago, the only noticable Trump additions are an oil painting of Trump in his tennis whites and photographs of his three children. Trump has also kept Marjorie Post's children's rooms intact.

Some of Dina Merrill's childhood scribblings still adorn the walls, which are made of hand-painted tiles displaying various children's fairy tales.

Trump took good care of Mar-a-Lago. But he and Ivana apparently lacked certain social skills. A dinner guest of the Trumps confided to journalist Linda Marx that Ivana never used any of the twenty-seven sets of Marjorie Post's antique china because "she is too cheap" and prefers caterers' dishes. "At dinner parties, the china used was rented and made for clods," another guest told Marx.

Reidun Sullivan, a former Mar-a-Lago maid, also has harsh words:

> I think about all the nice people in this country, and for the Trumps to be a symbol is too bad. They have no class. Mrs. Post must be turning in her grave. Donald shaved with disposable razors that he used over and over, kept hotel towels in the bathroom, watched television and ate fried chicken on top of a beautiful bedspread.
>
> Ivana was a tough cookie. Very demanding. She's got steel rods in her nose. If people came to dinner and Ivana thought they had AIDS, she would order the silverware be washed in Clorox, and that would ruin it. And they used cheap plastic ice buckets with the words *Trump Castle* on the antique furniture. All this mother-of-pearl inlay and you put plastic? No. I'm sorry. That tells you something right there.

While Trump knew few of his neighbors when he moved to Palm Beach, he was familiar with one of them, Leona Helmsley. The two detested each other. As far as Trump was concerned, the island was not big enough for the both of them.

"Leona Helmsley," he said, "is a bully who is driven mostly by a desire to intimidate others or to get away with something that other people can't. Being a good businesswoman is, to her, secondary to being a bitch on wheels."

Their longtime feud had broken out fifteen years earlier.

"When I was still a bachelor, I attended one of her parties with a young and very attractive fashion model as my date," Trump recalled in *Trump: Surviving at the Top:*

> As soon as Leona saw who was with me, she became incensed. "How dare you bring that tramp to one of my parties," she screamed, looking the girl directly in the eyes. At first I was shocked, but then all the things people had been telling me about Leona and her Jekyll-and-Hyde personality started coming back to

me. The rest of the evening Leona was all smiles and small talk, as if nothing had happened.

The next day, when I was in my office, she called and said, "You fucking son-of-a-bitch, I watched you politicking the room. Don't do that on my time. And don't bring pretty girls to my parties anymore, especially girls that make the other women in the room look like shit. Fuck you!"

Trump inadvertently brought Palm Beach unwanted publicity in February 1990, when he found himself in the middle of a breaking sex scandal. Gossip queen Liz Smith reported in the New York *Daily News* that Donald and Ivana were separating and that Trump secretly had maintained a young mistress for several years. Her name was Marla Maples, a twenty-six-year-old Georgia blonde who had won several beauty pageants and had attempted to break into acting. Her biggest role had been that of a hapless motorist crushed by a load of falling watermelons in the Stephen King–directed horror movie, *Maximum Overdrive.*

Within twenty-four hours, New York City's papers dispatched investigative teams to look into Trump's affair. And for two weeks, New York's papers relegated such internationally important stories as the unification of the two Germanys and the freeing of Nelson Mandela to the bottom of the front page, while Marla and Donald ruled the top.

The headlines said it all: SPLIT! THEY MET IN CHURCH. TRUMP SAYS: ADULTERY NO SIN.

The most famous headline appeared in the *New York Post*. It read: *Marla boasts to pals about Donald*: BEST SEX I'VE EVER HAD. A picture of an extremely pleased Donald Trump accompanied the headline. Trump was happy with the article. "You could take it as a great compliment," he told friends.

A week after the story broke, the Trumps visited Mar-a-Lago for a long-planned vacation with the children. But as the *Post* exclaimed on its front page, they stayed in SEPERATE BEDS. As investigating reporters learned, Donald and Marla had spent several secret weekends at Mar-a-Lago. Islanders began referring to the Post home as Marla-lago. Journalists descended on Palm Beach to try to dig up new information about the comings and goings of Donald and Marla.

Some believe Donald left Ivana because he is easily bored. Others said the developer was caught by a midlife crisis. Still others blamed domestic problems, specifically in-laws. One friend of the Trumps pointed a finger at Ivana's mother, Maria Zelnickova, who often visited

Mar-a-Lago, and who would reportedly follow Donald around, nagging him. Donald wanted to relax in his paradise; his mother-in-law wouldn't let him.

"I think that helped destroy the marriage," the friend said. "For example, he would leave the lights on in every room he inhabited. And her mother would complain loudly about waste. She also tattled to Ivana if Mar-a-Lago wasn't properly cleaned and vacuumed when Donald was there."

Trump did not care what the newspapers wrote about his personal life. But he was sensitive about articles chronicling his finances. And over the next year, as a recession began to sweep the nation, Trump took a beating. His newly opened casino, the Taj Mahal, declared bankruptcy, and *Fortune* removed him from its list of the nation's richest men, accusing him of overvaluing his wealth and possibly being in debt. Trump was forced to admit he was in trouble and had to reorganize his empire. He sold his airline, the Trump Shuttle; his yacht, the *Trump Princess*; his personal jet; and some of his stake in the Grand Hyatt Hotel. The banks he worked with to stay afloat ordered him not to talk to the press about the negotiations. For the first time in his life, Donald was silenced, humbled.

In 1991, Donald Trump's financial problems came to Palm Beach. He announced plans to subdivide Mar-a-Lago in order to reduce the huge tax burden. He would divide the property into eight lots, in addition to the main house and guest house already there, and build new luxury homes. He maintained the homes would be built in a way that would not destroy the dignity of the main house. But residents complained the project would not only destroy the splendor of Mar-a-Lago, but would also transform heavily-traveled South Ocean Boulevard into a traffic nightmare.

In April 1992, the Palm Beach Town Council voted unanimously to deny Trump's request for a subdivision. Society columnist Billy Norwich captured Trump's ugly mood as he pondered the news:

> Picture it: Easter weekend in the posh resort and the artmeister of the deal is hitting golf ball after golf ball off the lawn of Mar-a-Lago into the intracoastal waterway and talking to the press. He is being watched by his parents, Fred and Mary Trump, and his significant other, Marla Maples, who wears a bikini and who will later this spring film a video celebrating, Marla says, "positive thinking."
>
> "I gave the town an opportunity and they blew it," Trump began, "Now I'm going to get everything I'm entitled to. The way I

look at it, the town is going to be writing me a check at the end of a year or so for the damages they have cost me. The lawsuit against Palm Beach is going to be a no-brainer, the town is totally screwed up."

The battle could go on for years. But there is a growing feeling even among the old guard that Mar-a-Lago as it stands today, as it has stood since 1927, will eventually become a memory. An oldtimer who has lived on South Ocean Boulevard for more than sixty years and loves Mar-a-Lago says even he has come to accept the inevitable. "There's no question it's going to be subdivided. It's just a question of when and how. The days of Marjorie Post, God bless her, are gone, and Mar-a-Lago is just too prohibitively expensive. Even our own government couldn't afford it."

The use of Mar-a-Lago has already been divided by a divorce court. Under the prenuptial divorce agreement, Ivana was paid $25 million, given the couple's $7 million mansion in Greenwich, and is guaranteed a stay of one month per year at Mar-a-Lago. During that month, one or two weekends are reserved for an all-girl "pajama party" for her close friends. Among her guests have been gossip columnist Liz Smith; Houston socialite Joan Schnitzer; Helen Von Damm, the former ambassador to Austria; socialite and gardening columnist C. Z. Guest; New York superpublicist Vivian Serota; and Fran Freeman of *Atlantic City* magazine. The women lounge around the estate, get facials and body treatments, and gossip about who's sleeping with whom, says an observer who has attended. A year after the Trump-Maples affair became public, one of Ivana's Mar-a-Lago guests surprised the gathering by arriving in a Donald Duck costume. "It's Donald! It's Donald!" the women squealed as the costumed reveler ran around the room flapping her wings and beating her chest. Trump reportedly was not amused.

To Ivana's chagrin, Donald had made the master bedroom a bit homier, placing a small silver-framed photograph of himself and Marla Maples on a nightable on the left side of the bed.

In the spring of 1992, Ivana Trump released her first novel, *For Love Alone*, penned for her by a ghost writer. The book is a thinly disguised story of her marriage to Donald. To publicize her roman à clef, Ivana appeared on the cover of various magazines, including *Penthouse*, and posed for photos with men friends. One photo showed her wearing a sexy, shimmering dress and being hugged from behind by a ruggedly handsome fellow on the Mar-a-Lago beach. It made Trump furious.

"She's in magazines posing with this boyfriend nobody's ever heard of in Mar-a-Lago. My place. This guy's living in my goddamn house and I have to watch this? Let him get his own place," Trump told Cindy Adams of the *New York Post*.

A few weeks later, Trump filed a petition in Manhattan Supreme Court to cease all future alimony payments to Ivana, including $350,000 annual spousal support, $50,000 for household employees, and use of Mar-a-Lago every March. The reason, Trump stated, was that Ivana was now living with Italian playboy industrialist Ricardo Mazzucchelli full time.

Trump said, "Under our divorce agreement, once she is cohabitating, I no longer have to pay maintenance and other financial obligations. I mean, this guy is with her in houses I paid for, eating in kitchens I paid for, sleeping in beds I paid for, and I'm still supposed to pay for it?"

Trump's employees compiled a list of Mazzucchelli's comings and goings with Ivana, including his overnight stays. "This boyfriend's in my Trump Tower apartment, my Connecticut house, my Mar-a-Lago home. What am I, some kind of shmuck that I'm going to support his life-style?" Trump said. Ivana and her new beau "played house" at Mar-a-Lago from March 7 through 29, Trump alleged.

To bolster Trump's charge, his lawyer took an affidavit from Minna Laputina, Ivana Trump's former social secretary, who said that Ivana had often expressed her love for Mazzucchelli. Ivana allegedly told Laputina she intended to marry Mazzucchelli, but wanted to hold off for "at least another year so that bastard can pay me more money."

Ivana denied she was living with Mazzucchelli and insisted he had been only a "houseguest." The alimony battle could drag on in the courts for several years.

Marla, meanwhile, rode the neverending Trump publicity train all the way to the Great White Way. On August 3, 1992, she made her Broadway debut as Flo Ziegfeld's mistress in *The Will Rogers Follies*. Marla's reviews were mixed. Critics said she had a bright and sassy presence on stage but a weak singing voice. There was speculation that Trump had a direct hand in getting his girlfriend the role—not unlike the way Charles Foster Kane pushed Susan Alexander into the spotlight in *Citizen Kane*. Trump denied it.

Marla's debut gained additional publicity thanks to a bizarre scandal which had erupted a few weeks earlier. Her longtime publicist, Chuck Jones, was arrested and charged with the burglary of dozens of pairs of Marla's high heels from her midtown Manhattan apartment. Jones allegedly broke into her home several times over the past few years and stole the footwear to satisfy a weird shoe fetish. Marla had complained that for years her shoes, bras, and panties had been disappearing. After refusing to believe her at first, Trump finally set up a hidden video camera in her bedroom, and it caught Jones. After his arrest, Jones was released on five thousand dollars bail. The case is under investigation by the Manhattan District Attorney's Office. Jones had been an integral part of the original "coverup" of the romance between Donald and Marla. When the couple traveled together to Mar-a-Lago, to the ski slopes of Aspen, to Atlantic City, Jones faithfully issued "no comment" and vigorously denied the romance.

While Trump and Marla have been "engaged" for more than a year, it is hard to say when and if they will marry. Both have been evasive on the question of a wedding date.

There is no evasion, however, when you ask Trump whether he will remain a Palm Beach resident for the foreseeable future. As far as he is concerned, Mar-a-Lago is one of the last properties he will ever sell. Donald and Marla have not plunged into the Palm Beach social scene. Trump expects to remain an outsider, keeping away from the company of the island's jet-setting crowd. He sums up the island's endless stream of party people as "phonies," adding, "They are feeders at the trough."

24

Something to Sneeze At:
James and Jacquie Kimberly

In the spring of 1988, a one-story brick ranch home in Lake Clarke Shores—a racially mixed, middle-income community on the Florida mainland—briefly became a kind of tourist attraction among some of the rich and privileged of Palm Beach. The residence, located on two acres of lushly landscaped property dotted by palm and mango trees, was quite pleasant in appearance, although it certainly could not compare with any of the homes back on the island.

A number of Palm Beach people crossed Southern Boulevard Bridge and made the mile-and-a-half journey southwest to get a glimpse of the property. Upon their return they expressed their sentiments in the form of disbelieving questions.

"My God, isn't it a shame about Jim Kimberly?"

"Of all people, how could this have happened to Jim?"

They seemed to speak the name of Jim Kimberly as if he were dying or had passed away. Kimberly, however, was very much alive and quite healthy. He had recently purchased the peaceful, two-acre home in Lake Clarke Shores. At eighty-one years of age, with a full head of white wavy hair and a fit and trim physique, Kimberly had the handsome features and the zest of a man at least twenty years younger. He had been assured by his accountants that he would be "comfortable" for the rest of his life as long as he stuck to a "moderate" budget. And Kimberly was happily involved in a relationship with a stunningly beautiful divorcée about half his age.

From all appearances then, Jim Kimberly was somebody to be admired for his good fortune in life. But not to the residents of Palm Beach. Kimberly had once been one of them. Now in their eyes he was a pitiable and tragic figure. Only two decades earlier, James Holbrook Kimberly had nearly owned Palm Beach in wealth and in spirit. As one of the heirs to the fabulous Kimberly Clark tissue fortune, Kimberly commanded an inheritance of $50 million.

A consummate playboy, sportsman, and "swashbuckler," as he liked to think of himself, Jim Kimberly considered his adventurous nature his life's work. And while he rarely was employed during his adult life, he boasted an impressive if eclectic résumé: champion race-car driver, yachtsman, sport fisherman, big game hunter, entertainer of kings, world-class traveler, owner of homes all over the world, escort to some of the world's most beautiful women. It was not a life-style that could be maintained inexpensively, and yet, with the help of wise accountants and careful investments, he had managed to juggle all of his many "professions" and still retain a substantial portion of his holdings.

But now it was gone. A year earlier, Kimberly had found himself so much in debt that he had to sell his yacht, his sports cars, all of his homes, and some of the priceless furnishings he had collected over his lifetime. Even more humiliating, Kimberly had been forced to leave Palm Beach and seek cheaper accommodations. His new place in Lake Clarke Shores was located within the city limits of West Palm Beach, the city Henry Morrison Flagler had erected for his black workers in the 1890s. West Palm Beach shared part of its name with Palm Beach, but that was all it had in common, as far as Palm Beach was concerned.

"This whole house is the size of my last dining room," he says in an old man's rasp. "I have nothing left but this goddamned house and four dogs and five stray cats to feed every morning."

Jim Kimberly was viewed not merely as a tragic figure but also as one more example of how the mighty can fall in Palm Beach. A well-liked, unpretentious man, Kimberly had taken that fall hard, suffering a heart attack, enduring embarrassing newspaper headlines, and having nightly sobbing sessions over his crumbling empire.

Kimberly's friends had a simple explanation for his downfall: Jacqueline Trezise Kimberly. Jacquie had been Jim's third wife, a woman forty-three years his junior. A legendary spender, Jacquie's shopping exploits are still remembered along Worth Avenue. Her impulse buys could range from a two-hundred-dollar belt to a ten-thousand-dollar evening gown. Her sensational divorce from Jim Kimberly is still talked about. It was a divorce that followed the legendary breakup of businessman Peter Pulitzer and his wife. Some society watchers believed that lurid revelations produced during the Pulitzers' ruthless court battle spelled the end for the Kimberlys. According to one friend, the couples were torn apart by charges and countercharges involving lesbianism, orgies, incest, and rampant drug use. A lurid tale, but one that reveals the heart and soul of Palm Beach: Money talks and debtors walk. Jim Kimberly knows that painful truth.

Kimberly was born into money—money from his grandfather's fabulously successful paper-products business. The seeds of the Kimberly-Clark fortune had been planted back in 1864, when John Alfred Kimberly and five other investors opened a small paper mill in Neenah, Wisconsin. The mill manufactured print, book, and tea paper for distribution in Wisconsin and surrounding states. Kimberly, along with investor C. B. Clark, eventually bought out the other partners and within a decade turned the new Kimberly-Clark Company into one of the largest paper-products companies in the world. John Alfred, a conservative businessman who had run his company as president until the day he died, had long cherished a vision that his sons and grandsons and great-grandsons would guide Kimberly-Clark through the twentieth century and beyond, providing a lasting family legacy in the business world.

His third child, James Cheney Kimberly, fit well into that plan, assuming the role of corporation vice president soon after he graduated from college. James proved to have a lot of his father's business savvy; he went on to invent the world's first tissue paper, marketing it as Kleenex. The absorbent thin tissue was an instant success. No longer would people have to blow their noses into bulky cloth handkerchiefs and retain the unsanitary mess for the weekly wash. Kleenex tissues were convenient, disposable, and cheap. The Kimberly name became almost as famous as that of several other Wisconsinites: Georgia O'Keeffe, Alfred Lunt, Frank Lloyd Wright, and Harry Houdini.

It was only natural then that James, and his wife, Geraldine, wanted their son, James Holbrook Kimberly, to carry on in the family tradition as master businessman-inventor-innovator. Born in 1907, young Jim seemed initially to be the natural choice to follow in his father's and grandfather's footsteps. He was an active, outgoing youngster who excelled at sports and had many friends in school.

Jim, however, seemed ambivalent about his designated role in the Kimberly dynasty. He would shrug his shoulders when the subject came up. Jim was a daydreamer with an Indiana Jones–like imagination that would take him all over the world in search of adventure. He dreamed about the Curtiss NC-4 navy seaplane, in 1919 the first aircraft ever to cross the Atlantic Ocean; about Jack Dempsey's reign as world heavyweight boxing champ; about the heroic dog sled teams that plowed through treacherous Alaskan territory to reach Nome with an anti-diphtheria serum.

As a result, young Jim had a very difficult time keeping his mind on his studies. His father watched in frustration as Jim's grades hovered around the failing mark. He would be forced to send his son to six prep schools, including the prestigious Boston Latin School and Phillips Academy, before the youth would garner enough passing grades to graduate. "I was supposed to be preparing for MIT, but I was distracted by girls and football," Kimberly recalled.

After graduation, Jim avoided the immediate rigors of college by asking his father to let him work at one of the family pulp mills to learn the business. Delighted at the prospect that his son might be falling in line, James Kimberly found Jim a position at a Kimberly Clark mill in Kapuskasing, Ontario. He worked for the senior engineers running the plant's huge paper machines. Eventually bowing to his father's wishes, Jim entered MIT as the Great Depression hit in the fall of 1929. Again, dreamer Jim's desire for adventure and pleasure overshadowed the stuffy, dreary classrooms of college. He excelled on the school's rowing team but flunked English.

Kimberly recalled, "I had to sit down and talk to my dad about my depressing career as a student. . . . Here I was flunking my courses and the world around me was collapsing. People were selling apples in Manhattan to survive. Others were jumping out windows. I couldn't concentrate on my studies. Somehow I graduated in 1934, but I didn't have the grades or credentials my dad would have liked."

Returning to the Kimberly plant in Neenah, Wisconsin, Jim shunned his father's offer of a corporate job to work on the assembly line at the company's paper mill. He opted for the graveyard shift, so he could spend his days sailing at the Neenah Nodaway Yacht Club. Such was his love of sailing that he and four friends made a pact to each have one ear pierced and wear an earring, as mariners around the world had done for centuries. He still wears it to this day.

Because he could come and go as he pleased on the job, Kimberly also began taking month-long jaunts to Europe, where he lived the good life in the best hotels of Paris, London, and Rome and pursued the most beautiful young women he could find. As Kimberly once explained his outlook on women: "If you have the means to enjoy yourself, which I have, I've always thought it was more pleasant to surround yourself with attractive girls rather than ugly ones. It's like putting flowers, not rutabagas, in your vase."

In the early 1930s, Kimberly became fascinated with race cars. While working a short stint at one of his father's paper mills in upstate New York, he had listened to the ramblings of a coworker on the assembly line who dreamed of building a race car. The man, a former mechanic, had the blueprint for his vehicle. With Kimberly's enthusiasm and financial backing, the two embarked on the project.

Kimberly recalled, "We bought a World War One Hispano-Suiza aircraft engine and with Ford parts picked up in junkyards, built the whole thing ourselves. We raced it at some of the New York state fairs and it did so well that we finally hired a German lad to drive. He had a lead foot and no brains but he was a pretty good driver."

There was increasing concern in the Kimberly family that Jim would lead the Kimberly Clark empire. The only publicity he seemed to attract was for his numerous girlfriends. "Jim is remembered...as the black sheep of the Kimberly family," said Kirsten Schrang Afton, whose family once bought land from the Kimberlys in Neenah. "The rest of the family was straitlaced and serious, and Jim was wild, free-spirited, and tooling around the world buying Jaguars and Ferraris."

During his mid to late twenties, Jim's hair turned prematurely gray. That, along with his Romeo-like reputation, earned him the nickname the Grey Fox, a title he kept for life. Another title friends bestowed upon him, but which he did not boast about, was the Yachtsman Cocksman.

In 1934, on one of his returns from Europe, Kimberly stopped off in New York, where he dated Greta Garbo for a short while. His romantic exploits were referred to by his friends as "Jim's hanky panky." During his friendship with Garbo, Jim also met a young Manhattan office secretary, Ruth Bishop. "Ruth was a cute gal," Kimberly said, "and I was seeing her so much I had taken an apartment in New York. I decided we should get married."

The couple moved to Neenah and began a family that produced three daughters. Kimberly was soon restless again. To reduce his boredom with family life, Kimberly signed up with the U.S. Coast Guard during World War II. He was assigned to the position of assistant chief director of the Coast Guard Auxilliary, which helped monitor potential spy and smuggling activities around the nation's ports. Jim's long absences took their toll on his marriage, and in 1947 he and Ruth divorced. "I was traveling everywhere," he said, "meeting other girls, and losing touch with home life in general. I'm sorry I missed seeing my girls grow up. I hate myself for it now."

A bachelor again, Kimberly returned to Europe, where he went back to racing cars and chasing women. In 1949, while in Monte Carlo, Kimberly received a telephone call from Gloria Swanson, the former silent film star who had been the business partner and mistress of Joseph P. Kennedy some twenty years earlier. Jim and Gloria had known each other in New York, where they had dated a few times. Gloria, fifty and eight years Jim's senior, invited him to Nice. After a brief rendezvous, they decided to drive back to Paris, where she had to meet her daughter and he had to arrange to ship a custom-made Mercedes back to the states. Being a racer, Jim wanted to take the quickest route possible. But Gloria had other ideas. She insisted they take the romantic back roads.

"I told her the goddamned scenic route would take forever," Kimberly remembered. "And it rained like hell, so we had to stop for a long lunch at some filling station in a little town. We parked in a farmer's field and opened the glove compartment. Out of Mickey Mouse glasses we drank an eighty-nine cent bottle of Burgundy and ate sweet buns packaged so beautifully we hated to spoil them. Obviously we never made it to Paris that day. We stayed the lovely night in Lyons. Gloria was a regular person who was a lot of fun and, I must add, quite a number."

When the couple finally reached Paris, they spent a week together before parting to resume their separate lives.

Returning to the family's home base in Neenah, Jim's fascination for cars and women accelerated further. He won several racing championships. He dated celebrities like Ginger Rogers and figure-skating star Sonja Henie. During a sailing trip to the Hamptons on Long Island, Jim found himself in a whirlwind romance with a young blonde named Sharon Kuronhouse, to whom, in "a fit of absolute madness" friends say, he proposed marriage a month later. Nine months later Sharon gave birth to a retarded child. A year into the marriage, "we just didn't get along. I call it lack of facility," said Kimberly, who obtained a divorce, his second.

Single again, Jim returned to the racing circuit. In 1953 and 1954, he won six out of seven races in the United States and was named top American racer by *Car & Driver* magazine. Two years later he made the cover of *Sports Illustrated* after winning the Sebring International

Sports Car Classic. During one race at Pebble Beach, Kimberly's vehicle—moving at a speed in excess of one hundred miles an hour—flipped over three times in a spectacular crash. As flames and black smoke shot from the wreckage, Kimberly miraculously emerged, shaken but unhurt. It was the end for the professional speed demon. He retired a few months later, at forty-nine.

"I wasn't worried about me," Kimberly said. "I was worried about getting in someone else's way. Your reactions slow down. As professional drivers say, 'There are a lot of old drivers and a lot of bold drivers, but their aren't very many old, bold drivers.'"

In 1957, at the age of fifty, Kimberly moved to Palm Beach, purchasing an airy twelve-room villa on Lake Worth, a short distance from the Sailfish Club. Kimberly's first major concern—ahead of even the furnishings—was to build a dock for his yachts and racing boats.

In some ways, Kimberly never imagined himself marrying again. With two unsuccessful marriages and his thirst for yachting, racing, and traveling still unquenched, he did not want the pressures of a domestic life. And yet, with middle age arriving, the devil-may-care attitude he had cherished as a young man faded. Kimberly found himself fitting quite comfortably into the slower, quieter pace of the Palm Beach life with its charity balls, cocktail parties, and dinners. He enjoyed yachting up and down Florida's Gold Coast and occasionally whipping a speed-boat around Lake Worth.

Kimberly belonged to several of the island's discriminatory private clubs, although he was not a prejudiced man himself. As a sportsman, he realized that the color of one's skin and one's religion meant nothing. He also knew that his sentiments were the exact opposite of those of most people in Palm Beach. Still, he never made a fuss at the clubs he belonged to.

In 1967, Palm Beach society photographer Bob Davidoff introduced Kimberly to Roberta Jacqueline Trezise, a petite, dark-haired beauty—she weighed no more than ninety pounds—who had modeled for *Town & Country* magazine and worked as a part-time receptionist at an art gallery on Worth Avenue. Jacquie was seventeen. Kimberly was sixty. Jim was immediately taken by the tanned, coquettish teen. When he asked Davidoff to help find him a date for a party at the Everglades Club, the photographer arranged for him to meet with Jacquie and her nineteen-year-old sister, Marie, for lunch at Ta-boo.

Davidoff recalled, "He said Marie was too old, but Jacquie, seventeen, was just fine and unabashedly beautiful. And the name Kimberly was magic to Jacquie. After all, she was uneducated and naive."

Shortly after the party, Kimberly asked Jacquie to move in with him, and the impressionable teen agreed. A Palm Beach publisher said, "Jacquie knew her good looks knocked him over. She may have even thought she loved him at first. But she was so young that it was more of a father-daughter relationship, with parties, clothes, and cars thrown in for good behavior."

Dick Hurley, a longtime Palm Beach resident, saw it another way. "Jacquie's mother pushed her daughter—even though she was still a teenager—to attract Jim Kimberly. And it worked. She got him." Jim and Jacquie married two years after their first meeting.

The press wanted to know all about this little nymphet that old Jim Kimberly had married. But initial reports were wildly exaggerated. Articles said she had been born in London, in France, and in Connecticut. Her father, they claimed, was a successful investment banker. In fact, there was little glamour at all. Jacqueline Kimberly had been born in 1952 in a middle-class neighborhood in Pasadena, California. Her father, John Trezise, was an engineer, and her mother, Maria, was a writer. They had moved to Florida in the mid-1960s when John Trezise was hired by an engineering firm in West Palm Beach. Two years later, Jacquie and Jim married and Kimberly set about teaching Jacquie the social manners, the style, and the grace she needed to be a proper Palm Beach wife and party hostess.

He also showed her how to use credit cards and write checks. The couple bought a larger house, a more luxurious chateau-style, beach-front mansion on El Vadado. Despite their forty-three-year difference in age, the couple shared the desire for adventure and embarked on several around-the-world trips. As Jacquie told a friend: "I loathe any kind of boredom. Especially boring people. I'd rather be alone."

One of Kimberly's friends was King Hussein of Jordan, whom he had met in his world travels several years earlier. When Hussein was introduced to Jacquie during one of the couple's trips abroad, the king privately asked her if she could provide dates for a group of Jordanian government officials he planned to bring to Palm Beach. There was little doubt about what the word "dates" implied, but Hussein discreetly made it known that his cabinet members were all very rich. The fact made Jacquie's task much easier.

When Hussein's entourage of thirty aides and Secret Service men arrived, Jacquie was ready with ten beautiful young women she had recruited for a large dinner party in honor of the king. One ex-Twyla Tharp dancer, who did not want to be identified, described the scene to journalist Linda Marx:

"I was paired with a Jordanian general who I knew liked me because I was invited back the next day. I was honored when he gave me a gold cigarette lighter from Cartier, but I took it back and exchanged it for a diamond ring. Even though he was married, I dated him for seven days. We went on Jim's boat, we rented an entire theater in Palm Beach for an evening. We had lavish dinner parties at El Vedado. At the end of the week, the general gave me a six-thousand-dollar necklace that I exchanged for a bracelet. The whole week was like a scene from a James Bond movie."

Chuckled Joe Farish, Palm Beach's best-known divorce lawyer, "You could say that Jacquie pimped for King Hussein. No wonder Hussein gave her a one-hundred-thousand-dollar Ferrari Dino as a token of his appreciation."

In the early 1970s, rumors about Jacquie Kimberly's marital fidelity and sexual preferences surfaced. She was said to have had a "close friendship" with socialite Molly Anderson, the ex-wife of prominent Palm Beach banker H. Loy Anderson, Jr. Jim had heard the gossip but tried to ignore it. He was shocked, however, to hear of an alleged affair between Jacquie and a young, muscular male skydiver from Indiantown, Florida. When Jim confronted her, Jacquie became despondent. She attempted suicide with an overdose of prescription drugs but was saved by a paramedic who pumped her stomach. She entered a private sanitorium for a month.

Kimberly's anger over Jacquie's wanderings did not cool. In 1975 he filed for divorce, saying their vows had been "irretrievably broken." As the couple separated, Jacquie went to court and filed an affidavit for temporary support. In the document she said her living expenses totaled about $20,000 per month. That amount included $1,500 for clothing, $3,325 for tennis, $2,000 for food, $500 for flowers, $82 for toys for her pet Sheltie, $200 for a personal photographer, $200 for beauty salon visits, $150 for cosmetics, $40 for prescription drugs, $440 for parachute jumps, and $2,475 for flying lessons. She also requested unlimited use of their nine automobiles.

Jacquie said she had no other assets other than the Ferrari King Hussein had given her and $5,000 worth of jewelry. The court awarded her $750 per month.

Instead of a bitter divorce trial, both Jim and Jacquie softened. On Jim's side, his divorce action had been halfhearted. As he confided to Jacquie's lawyer, Joe Farish, "At my age, I don't know how many years I have left. I don't want to be alone at the end."

On Jacquie's side, she would be nearly destitute if she left Kimberly. A prenuptial agreement she had signed before their marriage would provide her with eighteen thousand dollars a year for seventeen years, a small sum by Palm Beach standards. In May 1976, the couple reconciled.

But Jacquie was still bored. One of Jim Kimberly's closest friends in Palm Beach was Herbert "Peter" Pulitzer, the multimillionaire businessman and grandson of newspaper publisher Joseph Pulitzer, after which the coveted Pulitzer Prize is named. Pulitzer had a similar problem with his wife, Roxanne. She was bored with the sedate, unchanging world of Palm Beach. Kimberly and Pulitzer agreed that their wives would probably hit it off. A meeting was arranged, and the two women immediately became friends. The women and their husbands were an inseparable foursome, dining and socializing and often vacationing together.

"I liked Jacquie from the start," Roxanne said. "I was awed and fascinated by her sophistication, her wardrobe, her manicures, her expensive lunches."

Soon the pair were jetting off to New York together to get their hair styled at Clive Summers's Fifth Avenue salon, facials at Georgette Klinger, and massages at Elizabeth Arden. There was no doubt that Jacquie was helping with Roxanne Pulitzer's transformation into a Palm Beach girl. Theirs was a friendship that would have a profound effect on both marriages. It was a friendship that would lead to the island's most publicized sex scandal until that involving William Kennedy Smith.

Like Jacquie Kimberly, Roxanne Pulitzer had also come to Palm Beach unsophisticated, not used to the abundance of wealth evident on the island. The oldest of three children, Roxanne was born in 1951 in Cassadaga, New York—a suburban community of five hundred residents about fifty miles south of Buffalo that Roxanne described as a "one-stoplight hamlet sandwiched between two trailer courts in the Allegheny foothills."

Her father, William Renckens, was an alcoholic prone to abusing his wife. When Roxanne was five years old, her mother, Marilyn, gave Renckens five hundred dollars and ordered him to leave. He did and never came back. That made Roxanne responsible for raising her kid sister Pam and younger brothers Keith and Kevin, while their mother worked two waitress jobs at a local restaurant and a tavern.

Former classmates of Roxanne have described her as the typical "all-American girl." She was an active youngster who excelled on her

baseball team. She also became an excellent swimmer. At Cassadaga
Valley Central High, Roxanne was a member of the student council and
played basketball, volleyball, and tennis. She was a member of the
cheerleading squad for four years and appeared in the lead role in the
Cassadaga High production of *I Remember Mama*. In her high school
yearbook, she listed "people who lie" as her pet peeve. It would turn
out to be prophetic.

Besides school activities and attending the local drive-in movie, there
was little to do in Cassadaga. On Friday nights, Roxanne and her school
friends hung out at Whim's Rollerskating Rink, eating hot dogs,
drinking Coke, and flirting with the guys.

During her senior year, Roxanne believed she had become pregnant
by her first boyfriend, a musician named John. As she prepared to tell
him about the pregnancy, he announced his own major piece of news: he
had joined the rock band Santana for a European tour and would be
leaving immediately. With John gone, Roxanne relied on a friend named
Peter Lowe Dixon to help her through the ordeal. Dixon was the son of
Lloyd Dixon, a wealthy and respected businessman who owned a
voting-machine-manufacturing company in nearby Jamestown, where
Roxanne had a part-time job as a secretary.

Roxanne told Peter she was going to have an abortion, that she could
not have John's baby. On the day they drove to her doctor's office,
Roxanne was relieved to find out that she was not pregnant. After her
doctor lectured her about the importance of taking precautions, he
wrote her a prescription for birth-control pills.

In the weeks and months following her pregnancy scare, Roxanne
poured her heart out to Peter, using him as a confidant and a shoulder to
cry on. As far as Roxanne was concerned, she and Peter were only
friends. And so she was flabbergasted one night when, over a few beers
at a local pub, he produced a box containing an engagement ring.
Although she was not sure she loved him—and still pined for her old
boyfriend John—she accepted the ring.

On the night before her wedding, John—back from his tour—
appeared at her apartment, told her he had heard about her wedding
plans, and begged her to back out and marry him.

As Roxanne recalled in her autobiography, *The Prize Pulitzer*:

> I knew John well enough to realize he was proposing out of a sense
> of duty. Marriage at this point would have halted his career. We
> made love that night with a bittersweet passion that I have still not
> forgotten, as though we were trying to turn back the clock through

sheer physical energy. Afterward he begged me again not to marry Peter, even though he knew as well as I that there was no turning back. I fell asleep crying. . . . The only thing that could have made that night more melodramatic was if we had both drunk poison afterward in Romeo and Juliet style."

The marriage proceeded as planned July 26, 1971, although Roxanne was exhausted from her marathon sex session with John the night before.

"In truth, looking back," Roxanne admitted later, "I'm ashamed to say that escaping Cassadaga was probably an underlying motive in my decision to marry Peter."

Peter Dixon was wealthy. His family owned an island in Canada, a farm in New York, and a winter home in Lake Worth, West Palm Beach. When Peter enrolled in Florida Atlantic University, he and Roxanne moved into the Dixon's Lake Worth condo in Florida and eventually into their own home. Roxanne enrolled part time in Palm Beach Junior College.

Her grades were passable, but her husband's were not. He floundered along, doing very poorly. Dixon's family also began to unravel. In 1973, his father resigned as head of his Automatic Voting Machines Company amid a financial scandal. He was later convicted of mail fraud and failing to report to the Securities and Exchange Commission a twenty-thousand-dollar loan he had secured from his company. Embarrassed by the scandal, Peter's older brother, Lloyd Dixon III—who also worked at the company—committed suicide.

Peter Dixon was not all he seemed, either. As he continued to get poor grades, Peter professed to be studying harder and harder in school and trying to do better. On the day of a big chemistry test, Roxanne wished her husband good luck as he went off to tackle his toughest subject. But midway through the afternoon, Peter's chemistry professor called. Did Roxanne know where he was? Roxanne soon discovered her husband had been skipping his chemistry classes for most of the semester. Instead of attending, he had gone off for afternoon sex sessions with one of her closest girlfriends.

A doubly betrayed Roxanne made plans to divorce her cheating husband, but as she did, another surprise was about to occur. After missing one of her menstrual cycles, Roxanne learned she was pregnant. She did not tell Peter and went off to Miami for an abortion. Ironically, her relationship with Peter ended as it had begun, with a trip to an abortion doctor.

The year was 1973. Twenty-one years old, divorced, and alone in West Palm Beach, Roxanne considered her options: return to Cassadaga, the town of long winters and well-meaning but tame people, or stay in Florida and start anew. She knew there was only one choice. Searching through the want ads, Roxanne answered an ad for the position of insurance sales trainee for Gulf Life Insurance in West Palm Beach. She was assigned to work with one of the office's top salesmen, Randy Hopkins, an heir to the Listerine mouthwash fortune who lived in Palm Beach. They began dating casually, a welcome diversion for Roxanne.

A few months into their relationship, Randy told Roxanne one evening he would have to drive by a client's home on the north end of the island at 410 North Lake Way to have him sign some papers. As they entered the cypress-shingled house of Randy's client, Roxanne recalled, "Standing in the center of the room . . . were two of the thinnest, tannest, most beautiful people I had ever seen. They looked like models for one of those Puerto Rican rum ads—you know, sophisticated but understated in their faded blue jeans," Roxanne recalled. Randy introduced the couple as Peter Pulitzer and Susie Caldor.

Roxanne continued, "Susie tossed her mane of long brown hair, arched her eyebrows as if to say, 'Who are you?' and gave me a cool hello. I felt as if I had just stepped off the bus from Cassadaga on my way to a Miami Beach convention of Future Farm Girls of America." Peter turned out to be Herbert "Peter" Pulitzer, the millionaire businessman, hotel and restaurant owner, and Susie was his longtime girlfriend.

Despite the shaky beginning, Randy and Roxanne and Peter and Susie became friends. Roxanne enjoyed Peter's company because he always seemed to be in command. He was an excellent conversationalist, and at parties he was often the center of attention. Roxanne thought she would not mind dating Peter, but it was out of the question. Susie kept saying that she and Peter would soon be married.

One night, as the two couples dined at Maurice's, a popular Italian restaurant, the conversation turned to sex and a kind of truth-or-dare game. The first question: What did everybody like best about sex?

Peter Pulitzer answered first. He liked making love with the lights on. Then it was Susie's turn. She was shy and it took a while to coax an answer out of her. But finally Peter's girlfriend answered, saying in whispered tones that she liked sex in the dark, and then in the missionary position. A bit outraged by Susie's milquetoast answer and somewhat intoxicated, Roxanne prepared her answer. What she liked, she said matter-of-factly, was oral sex. Everybody at the table was silent, almost in shock, except Peter. He roared with laughter.

"Then as he reached into his pocket to pay the bill, he turned to me and said, 'Look, break up with Randy, because I would like to go out with you.'"

Three days later, at a party the two couples attended, Roxanne suddenly found Randy storming toward her, his face contorted in rage. "He said, 'Come on, we're getting out of here.' Ugly scene, very embarrassing. We drove to his place and he was shouting, 'You've been fucking Peter Pulitzer. He says you're planning to go out together. He told me the whole story.'

"Our plan to go out together was true, but we most certainly had not slept together," Roxanne said. With his accusatory words echoing in her ears, Roxanne stormed out. She had been living with Randy on a part-time basis. Now she was without a place to stay and nearly broke. She decided to return to Cassadaga.

But first she had to talk to Pulitzer to find out why he had provoked a confrontation with her boyfriend. "Because Randy asked me point blank if [I liked you] and I couldn't lie," Pulitzer answered quickly. Then he asked Roxanne out. When she explained her predicament and intention to leave Florida, Pulitzer had another suggestion. He was driving to Miami to drop Susie at the airport for a trip she was taking to Africa, where he was supposed to join her in a few weeks. Why not meet him at the Howard Johnson's hotel he owned in Miami and they could discuss the situation?

Roxanne agreed, and minutes after she arrived, the two were relaxing over wine in Peter's penthouse suite. They spent most of the night talking, until Pulitzer suggested they go to bed. Roxanne agreed. They made love, and within a few weeks were living together.

Over in Africa, a few weeks passed and Susie Caldor realized that Peter had unceremoniously dumped her.

Roxanne Dixon's new boyfriend, Herbert "Peter" Pulitzer, Jr., had been a child of Palm Beach. His parents, Herbert Pulitzer and Gladys Amory Pulitzer, had moved to the island in 1930, the year he was born. His father had been Joseph Pulitzer's choice to succeed him in running the family newspaper business, which included the *New York World* and the *St. Loius Post-Dispatch*. But Herbert Sr.—not unlike Jim Kimberly and his feelings about the Kimberly paper products business—showed little interest in the newspaper business. He was dedicated more to the pursuit of pleasure: yachting, lavish parties, travel. It was a pursuit he could easily afford, thanks to Joe Pulitzer's generous remembrance in his will.

By the time Peter Pulitzer was born, his father was worth $6 million. Young Peter would grow up with memories of wealth in Palm Beach, but with little memory of his parents. His mother died of tuberculosis when he was eight, and his father went off to England to serve in the Royal Air Force during World War II.

Peter was raised by a nanny; then, at age fourteen he was sent to St. Mark's prep school in Massachusetts, where he was expected to excel in preparation for Harvard, the school where all Pulitzer men went. But after graduating from St. Mark's, he enrolled at Stanford University instead and transferred to the University of Virginia a year later. After a single semester in Virginia, he dropped out. School was not for him. He returned to Palm Beach and found that his father was in deep financial trouble, barely able to keep the house maintained. At age twenty, he borrowed a few thousand dollars and opened a small wine and liquor shop. It was successful enough so that young Peter could keep the creditors away.

A year later, in 1951, Peter turned twenty-one and received a $110,000 inheritance from his grandfather's estate. He invested the money in vacant land along the Florida coast and in orange groves. He made a large profit when he was forced to sell some of the land to the U.S. government for its I-95 superhighway project.

Palm Beach Life magazine wrote about him, "Peter is one of the new breed of international playboys with the significant difference that work is their play. They live well but quietly. Simulation comes primarily from discovering and pursuing the new and challenging."

Peter was also considered one of the most eligible bachelors in Palm Beach. He dated steadily and briefly went out with Grace Kelly and with Jacqueline Bouvier a few years before she married Jack Kennedy. But Peter really had never been in love. That changed when he met Lilly Lee McKim, whose stepfather was Ogden Phipps of the Bessemer steel and real-estate fortune and one of the leaders of Palm Beach society. They eloped in 1952, and within three years, Lilly bore two daughters and a son.

After his father died in 1957, Peter inherited $1.5 million of Pulitzer family stock, some of which he sold and invested in more orange groves and a waterfront parcel in Miami, on which he built a Howard Johnson's hotel. While Peter was building his real-estate empire, his wife decided to channel her energies by opening a small fruit and juice stand in Palm Beach. She tailored her own uniform for the job, a colorful, sleeveless, beltless dress that would not show juice stains. When customers began complimenting the outfit, she duplicated it and sold "Lilly dresses" from her stand.

Jacqueline Kennedy was photographed wearing a "Lilly," and the dress became an overnight national sensation. Lilly branched out and created Lilly Pulitzer, Inc., a sportswear line for men and women. The company became a multimillion-dollar enterprise. Their separate businesses were very successful. Peter had gone to Europe to arrange with KLM airlines to build hotels in Amsterdam and Indonesia. He rarely saw his wife. When he returned home from one of his trips, she filed for a divorce. The couple reached an out-of-court settlement, and Lilly received custody of the children. A few months later, Lilly married one of Peter's best friends, Enrique Rousseau, an exiled Cuban aristocrat who managed Pulitzer's Howard Johnson's hotel in Miami.

After Roxanne moved in with Pulitzer, she conducted a little research and found out he had been dating Susie for a year and a half before rejecting her. That would not happen to Roxanne, she vowed. "If we're not married at the end of six months, then I'm not going to waste my time," Roxanne said. "I'm not going to give you any eighteen months like Susie gave you."

Her nervy ultimatum worked. Exactly six months later, as the couple sat in the back seat of the Pulitzer limousine, returning to Palm Beach from Miami, Peter produced a bottle of champagne, filled two glasses, toasted, and said, "Will you marry me?" On January 12, 1976, before an intimate gathering of friends at Pulitzer's waterfront home, forty-five-year-old Peter and twenty-four-year-old Roxanne married.

Now the wife of multimillionaire Peter Pulitzer, Roxanne was propelled suddenly into Palm Beach's "inner circle." The imposing mansions she had passed so many times along South Ocean Boulevard became the scenes of dinner galas, luncheons, and cocktail parties to which she was invited. Socialites she hardly knew asked her to join charity organizations and planning committees for social events. A few days after she returned from her honeymoon, Roxanne was being invited to luncheons all over town. She dined with the girls at Café l'Europe and played tennis at the Everglades Club and the Bath and Tennis Club. Roxanne realized that the sole reason for her instantaneous social elevation was her new identity as Mrs. Peter Pulitzer. She was now a hot ticket.

Roxanne soon learned, though, that Palm Beach had its own set of restrictive rules and standards that she could never have dreamed of back in upstate New York.

25

Not a Pulitzer Prize:
Roxanne, Peter, and a Count

When Roxanne Renckens Dixon became Mrs. Peter Pulitzer, any lingering characteristics of the cute little cheerleader from the backwoods town of Cassadaga soon vanished as her husband began molding her into a Palm Beach wife. Like many of his other male friends on the island, Peter Pulitzer asked his brunette, blue-eyed wife not to work. He wanted her available, at his whim, ready for his sudden trips. He placed her on allowance of one thousand dollars a week, a sum that, at first, Roxanne thought to be a queen's ransom. She soon realized differently.

"I became acutely aware that the Palm Beach dress code didn't cover much that was in my wash-and-wear wardrobe," Roxanne said. "A $200 pair of Gucci loafers, de rigueur for just kicking around, or a $300 Louis Vuitton handbag...were essential to fitting in." To complement her new image, Roxanne, at Peter's suggestion, signed up for tennis and French lessons for "a little refinement." She also began reading books from the *New York Times* nonfiction bestseller list to learn adequate material for conversations at parties.

However, Roxanne said, "tennis elbow was the one type of dinner-party conversation I found to be of almost universal interest. For all its social pretensions, I learned that Palm Beach has justifiably few intellectual ones."

Her social transformation was not without its problems. One afternoon, after Roxanne brought a girlfriend to the Bath and Tennis Club to play a few matches on the courts, she arrived home to find Peter waiting pensively. "'They called from the club,' he said. He then told me it wasn't a good idea to bring Jews there," Roxanne recalled. "Not only didn't I realize that, I told [him], I didn't know my friend was Jewish. 'What's her name?' he wanted to know. 'Rosenthal,' I said. 'And that didn't give you a clue?' he asked incredulously."

One area in which Roxanne and Peter felt a strong attraction was sex. They had a very active sex life and, as Roxanne told *Playboy* magazine, "We made love everywhere you could make love." They enjoyed collecting adult movies and sexual paraphernalia. "We belonged to an X-rated movie club in West Palm Beach. We had an enormous collection of pornography—thousands of dollars' worth of dirty books, magazines, movies, paraphernalia. Vibrators, inflatable dolls, all kinds of weird gizmos. We bought them as jokes."

One of the couple's favorite romantic spots was the bedroom aboard his seventy-three-foot yacht, the *Sea Hunter*. The vessel's huge brass bed was complemented by mirrored walls and ceilings.

Their frequent couplings resulted in Roxanne's pregnancy in early 1977 at age twenty-five. Late in the year she gave birth to twins, MacLean and Zachary. Parenthood did not remove the Pulitzers from the fast lane. Aside from a healthy sexual appetite, the couple had developed a desire for illegal narcotics, particularly cocaine. They were not alone. In the late 1970s, the country witnessed the emergence of two cultural phenomena, disco music and the use of cocaine among the wealthy. Florida's enormous coastline provided easy access for the importation of illegal drugs, guaranteeing Palm Beach an ample and endless supply.

Cocaine, of course, had been a rich man's drug since the days of Henry Morrison Flagler. But following its turn-of-the-century use as a legal, recreational stimulant, the government had cracked down on the narcotic. Heavy jail sentences and fines now awaited those convicted of importing or using the mind-numbing substance. The legal danger of using cocaine gave it a particularly forbidden aspect, which made it perfect for the sophisticated jet-setters of Palm Beach. The powder seemed to be everywhere. At private parties, wealthy Palm Beach residents snorted it in the open. At restaurants and nightclubs, they waltzed off to the stalls of the bathrooms to snort up.

On Roxanne's twenty-eighth birthday, Peter gave a dinner party for his wife. At one point, before a group of cheering well-wishers, a waiter produced a silver serving tray that he laid at Roxanne's table. On the tray, the words HAPPY BIRTHDAY ROX were spelled out in large, long lines of cocaine. The guests took turns sniffing the gift.

Roxanne recalled in *The Prize Pulitzer*, "Cocaine was something we identified with going out on the Palm Beach social scene. And, eventually, it became just as indispensable to a night of partying as donning evening clothes. Fueled by cocaine and a nagging feeling that the real fun was sometimes eluding us, a kind of post-party party crowd evolved of reckless revelers who were hell-bent on high times."

Hopping into their sports cars, the party folk zoomed off to the latest discos—West Palm Beach's Marrakesh or Fort Lauderdale's Studio 51— often snorting cocaine along the way. Everyone always ended up at the mansion of whomever had the biggest drug supply at the moment.

"By the dawn's early light, they would stagger home and into bed— some with their original partners, some with different ones," Roxanne said.

If there were any seams showing in the Pulitzer marriage, they were invisible to Palm Beach society. When Roxanne and Peter were seen out on the town, it appeared that they were having the time of their lives. Roxanne, however, was growing bored by the endless string of dinner parties and galas. As she described it, residents did not routinely entertain to be neighborly. Rather, they did it to show off their art collections and antiques and their chefs.

One of the few collections Roxanne remembered was one owned by Patrick Lannon, the seventyish, retired chairman of the board of ITT and Palm Beach's premier collector of museum-quality contemporary art. One evening during a dinner party at his home, Lannon asked Roxanne to view one of his collections in another wing of the house. It was not the treasure-trove of modern artwork Roxanne expected to see. Roxanne said, "Mounted on red walls like works of art were leather dominatrix outfits, complete with whips, special love chains and handcuffs, erotic paintings and sculptures [and] what appeared to be an authentic medieval chastity belt."

In addition to the dull parties she was forced to attend, Roxanne was disturbed by a rivalry for Peter's affections with his beautiful daughter, Liza, who was five years younger than she and married to a wealthy stockbroker. "I feel sorry for you, Rox," she had told her stepmother. "It's so obvious how much you love [my dad] and how he's number one in your life. But you'll never be number one in his. You're always going to be number two, because if I weren't his daughter, he would have married me."

According to Roxanne, another strain on the relationship was Peter's growing interest in expanding the perimeters of their sexual experiences. Pulitzer, she said, began asking her to participate in a threesome involving another woman. Roxanne had grown used to some of Peter's requests. She had consented to not shaving her underarm hair because Peter insisted that the "European look" was sexier. She and Peter had also hired a beautiful Thai masseuse to rub them down as they made love together.

Still, she said, as he brought up the idea of three-way sex again and again, she worried that if she didn't submit to it, he would wander. After weeks of agonizing, she came to her decision. She would participate in a ménage à trois. But who to ask. She finally decided Jacquie Kimberly was the only woman she could trust.

Over a champagne lunch, Roxanne asked Jacquie if she would participate. "At least I know you're not going to run off with him," Roxanne said. "No question that you can count on me not running off with him. [Peter's] not my type. But for you, Roxy, sure, I'll do it," Roxanne quoted Jacquie as saying.

To make sure nobody—servants or friends—would find out about the planned event, Pulitzer rented a suite in a Holiday Inn in South Palm Beach.

As Roxanne described the encounter in her autobiography: "Jacquie slowly began unbuttoning my blouse and slid it off my shoulders. Then she unbuttoned her blouse. Jacquie gently pushed me back onto the bed and began caressing me and kissing me. Even though I told myself to relax, that this was my best friend, my heart was pounding. She was kissing me on the breasts, letting her hands wander, tracing the curves of my body with her fingers. [Peter] was undressed now. Jacquie began to gently caress [Peter]. Then I rolled over on top of [Peter] and we made love."

One person not invited to the festivities was Jim Kimberly. Nor had he been told about the secret tryst. Jim Kimberly came from a different generation. And while he was open-minded about many things, sex was not one of them. It was something to be done in the privacy of a bedroom between a man and a woman. Orgies, threesomes, men with men, women with women, decidedly were not for him. All three of them knew Jim would be greatly hurt to learn of the ménage à trois.

A second encounter occurred a few weeks later, according to Roxanne, onboard Peter's yacht. This time, however, a new wrinkle occurred in the sex play. "Suddenly, we were all in bed, naked, touching, entwined," Roxanne recalled in her autobiography. But after Roxanne momentarily left to go to the bathroom, she returned to find her husband and Jacquie in the throes of passion. They were "greedily going at it as though they were devouring each other's bodies."

In her own mind, Roxanne blamed Peter. She said he had promised her such a scene would never happen. According to Roxanne, Peter said he was mainly interested in watching her and Jacquie make love, after which he would make love with his wife.

"Never before had it crossed my mind that [he] would fuck Jacquie," she said.

Roxanne said Peter later assured her it would never happen again. "I couldn't help it... I was drunk and high and turned on. It just happened."

The threesome, according to Roxanne, was the beginning of a "tailspin" from which she and Peter would not recover. The couple fought bitterly—over Jacquie, over Liza, over drug use. Other, darker reasons would eventually emerge. In early 1982, Peter Pulitzer filed for divorce and requested custody of his two children by Roxanne, Mac-Lean and Zachary. Palm Beach Circuit Court Judge Carl Harper was assigned to hear the case in what would be a nonjury trial.

Word had spread among the press that this was going to be a "hot" trial, and dozens of reporters converged on the courthouse. In previous years, warring couples had strived to keep their names out of the papers. Out-of-court settlements were more common. But in the "sky's the limit" atmosphere of the prosperous 1980s, no accusations or tactics were out of line when large fortunes were at stake.

The trial opened to a packed house at the Palm Beach County Courthouse in West Palm Beach on September 20, 1982, and immediately turned nasty when Pulitzer's lawyer, Robert Scott, and Roxanne's lawyer, Joe Farish, squared off in their opening statements. Scott charged Roxanne with adultery, lesbian affairs, and rampant cocaine use, saying all that had destroyed the marriage.

Farish labeled Peter a drug user and pusher who transported cocaine from Colombia aboard his yacht and who dropped bales of marijuana from his plane to one of his orange groves. "He liked that coke," Farish told the court. Both Roxanne and Peter charged each other with being unfit to raise Mac and Zac, and it quickly became clear that the divorce battle would be over the children first and Pulitzer's money—of which Roxanne wanted $1.5 million—second.

The opening left Palm Beach Circuit Court Judge Carl Harper with no illusions about the chance for a reconciliation, which both parties had hinted was still an outside possibility. "If it's not broken now, it will be by the time the trial's over," he quipped.

Both Peter and Roxanne took the stand to tell damaging stories about the other's behavior. Each admitted to having used cocaine but said it was the other who had introduced the drug. According to Roxanne, Peter had once threatened to commit murder-suicide with a pistol unless she sought help with kicking her cocaine habit. "He put the gun at my temple and cocked the pistol. And I just closed my eyes and sat there and then he didn't do anything. He sat down and then he turned and he put the gun in his mouth with it cocked and said, 'Do you want me to kill myself?'"

Pulitzer's lawyers hammered away at Roxanne's drug use. As she testified about getting high, Roxanne revealed her favorite alternative to snorting the drug: drinking it in a mixture of three-quarters of a gram of cocaine and three-quarters of a bottle of champagne. Roxanne also testified that she had been corrupted by Pulitzer. "I used to drink milk at dinners. I embarrassed him. He told me to have a glass of wine or champagne, even if I didn't like it."

Pulitzer testified that he had only used the drug to keep up with his wife, who, he said, wanted to go out nightly and party. "It just got to the point where it was the only thing that could keep me awake."

While the Pulitzers' drug history was certainly titillating, it paled in comparison with their accusations about each other's alleged sexual perversions. Roxanne Pulitzer testified that her husband had once admitted to having slept with his daughter, Liza, and that she had seen them involved in incestuous behavior.

"They would lie on the same bed together drinking champagne and kissing. In the Bahamas on our yacht, I saw them lying kissing while Liza was topless. This was in front of our twin boys," Roxanne testified. "When I confronted him about it, he said, 'I'm just hugging my daughter.' He told me he still loved his first wife Lilly and that he saw Lilly in Liza. Before we were married Peter told me he had been to bed with his daughter. He felt embarrassed about it. Liza told me she wanted me out of the way. She wished she wasn't Peter's daughter." Roxanne claimed that the incestuous relationship had developed when Liza was sixteen and lasted for about two years.

Peter Pulitzer said of the allegation, "That's the sickest thing I've ever heard in my life." The incest charge also was vehemently denied by Liza. "It's a disgusting lie," she testified. "Roxanne's tried to turn a wholesome father-daughter relationship into something dirty and disgusting." Liza then returned fire. She told the court that as she and

Roxanne sniffed cocaine in the bathroom of the exclusive Club Mar-
akesh disco in West Palm Beach one evening, Roxanne had propositioned her. "She said to me that if I ever felt I wanted to get involved in a
lesbian relationship to let her know because she wanted to be the one,"
Liza told the court.

Peter Pulitzer, in a sworn statement made before the trial, had
admitted to getting into bed with his wife and Jacquie Kimberly "two or
three" times to share sex and cocaine. He also said his wife had told him
that she had slept with Jacquie. But he said nothing of Roxanne's claim
that he had instigated the activity. Pulitzer's attorney Robert Scott
grilled Jacquie on the subject.

"Have you ever had sexual intercourse in a lesbian way with Mrs.
Pulitzer," asked Peter Pulitzer's attorney Robert Scott.

"It's an absolute lie, unfair, cruel, and malicious," Jacquie fumed on
the witness stand.

"Have you ever been in the first-floor bedroom [of the Pulitzer home]
in the bed, naked when Roxanne Pulitzer was also in the bedroom
naked?" Scott continued.

"You're disgusting!" Jacquie shrieked.

Obviously, somebody was not telling the truth. A corroborating
witness was called in by Pulitzer's side. Dick Hurley, a longtime Palm
Beach resident and a bartender at the Palm Beach Yacht Club, testified
that he had witnessed Roxanne and Jacquie sitting on a couch at the club
holding each other. "The kind of thing you see a boy and girl do.
Touching each other. My interpretation would be physical affection."

The testimony involving the alleged "unnatural sexual practices" of
both Peter and Roxanne titillated Palm Beach. On the days testimony
appeared on the front pages of the island's newspapers, they sold out
within an hour. The Pulitzer trial was also the hottest show in town.
Spectators began lining up outside the courthouse at seven A.M. each
day in an effort to obtain one of the courtroom seats. Those who stood
on line spanned the spectrum in age, wealth, and social status.
Dowagers, stockbrokers, cooks, and porters all wanted a glimpse of
what many were calling a "freak show."

"The way it's coming out, it seems like all we have here are a bunch of
drug addicts and sex maniacs," one disgusted Palm Beach town
employee remarked.

At times, Judge Carl Harper seemed to grimace in distaste. "This
case really makes me appreciate my wife. I go home every night and
give her a big hug," he remarked after one particularly steamy session.

Pulitzer's lawyers attempted to prove that Roxanne had been involved in a series of affairs during the marriage. Psychic Janet Nelson, who once advised Roxanne about the future but had had a falling out with her, now took the stand to testify for Peter's side. Nelson said Roxanne had told her about two men she had had affairs with—Palm Beach handyman Brian Richards and local real-estate salesman James Murdock. According to Nelson, Roxanne said she had made love to Murdock in a nearby motel.

"I told her she shouldn't have sex. She said Mr. Farish told her she could have all the sex she wanted," Nelson said, as the courtroom burst into laughter.

Farish attempted to ridicule the psychic. "You say you can tell things in the future? Well, the Florida Gators have a seven-point spread against LSU next week. You think that's a good bet?" Farish asked. An objection was shouted and Farish never received his tip.

Jacquie Kimberly also took the stand for Roxanne's side and denounced Nelson. "She told me she wanted to get even with Roxanne," Jacquie testified. Peter's side also accused Roxanne of having affairs with Hubert Fouret, owner of a Palm Beach pastry shop, and with Belgian race-car driver Jackie Ickx. Witnesses testified that they had seen Roxanne and Jackie Ickx kissing on the beach in full view of her twin boys.

The four men admitted knowing Roxanne, but denied having affairs with her. Roxanne also said she had not slept with any of them.

One of the most bizarre newspaper stories to come out of the trial followed Roxanne's testimony about a three-foot-long silver cylindrical trumpet she said she kept in her bedroom. Roxanne said she was given the instrument as a gift and that when covered with a black cape and taken to bed, it supposedly was capable of calling forth spirits of the dead. Pulitzer's lawyers alleged that Roxanne had indeed used it in "strange and bizarre religious rites."

The following day, the *New York Post* front page raged: *Pulitzer Sex Trial Shocker:* I SLEPT WITH A TRUMPET! A cutline under a photo continued: "The 31-year-old beauty shocked the courtroom when she admitted that she usually went to bed with a 3-foot trumpet wrapped in a blanket. All the sizzling details on Page 7."

Roxanne was furious. She charged that the article implied that she had had unnatural sexual relations with the instrument. The newspaper stood by its story. A few days later, she filed suit against the newspaper for libel, but the case was later dismissed.

After eighteen days, thirty-five witnesses, and ninety-five hours of testimony, the case of *Pulitzer vs. Pulitzer* concluded. The outcome was now up to Judge Harper. Peter and Roxanne agreed on almost nothing during the court proceedings, but they both criticized press coverage of the event as far too sensational. Roxanne referred to some of the journalists as "scum." The irony of their anger did not escape many of the two hundred reporters in attendance. It had been Pulitzer's grandfather, Joseph Pulitzer, who had made his fortune at the turn of the century splashing scandals and other people's misfortunes in giant headlines across his front pages. Perhaps the biblical promise that the sins of the fathers shall be visited upon the sons unto the third generation had come true in the Pulitzer case.

One journalist whose reports were particularly vivid was Dr. Hunter S. Thompson, the eccentric and unpredictable creator of so-called gonzo journalism and author of the cult book *Fear and Loathing in Las Vegas.* Thompson, covering the trial for *Rolling Stone* magazine, described the principals in the Pulitzer trial in most unflattering terms.

On Roxanne: "At age thirty-one, she looks more like a jaded senior stewardess from Pan Am than an international sex symbol."

On Peter: "A millionaire playboy who bore a certain resemblance to Alexander Haig on an ether binge."

On West Palm Beach residents: "These are servants and suckfish and they don't really matter in the real Palm Beach, except when they have to testify."

On December 28, 1982, Judge Harper issued his final decision in *Pulitzer vs. Pulitzer* and, as many had predicted, Roxanne lost resoundingly. She was awarded forty-eight thousand dollars in "rehabilitative alimony" to be paid in installments of two thousand dollars a month, sixty thousand dollars' worth of jewelry, a twenty-thousand-dollar Porsche, and a seven-thousand-dollar cash equity in the couple's pleasure boat. Most devastating, however, was the custody ruling regarding Mac and Zac. Peter received full custody of the children, allowing Roxanne limited visitation rights.

The judge based his decision on a legal doctrine that it is "improper to permit an errant spouse to destroy a marriage and then to claim benefits equal to those which would have been enjoyed had the marriage remained intact."

Judge Harper attacked Roxanne in his own words: "The wife's exorbitant demands shock the conscience of this court, putting the court in mind of the hit record by country music singer Jerry Reed, which laments, 'She Got the Gold Mine, I Got the Shaft.'"

As to Roxanne's moral character, the judge added, "This court finds that the wife's conduct involved more than isolated, discreet acts of adultery."

The question about Peter's alleged infidelities with his daughter, Liza, and his alleged role as a Svengali-like sex guru seemed of secondary importance to Palm Beach society. The real issue was whether Roxanne had committed an inexcusable indiscretion in accusing her husband of incest.

Liza's husband, Robert Leidy, said, "Roxanne will never be forgiven for what she said. As far as Roxanne's social situation goes, I'm afraid she's had it."

And so Roxanne Pulitzer became an outcast, shunned by many of the people she had once counted as good friends. Her name was crossed off guest lists. Invitations to dinner parties and charity events ended.

According to David Field, editor and publisher of the *Palm Beacher* newspaper, which, incredibly, did not run a single article on the Pulitzer scandal, "Peter Pulitzer is landed gentry. The trial doesn't touch his social position. His friends will still be his friends. Nobody's going to cut him off. The feeling is that Pulitzer got hung up on a broad who was much beneath him in every way. She's just a kid who got too much too soon and didn't know how to handle it."

Many prominent Palm Beach residents literally avoided Roxanne, going as far as to refuse eye contact. Some, though, had no inhibitions about telling her what they thought of her to her face. As she pushed a shopping cart around one afternoon in Palm Beach's only supermarket, Publix, one socialite she knew marched up to her and screamed, "Get out of town, you tramp! You have ruined the Pulitzer name!"

Roxanne, however, did not leave the island. Much to her credit, she stayed and began contemplating life without Peter Pulitzer and her two sons. In 1985, she was approached by *Playboy* magazine to do a "tasteful" nude spread. She agreed and was paid seventy thousand dollars for the pictorial, which consisted mainly of topless shots. In one photo, she mocks her infamous divorce trial by holding a copy of the I SLEPT WITH A TRUMPET! front page over her naked body. She began writing her memoirs. Roxanne, although far from being wealthy, was picking up the pieces, and she was doing it in Palm Beach. Many society women, while openly shunning her for appearance' sake, secretly admired her for having the courage to remain on the island.

Incredibly, not long after the divorce, Roxanne and Peter began meeting for occasional sex. "That part of the relationship did not die with the divorce," Roxanne explained. Some of her friends believed that, in fact, her self-esteem had died.

Meanwhile, Jim Kimberly was not doing well at all. He felt betrayed and heartbroken over the embarrassing revelations at the trial. He had avoided attending the debacle and remained indoors for several weeks after it ended. Although Jacquie had denied it all, the mere thought that his friend, Peter Pulitzer, had planned and executed a sex session involving himself, Roxanne, and Jacquie was abominable. And then to hear that Pulitzer had enjoyed a solo encounter with his wife. Kimberly was depressed, confused, and stressed out.

Remarked Dexter Coffin III, an heir to the fortune made by the inventor of the Flow-Thru teabag, "[It's] pretty embarrassing for him to get out of his Maserati on Worth Avenue and know that everyone has read that his wife shacked up with another woman, whether the testimony is true or false. He is one of the saddest figures in this whole divorce business."

Jim was further devastated by his resounding 2–1 defeat for reelection to the Palm Beach Port Commission, despite a spirited campaign. Friends said Jim blamed his loss partially on the Pulitzers for dragging the Kimberly name through the mud at their trial.

Causing further angst was his wife's new friendship with a chunky, big-boned woman named Susan Lynch, a former gardener to King Hussein who favored jeans, suspenders, and combat boots over the more stylish fare of Worth Avenue. Jacquie quietly moved out on Jim and into the small guest house on their property. Susan Lynch moved in with her.

In October 1984, Jim Kimberly suffered a heart attack. Three months later he underwent triple bypass surgery. At least he still had a heart, his friends joked. That was more than they could say for Jacquie. While Jim recovered, Jacquie and Susan moved in together at the Warwick Hotel and ran up a seventeen-thousand-dollar tab.

"Jim said Jacquie handled all the paperwork and took care of everything," remembered a friend, "but she and Susan treated the ordeal like a grand old party."

As Jim convalesced at home, Jacquie and Susan jetted off to Boston, checked into the Ritz Carlton, and spent $8,000 in a single weekend. Next it was on to the Ocean Key Club in Key West, where they charged several thousand more to Jim's account. Jacquie's devil-may-care spending spree resulted in a bill that topped $31,000 in one month—an amount that far exceeded Jim's already reduced monthly budget of $4,500. To pay the tab, Kimberly was forced to sell $44,621 of his stock investments, further crippling his already weak financial portfolio.

The ongoing cash drain caught the eye of one of Kimberly's lawyers, Gus Broberg, Jr., who wrote to Jacquie, pleading with her to ease up on her spending which he calculated at about $500,000 a year.

"At the rate money is being spent," Broberg wrote, "Jim would be without funds by the end of the year. I ask you to promise me that you will treat Jim with kindness and cut down drastically on expenditures. I urge you to change your ways and resume your life with Jim without the interference of Susan Lynch.... There is no more money.... Jim is not only suffering financial remorse, but is in a moral depression while attempting to recuperate from open heart surgery.... It is not proper for Jim to be left alone in his house with no companionship and having to fend for himself including the preparation of his own meals."

The letter had no effect. Two months later, Jacquie filed for divorce. Recalled Shannon Donnelly, former society editor of the *Palm Beach Daily News*, "Jim was flabbergasted when Jacquie filed for divorce. He had no idea she was going to do it to him. I had lunch with him the day he found out, and he was crushed. I felt so bad because he is the nicest person."

In her divorce papers, Jacquie charged that Kimberly had threatened her with a gun, menaced her with a knife, eavesdropped on her telephone calls, and opened her mail.

Kimberly told friends, "I love Jacquie, still care for her, and want to stay married."

Near groveling, the crushed Kleenex heir wrote her a love letter.

Darling Jacquie, I am so sorry I caused you so much unhappiness and misery. Please remember one thing. I am your friend—and I want you to be mine—please! In defense of my actions and conduct, I do receive and digest a lot of criticism—please think of that.... The bottom line is: I love you. I am going through difficult times—financially particularly—and it makes me ill. I know it is the result of my stupidity concerning many things and unfortunately it irritates me, which I should control. I can only try. I truly want to be a better person and I hope I can succeed.... God love you, I do, Jim.

Jacquie asked the Palm Beach Circuit Court to award her temporary alimony payments of fifty thousand dollars a year for a rental home

("Ours has rats," she insisted) and fifteen thousand a month for clothes, food, servants, and other expenses. The request was far more than the eighteen thousand a year provided for in a prenuptial agreement she had signed with Kimberly in 1969, but Jacquie insisted she had been "too young" to understand the marital contract when she signed it.

Her lawyers bolstered her demand with a tip of the hat to George Bernard Shaw and *Pygmalion*. They claimed Jacquie was a real-life Liza Doolittle, a poor, coarse woman taught culture and refinement by a wealthy man and that she therefore should not be deprived of that lifestyle.

Unfortunately for Jacquie, Palm Beach County Circuit Court Judge William C. Williams III knew his Shaw better than the lawyers did. "Although the Cinderella aspect of *Pygmalion* is charming, George Bernard Shaw, in an epilogue not meant for the stage, reveals Liza's destiny. Liza did not marry Henry Higgins or a duke or other nobility, but Freddie, and her destiny was working in a florist shop. The question, therefore, left remaining is: Was it sound sense on Shaw's part or ultimate irony that Liza should end up spank in the bosom of the bourgeoisie."

The judge upheld the terms of the prenuptial agreement and added his own personal sense of outrage at the amount Jacquie had requested. "While it may be true that for the past fifteen years the parties have enjoyed a lavish lifestyle at twelve hundred dollars a day, who couldn't? And while it may or may not be true, as Cleveland Amory once said, that 'Palm Beach is an island just off the east coast of the United States,' it is still on this planet," Judge Williams concluded.

Another judge later granted the divorce and upheld the amount in the prenuptial agreement. As Jacquie and her lawyer left the courtroom, their faces long and sad, the attorney told reporters, "Well, we gave it our best shot. *Qué será, será.*"

Jacquie's mother, Maria—who some believed pushed her daughter to marry Kimberly—has little sympathy for him now. "When they married, she was a little girl playing grownup. Now she has outgrown Jim."

While Kimberly may be pitied by many of his Palm Beach friends, the former playboy, bon vivant, and girl chaser sees his golden years as yet another adventure in his long life. He told journalist Linda Marx, "You know, I probably shouldn't say this. But I've reached a serenity, an inner peace. I have never been comfortable being a Kimberly where people know the name means money. Now when people call me on the phone or invite me to lunch, it's because they really like me personally.

Not who I am or what I can do for them. It's a damned nice feeling," he said. Eighty-one-year-old Kimberly is also madly in love with Chris Kornhauser, a stunning Palm Beach divorcée in her late thirties with a thirteen-year-old son.

"The goodness inside Jim's heart is not like you find in most people," Kornhauser said.

Jim's heart did find room to forgive Jacquie, who now lives with Susan Lynch in Delray Beach, twenty miles south of Palm Beach, where they also work together in a clothing shop. "I loved her. I still like her. We talk on the phone. I have no hard feelings. She now realizes that life is hard and people need to work to support themselves. The divorce has been good for her."

Jim is also understanding of her apparent bisexuality. "I've traveled everywhere and met many unusual people. But I've long since avoided accounting for the tastes of others."

The same forgiveness is not evident when the subject of Peter Pulitzer comes up. "Peter has gone berserk sexually...and I just don't see him anymore," Kimberly said. (Pulitzer has since remarried and moved to Okeechobee, Florida.)

After Jim Kimberly's move from Palm Beach to Lake Clark Shores, his name began appearing far less frequently in the Palm Beach papers. The same could not be said for that of Roxanne Pulitzer, whose autobiography, *The Prize Pulitzer,* was a best-seller in 1987.

In 1990, Roxanne became a central figure in yet another scandalous divorce. This one involved a swarthy, thirty-year-old French race-car driver named Count Jean de la Moussaye, a man who traces his lineage back to Louis XIV, and his thirty-four-year-old wife of five years, Francine McMahon, millionaire heiress to the fortune of her late father, Canadian oilman and industrialist Frank McMahon. It was a divorce that would rival—and some would say top—Roxanne's divorce trial.

The trouble began in October when Jean's wife threw him out of their home on Osceola Way and changed the locks. She accused him of having an affair with Roxanne Pulitzer. A month later, de la Moussaye—now living in the Chesterfield Hotel—retaliated, filing for divorce and asking for custody of the couple's three-year-old daughter, Alix, and one-year-old son, François. Jean charged that his wife was a violent alcoholic, a drug abuser, and a bisexual who was incapable of caring for their children.

Francine countercharged that de la Moussaye was an "irresponsible" husband who had no assets, no steady job, and who had a criminal record in France. Furthermore, Francine charged, Jean had had affairs with numerous women, the last of whom had been Roxanne Pulitzer, who was now supporting him.

After first denying the romance, Roxanne and Jean admitted they were lovers, but added that their involvement had followed a long friendship. The couple said they had initially met at Lulu's restaurant in July 1990, after their publicists devised a promotional gimmick to advertise Roxanne's novel, *Twins*, on the hood of de la Moussaye's race car.

Roxanne remained by de la Moussaye's side as the divorce battle reached Palm Beach Circuit Court in May 1991. Very quickly Roxanne and Francine squared off against each other on the witness stand. Under oath, Francine charged that Roxanne was turning her children against her. She said her daughter Alix had marched up to her and said, "You're a bitch! Roxanne's my new mommy!"

Roxanne angrily denied the accusation, countercharging that Francine had taught Alix to call her "the slut, the whore and piggy. She says it with a smile. I don't think she means it or knows the meaning of at least two of those names."

The trial also quickly became made-for-television soap opera, thanks to a steamy videotape. Francine had alleged that de la Moussaye had had a string of affairs during their marriage. One of them allegedly involved Kirsten Thompson, a lingerie model who had posed nude on top of his racing car in a session that had been videotaped. The tape was obtained by television's tabloid news shows, which quickly transformed the de la Moussaye trial into a nationwide story. The footage of Thompson writhing on Jean's car was broadcast with her private parts electronically obscured. "Roxanne Divorce Explodes! Race Car Beauty Exposed! Naked Video Revealed! Wife Left in Tears!" was how "Hard Copy" promoted its story.

Not to be outdone, "A Current Affair" promised the "exclusive story of America's dirtiest divorce," which would fill "another scandalous page in that overheated little town of Palm Beach."

In a TV interview, the sexy model said she had made love with de la Moussaye three times, once directly after the modeling session on his car. Thompson gained the nickname, the X-rated Hood Ornament.

Back in the courtroom, Francine's side alleged that Jean had taken part in a ménage à trois in a Miami hotel room; given his wife herpes; been caught straddling Roxanne in the front seat of his Porsche outside a West Palm Beach nightclub; refused to let her shop at K-mart "because blacks and Hispanics shopped there"; introduced her to cocaine; been convicted in France of receiving stolen French and Spanish royal jewelry in a scheme to resell it. De la Moussaye admitted the last allegation.

Jean's side argued that Francine had deliberately carved a star pattern into her left foot with a piece of broken glass while in a drunken stupor; had an affair with a lesbian and taken nude beach strolls with her; threatened to kill herself and her daughter; partaken in a marijuana-and-cocaine party with a half dozen homosexual men; given Jean herpes. Francine denied the charges.

In addition to the accusations, a bizarre blackmailing scheme emerged involving a former Palm Beach official. De la Moussaye said that shortly before the divorce trial began, he was approached by former Port of Palm Beach Commissioner Sandy Klein, photographer Garvin Smith, and carpenter Jeffrey Diamond, who warned him they had revealing videotape and photographs of him with other women that would damage his case. They offered to sell the evidence to him for fifty thousand dollars and "stay loyal" to him during the divorce proceedings. De la Moussaye said the men told him if he did not pay up, they would sell the evidence to the *National Enquirer.* Jean, who had counted Klein among his best friends, was stunned by the scheme and went to the police.

Detectives set a trap for the blackmailers. They wired the room where de la Moussaye was supposed to meet the trio for the payoff. During that taped conversation, the men lowered their price to sixteen thousand dollars. When de la Moussaye handed over some money—specially marked bills given to him by police—officers rushed in and arrested the three.

In January 1992, the de la Moussayes were granted a divorce, and Jean was awarded custody of the two children. In true Palm Beach style, Francine McMahon de la Moussaye remarried a few hours later, barely allowing the ink to dry on her divorce decree. Even though he had awarded custody of the children to Jean, Circuit Court Judge John Hoy let it be known he was not pleased with the Frenchman's character. The judge called Jean "immature...not a model of diligence and hard work."

Still, the judge said, Francine's terrible drinking problem ruled her out as a responsible parent. "On three occasions in little more than three years she drank herself into a violent state of intoxication which required police or medical intervention," the judge wrote. He ordered Francine to pay Jean fifteen hundred dollars a month in child support.

Francine, now married to commercial airline pilot Jay Andrew Ryan, has vowed to fight for custody.

Three months after the de la Moussaye divorce, Jean and Roxanne became engaged. It has not changed their life much. They are still mainstays at Au Bar. Roxanne continues to write, and she has made a comeback on the Palm Beach social scene. She and Jean are night creatures, often staying into the early morning hours at the table they reserve once or twice a week at Au Bar. Roxanne is a celebrity there, occasionally signing autographs or a book jacket. The mean-spirited glances and comments that followed her after her divorce battle with Peter are gone. Still, she cannot go anywhere without heads turning and people whispering, "Look, it's Roxanne Pulitzer."

She often hears her name called and smiles sweetly. But there are no doubt a few daggers behind some of those smiles. Her second novel, *Façade*, released in June 1992, is set in Palm Beach, and the blurb on the book jacket promises a roman à clef:

> It is the 1980s, and sex and sin under the scorching sun and seductive skies of Palm Beach—the playground of the Atlantic— are as rampant as ever. In this deliciously decadent city, sexual license and self-indulgence aren't just a way of life—they are the very essence and meaning of life. . . . Nothing is honest or true in a world fabricated on deceit and deception, a world where lust dominates love, reality crushes dreams, and money reigns supreme.

And on occasion, the combination of love and money and power, brought more than just sex scandals, sleazy divorces, and saucy headlines. Sometimes it brought sudden death.

26

"I Can Get Away With Anything": James and Suki Sullivan

On the morning of January 16, 1987, James Vincent Sullivan was in his magnificent two-story oceanfront mansion on South Ocean Boulevard in Palm Beach. The $5 million, nine-bedroom Casa Eleda was one of the island's original grand homes. Designed in 1929 by Maurice Fatio, Casa Eleda is built around a coral-rock courtyard, features Italianate Tuscan columns and Palladian windows, and spans two hundred feet of beach. When Sullivan purchased Casa Eleda, he spent nearly one year—and several hundred thousand dollars—meticulously restoring the historic mansion to its original condition. The sensitive renovations ultimately helped him obtain a coveted appointment to the island's influential Landmarks Preservation Commission.

As the native Bostonian awakened to the sounds of the Atlantic ocean outside his magnificent home, a series of events began to unfold in Georgia that would forever alter Sullivan's life. At 8:20 A.M., a delivery-man carrying a box of roses arrived at the Atlanta home of Sullivan's estranged wife and knocked on her door. When she opened it, the "deliveryman" pulled out a powerful revolver and shot Lita Sullivan several times in the head. As she fell backward mortally wounded, the messenger dumped the flowers over her body and fled.

Forty minutes later, a collect long-distance telephone call was made to Sullivan's oceanfront mansion. The police traced that call to a rest stop on Interstate 85 near Atlanta. By then, the authorities knew that a judge presiding over Sullivan's divorce was to rule that afternoon on whether Lita Sullivan was entitled to one-half of her husband's estate, including his beloved mansion. The first question the police and the Federal Bureau of Investigation wanted to answer was: Who is James Sullivan?

From the start, the agents learned that Sullivan had embellished his background. Born in 1942, James Vincent Sullivan was raised in a tough working-class Irish neighborhood of wooden triple-decker homes in Boston. Sullivan's father was a typesetter with a small Boston news-paper—although he later told his in-laws and business associates that his dad was a publisher.

As a teenager, Sullivan appeared to be just an ordinary curly-haired, red-headed boy in an Irish Catholic town teeming with red-headed youngsters. But Sullivan early on exhibited a drive and perseverance that demonstrated he wanted more from life than an unskilled job that would confine him in his neighborhood. While his friends played stickball during the day and roamed the streets at night, young Jim Sullivan remained in his room studying long into the night. He eventually graduated in the top percentile in public school and earned an appointment to prestigious Boston Latin, a preparatory school whose alumni include many of the city's influential politicians, lawyers, and physicians. At the competitive prep school, Sullivan continued to excel and earned another full scholarship, this one to Holy Cross College in Worcester.

In 1962, Sullivan graduated from Holy Cross with a degree in economics and enrolled in the graduate business program at Boston University. Inexplicably he dropped out in less than a year. To support himself, he accepted a mundane position in a small accounting firm. Four years later, he married Catherine Murray. The couple quickly had four children. Living in Boston with the responsibilities of a large family, James Vincent Sullivan now had become the type of man he did not want to be.

But an opportunity arose in 1974 that rekindled his dream of a life beyond the neighborhood. James Sullivan received a call from an uncle, Frank Bienert, who owned a million-dollar liquor distributorship in Macon, Georgia. A few years earlier, Uncle Frank had provided a position to Sullivan's brother with the hope of grooming him to take over the company. Uncle Frank now was on the phone saying that he had fired Sullivan's brother because he had failed to live up to expectations.

"I'm in my sixties, getting close to retirement, and I have no children to leave the business to," the sixty-five-year-old Bienert said. "Come help me run the place and I'll give you a share of the business."

Rather than accept Bienert's offer, Sullivan perceived an opportunity to bargain with his aging and often difficult uncle. After intensive negotiations, Bienert gave 10 percent of Crown Beverages to Sullivan and agreed to a sliding-scale provision that eventually would increase his nephew's stake to 48 percent. Bienert also agreed to revise his will—making Sullivan sole owner of the distributorship in the event of his death. Before Sullivan moved to Macon, he bragged about how he had cut a lucrative deal with his uncle.

But within months of his arrival in Macon, it appeared that Sullivan—like his brother before him—would not be able to meet Uncle Frank's demands. Crown employees told journalist John Connolly that they often saw Bienert visibly angry with Sullivan and heard him complain about Sullivan's rude and condescending manners. On at least one occasion, they heard Bienert threaten to dismiss Sullivan outright. By the end of 1974, Bienert was discussing openly the possibility of removing Sullivan from his will.

In a letter Bienert planned to deliver to Sullivan, Uncle Frank wrote, "I am [writing] this statement as an indictment to record the poor performance of your tenure. Many unsatisfactory and unresolved problems of your operational management—the worst of any I have experienced—was leading to chaos. You haven't carried your weight, earned your keep...or made our lives easier, better or happier.

"On the contrary," Bienert continued, "you have made things harder for just about everyone...and have put a serious and undue strain upon me and my family's well-being.... You have made our relationship a one-way street—your direction only. In short, you haven't been a good relation."

Bienert also drafted a codicil to his will, stripping Sullivan of any claim to his company or estate. But the scathing written indictment and the codicil were never acted upon. On January 3, 1975, Frank Bienert, a vibrant businessman with an unblemished health record, suddenly collapsed at the dinner table. He began to vomit and gasp for air. Rather than summoning an ambulance, Bienert's wife, Agnes, a devout Christian Scientist, waited for his violent wretching to end.

When the heaving subsided, Agnes put Bienert to bed and waited for the Lord to heal her seriously ill husband. But during the next five days, his health only worsened. Finally, Bienert telephoned a trusted aide who, according to Connolly, rushed him to a hospital. By then it was too late.

Frank Bienert succumbed to his illness on January 8, 1975. Physicians said he died from heart failure. Bienert's lawyers adhered to the will he had prepared before Sullivan arrived in Macon. In accordance with Bienert's "wishes," James Sullivan—the terrible "relation"—was officially named executor of Uncle Frank's estate.

Among Sullivan's initial instructions as "executor" was to have Uncle Frank's body prepared for cremation and shipped quickly to Boston. "The fat old bastard keeled over from a heart attack, right onto a pallet of vodka!" Sullivan later told Connolly at Casa Eleda in Palm Beach.

Connolly, a former New York City cop, suggested that Sullivan might have poisoned his uncle. But Georgia law-enforcement authorities who looked into Bienert's death failed to turn up any evidence to substantiate such a charge.

Curiously, within ten days of Bienert's death, James Sullivan's wife emerged from their newly inherited twelve-acre estate in Macon with her luggage packed and their four children and moved back to Boston. Catherine Sullivan sued for divorce in March, claiming that her marriage "was irretrievably broken" and that her husband was no longer a partner in their relationship. In January 1976, they officially divorced after ten years of marriage. Catherine was awarded custody of the children. But the suddenness of their separation and divorce did not faze Macon's newest millionaire.

Sullivan immediately started to date Lita McClinton, the elegant twenty-six-year-old daughter of a politically connected black family in Atlanta. Lita was an attractive, bright young woman with a generous nature and a lust for life. Lita's mild-mannered parents—her father was a government official, her mother was a housewife—raised their children to "judge people as individuals" regardless of race.

As a child, Lita McClinton attended parochial school, and then the prestigious Spelman College in Atlanta, where she made the dean's list and graduated with honors. After college, Lita, with a passion for clothing, took a position in a fashionable boutique in Atlanta, where she met—and fell in love—with Sullivan.

In proposing marriage to Lita, Sullivan recognized he possessed a vanity that compelled him to show the bigots of the South that there could be no limitations on what he could attain or achieve.

"Hubris!" Sullivan later explained. "I wanted to show people I could get away with anything."

Lita's parents did not approve of the engagement. But their concern had little to do with the obvious hurdles their daughter would face married to a white northerner in Georgia. Her mother, Jo Ann, said she was uncomfortable about the ten-year age difference between Lita and Sullivan. And her daughter knew too little about him.

"We did not like Jim from the beginning, but we always told our children: 'Don't judge a person by his race, you judge him as an individual.' She said she loved him. That was the thing."

On December 29, 1976—less than ten months after Frank Bienert's death and six months after Sullivan's divorce—James Vincent Sullivan married Lita McClinton. Lita's great-uncle conducted the ceremony. "If you'd meet Jim, you'd think he's charming and well-spoken," Jo Ann McClinton said. "He could act kind of thoughtful, and if you don't know him, he has a way of bowling you over."

Despite his "hubris," Sullivan quickly decided that his business might suffer if he brought his black wife home to Macon. He voiced his concerns after the wedding and convinced Lita to remain in Atlanta while he lived during the week at the estate in Macon, ninety miles away. When people in Macon asked Sullivan if he was married, he said he was single. But after a year, Lita insisted the two-city charade end. Sullivan acquiesced.

Within days of Lita's arrival, racists dumped a small mound of garbage on the Sullivans' lawn and delivered a truckload of watermelon rinds to Sullivan's office. Phil Walden, a recording executive and neighbor, recalled that he admired Sullivan and Lita for their courage.

"They were in love and had the guts to get married in a town that small." Walden described Sullivan as "bright," but "opinionated." He said Sullivan showered his wife with gifts early in their marriage—Lita was always elegantly clothed.

"She had a great sense of humor, and God knows she needed it as the wife of a white man in Macon," a friend of Lita's said.

Lita's friends saw Sullivan as a calculating man who was very selective about with whom he shared his time and charm. "He had no energy and no time for anyone who can't do something for him," another friend told the *Fort Lauderdale Sun-Sentinel.* "He was harsh in business, cold to people whose favor he didn't care to cultivate, but he could be very pleasant, even generous to those he did."

Sullivan's "condescending" and "rude" manners—the ones Bienert had criticized years earlier—worsened as he grew secure as a millionaire businessman. People said his high-minded superiority and his tendency to treat people shabbily intensified. "Jim didn't much like Georgia, not Macon, not Atlanta," an acquaintance told a reporter. "He didn't think people here had the intellect he appreciated." Then he began to treat his wife shabbily as well.

Employees at Crown Beverages said Sullivan placed severe restrictions on his wife's freedom. At one point, they recalled, Lita Sullivan had to ask her husband for money to have her hair coiffed.

And the humiliation did not end there. Soon the workers watched in silence as Sullivan cheated on Lita, according to Connolly. One employee recalled how Sullivan used his wife's car to visit a lover because his own Rolls-Royce was too conspicuous in Macon. When Sullivan returned from his mistress, he tossed the keys cavalierly to Lita and said: "You need gas."

Sullivan began to look for a new place to live: one that was better suited for his refined mind and dignified manner. In 1981, he found—and purchased—the landmark Casa Eleda. Situated on the most expensive mile of beachfront property in America, the mansion cost $2 million.

"When my husband purchased the Palm Beach home, he did so over my objections," Lita later said. "I did not intend ever to make Palm Beach my home as I was not accepted in the social community."

Casa Eleda was affectionately known in Palm Beach as the "Ham and Cheese House" thanks to rows of red bricks that are sandwiched across the villa's coquina stone. Because of its unusual and historic importance, the gentry of Palm Beach were concerned about how the mansion's new owner would renovate Casa Eleda.

Sullivan quickly allayed their fears. He tended to Casa Eleda with attention he had rarely shown to anyone or anything. He hired the island's most respected contractors, and he spent several hundred thousand dollars to ensure that the estate was carefully restored to its original condition. His efforts were not overlooked.

"What Mr. Sullivan did to his house was a marvelous piece of work," Yvelyne "DeeDee" Marix, the Palm Beach mayor, later said. "It looks exactly the way it must have when it was built."

By 1983, Crown Beverage was worth approximately $5 million. And James Sullivan—with his Boston accent, Holy Cross degree, and preparatory-school background—felt he deserved to live permanently in Palm Beach, a town that was worthy of his wealth and breeding.

"Jim always had grandiose ideas," said Jo Ann McClinton, Lita's mother. "I remember he told us that his father was a publisher for

Hearst in California. It turned out his father was working class, blue collar. There's nothing wrong with that, so why lie about it! But he was always looking for social acceptance."

She also remembered how her son-in-law often said he was embarrassed by his hands. He would lament that his fingers were short and stubby rather than long and elegant "like a gentleman's should be."

Sullivan sold his liquor distributorship and moved into his mansion at 920 South Ocean Boulevard. Perhaps it was his arrogant "I can do anything" attitude that led him to believe that—with a black wife—he could join Palm Beach society, a society arguably as racist as Macon. From the start, Lita predicted she would be forced away from a community that was created exclusively for America's wealthy, "white" aristocracy.

Lois Terry, a friend and neighbor of the Sullivans, later said: "There is still that feeling here that it's all right if your gardener's black, but you're not going to invite him over for cocktails."

As an avenue into Palm Beach society, Sullivan became a spirited supporter in Marix's mayoral campaign in 1984. When the charming Marix won election, Sullivan sought his reward—a seat on the Landmarks Preservation Commission. Sullivan recognized that the commission held virtual authority over all zoning, development, and architectural alterations on the island. Therefore, anyone who held a seat on the commission had social cachet in Palm Beach.

When a seat became vacant in May 1985, Marix named Sullivan to the commission. His expectations of instant social status soon materialized. Even the most respected figures in Palm Beach began to notice him as he attended charity balls in his custom-made black tuxedos.

Palm Beach's response to Sullivan energized him in his work on the commission. He immersed himself in the newfound post. Associates said he rarely missed a commission meeting—and the attendant charity balls and dinner parties. Soon Sullivan was regarded as an astute, effective, and knowledgeable board member. He had invested time studying the history of Palm Beach and became a "potent political force," one observer said.

"That commission was his whole claim to fame," another said. "That seat on the commission was his key into society."

To the keepers of the island's social register, James Sullivan was warm and generous, always eager to donate time and money to charity. For the powerbrokers and haute society members, he was the charming New Englander with a quick wit, carefully chosen word, and a glint in his eyes. His picture seemed to end up in the *Palm Beach Daily News* two or three times a week. But always Sullivan was photographed alone. In fact, he rarely was seen with his wife at all.

One Palm Beach regular who knew Jim and Lita Sullivan said that if someone were meeting his wife for the first time, he might think she was simply a domestic from West Palm Beach because of the way Sullivan treated her. People who noticed Lita's rough hands believed they were the result of housework.

By the time Sullivan was appointed to the commission, Lita already was spending long weekends in Atlanta, which eventually stretched into weeks. She rarely returned from their $450,000 townhouse in suburban Buckhead. Sullivan did not mind. Lita's preference for Atlanta made it easier for him to make the rounds of Palm Beach society. On the occasions when she visited Palm Beach, Lita felt abused and complained that her husband again was using money "as a weapon which he would cut off whenever he became angry." Then she discovered that her husband was sleeping with various women on the island.

On August 12, 1985, Lita McClinton Sullivan packed her clothes, antiques, crystal, porcelain, and sterling silver and loaded it into a U-Haul trailer attached to a 1973 Mercedes and left Casa Eleda. She drove to her Atlanta townhouse at 3085 Slaton Drive in the Coaches. Two days later, she filed for divorce. She claimed that Sullivan had become so hostile and unpleasant that she could not stay with him.

"It's only later you learn he's a ladies' man, that he's practiced and perfected that over the years," Lita's mother said.

In her divorce papers, Lita requested twenty-three hundred dollars a month alimony and one-half of Sullivan's estate. Rather than challenge the divorce, Sullivan actually contacted Lita and pleaded with her to return to Palm Beach. Some of their friends and acquaintances said Sullivan's attempt at reconciliation was genuine. But they were unaware of another possible motive. When Lita left her millionaire husband, he could little afford a costly divorce.

Nearly $3 million of the $5 million he received for the sale of Bienert's distributorship was invested in Casa Eleda. In addition, he was paying the mortgage on Lita's $450,000 home in Atlanta. And he was spending heavily to support his lavish Palm Beach life-style, which now included country club memberships, large dinner bills—and expensive girlfriends.

Putting an even tighter crimp in his bank account, Sullivan invested virtually all of his "ready" cash with a smooth-talking couple from Orlando whom he had recently met. The couple, George and Pilar

Bissell, told Sullivan they were starting a retail business that sold rare palm trees and orchids. Over several dinner meetings at Casa Eleda and at the Bissell's home, Sullivan was persuaded to invest more than $1.5 million in the Bissell's DewKist Nursery.

The investment did not pay off immediately—and it never would. The Bissells were professional swindlers. With no appreciable income from his Palm Beach commissioner's position, Sullivan, in short, could not afford to dispose of Lita.

And Lita was not cooperating. She told Sullivan she would return to Palm Beach only if he instructed his attorneys to draw up an agreement that provided her with half their property. "If I own part of his property he'll be nice," Lita said.

But Sullivan refused—and he countersued for divorce, angrily accusing his wife of being an adulterer and a drug-abusing thief. He then started to tell people that he had never loved Lita. "It was only lust," Sullivan said.

Despite the prospect of an acrimonious divorce, Sullivan never missed a step in his busy social whirl. He continued to travel among the fun-seekers who dined regularly at Chuck and Harold's, Nando's, and Club Colette. His crowd included the debonair Leonard Rogers and his gorgeous Korean-born wife, Suki.

The forty-eight-year-old Rogers and his twenty-five-year-old Suki had their own stormy times. Rogers was a member of Palm Beach's old guard. A former senior vice president at Gulf & Western, Rogers had a condominium in Palm Beach and homes in New York and Palm Springs, California. In 1977, he came out of retirement, launching a financial investment corporation in Florida and the Bahamas.

The *Palm Beach Daily News* described Rogers then as "an immaculate dresser who was handsome, charming, cool, intelligent, articulate and most of all smooth, calm and at ease at all times." He also was divorced—and he "loved" being single. "It's marvelous to be a bachelor and live in Palm Beach," Rogers said.

The dashing Rogers was having cocktails in the main lobby lounge of the elegant Colony Hotel on Worth Avenue in 1981 when the stunning and mysterious Hyo-Sook "Suki" Choi arrived. Suki was the image of a perfectly sculptured Oriental figurine. Barely five feet tall and weighing less than one hundred pounds, Suki had long, flowing black hair that seemed to trace the contours of her shapely figure. She dressed meticulously in custom-made clothes and fashionable high-heels, which only enhanced her exotic beauty.

Little was known about Suki then—or now. What little is revealed about the exotic Suki comes from her own three divorces. Hyo-Sook Choi was born in Seoul, Korea, on May 18, 1952. She studied English in public school, but failed to master it. She graduated from high school in 1971 and emigrated to the United States two years later, settling in Chicago with friends. It is unclear how she supported herself during her initial years in Chicago.

In 1978, Suki met and quickly married James Schinder, a Chicago financial consultant. They soon talked about moving to the Palm Beach area. After one year of marriage, the Schinders left Chicago and relocated to North Palm Beach, about ten miles north of the island on the Florida mainland.

Suki Schinder took a job behind the counter of Kaufman Jewelers in the Palm Beach Mall off Belvedere Boulevard to help with the bills. But her hands were destined to wear diamonds, not display them. Suki quickly quit her job at Kaufman Jewelers, divorced her husband, and was in the circuit of Palm Beach nightlife—all before the year had ended.

By the spring of 1980, the exotic twenty-seven-year-old Suki was dating Rogers, the "contented bachelor." On December 15, 1980, they married. Leonard Rogers, fifty-one, presented his bride with a diamond- and ruby-studded ring. He also presented her to Palm Beach society. Their marriage lasted seven months.

But in the odd, seemingly inexplicable, marital machinations of Palm Beach, Suki Choi and Leonard Rogers reconciled and married a second time, on New Year's Eve, December 31, 1982. They moved to a splendid home on Tangier Avenue. They were photographed frequently on the cocktail party circuit and were seen beaming from the pages of the *Shiny Sheet*—Rogers in black tie, Suki in a gown with babies' breath tucked in her hair. Suki even enrolled in a course at Palm Beach Community College to help polish her English, but her social schedule with Rogers interfered.

"The classes were at a bad time," she later explained. "I have to get up at six thirty and [classes were] always during the [social] season, and we go out at night and we come home maybe twelve o'clock—it's hard for me to go out and get up at six thirty."

But Rogers's successful investment company demanded that he travel out of town on business. After several years of apparent marital bliss, their marriage deteriorated again. Suki divided her evenings between knitting and the Palm Beach "scene." Rogers became suspicious that she slept with other men. He did what most millionaires on Palm Beach in his position do when they think their wives are cheating—they hire private detectives.

One afternoon, detectives stood outside Rogers's Tangier Avenue home. They watched as the garage door opened and Suki moved her husband's Mercedes into the driveway. She was making room for Sullivan and his convertible Rolls-Royce, the one that was too conspicuous to drive in Macon.

The sleuths remained outside the Rogers home until morning, when Sullivan finally left in his Rolls. The investigators dutifully reported their findings to Rogers. He divorced Suki on October 1, 1986. Suki received $120,000 in alimony, a 1983 Cadillac El Dorado, and an investment portfolio worth nearly $135,000, which quickly grew to $300,000, thanks to Rogers's investment acumen.

Sullivan, who was still married to Lita, refused to testify at the Rogers divorce proceedings. As soon as the divorce was final, the slender five-foot-ten Sullivan began to squire "his" Suki around Palm Beach. Sullivan's many friends and acquaintances simply assumed he had found "another exotic." But Sullivan's infatuation for Suki was more akin to an obsession. "She was the love of my life," he later said. "He was mad about her," another added.

Sullivan showered Suki with attention and gifts. He took her to dinner every night. He often shopped with Suki on Worth Avenue, insisting on accompanying her into the dressing rooms, to the chagrin of the management. They vacationed together in Europe and Asia. Nothing was too good, or expensive, when it came to his "exotic" girlfriend.

"They traveled extensively, dined out frequently, attended parties and, in general, had a grand time," Judge Hubert Lindsey later said at their divorce. "They were consumers in the true sense of the word...the sort of life-style which a considerable portion of the population does not have—but wants."

Ironically, while James Vincent Sullivan had become the influential millionaire he dreamed of being as a youngster, he was learning the high price of sustaining such extravagance. To balance his passion for Suki and his bank account, Sullivan scaled back his life-style in other, less necessary, places. Parties at Casa Eleda became flinty affairs.

"He's the tightest guy in the world," one Palm Beacher told the *Sun Sentinel*. "A party at Sullivan's was one hors d'oeuvre and forty-watt bulbs in the lamp."

Some people noticed that he started to neglect Casa Eleda. These critics expressed annoyance that a man with authority to tell them how to treat their homes was allowing his own to grow shabby.

As 1987 approached, Sullivan's money woes could no longer be juggled by serving hors d'oeuvres rather than a full-course meal. His $1.5 million investment with the Pillars was lost. There was the monthly mortgage payment on his $900,000 home loan. By coincidence, another $1 million loan he had taken from a employee-retirement plan was coming due. These three heavy financial realities were converging as Lita's lawyers demanded he surrender their $425,000 townhouse in Buckhead.

Sullivan applied for a $1 million loan at a Florida bank. He offered Casa Eleda as collateral. When he filled out the application form, Sullivan claimed he was single, according to Connolly. Investigators suspect he lied because he feared the bank officials were reluctant to lend money to an applicant involved in a divorce.

Before the loan money was issued, Atlanta Judge William Daniel, meanwhile, set January 16, 1987, as the day when he would make a pivotal ruling in Sullivan's divorce case. He said he would decide whether Lita Sullivan was entitled to twenty-five hundred dollars per month in alimony or whether she was entitled to half of everything her husband owned, including the mansion.

As Lita awakened early that morning to prepare for her appearance in court, three men were already outside a Peachtree Road flower shop, purchasing a box of pink roses. At about eight A.M., they drove from the florist in a white Toyota to Lita's home, which was only three blocks from the governor's mansion. At about 8:20, a tall, balding, middle-aged man got out of the car. With the box of flowers in one hand and a nine-millimeter revolver in the other, he knocked on Lita's door, and then fired three hollow-pointed bullets into Lita's head.

Forty minutes later, a collect call was made from a rest-stop pay phone on Interstate 85 north of Atlanta near Suwanee. The call was made to historic Casa Eleda mansion in Palm Beach.

Mayor Marix was stunned at the news. "I am absolutely shocked at what a terrible thing this is. I feel terribly sorry for him. Obviously, when one has been married to someone for a time and something like this happens, it must come as a terrible shock."

When word of Lita's murder spread throughout Palm Beach, concerned residents found the slain woman's husband on a tennis court, wearing his whites and in the middle of a match. Later that evening,

Sullivan was again seen in public. He went out for a cozy dinner with "his" Suki at a Palm Beach bistro. The two lovers appeared calm and unaffected by the news of the day, as though nothing extraordinary had happened, according to newspaper accounts.

Lita's mother, Jo Ann, recalled how Sullivan—despite nearly ten years of marriage to her daughter—never called to express his regrets or send flowers or attend Lita's funeral. And when family members asked Sullivan whether they could donate Lita's organs to an Atlanta burn center, he flatly refused to give his permission, without providing a reason. Lita's friends and relatives pooled their funds, posting a fifteen-thousand-dollar reward for information about her murder. Sullivan did not contribute to the reward money.

People who knew Sullivan remarked how—for a second time in his life—death had come at a most opportune moment. Within two months of Lita's murder, Sullivan, now truly single, received his bank loan. He used the $960,000 loan to pay off the two notes on his mansion. The "good timing" of Lita's slaying did not escape the police, who instantly recognized that Sullivan had motive.

Sullivan denied any involvement in his estranged wife's murder, and his lawyers challenged the cops to disprove him. "What husband would be foolish enough to have his wife killed on the very day there is to be an important court decision?" Sullivan, puffing on a cigar, coolly asked *Spy* magazine writer John Connolly one night.

A few days later he bragged that he had slept soundly each night since his wife's murder, never rising before nine in the morning. "That's either the sign of a clear conscience," Sullivan said, now lowering his voice to a whisper, "or no conscience at all." When the detectives asked Sullivan about the collect phone call from Suwanee after Lita's murder, he and his lawyers said he knew nothing about it.

Five weeks after his wife's killing, Sullivan hosted a fund-raising party for his alma mater, Holy Cross College, at Casa Eleda for one hundred alumni who reside along the East Coast. The Reverend Francis Miller, the school's vice president for development, recalled Sullivan as a "very gracious host."

Seven months later, Sullivan married Suki Choi Schinder Rogers. The September 26, 1987, edition of the *Palm Beach Post* announced: SULLIVAN WEDS; HAS PALM BEACH TONGUES WAGGING. Atlanta homicide police lieutenant Horace Walker told columnist Thom Smith that Sullivan was a prime murder suspect on his wedding day, but "it's not against the law to get married. We wish him well."

Despite the controversy surrounding Sullivan, his reputation in Palm Beach was not diminished by the whiff of scandal. The following May, when his term on the Landmarks Preservation Commission ended, Sullivan was not only reappointed to the board—but he was named its chairman. The designation was truly the penultimate moment of Sullivan's life. But it also marked the heights from which he might fall.

On March 8, 1990, Sullivan's Rolls-Royce was involved in a seemingly harmless fender-bender. But the police discovered he was driving with an expired and suspended license. Rather than plead guilty to the embarrassing violations, Sullivan—with his "I can get away with anything" attitude—enlisted Suki in a coverup. She claimed she had been the driver—even though witnesses said Sullivan was alone in the car. When the deception was unmasked, Sullivan—and Suki—were charged with perjury. Suki did not enjoy the prospect of facing the more serious charge.

On June 11, 1990, Sullivan left his mansion to attend a meeting of the Palm Beach Town Council and walked headlong into a row. Town Council President Bernard Heeke said that he had received "a lot of calls at home from people asking, 'How can the town let a man like that serve on the commission?'" Sullivan was forced to resign his post, for "personal reasons."

He returned home to an empty mansion. Suki had collected her belongings—including hundreds of pairs of pantyhose she had stashed under the bed—and moved out. The following morning Sullivan awoke to his third divorce action. Suki had filed for divorce. She claimed she was "deathly afraid" and was in hiding.

"A year ago, he told me that I was dealing with a dangerous person (him) in a dangerous game and that I had better watch out," the divorce complaint said. She described Sullivan as a foul-mouthed, violent-tempered husband who scrutinized her every move and counted "every penny I spent."

On September 18, 1990, Suki Sullivan testified at her divorce trial and stunned the courthouse. She said her husband James Sullivan had confessed to her that "he hired someone to get rid of Lita—he did it to his second wife!"

The diminutive Suki recalled that after the car accident she tearfully told Sullivan she did not want to commit perjury. "I said I was afraid to go to jail. He turned the volume on the television high up so no one could hear our conversation. He said he had 'made terrible mistakes and that God would punish him.'"

"He [made] me [commit] perjury because he was afraid he's never going to come out of jail because he did it to his wife. He told me he hired someone to murder Lita, to get rid of her. He said, 'Let's sell this house as quick as possible, and we'll move to a different country.' I was afraid I'd be next. I knew I had to do something."

Instead of immediately leaving, Suki remained with Sullivan for sixteen days, going out to dinner and visiting friends. "I did not know what else to do," she said. Suki testified a second time before a federal grand jury in Atlanta. The panel had been investigating Lita's death under a federal statute covering the use of interstate commerce—telephones—to commit murder.

Sullivan took the stand at his own divorce. He denied Suki's allegations and his attorneys argued that Suki was a golddigging "black widow," who would say anything because her only true love was money. The *Palm Beach Post* shared that opinion: "In her ten years on Palm Beach, Suki had refined the art of marrying well and living better."

On December 11, 1990, Judge Hubert R. Lindsey rendered his verdict in the divorce. The *Miami Herald* told the story: SUKI SULLIVAN A LOSER IN DIVORCE DECISION. James Sullivan retained everything—his mansion, his Rolls, his silver Mercedes, even Coco, their Maltese dog. And he did not have to pay alimony. The judge noted that during their thirty-three-month marriage, Sullivan's net worth plunged $2 million while Suki's increased from $421,000 to more than $600,000.

Suki, now a single woman whose perjury charge was dropped, returned to the nightlife of Palm Beach. She continued to make the rounds of the island's restaurants and clubs that included a "new" nightspot called Au Bar. On April 5, 1991, Suki was in Au Bar drinking champagne. A rape scandal involving the Kennedys had catapulted the obscure Au Bar to national attention.

While Suki returned to the Palm Beach "scene," Sullivan was sentenced to one year under "house arrest" for lying to the court about the traffic accident. He was confined to one half of his seventeen-thousand-square-foot Casa Eleda with his movements monitored by an electronic ankle bracelet. Because of the size of his "prison," Sullivan paid the $250-a-month costs of his own confinement.

The debonair millionaire spent his days shuffling around in slippers. He lost weight from his already spindly frame. And he allowed the inside of his mansion to become increasingly unkempt and the lawn to be overgrown. The former head of the prestigious Landmarks Preservation Commission's own home appeared dank, dirty, and in disrepair.

Connolly visited Sullivan for a week in August. He reported that Sullivan refused to turn on the air conditioning during the sweltering summer days in order to save money. He kept the front door locked at all times and only used a rear entrance. And on one nightstand, Sullivan had two books: one was *The Burden of Proof*, a story of a man presumed guilty of murder; the other was a collection of poetry on death. Connolly reported one other interesting quirk about Sullivan to the authorities: he kept meticulous diaries.

On September 6, 1991, federal agents conducted a six-hour raid of Sullivan's mansion. They found—and photographed—the diaries, which Sullivan compulsively kept. They also found four weapons—two shotguns, a rifle, and a .38 handgun. Sullivan denied knowledge of the firearms, but he was returned to jail. A few weeks later, he sold Casa Eleda to an "out-of-state" couple for $3 million, $1.5 million less than the original asking price.

On November 8, 1991—nearly four and a half years after Lita Sullivan was executed at her home—the Federal Bureau of Investigation implicated Sullivan in the murder conspiracy. The court affidavits revealed that a convicted forger had identified the man who placed the mysterious call to Sullivan's home after Lita's murder as a Georgia man with a lengthy criminal record. The informant also told the FBI that a former neighbor of Sullivan's was "involved in the murder of a black woman living in Atlanta who was married to a white millionaire in Florida." The FBI identified the former neighbor as a black former state trooper.

The FBI said Sullivan had described the murder weapon, a nine-millimeter automatic revolver, to a neighbor of Lita's—even though "no one in the Atlanta police department recalls telling Sullivan about the weapon." And only days after Lita's murder, Sullivan told a former mistress in Atlanta: "I told you I'd take care of things where you wouldn't have to testify."

On January 10, 1992, the federal grand jury in Atlanta indicted James Vincent Sullivan on charges that he had arranged Lita's murder. The indictment was handed up only five days before the federal statute of limitations would have expired. United States Attorney Joseph Whitley declined to reveal how much Sullivan allegedly paid for Lita's murder.

"James Sullivan was the primary suspect as far as my family was concerned from the beginning," Jo Ann McClinton said. "Our contention was that he initiated and orchestrated the murder."

Although he had been nine hundred miles away from Atlanta on the day of Lita's death, Sullivan is the only person under indictment in her murder. The FBI and U.S. attorney say their investigation is continuing. There may be more arrests.

Sullivan swears he is innocent of the charges against him. "He had nothing to fear from Lita's divorce case," Sullivan's lawyer, Edward Garland said. "The idea he had a motive to kill Lita is nonsense. He had ample resources to divorce Lita. And the phone call to the mansion does not prove a thing, and I tell you it can be explained by any number of things."

Garland says the trial of the one-time influential chairman of the Palm Beach Landmarks Preservation Commission will be Sullivan's salvation and vindication. The Atlanta lawyer said he will show in court that there were other men in Lita Sullivan's life who might have motive to murder her. Then the defense attorney paused. And, in a slow, sweet-as-syrup, southern voice, he insisted: "James Sullivan has been hounded for years with this false charge. But his day will come!"

On April 4, 1992, James Vincent Sullivan was released from prison on the perjury charge. But his assets of $2.8 million were frozen by the court. He was given a monthly allowance of $8,000. When the Palm Beach millionaire left West Palm Beach county prison, he was met by his "new" girlfriend, Karen Griner, an attractive thirty-eight-year-old realtor from Macon. She said she had known Sullivan when he owned Frank Bienert's liquor distributorship.

As the fall of 1992 approached in Palm Beach, James Sullivan, the scruffy kid from Boston who once dreamed of a millionaire's life, planned to move into a fifteen-hundred-dollar-a-month rented "garage" apartment with his girlfriend, a short drive from Casa Eleda on the ocean. But the landlord canceled the lease at the last moment, forcing his infamous tenant to find lodgings elsewhere. In the end, James Sullivan, the once powerful commissioner who had held sway over the owners of America's most expensive mansions, left the island and moved into a home on the mainland, forty miles south of Palm Beach, in Boca Raton.

27

Under a Raging Moon: William Kennedy Smith and Patricia Bowman

At about three A.M. on Saturday, March 30, 1991, an attractive young couple strolled along the beach outside the historic Kennedy estate on North Ocean Boulevard in Palm Beach. The two figures—William Kennedy Smith, a medical student, and Patricia Bowman, a single parent—held hands as they walked beneath the clear Florida sky. As the ocean tides lapped against the shore, they paused and then kissed softly. This gentle embrace, however, became their last moment of peace together. What happened next between these two moonlit strollers in Palm Beach became the mystery all of America wanted to solve.

Patricia Bowman, the stepdaughter of a gritty midwestern industrial-ist who had founded the General Tire Corporation, recalled that she "was enjoying" herself with Smith, the nephew of former President John F. Kennedy. They had just met for the first time that night at a Palm Beach nightspot. "I felt no fear," Bowman said. "I was at the Kennedy mansion. I thought there would be security."

After their kiss beneath the stars, Smith asked Bowman if she wanted to go for a swim in the nude. She declined. When Smith took off his clothes and plunged into the surf, the twenty-nine-year-old Bowman timidly turned and walked away. But as she reached the top of a concrete staircase leading from the beach, someone grabbed her ankle from behind. The predator was not some intruder on the Kennedy grounds. It was William Kennedy Smith, she said. He had undergone a "surreal" transformation.

"I couldn't understand why my leg was being grabbed. I thought maybe he was playing. I can't play that way. My neck was broken years ago [in a car accident]," Bowman said. She broke free of his grasp and ran across the lawn. "I started running, to get away," but Smith chased and tackled her near the pool. He held her to the ground with his six-foot-three-inch body.

"He was on top of me," she said. "I was trying to get out from underneath him because he was crushing me. He had my arms pinned. I tried to arch my back to get him off of me and he slammed me back into the ground. I was yelling 'No!' and 'Stop!' I was screaming 'No!' I was struggling and he told me to 'stop it, bitch!'"

Then Smith pushed aside her dress and raped her as she continued to scream in vain for help. Afterward, Smith smugly informed Bowman that no one would ever believe her if she accused him of rape. "I thought he was going to kill me," Bowman said.

News of "alleged sexual battery" behind the walls of the Palm Beach home once known as President Kennedy's beloved "Winter White House" attracted media attention instantly around the world. As the "suspect" was tentatively identified as a "Kennedy"—rather than a family friend or distant relation—dozens of investigative reporters and television correspondents were dispatched to Palm Beach. The media's interest heightened when the "Kennedy" became William Kennedy Smith—grandson of bootlegger Joe Kennedy and the son of a sister of President Kennedy, Senator Robert Kennedy, and Senator Ted Kennedy. But the story soared to unprecedented levels when it was revealed Ted Kennedy was directly involved in the "Easter Weekend Rape Scandal" in luxurious Palm Beach.

Senator Edward Moore Kennedy, the youngest of Joe Kennedy's four sons, was a notorious, hard-drinking womanizer and rake. As a young senator, Ted Kennedy was viewed as a "shoo-in" to become president and return "Camelot" to the White House. But in 1969, a car he was driving plunged off a bridge at Chappaquiddick. Critics later claimed there was a "Kennedy cover-up" when Kennedy failed to report the crash for eleven hours, but was allowed to plead guilty to leaving the scene of a fatal accident and served no jail time. In 1980, Kennedy made a final bid to win the Democratic presidential nomination. At one campaign fund-raising party at New York's trendy Magique discotheque, a young Brooke Shields was photographed dancing intimately for hours with Smith, then a puffy eighteen-year-old. The senator's campaign was unsuccessful. Two years later, Kennedy and his troubled wife, Joan, divorced.

While Kennedy supporters defend Ted Kennedy as a tireless public servant and influential standard bearer for liberal causes, his detractors characterize him as an debauched "partymeister." Since his divorce, Kennedy has cavorted shamelessly with women in public—in bars and restaurants, on boats and planes. Occasionally photographers captured his bawdy public displays. One photograph published in a respected national magazine showed the senator clutching a woman from behind on a yacht, with his arms draped around her bikinied body. The picture prompted one midwestern senator to remark: "I'm glad to see the good senator from Massachusetts has changed his views on off-shore drilling!"

Despite the considerable influence of the Kennedys, they were never embraced by Palm Beach society. The rough-edged Kennedys were perceived as arrivistes on this insular tropical island, even after John Kennedy was elected president. The Kennedys, in turn, preferred Martha's Vineyard and Nantucket to Palm Beach. Family members merely rotated shifts at the Kennedy compound. They treated the sixty-nine-year-old, Addison Mizner–designed mansion like an oceanfront college dorm.

But when the winter season arrived in Palm Beach in December 1990, Senator Kennedy began to spend an uncharacteristic amount of time at La Guerida, as the Kennedy estate is officially known. Since his divorce, the barrel-chested six-foot senator had been romantically "linked" by gossip columnists over the years, but none of the relationships was ever serious. But Kennedy now was dating a beautiful thirty-six-year-old Palm Beach divorcée, Dragana DuPont Lickle. And this relationship was significant.

Dragana Lickle was the daughter of a Yugoslavian physician in Cleveland. For six years, Dragana was married to Garrison DuPont Lickle, an attorney and an heir to the DuPont fortune. The Lickles divorced in 1984, with Dragana awarded custody of their two children. A fanatic tennis player, Dragana works for Sotheby's exclusive real-estate office in West Palm Beach. By coincidence, she lives in a house on a street that faces the Kennedy compound.

The senator and Dragana Lickle met on the Palm Beach "social circuit" and started to date seriously around Christmas 1990. Acquaintances of the couple recalled how they could not contain their amorous affection in public. "He really worshipped Dragana," said Susan Kennedy, the editor of the *Palm Beach Social Register* and no relation to the senator. Shortly before Christmas, Kennedy flew Dragana to Massachusetts to meet Rose, the family matriarch. Ted Kennedy had never formally introduced any woman he was dating to Rose Kennedy.

On Valentine's Day, 1991, Ted Kennedy organized a large Palm Beach–style party at the family's compound. His "sweetheart" Dragana Lickle served as "hostess." But during cocktails, a process server came to the door with a subpoena for Kennedy. It had been sent by Joseph Farish, a lawyer working for Dragana's ex-husband. Garrison Lickle was in court attempting to win back custody of his children, charging his wife was exposing the young Lickles to "the lifestyle of the jet set" and "to notorious characters... of questionable background."

A judge later ruled that the subpoena had been improperly served and Kennedy did not have to testify. But the subpoena seemed to rupture Ted and Dragana's relationship. Newspaper gossip columnists such as Cindy Adams said there were public rows between the two in Palm Beach. One Palm Beachite said that Kennedy and Dragana had a loud argument at Au Bar only days after Valentine's Day and that he had stormed out of the nightclub without paying his bill—which was his habit.

A few weeks before Easter, 1991, Dragana DuPont Lickle broke off her relationship with Kennedy. "She dumped him," an acquaintance said. "Everyone believes it was because keeping custody of her children, whom she loved, was far more important than a relationship with Ted Kennedy."

Dragana's abrupt exit left the fifty-nine-year-old bachelor crestfallen—and alone on Palm Beach. Kennedy resumed his hard-driving "single" lifestyle with vigor. Some say he drank and played to distract himself from thinking about Dragana. Kennedy was seen on the Palm Beach evening circuit, making the rounds of the saloons and nightspots such as Chuck & Harold's restaurant, Bradley's, Dempsey's, and Au Bar.

One afternoon, Kennedy chartered a yacht belonging to the owner of a popular Palm Beach eatery. He and the yacht owner invited about a dozen men and women friends for a cruise and brunch aboard the ship. Once the ship was plying the waters of Lake Worth, Kennedy and a female companion began to drink in the warm Florida sun and then they kissed. Within minutes, their kisses became so amorous they decided to retire to the cabin. But they barely stepped beyond the last rung before they started to embrace. The woman then pulled down Kennedy's shorts. In view of everyone on deck, the woman pleased the glowing senator from Massachusetts.

When Easter week arrived, the senator was joined at the mansion by his son, Patrick, a twenty-three-year-old Rhode Island legislator. On Wednesday, March 27—two nights before the "alleged sexual battery"—Patrick Kennedy arrived in Palm Beach. That evening, he and his father went to Au Bar for drinks. They arrived at about eleven P.M. Dave Janos, the assistant manager, motioned the two generations of Kennedys into the club. The senator immediately recognized Ivana Trump and exchanged a fleeting hello with the former wife of Donald Trump. The senator then stepped up to the bar and ordered his "usual" double Chivas Regal from the handsome blond bartender, West Shoaf. Within an hour, the Kennedys were joined by two young women, who followed them to the mansion.

One of the women stayed with Patrick for an hour before he called a cab to take her home. The other woman, described only as a blonde, remained with the senator for an hour and a half. She apparently was unable to drive. Kennedy asked Dennis Spear, a "caretaker" at the estate, to drive the woman—and her car—home. Spear put a bicycle in the trunk of the woman's car and drove off with her as Ted went to sleep. Spear used his bicycle to peddle back the few miles to the compound. Both Patrick Kennedy and Ted Kennedy later refused to discuss their Au Bar evening.

By Good Friday, March 29, the Kennedy mansion was bustling with guests. William Kennedy Smith and his mother, Jean Smith, had joined Ted and Patrick for Easter weekend. Also there were William Barry, a close family friend and longtime security chief, and his wife, Mary, and their son, Stephen, and daughter-in-law, Karen Disalvatore, both prosecutors with the Manhattan District Attorney's Office.

That evening the large Kennedy gathering shared a sumptuous turkey dinner and a few bottles of wine. After dinner, the younger Kennedys were joined by two girls, Brigette and Cara Rooney, granddaughters of Art Rooney, the owner of the Pittsburgh Steelers football team. They played charades and then went out to a discotheque, Lulu's, on Cocoanut Row.

The older Kennedys, meanwhile, had retired to the veranda, where they reminisced about Willie Smith's father, Stephen Smith, who had died of cancer the previous August. To longtime Kennedy observers,

Stephen Smith was the family member who skillfully managed "damage control" whenever there was another Kennedy scandal. The 1991 Easter weekend marked the first time Ted Kennedy, his sister Jean, and Willie Smith had been together since Stephen Smith's funeral.

Senator Kennedy later explained, "The conversation was very emotional, very difficult, and brought back a lot of very special memories to me. We lost a brother, Joseph, in the war. When Jean married Steve we had another brother, and when Steve was gone something left all of us—when we buried him. I found at the end of the conversation I was not able to think about sleeping. It was a very draining conversation, a whole range of memories came as an overwhelming wave in terms of emotion and I thought 'I can't possibly sleep.'" Kennedy emphasized that he felt he needed to talk with his son and nephew.

The senator found the young Kennedy men preparing for sleep in a bedroom they shared for the weekend. Patrick and Smith had just returned from Lulu's, where they had been drinking and dancing for a few hours with the Rooney sisters and two other friends, Martha Dolan and Kerri Allison. Although Ted Kennedy said he needed to talk, he suggested that Patrick and Smith accompany him for drinks at the raucous Au Bar. "I wish I'd gone for a long walk on the beach instead," the senator would later lament.

In less than twenty minutes, the three Kennedy men were inside the pulsating Au Bar on Royal Poinciana Way near the Lake Worth waterway.

Au Bar was a new club that had first opened earlier that season. The owners were offering private membership to island residents, but because the interest proved only modest they quickly welcomed a broader clientele to bolster business. One of the Au Bar principals was well-known New York nightclub owner Howard Stein, the son of one of the Big Apple's infamous loan sharks. Stein's father, Charles "Ruby" Stein, was a multimillion-dollar Mafia associate who ran the city's numbers rackets before he disappeared. His torso washed up in Jamaica Bay, Queens, on May 15, 1977. The FBI once secretly recorded Ruby Stein at the Hilton Hotel asking Anthony "Fat Tony" Salerno, the head of the Genovese crime family, for $500,000 to bankroll his young son, Howard, in the nightclub business. Law enforcement officials believe "Fat Tony" helped launch Howard Stein's career, although Stein, a respected businessman, vigorously denies the allegation.

Ted Kennedy ordered his double Chivas Regal, and then he and Patrick sat down at a table near the small wooden dance floor. As the music pounded around them and women's skirts whirled before them, a series of seemingly innocent encounters occurred.

Patricia Bowman, searching for a ladies' room, accidentally "bumped into" the bulky, six-foot-three-inch Smith near the entrance to Au Bar. Bowman remembered feeling embarrassed. While offering an apology, she and Smith started a conversation. Bowman lived in a $150,000 home her stepfather had purchased for her in nearby Jupiter, an affluent community north of Palm Beach adjoining Singer Island. Bowman said she had not been "out" in the Palm Beach scene since her daughter had been born two years before. In fact, she said she had gone out for dinner that evening with friends at her mother's urging. She and a friend had stopped at Au Bar for a nightcap.

Because Smith was about to become a doctor, she said the conversation gravitated quickly to her daughter's fragile health. Eventually they danced. "I really felt like I could trust him. He seemed to be an intelligent man, a likable man. We were carrying on a conversation that to me had no fearful attitudes. During our dancing he never laid a hand on me. He had never done anything suggestive at all."

Senator Kennedy and Patrick, meanwhile, were introduced to Bowman's "friend," Anne Mercer, a tall, sharp-tongued thirty-three-year-old blonde. She was rude to the Kennedys and her brusque manner drove Patrick to the bar, where he met Michele Cassone, a wide-eyed, pudgy waitress at nearby Testa's Italian restaurant. Patrick Kennedy and Michele chatted and then danced.

Sometime between two and three A.M. the senator and his son left "the establishment"—as Ted Kennedy later called it. Again, he had not paid his sizable bar bill. Kennedy said, "I asked Patrick, 'Where is Willie?' and he indicated that he split, which in the parlance of our times meant that he had gone home, made other plans." Michele Cassone, at Patrick's invitation, followed the Kennedys in her car to the Kennedy compound.

The kleig lights at Au Bar were turned up about three A.M., signaling closing time. Smith, now without a ride, asked Bowman if she could drive him home.

"I thought they would have security there. There was a senator there. I did not feel I was in any danger going to the Kennedy home."

When she pulled into the driveway of the estate, Smith invited her for a tour of the historic mansion. "I was enjoying his company," Bowman later said. "I felt no fear." Once inside, however, the couple moved quickly from the house to the beach for a walk.

The senator, Patrick, and Michele, meanwhile, had made their way to a veranda at the edge of the lawn that overlooks the ocean. There, under the clear starry night, they sipped wine, chatted, and listened to music from a portable "boom box" radio. Ted Kennedy spent twenty minutes on the veranda with Patrick and Michele before he returned to the mansion. He said he had a "snack" in the kitchen and then went to his first-floor bedroom, where he undressed. Instead of climbing into bed, however, Kennedy, now pantsless and wearing only a long "nightshirt," went to his son's room to say good night. His sudden appearance startled Patrick, who was fondling Michele. And the sight of a trousersless Senator Kennedy frightened Michele. "The senator had this weird look on his face!" she later said. "I was weirded out."

As the senator retreated, Patrick calmed Michele and suggested they take a walk on the beach. Grabbing a blanket, Patrick and Michele went to the shore, where "we necked a little bit." Patrick noticed his cousin Willie, alone, in the moonlight.

"I don't know exactly what he was wearing, but he wasn't naked," Patrick said. Patrick also recalled seeing his father strolling the lawn when he escorted Michele to her car. But Patrick said he never heard Bowman's screams for help. And neither did Michele or the senator—or anyone else at the mansion that night.

Bowman said she screamed and "could not understand why no one was helping me. I knew there was a senator inside." After the attack, she fled into the mansion and hid in the pantry, afraid Smith might kill her. "I was a mess. I'd never been raped before. I didn't know what to do. I was afraid he was going to come after me. Everything was shaking. I was just trying to get my body to stop shaking."

Sandwiched between two cupboards, Bowman composed herself. She noticed a telephone on a nearby table and called Anne Mercer. "I was in the Kennedy home and...all I knew is I wanted to feel safe. I wanted somebody to come and help me feel safe. And I didn't know that the police would care or would come. I had just been raped by a Kennedy and I didn't know what power they held. I was more comfortable calling a friend."

She heard Smith calling for her and then he found her. "He grabbed me again. I thought he was going to kill me. I didn't know what he was going to do to me."

Smith pulled her into a room. He appeared calm. "He was real different. I was telling him, 'You've raped me. How could you do this?'"

At one point, she was so upset she mistakenly called him by the wrong name, Michael. When she said she would call the police, Smith just sat in a chair and smugly said: "No one will believe you."

Mercer arrived at the compound at 4:15 A.M., about fifteen minutes after Bowman's "hysterical" call. "Patty said she had been raped." Mercer had brought along her boyfriend, Chuck Desiderio. Mercer said Bowman "was literally shaking and she looked messed up, her hair and makeup were running." Mercer said Bowman asked repeatedly that she find her shoes. Mercer asked Smith, "What did you do to my friend" before setting off with him in a search through the house and beach for the shoes.

Finally, Mercer returned to the mansion to get Bowman. "I said, 'Let's get out of here.'" Desiderio grabbed an urn and a photograph from a table. He later said he took the valuables so Bowman could have proof that she had been at the Kennedys' mansion.

In a few minutes they arrived at Mercer's house. Patty "had her knees up to her chest, and when we tried to talk to her she would jump like she didn't want someone to touch her," Mercer said. She eventually went to Good Samaritan Hospital and spoke with a county rape counselor. Then the police were notified. She did not want "to be responsible for [Smith] doing it to someone else."

About nine hours after the alleged sexual battery, Patricia Bowman sat curled up in the fetal position on a chair in the Sheriff's Office in West Palm Beach. She trembled and shook—and again she recoiled when someone tried to touch her. Now, for the first time, she tearfully told detectives that she had been raped at the Kennedy mansion by William Kennedy Smith.

"I felt so disgusting. I felt all this fear and this dirtiness," she later said. "I was just so afraid and confused by everything that had happened to me. I was a mess."

The following morning, Easter Sunday, Ted Kennedy and his son went to Chuck & Harold's for brunch. Kennedy drank a Screwdriver and a Bullshot, a combination of boullion and an ounce of vodka. His son had a Long Island Ice Tea, a concoction of several liquors. The Kennedy men discussed the "incident" between Smith and Bowman.

Early in the afternoon, detectives from the Palm Beach Police Department arrived at the Kennedy compound to speak with Smith and the senator. Although Kennedy had returned to the mansion, William Barry, a former FBI agent and bodyguard for Robert Kennedy, told the police Ted was not there. Barry promised the detectives that the senator would contact them later. Kennedy never did.

An hour later, Smith left Palm Beach on a previously scheduled flight to Washington. He was supposed to take his final medical boards at Georgetown Medical School that week. At about six P.M., Smith telephoned Uncle Ted. He wanted to tell the senator what had occurred between him and Bowman, but Kennedy cut him off. The senator, an attorney and experienced hand in criminal procedure, knew that if Smith told him the story he would have to reveal the conversation to prosecutors.

"Ted has been around the block a few times and he knew enough not to talk to Willie," a family acquaintance explained.

Senator Kennedy instructed Smith to call Marvin Rosen, a Miami lawyer in the firm Greenburg, Traurig, Hoffman, Lipoff, Rosen and Quentel. Rosen was a longtime Kennedy friend and supporter. He told Smith to speak with Mark Schnapp, a new partner at the firm.

Schnapp had recently served as the head of the U.S. Attorney's criminal division in Miami. He was credited with helping lodge criminal charges against Panamanian dictator Manuel Noriega who retaliated by putting a voodoo curse on him. Schnapp interviewed William Kennedy Smith on Monday, April 1—two days after the alleged sexual battery. Schnapp now became the first person to hear Smith's version of the events of March 29. He was eager to meet with Palm Beach police and the state attorney.

Having heard Smith's story, Schnapp went to Palm Beach to convince the detectives that there was no case to prosecute. But this case involved a Kennedy. Word of the "incident" had spread through Palm Beach and leaked to the press. The media interest was intense. The television networks were already starting to refer to the story as the "Rape at the Kennedy Compound." It was quickly becoming one of the largest news events in a decade. And the state attorney, David Bludworth, once criticized for his handling of the overdose death of David Kennedy, was not about to treat the case cavalierly.

There was one peripheral player around the case who sensed its importance from the outset: Leonard Mercer, who was Anne Mercer's father and a close associate of Philadelphia Mafia boss Nicodema Scarfo. Leonard Mercer had recently served one year of a four-year federal prison sentence for obstructing justice, giving kickbacks, and evading taxes, according to former U.S. federal prosecutor Joseph DeMaria.

The fifty-eight-year-old silver-haired Mercer is a colorful and widely recognized Palm Beachite. He once owned Ta-boo and La Petite Marmite, two popular restaurants on exclusive Worth Avenue. Mercer also owned a \$3.7 million oceanfront estate on South County Boulevard until 1988, when he transferred title of the property to Anne. In that same year, another oceanfront house Leonard Mercer owned in Fort Lauderdale was nearly seized by the federal government because it mistakenly believed the house belonged to Nicodema Scarfo. The government had come to its belief honestly; Mercer had allowed Scarfo to live in the four-bedroom house for years.

In addition to his Palm Beach real-estate dealings, Mercer built the luxury 725-unit Ocean Club condominiums in Atlantic City, and at one time he owned three hotels in Fort Lauderdale, including the Galt Ocean Mile, once the spring training headquarters of the New York Yankees. Ultimately, Leonard Mercer served a year in prison for paying kickbacks to two men who illegally loaned him \$500,000 in Teamsters Union pension funds to buy Ta-boo. One of the other two men, former New Jersey state senator David Friedland, is still in jail.

At about the same time Schnapp was questioning Smith, Leonard Mercer was having lunch with Patrick McKenna, a local private detective. McKenna had known Mercer for several years. The detective, who once worked as a parole officer, helped write Mercer's presentencing memorandum following his federal conviction. "I always liked Leonard," McKenna said. "He was the kinda guy who would bring 'big-time swindlers' to a table, screw them all out of money, and they'd walk away in amazement saying, 'Goddamn it! Leonard, just gave us a major fucking.' Leonard's great!"

Mercer asked McKenna if he had been hired to work on the rape case. He had not yet been retained. "I knew Leonard was talking to the tabloid papers," McKenna said. "He already had a business card from the *National Enquirer* in his billfold. I think he was seeing where the case might go and how he could drive up the price for 'Anne's Story.' He and a lot of other people never thought the case would go as far as it did, that there would be some kind of settlement early on and the charges dropped. Leonard was playing poker, upping the ante."

By Monday night, April 1, two days after the alleged sexual battery, dozens of reporters began to descend on Palm Beach as media tipsters spread the news for "finder fees." Journalists from across America and as far away as Germany, England, and Brazil were dispatched to the island to capitalize on the allure—and selling power—of the Kennedy name. Hotels such as the Brazilian Court, the Colony, and the Breakers were quickly filled. The media proved a boon to the local economy. Ultimately nine hundred newsmen and women—writers and photographers from the "lowly" supermarket magazines to the "lofty" *New York Times*—camped on Palm Beach. And the *New York Post* led the competitive field.

With exclusive reports and its unique style of headline writing, the *New York Post* set the tone during the initial tumultuous weeks. The *Post* edition of Wednesday April 3 declared: BACHELORS PARTY and carried pictures of Senator Kennedy, his son, and Smith on the front page with an insider's view of their "Good Friday" evening in Au Bar. The next day's *Post* headline shouted: I WANT JUSTICE! and reported that Bowman had spurned offers to tell her story.

But Friday's *Post* exclusive was the one that startled America—providing the public with the first account of a "pantless" Senator Ted Kennedy and a stunned Michele Cassone. The story was accompanied by a "classic" headline: TEDDY'S SEXY ROMP! The article ignited the media.

That night—exactly one week after Smith met Bowman—Mark Schnapp, Smith's attorney, decided to "inspect" Au Bar. He paid his first—and last—visit to the "trendy, chic, new" nightspot after feeling ill at ease and somewhat overwhelmed at the crush of celebrities, socialites, and reporters who were whirling about. "It was incredible." Mark Schnapp later told a friend.

The Florida state attorney by now had selected Moira Lasch, a tenacious "go for the jugular" assistant, to lead the prosecution. The forty-year-old Lasch was a magna cum laude graduate of Vassar College who had earned her law degree at the University of Maryland. She was an attractive woman with a soft-angled face, moist eyes, and short straight hair. But her chilly, straightforward manner signaled she had little time for small talk or casual pleasantries. Lasch, a vegetarian who is married to a dentist, kept a miniature electric chair, complete with matching tiny helmet, on her desk. Once, when she was in court, a serial killer had screamed that she was "a pointy nosed... white bitch." Lasch's response: "I don't have a pointy nose."

From the start, Lasch supported Bowman and her gripping account of the alleged sexual battery. And she was acutely aware of the Kennedys' reputation for engaging in "cover-ups." Determined that Patricia Bowman would receive her "justice," the bright prosecutor employed an extremely methodical approach to the case. She was zealous—perhaps to a fault.

By contrast, the Kennedy advisers were loose-knit and far-flung, with connections reaching in myriad directions. Schnapp entered the case by way of Senator Kennedy. But Jean Smith had retained Herbert Miller, the Washington lawyer who was head of the Justice Department's Criminal Division when her brother Bobby was U.S. attorney general. Given the long history of the Kennedys in politics—and in public scandals—there was a retinue of public-relations specialists, political consultants, and media analysts volunteering advice. "You cannot imagine how Smith was getting led around in every direction," an insider recalled.

Despite the inherent confusion, the nucleus of what became known as "the Kennedy team" was in place. In addition to Schnapp and McKenna, there was Holly Skolnick, a Harvard trained attorney, and investigators Tom Myers, a former FBI agent, and Steve Roadruch, who was known as "Dr. Dirt" because of his unflinching ability to uncover scandalous personal information about an adversary.

On Saturday, April 6, Smith went to Miller's office in Washington, where he sat through a grueling, four-hour, three-party telephone interview with Schnapp and his investigators in Palm Beach. "My sense was Willie was nervous, scared," McKenna recalled. "He was uncertain what would happen. But he was bright, intelligent, and he came across honest. We already knew what Patty had said and, by then, we heard certain things about her personal life. I believed right there and then that Smith was getting a screwing."

The following morning the team met at the Kennedy mansion. Schnapp stood on the lawn. McKenna was on a balcony. "Mark was speaking in his normal voice as he walked around. He was saying: 'Can you hear me? Can you hear me?' The hedges acted like a megaphone. I could hear his voice as clear as a bell. It came right up the staircase and not just up from the lawn. I wondered: How come no one heard Patty scream. I swear it was like an echo chamber there."

The unscientific acoustic test only made Schnapp and the rest of the Kennedy team more confident in Smith. They waited for an opportunity to persuade the prosecution that there was not a case. The opportunity never came.

"Generally, it does not hurt the prosecutor to listen to the defense because they may learn something they do not know," an observer said. But Lasch was not interested in what the Kennedy lawyers had to say. "It is routine for the defense to make a pitch for dismissal," one participant recalled. "We were not even allowed to ask. Like, 'Don't bother!'"

Both sides hunkered down for combat. Smith's investigators criss-crossed Palm Beach county with a vengeance, searching for "dirt" on

Bowman. The Palm Beach police and Bludworth's investigators set off with equal zeal. But the media stayed one step ahead of them all.

The supermarket magazines and the television tabloid shows were paying tens of thousands of dollars for photographs and information about Bowman and Smith and the alleged sexual battery. Bowman's attorney, David Roth, revealed that the television show "Hard Copy," had offered $500,000 for an interview with Bowman. He was unaware that the tabloid show was actually prepared to pay between $800,000 and $1 milliion, thanks to a consortium deal they had arranged with several international media organizations as far away as Australia.

Each evening, the irrepressible Steve Dunleavy of "A Current Affair" and Diane Dimond of "Hard Copy" were broadcasting live from Palm Beach, using the island's trees, beaches, and nightclubs for backdrop. By now, Michele Cassone—the "other woman" in the scandal—provided interviews to anyone holding a notebook or microphone. She embarked on a whirlwind "talk show" circuit. She went from Curtis and Lisa Sliwa's radio show in New York to the extraordinary Jack Cole's show in Florida to "A Current Affair" to "Geraldo" and to "Sally Jessy Raphael" before her "fifteen minutes of fame" ended.

But it was the *London Mirror*, a tabloid featuring scandal, that published Bowman's name and a photograph. The British magazine's decision came in direct opposition to the accepted practice in America, where the press historically withholds the identities of sex crime victims. On April 14, 1992, the *Midnight Globe*, an American super-market magazine, broke with that tradition and followed the *Mirror's* lead.

Two days later, Bowman's name was broadcast during "NBC Nightly News." Michael G. Gartner, the president of NBC News, said: "We believe in this case, as in all news events, the more we tell our viewers, the better informed they will be in making up their own minds about the issues involved. We do not mean to be judgmental or take sides. We are merely reporting what we have learned."

Immediately following the broadcast, editors at the *New York Times* inserted Bowman's name quickly into a "profile" article that was published that evening for the next morning's editions. The article presented an unusually harsh portrait of Bowman and included anony-mous remarks about her "poor academic record" in high school and her "little wild streak."

In explaining their decision to reveal Bowman's name, the *Times* said: "Like many other news organizations, the *New York Times* ordinarily shields the identities of complainants in sex crimes, while awaiting the courts' judgment about the truth of their accusations. The *Times* has withheld Ms. Bowman's name until now, but editors said yesterday that NBC's nationwide broadcast took the matter of her privacy out of their hands."

The *Times*'s decision sparked a bitter controversy about journalistic ethics, privacy issues, and the rights of victims and the people they accuse. Several newspapers followed the *Times* and published Bowman's name. But most did not. The *Times* later reversed itself. One editor lamented that she wished the paper at least had prepared a comparable profile on Smith. Despite the *Times*'s mea culpa, the damage was done as far as Bowman was concerned.

Patricia Bowman, who was in hiding, sobbed when she learned her name had been revealed by the *Times* and NBC-TV. "I felt victimized a second time. Reporters from the *New York Times*, the nation's most reputable newspaper, stood outside a two-year-old's window. I believed there was this wide chasm between supermarket tabloids and the *New York Times* and NBC News, reputable news organizations. I saw that chasm gone. Why? Why me? How did publishing my name make anyone more informed?"

On May 9, forty days after the alleged rape, William Kennedy Smith was formally charged with one felony count of second-degree sexual battery, the Florida equivalent of rape, and a second-degree misdemeanor count of battery. Although a warrant was issued for Smith's arrest, Bludworth and the Palm Beach police arranged with Smith's lawyers in Washington for the thirty-year-old medical student to surrender the following week. Two days later, Smith surprised Palm Beach and the press. He arrived with his mother and Schnapp to be "booked," fingerprinted, and photographed by police.

Inside the Mediterranean-style, red-tile-roofed police headquarters, Jean Smith greeted the police officers and support staff as though she were on a campaign trail. She earnestly shook hands and told each person how she admired people in public service. A police officer asked Smith if he wanted to make any statement. "Yes," Smith answered. As he started to explain his side of the alleged sexual battery, Schnapp cut him off.

Smith left police headquarters through a throng of reporters and was driven five miles to the West Palm Beach courthouse, where he officially pleaded innocent to Bowman's charges. Outside court, Smith, enveloped by reporters and cameramen, spoke publicly for the first time. He called Bowman's allegation "an outrageous lie ... a damnable lie."

"I did not commit an offense of any kind," the grandson of Joseph Kennedy said. "Her statements represent an attack on me, on my family and on the truth. I'm very much looking forward to a trial where I can testify and where the truth can come out. I have no question that will happen."

Smith spent the next afternoon—Mother's Day—in New York at his mother's elegant slate-gray town house on the Upper East Side. On the street that morning, Smith said "I just plan to spend Mother's Day with mom. It's not like I'm running for public office." His mother, dressed neatly in white, said she was "having a lovely day." Then she grabbed her son's hand and said, "We're hoping for a nice quiet supper. After all, it is my day."

A report from London that afternoon was anything but the kind of news a mother wants to hear about a son, much less on Mother's Day. A British woman said Smith had sexually attacked her six years earlier at a New York party. The attack allegedly occurred when she had resisted Smith's advances.

London columnist Taki Theodoracopoulos, who was a friend of the British "victim," wrote that the woman had bad bruises and marks on her face from the pummeling. The writer said he urged his friend, then twenty-one and single, to file charges with police, but she said she was frightened of the influential Kennedys. Instead, she left America and never returned. Taki's report received little public attention in the United States at the time.

On May 21, Anne Mercer "broke her silence" on "A Current Affair" for $25,000. The fee was considerably less than the $150,000 she was initially offered. The value of her story had plummeted recently with the release of transcribed interviews from police files with her and other principals and witnesses. Mercer's "paid" appearance was viewed by millions, including the Kennedy team. Her credibility had been damaged because jurors might wonder whether she altered her account for cash.

On June 1, Smith pleaded not guilty at his arraignment before Judge Mary E. Lupo. The graduating medical student could have submitted a written plea, but he wanted to appear in person. "It was important for me to come down and look the judge in the eye and tell her I'm not guilty," Smith told reporters. "I get so frustrated that I can't tell my side of the story. Every time I pick up the newspaper, I see something else about the case. But I've been given strict instructions not to say anything."

To Moira Lasch, "instructions" meant Smith was being handled by the Kennedy machine. The stern prosecutor walked into Palm Beach County Court on June 14. In her briefcase was a copy of the 1988 best-selling book *Senatorial Privilege: The Chappaquidick Coverup.* Lasch submitted the scathing investigative report for the record, claiming the book was evidence that the Kennedy family manipulated politicians, and justice.

Arguing against a motion by the defense that a gag order be issued, Lasch said, "That book is relevant because it shows the fact that public officials can come under the influence of Kennedy lawyers. They attempt to intimidate officials and try to control the dissemination of free information. The Kennedys try to avoid the close scrutiny of their own conduct."

She claimed that lawyer Herbert Miller was again using the Kennedy family machine to try to influence the court and public opinion. The prosecutor later also accused Judge Lupo of being against her and said that the judge had demonstrated her feelings through "negative facial expressions" and scowls.

Mark Schnapp vehemently objected: "This is not a forum for Ms. Lasch to trash Senator Kennedy in public!" He disputed Lasch's claim that she had given him notice of her intention to submit *Senatorial Privilege* into the record.

Buttressing his argument for a gag order, Schnapp produced articles about the case from a newspaper published in Hong Kong.

Lasch responded: "We are not going to select jurors from China."

Judge Lupo ultimately imposed strict restrictions on out-of-court-room comments. "I think we're almost at the point of a clear and present danger" of being unable to empanel an impartial jury, Lupo said.

Ten days later, Kennedy defense lawyer Herbert Miller removed himself from the case. Whether the negative publicity attendant to the book, and therefore to Miller, played a role in his departure depends on whom you believe. Some observers speculated that Miller was an unpleasant reminder of the Kennedys' checkered past. Others insisted his exit was dictated solely by the needs of the case.

Miller's departure came at a time when William Smith and his family were confronted with a most important decision. They had to select a trial attorney to lead the criminal defense in court. The choice was complicated. Numerous Kennedy "advisers" offered suggestions, and the list of candidates became daunting. "You could not believe the number of people leading Smith around," an insider said. Jean Smith and her son's lawyers even spoke with Linda Fairstein, the New York prosecutor with a national reputation in rape and sexual assault cases, and a family friend.

Initial discussion centered on whether Smith had to be represented by a woman. The logic in hiring a female attorney was twofold: her presence would enhance Smith's image with the jury and would counterbalance any advantage the prosecution enjoyed because Lasch was a woman. But the list of qualified female criminal lawyers was slim. And the best were still prosecutors or they specialized in federal law. Everyone finally agreed gender was irrelevant. They wanted the "best" lawyer for "this" case.

A revised list was compiled. The candidates included many nationally recognized names. William Kennedy Smith was fully involved in the process and he personally conducted interviews. Two criteria were established before a selection was made. First, the choice had to be an attorney familiar with the laws and criminal justice system of Florida. And second, the final decision would be Smith's alone.

The charges were incredibly serious and insiders believed it was only fair for Smith to make the choice. They felt Smith had to have a chemistry with whoever was chosen to defend him.

Smith decided upon Roy E. Black, a prominent, forty-eight-year-old criminal attorney from Miami. Black, known as "the Professor," had a penchant for unsympathetic clients. "Because he has the image of a quiet college professor, people miss how devious he can be, and I mean that in a complimentary sense," said John Hogan of the Dade County State Attorney's Office.

David Margolick, legal affairs writer for the *New York Times*, aptly described the bookish Black as having a "finely calibrated personality" capable of moving skillfully from "charming country-lawyer" to "slashing, contemptuous," cross-examiner to "low-key" interrogator. Ultimately, Black is capable of demonstrating a "proficiency at work that many people would have neither the stomach or soul to do," Margolick wrote.

Black, and a colleague, Mark Seiden, were retained for $250,000. The fee was formally paid by the Joseph P. Kennedy Foundation, which adminsters trust funds for the Kennedy family heirs.

"Roy Black's law practice is very unique in that it is designed solely for him to be in court trying cases," an acquaintance said. "Roy knew from the start what he was walking into." The legal defense eventually cost in excess of $1 million.

Black attended his first "team" meeting on July 2 at the Greenburg law office in West Palm Beach. He was briefed on the status of the investigation. He barely spoke and basically polled the participants on what they thought had to be done. "There was never a doubt we would lose the case," one participant recalled of the meeting's mood.

But their unyielding confidence was soon seriously tested. On July 24, Moira Lasch submitted into the record the sworn statements of three women. Each claimed she was sexually assaulted by William Kennedy Smith. One woman accused him of rape. In each case, the women described Smith as a gentle man who strangely transformed into a ferocious sex attacker. Their accounts resembled Bowman's. But these new "accusers" did not resemble the portrait the Kennedy team tried to paint of Patricia Bowman as a "troubled, drug-abusing single mother who flipped out after consensual sex."

These accusers were a doctor, a medical student, and a law student. None had previously reported their experience because they feared the Kennedy name. The twenty-six-year-old medical student accused Smith of raping her in his apartment after she became drunk at a party in 1988. She said that Smith had offered her a ride to her home from the party, but took her to his home instead.

"I trusted him—a friend," she said. "He was somebody I knew. So I figured, well, he isn't going to do anything terrible to me. He is Willie. But then he started kissing me and stuff and I said: 'Leave me alone. Get away. No. I want to go to sleep.' He was on top of me and I could not push him off. He [had] such a ferocious . . . almost animal-like look. It was just horrible."

The doctor, who now practices medicine in Alabama, told Lasch that she was attacked by Smith in 1988 while she was a student at Georgetown Medical School. She said he threw her over a couch in his apartment and began to kiss her wildy. "I was pinned down by the wrists. I was very frightened. I thought if I struggled, he probably wouldn't let me up. I told him; 'Willie, you've misunderstod why I'm here. I think you need to let me go.' Evenutally he did."

Perhaps the most damaging account came from the law student. She said she was the girlfriend of Smith's cousin, Matthew Kennedy, a son of the late Senator Robert Kennedy, when Smith attacked her. The assault took place in Smith's mother's home.

According to the law student, she, Smith, and a few friends had gone to a Diana Ross concert in Central Park in 1983 and then to Jean Smith's home after the show. Smith, who had been drinking, twice lunged at her, pushed her onto a bed, pinned her beneath him, pushed up her dress, and began fondling her breasts. She said she fought Smith off by "being pretty aggressive, pretty hostile."

Smith apologized and said he "had just gotten a little carried away and made a pass at me. [But] this was much more than a pass." The law student later told her boyfriend Matthew about the assault, but he "minimized" the incident. Matthew said Smith had already called and apologized for making a pass at her.

Eight years later, after Bowman accused Smith of raping her in Palm Beach, the law student received a telephone call from Matthew Kennedy. He apologized for downplaying her encounter with Smith. "It sounds like Willie has psychological problems and that he should get some help to deal with his feelings toward women," Matthew said.

Lasch maintained that these new "accusers" should be allowed to testify. "The truth of [Smith's] statements cannot be judged in a vacuum," Lasch said. "This is not an isolated event in his life. These are real people who have been victims. This is very compelling evidence, very similar evidence, very striking evidence."

But Smith's lawyers argued that the allegations were "ludicrous" and "garbage," made by copycats who "crawled out of the woodwork." "Their own statements raise substantial questions as to what actually happened and why," the Kennedy lawyers said. Using charts and methodical logic, Black later delineated the differences between these incidents and Bowman's story, including whether they occurred indoors or outdoors, or followed a kiss.

Judge Lupo sided with Black. She ruled the accounts were inadmissible. It was a decision considered by many to be the most important ruling in the case. Lupo's decision, however, held little sway in the court of public opinion. Their verdict was clear. Polls showed sentiment shifted dramatically away from the nephew of President Kennedy and the grandson of Joe Kennedy.

His Uncle Ted's reputation also reached an all-time low. The senator remained a public spectacle—albeit a silent one—when the country turned its attention to the next nationally televised American scandal, the Clarence Thomas hearings. Thomas, a nominee for the Supreme Court, had been accused of sexual harassment by a former assistant, Anita Hill, a law professor. Kennedy was a panel member considering the nomination and the allegations of Thomas's former associate. Because of the controversy surrounding him, Kennedy was forced to play the impassive observer. And his presence was a constant reminder of his role in the sensational Palm Beach rape case.

In the days before jury selection, lawyers on both sides took final depositions. Among the last people questioned by the Kennedy team was Patricia Bowman. It was their initial meeting. Considering the negative "dirt" they had sifted, they were surprised at how articulate and well-spoken Bowman was. She completed two days of interviews on June 31. But it was something she failed to mention rather than what she said that was important.

Black sent McKenna the next day to find Tony Liott, a handsome Palm Beach bartender who had worked at Ta-boo. Liott was a loyal friend of Bowman's, and he volunteered little beyond pleasantries. The Kennedy investigators "dropped in" on Liott several times. On one occasion they brought along a beautiful female investigator, hoping vainly that her presence would "loosen him up." They only thing they learned was that Liott—like many people in the Palm Beach area— wagered on the dog races at a nearby track. The track is owned by the Rooney family. McKenna had found Tony Liott there.

Liott said he had met Bowman in 1982. Since then, he and Bowman had met intermittently over the years. Their relationship was strictly platonic. Liott said he "liked Patty very much" and described her as "a little bit shy." A few days before Easter in 1991, Bowman suggested that they get together on Good Friday evening. "It was not a 'date date' type of thing." Bowman telephoned him that evening to confirm the meeting. She stopped by Ta-boo and visited with him at about 1 A.M. She did not appear "drunk" and did not have a drink. She left after "fifteen or twenty minutes"—nearly three hours before the alleged sexual battery. His tale was simple, but immensely significant. Bowman—in all her statements to law-enforcement authorities and the Kennedy lawyers—had never mentioned her visit to Ta-boo. The defense saw the omission as further proof that Bowman's memory was selective and unreliable. The defense felt Patty's omission had "cracked the case."

Jury selection began on Halloween amid concern that the enormous media attention had made it impossible to find six impartial jurors. One Palm Beach judge remarked that scientists in igloos at the South Pole monitored the case. Margolick in the *New York Times* wrote: "It is not uncommon in cases of great notoriety for jury selection to be both arduous and tedious. The task in Palm Beach could prove even tougher, since the cast of characters is better known, the story starker, the facts far more widely disseminated and arguably, the composition of the panel even more critical."

To assist in the process, Black hired Cathy E. Bennett, a nationally known jury consultant from Galveston, Texas, to the Kennedy team. Cat, as she was called, was suffering from lymphatic cancer, which ultimately claimed her life the following June. But, at the time, the brave Bennett agreed to join the team after she met Smith and became convinced of his innocence. Bennett was said to have a "sixth sense" about potential jurors. She suggested open-ended questions for Black to ask in order to elicit hidden prejudices.

When the selection process began, Black started to introduce William Kennedy Smith to potential jurors as "Will" Smith—providing a softer, less threatening edge to Willie's name. "Will" Smith also posed for "select" photographers at staged events that included his dog Shane and a football, hoping to evoke past positive images of President Kennedy and his brother Bobby playing touch football in Hyannisport. Prominent Kennedy clan members suddenly began to arrive "to support Will" as well. John F. Kennedy, Jr., son of the former president and a prosecutor in the Manhattan District Attorney's Office, came to Palm Beach to show "support."

The Kennedy brood was under strict orders to remain at the mansion at night and never venture into any bars in town if they had to go out. "It was the height of paranoia then," an insider recalled. But John Kennedy, Jr., one evening decided he wanted to meet a friend from Miami for dinner. Roy Black and the team agreed, but only grudgingly. They insisted JFK Jr. dine at the quiet Rain Dancer, a restaurant in West Palm Beach. They even provided detailed directions so he could not get lost.

But JFK Jr. went instead to crowded Chuck and Harold's, where many reporters were eating or drinking. Several even approached JFK Jr., who was wearing a T-shirt and the sort of cap worn by bicycle riders. When he returned to the mansion and said he had met up with reporters in Chuck and Harold's, "everyone's eyes turned the size of bowling balls. No one said it, but they wanted to strangle him. Fortunately, nothing happened."

It was somehow fitting, however, that the Kennedy "supporters" were in court for jury selection. The questions centered on the history of their family. Black, acting the charming country lawyer, casually asked potential jurors what they thought of when the heard the Kennedy name, how they felt the Kennedys treated women and whether the Kennedys believed they were above the law.

The pool of jurors roundly viewed Ted Kennedy as the least respected

Kennedy. One woman, Dorothy Wixted, of Delray Beach, faulted Ted Kennedy over Chappaquidick. She also never "cared for" Jacqueline Kennedy after she married Aristotle Onassis, felt Joe Kennedy's views on Nazi Germany were "awful," but she thought President Kennedy "was great." Another, Priscilla Roper, said the Kennedy family wealth came from "bootlegging liquor." And still another, Florence Orbach, said "the worst thing I ever heard about the Kennedys is that they are very smart but when they get horny, their penis takes over and their brain closes." Everyone—except Lasch—laughed.

The prosecutor added questions about women's rights: "Do you think a woman gives up her right to say 'No' to a man's sexual advances if she goes to his home...if she walks on the beach with him...if she kisses him? Do you think where a woman buys her underwear has anything to do with rape?"

After sixteen grueling days, there were thirty-seven candidates from which to chose. Lupo "broke" for Thanksgiving weekend, leaving the final selections for the following Monday. The Kennedy team returned to the mansion for a turkey dinner. As they chatted and joked, the mood became "giddy." Suddenly, William Kennedy Smith put out his arms and started to impersonate Arnold Schwarzenegger.

Evincing Schwarzenegger's distinctive Teutonic voice, Smith now pretended to question potential jurors. "Vat do you think about de Kennedys?" Smith bellowed in Schwarzenegger's voice. "And vat are your feelings about Maria?" he added, referring to his cousin Maria Shriver, the television personality married to Schwarzenegger. As Smith continued to impersonate the star of *The Terminator*, the overworked team roared with laughter.

Following the Thanksgiving recess, a jury of four women and two men was selected on Monday, December 2, 1991. Television cameras already were set up inside the courtroom for "gavel-to-gavel" coverage to be broadcast across America and to countries around the world. Outside the four-story courthouse, the media had erected a small city of mobile satellite trucks. Only sixteen passes were available on a rotating basis each day for reporters to watch the proceedings in the tiny courtroom. The remaining journalists were forced to cover the trial from television monitors and from Cable News Network and Court TV. Each day, hundreds of spectators arrived to jeer—but mostly cheer—William Smith.

The prosecution called Anne Mercer as its first major witness. Her appearance on the opening day of the trial surprised most court observers. Lasch apparently recognized Mercer as "damaged goods" because she had accepted the twenty-five-thousand-dollar fee in June from "A Current Affair." By putting her on the stand first, Lasch was able to get the best—and worst—out of the way early. But Mercer was even more devastating to the prosecution than Lasch could have imagined.

Under Black's "contemptuous" cross examination, she admitted she had accepted a total of forty thousand dollars—including fifteen thousand more from "A Current Affair"—for a second interview to be aired that night. She said she had spent the money on a Mexican vacation with her boyfriend. The audience gasped at the news. Mercer even acknowledged that in her initial interview with police she said she had not known Smith's name. Black demanded: "It became 'William Kennedy Smith' when you realized how you could cash in on the Kennedy name, isn't that true?"

Mercer was nervous, terse, and monotonic even when Lasch questioned her. When her testimony ended, Anne Mercer left the courtroom in tears. She hid her eyes behind sunglasses and exited the courthouse, with Steve Dunleavy (from "A Current Affair") and her attorney, Raoul Felder. Dunleavy said Mercer "once was a poor little rich girl who was used to getting her way with everything. She still had this air that she was rich, famous and arrogant. There was this attitude, 'Who are you to question me!' It was that attitude that killed her on the stand."

Lasch—her case off to a disastrous start—called Patricia Bowman to the stand the next day. Bowman's early arrival was surprising. But her testimony restored credibility to the case.

Bowman's appearance—her face was covered on television by a fuzzy, blue dot—proved spellbinding as she offered her tearful, anguished account. Throughout much of her testimony, she managed to remain composed, but occasionally she broke into tears when she discussed details of the "alleged sexual battery."

Asked several times if she needed a recess to regain her composure, Bowman, in quiet, choking voice, insisted: "No, I will get through this. This has been a nightmare for me. I want this over."

During cross examination, Bowman required several recesses. When Black questioned her "memory lapses," Bowman replied, "I was trying as hard as I could to forget everything that had happened to me," Bowman responded. "What he did to me was wrong. I have a child. It's not right and I don't want to spend the rest of my life in fear of that man.

And I don't want him doing it to someone else.... Your client raped me."

During Bowman's wrenching testimony, Ethel Kennedy and Eunice Kennedy Shriver were noticeably uncomfortable, and they had difficulty watching her. They fidgeted nervously in their seats.

After two days of testimony, Bowman left the stand, and Smith walked out of the court to face reporters. He stepped up to a phalanx of microphones. "Obviously we saw some very sad and some very dramatic testimony," Smith told reporters. "But I've been living with these allegations, with this damnable lie for eight months, and I hope everyone will be patient, as I have been, and allow me the opportunity, with Roy's help, to defend myself in the coming days."

Despite the remarks, Smith and the team were severely shaken by Bowman's testimony. None said so aloud, but their mood was somber. For nearly five months, the team ate together each night and stayed afterward to talk. "No one verbalized it, but there was concern," one insider said. Smith said he was going home to the mansion. Black also skipped dinner and returned to the house he had rented on Palm Beach. Jean Smith wondered whether Bowman had come across as believable. Cat Bennett, who had had a difficult chemotherapy session the previous day, was drained.

By comparison, the mood around Bowman was jubilant. That evening, Patricia Bowman, her family, and supporters went to the Cobblestone Restaurant in Tequista, where they savored her moment in the spotlight. They toasted her success and perseverance, and they celebrated the fact that she finally had her opportunity to "get the Kennedys" in court.

Bowman's testimony guaranteed that Smith would have to testify in his own defense—regardless of all the expert scientific, forensic, and medical evidence to come. It would be his word against hers.

On Friday, December 6, Ted Kennedy flew into Palm Beach, called by the prosecution. The senator appeared reasonably fit, having curtailed his drinking and diet. He had trimmed nearly thirty pounds from his bloated girth. He was met by his sisters, Jean Smith and Patricia Kennedy Lawford. The three elder Kennedys "goofed around" about how they had aged, "about how their teeth looked. They seemed extremely confident." They ate soup and sandwiches.

Ted Kennedy was driven to the prosecutor's office behind the courthouse. He was spotted by the press and his car was surrounded by reporters and photographers. He waved them off as though on his way to deliver a speech.

Kennedy waited alone for twenty-five minutes in a Spartan government office and then was driven 275 feet around the corner to court.
After ten months of disastrous publicity, Kennedy finally took the stand.
People had speculated that Lasch might try to further tarnish Kennedy's
already badly damaged image. But she surprised everyone—including
Kennedy. She barely questioned him. But the few questions Lasch did
ask provided Kennedy, the skilled politician, with an opportunity to
evoke the "magic" of the Kennedy legend.

After forty minutes of testimony, the senator was gone. "It was a walk
in the park for him," a Kennedy aide said. "He just did it. To him it was
something he had to do. It was like he had to give a speech."

Kennedy was driven from court to the West Palm Beach airport,
where he said he wanted to watch his son, Patrick, testify. Someone in
the Kennedy party gave twenty dollars to a bartender to open early, and
he asked that the television be turned on. As Kennedy sipped a beer, he
impassively watched his son's testimony on CNN.

There had been concern about how the younger, less experienced
Kennedy would handle the pressure. Earlier in the week, the *National
Enquirer* disclosed that Patrick had had a cocaine habit when he was
sixteen years old and that he had undergone drug rehabilitation. Patrick
appeared nervous on the stand, often inhaling deeply to remain calm.

The twenty-four-year-old Kennedy compared Bowman to the obsessive, crazed female character in the movie *Fatal Attraction* who "you
couldn't get rid of." He said that on the night of the incident he had met
his cousin in the parking area outside the mansion. He said Smith
appeared to be saying good-bye to Bowman.

As she drove off, Smith "told me he was quite exasperated because
the woman was saying all sorts of strange things." She had even referred
to him as "Michael" and demanded that he produce his driver's license
to verify his real name. Patrick said he and Smith returned to the
mansion together, only to be "startled" at the sight of Bowman now
standing in a hallway after doubling back. Smith took Bowman
"amiably" into a room, where they remained for forty-five minutes. "She
was really strange," Smith later told Patrick.

Patrick Kennedy's testimony ended in about two hours. Despite his
nervous appearance, the Kennedy mettle came through. The expressionless senator watched his son's entire performance and then, without
saying a word, walked confidently to his plane.

On Tuesday, December 11, 1991, Roy Black called William Kennedy
Smith to the stand. It was the moment everyone had anticipated. For
the next twenty-nine minutes, Smith explained his side of the Palm

Beach story in a generally calm, unemotional voice. The courtroom was hushed and the audience spellbound. Tens of millions of Americans watched on television. Insiders swear the defendant was prepared to testify, but that he was not "coached."

Smith's account portrayed Patricia Bowman as anything but a rape victim. He said she was an eager, sometimes aggressive, participant in a consensual tryst. She later turned into a hysterical, erratic, and accusatory "nut" when he failed to show any lasting interest in her.

"I was standing at the bar and felt someone brushing against me on the other side," Smith began. "She was standing quite close to me, very close to me. We started talking. I asked her if I could buy her a drink and she said 'yes.'" They danced and during the slower songs, "we were kissing and were very close together. I was feeling that I had gotten picked up."

When Ted and Patrick left Au Bar with Michele Cassone, Smith said he told Bowman: "There goes my ride" and she offered to drive him to the estate. Once there, they quickly went inside and then through the mansion to the lawn. Bowman, he said, began to act strangely, claiming she had been there before and alluding to something embarrassing in her family's past. Then she said: "I wouldn't expect you to understand, Michael." Smith told her his name was William and she demanded to see his driver's license as proof.

Smith asked her if she wanted to swim. She did not. Instead she suggested walking to the ocean. Smith grabbed a beach towel, kissed her, and they walked arm in arm to the sand. "I thought we were going to have sex."

At this point in his testimony, Smith paused. "This is not easy for me to talk about," he said turning to the jurors. But then he continued with barely a hint of discomfort. They began to neck. Then she unbuttoned his pants as he removed her underwear—"with her help."

He asked about birth control and she said, "We better be careful." They started to fondle and stimulate each other. Smith said he ejaculated and then quickly dove into the surf for a swim.

Emerging from the ocean, Smith walked onto the lawn where he found Bowman. He said he wanted to go into the house, alone, but Bowman became flirtatious. As they embraced, they laid down on the lawn. Smith penetrated Bowman, with the help of her hand. As they were engaged in intercourse, Smith thought he might ejaculate. "I held her very tightly and I stopped moving and I told her to stop it and I called her 'Kathy.' I knew it was a mistake and I just hoped she didn't hear it. She sort of snapped. She got very, very upset, told me to get the hell off her and hit me with her hand."

Smith said he got off Bowman, and went directly to the pool "for a couple of laps." He got dressed and walked Bowman to her car. "Try not to worry about what happened back there because I was pretty careful," Smith said.

Bowman replied, "You're the one who better worry. You raped me, Michael." She pulled away, then stopped, rolled down her window, and said, "I'm sorry I got upset. I had a wonderful night. You're a terrific guy." They kissed good night and she asked for his number.

When he said he did not know it, Bowman barked, "Tell it to Kathy!" and drove off.

Smith met his cousin Patrick walking back to the mansion. Bowman had returned and was standing in a hallway. They went into a den. Smith said Bowman once again told him that he was "really nice" before starting to shake and cry, repeating that "Michael" had raped her.

"I said, 'Who's Michael?' and she said 'You showed me an I.D. that said 'Michael' and I said 'That's ridiculous.'" Smith then took out his wallet. "'It says William Smith, William Smith, William Smith.'" Finally, she left. This time with Mercer.

Lasch stepped to the lectern near the jury box and spent the next three hours trying to rattle Smith. She was sarcastic. She was biting. She was accusatory.

About being "picked up" by Bowman, Lasch demanded, "Is it your animal magnetism?"

About reaching two orgasms, "What are you, some kind of sex machine?"

About Smith's contention that Bowman actually helped him enter her, Lasch asked, "What are you saying, that she raped you?"

At one point, the prosecutor suggested Smith's relatives were unduly loyal, and Smith snapped, "If you're implying that my family is lying to protect me, you're dead wrong." At another juncture, Smith asked Lasch to repeat a question that he did not understand, and Lasch countered, "I didn't understand your testimony!"

Despite her exhaustive, sometimes flailing, sometimes repetitious cross examination, Lasch was thwarted. Her frustration showed after lunch when she returned to court. Walking past a group of photographers snapping her picture, Lasch repeated: "Click, click, click,

click, click!" Finally, at the end of her cross examination, she asked Smith why he thought Bowman would fabricate a charge of rape. It was a question she should not have asked.

"Miss Lasch," he replied. "I've searched myself since March 29 to try to find out why [she] would make an allegation against me that's not true, that's going to destroy my family, destroy my career, possibly send me to jail for fifteen years. I don't understand why she would do that. I don't understand why anyone would do that."

Smith pointed to Bowman's checkered past and her daughter's health problems, suggesting the strain was too much. He said he even felt "very sorry" for her.

"But that's not the issue here," he declared. "The issue here is I'm innocent. And how do you defend yourself from somebody who says the word *rape* over and over again. I'd like you to tell me how to deal with it."

Jury deliberations began on December 11, 1991. And, in seventy-seven minutes, the six-member jury reached a verdict: Not guilty. As the verdict was announced, Smith placed his forehead in his right hand, smiled, and then stood up and hugged Roy Black.

Bowman, who was nearby with friends, collapsed at the news. "I just fainted, and the next thing I knew I was on the floor." Lasch, meanwhile, remained expressionless, writing on a yellow notepad. She later refused to make a statement.

Two jurors, Lea Haller, a lovely cosmetics executive, and Thomas Stearns, a Vietnam veteran who had won seven Purple Hearts, wiped tears from their eyes. Haller later said Smith's account "supported the evidence much more than Bowman's did, and it didn't seem nearly as contrived."

Smith emerged from court triumphant and faced a crowd of hundreds of spectators—some chanting "Willie! Willie! Willie!" He then addressed a huge semicircle of about 250 reporters and cameramen. "I have an enormous debt to the system, and to God, and I have a terrific faith in both of them. And I'm just really, really happy."

Smith then got into a car and was driven back to the mansion, where the team celebrated with beer and pretzels. At one point they held hands as a priest said a prayer for Bowman.

Smith returned to Palm Beach the following Easter, but the weekend was uneventful. In June 1992, Smith became a twenty-five-thousand-dollar-a-year medical resident at the University of New Mexico.

Bowman also issued a statement following the verdict, reminding the public that "not guilty" does not mean "innocent": "I pray that my decision to proceed was not in vain, and that in some small way I have contributed to a reasoned consideration of the critical issues," Bowman said.

The following evening, Roy Black appeared on CNN's "Larry King Live." He suggested Bowman had fabricated the rape story because she was mentally disturbed. His insensitive remarks prompted Lasch to make her only posttrial observation. Cornered in an elevator, the prosecutor bitterly told reporter Joe Nicholson, "He's trying to finish her off now."

Black's comments helped to convince Bowman to emerge from behind "the Dot." On ABC-TV's "Prime Time Live" with Diane Sawyer, Bowman declared: "I am not a blue blob." She detailed her "terrifying" ordeal to "be in the same room with the man who raped you" and "then hear what he said on the stand."

She later was photographed by Annie Leibowitz for a *Vanity Fair* article written by famed author Dominick Dunne. She ultimately began to work as a rape counselor and spokeswoman for the National Victims Center in Arlington, Virginia.

Senator Kennedy eventually issued a public apology for his distasteful transgressions, "the faults of my private life." The following March, Kennedy announced his engagement to Victoria Reggie, a thirty-eight-year-old Washington lawyer. The Kennedys and Reggies had known each other for years. "Vicki was Ted's solace away from the storm," a friend said. She was described as bold, independent—nothing like the "vulnerable" Joan. Reggie's father, Edmund, ran Kennedy campaigns in Louisiana. When Ted and Vicki announced their engagement, Reggie's father was under federal indictment on eleven counts of alleged bank fraud for $4 million in questionable transactions.

On July 3, Vicki Reggie married Ted in a civil ceremony attended by thirty close relatives in the Kennedy house in McLean, Virginia. On September 26, Ted's new father-in-law was convicted of stealing $4 million from the savings and loan he founded—and faced up to ten years in prison.

But immediately after the verdict, it was business as usual at the Au Bar. Nearly nine months after Bowman had "bumped" Smith, the Rolls-Royces and Mercedes-Benzes continued to pull up. Middle-aged men in silk shirts, ascots, and blue blazers sauntered into the club, where they raised their glasses to sleek young women. The older female patrons, turned out in Armani and Gucci attire, similarly raised their glasses in their never-ending search for affection. But their glasses were hoisted toward the younger, well-tanned men. The dance floor was crowded with couples gyrating to the pulsing music. Clarence Carter could still be heard singing "I'm strokin' with the woman that I love the best! I'm strokin'!" And the distinguished "Neil" was also present. His mustache was neatly trimmed, his blazer smartly pressed. And his skirt was hemmed fashionably at the thigh.

The abrupt conclusion to this extraordinarily publicized Palm Beach story came at a most convenient time of year. Christmas was barely two weeks away. The Yuletide holiday traditionally marks the advent of a new winter season on the tropical island Henry Morrison Flagler had created for the rich, one hundred years before. With the trial of William Kennedy Smith over, and the unwelcome scrutiny of the media gone, the Palm Beach society of wealth and privilege looked forward to returning to its endless cycle of cocktails and dinner parties, charity balls and galas.

The day after the verdict, Worth Avenue was abuzz with activity. Tiffany & Company was celebrating the opening of their shop there. Standing outside the jewelery store were William Weinberg, a Town Council member, and Martha Smythe, executive director of the Worth Avenue Association.

"This is the time of year for season openings, for cocktails, for the events that say 'Look at me, I'm here!'" Weinberg said. And then as the five Tiffany's trumpeters played on, Martha Smythe observed: "Everything is normal! Everything is great!"

Afterword

With the Smith trial completed, the media lost interest in Palm Beach and departed the island as quickly as they had descended upon it in April. The courthouse, which had been surrounded for weeks with onlookers and reporters, now was relatively quiet.

Then, two days after the verdict, on Friday, December 13, another six-member jury in Palm Beach County was handed a case. This one involved Jeffrey Diamond, a Palm Beach resident and former town council candidate. Diamond and two other men, Sandy Klein, the former Port of Palm Beach commissioner, and Garvin Smith, a Lake Worth photographer, had been arrested in October 1990 for attempting to collect fifty thousand dollars in blackmail from Roxanne Pulitzer's fiancé, Count Jean de la Moussaye.

The three men allegedly tried to blackmail de la Moussaye while the count was involved in his high-stakes divorce proceeding with Canadian newspaper heiress Francine McMahon. Diamond approached de la Moussaye and told him that Klein had damaging information about him that could undermine his divorce case. And making matters worse, Diamond said Smith had photos of the count posing with a partially nude model, which he planned to sell to a national publication.

But to prevent the scandal, Diamond said he could bring the four men together for fifty thousand dollars to work out a deal to buy Klein's silence and keep Smith's photos out of print. The count balked at the price and negotiated a payoff of sixteen thousand dollars.

Instead of quietly paying the bribe, de la Moussaye went to the Palm Beach police and agreed to participate in a sting operation. At his Worth Avenue office, with police tape recorders monitoring the scene, de la

Moussaye handed over sixteen thousand dollars in marked money. With the money firmly in the grasp of the three unsuspecting men, the police moved in. They found Klein with five thousand dollars in bait money, Smith with ten thousand, and Diamond with one thousand.

Diamond was the first suspect to stand trial. It took prosecutors four days to present their case. In thirty minutes—less than half the time it took the Smith jury to reach a decision—the Diamond panel announced it had a verdict.

"Guilty!" the jury foreman announced.

That evening, Roxanne and her triumphant count went out in Palm Beach to celebrate the victory. Of course, they headed to Au Bar, where they sipped champagne at their "usual" table, situated perfectly between the wrought-iron-and-glass front doors and the club's small wooden dance floor. The music was pulsating. The marble bar was surrounded.

Another Palm Beach season was underway.

Bibliography

Akin, William. *Flagler: Rockefeller Partner and Florida Baron*. Kent State University Press. 1988.

Amory, Cleveland. *The Last Resorts*. Harper & Brothers. 1948.

Anger, Kenneth. *Hollywood Babylon*. Straight Arrow. 1975.

_____.*Hollywood Babylon II*. Dutton. 1984.

Birmingham, Stephen. *Dutchess: The Story of Wallis Warfield Windsor*. Little, Brown. 1981.

Bishop, Jim. *The Murder Trial of Judge Peel*. Trident Press. 1962.

Brandon, Ruth. *A Capitalist Romance: Singer and the Sewing Machine*. J. B. Lippincott Co. 1977.

Brenner, Marie. *House of Dreams: The Bingham Family of Louisville*. Random House. 1988.

Chambers, Andrea. *Dream Resorts*. Potter. 1983.

Chandler, David. *Henry Flagler: The Astonishing Life and Times of the Visionary Robber Baron Who Founded Florida*. Macmillan. 1986.

Chellis, Marcia. *The Joan Kennedy Story—Living With the Kennedys*. Simon and Schuster. 1985.

Collier, Peter, and Horowitz, David. *The Kennedys, An American Drama*. Warner Books. 1984.

Damore, Lee. *Senatorial Privilege: The Chappaquiddick Cover-up*. Regnery-Gateway. 1988.

Davis, John H. *The Kennedys: Dynasty and Disaster*. SPI Books. 1984, 1992.

Desti, Mary. *The Untold Story: The Life of Isadora Duncan*. DaCapo. 1929.

Duncan, Isadora. *My Life*. Horace Liveright, 1927.

Genthe, Arnold. *Isadora Duncan*. Ayer Co. 1929.

Gibson, Barbara, with Latham, Caroline. *Life With Rose Kennedy*. Warner Books. 1986.

Gold, Sylvia. *A Selection of Isadora Duncan Dances*. Sutton. 1984.

393

Heymann, David C. *Poor Little Rich Girl: The Life and Legend of Barbara Hutton.* Lyle Stuart. 1983.

———.*A Woman Named Jackie.* Lyle Stuart. 1989.

Jahoda, Gloria. *Florida.* W. W. Norton. 1976.

James, Henry. *The American Scene.* Indiana University Press. 1905.

Johnston, Alva. *The Legendary Mizners.* Farrar, Straus and Young. 1953.

Latham, Caroline, and Sakol, Jeannie. *The Kennedy Encyclopedia.* Plum. 1989.

Linton, Calvin D., editor. *American Headlines Year by Year.* Nelson. 1985.

Lundberg, Ferdinand. *The Rich and the Super-Rich.* Lyle Stuart. 1968.

Manchester, William. *American Ceasar: Douglas MacArthur 1880-1964.* Dell. 1978.

Martin, Sidney Walter. *Florida's Flagler.* University of Georgia Press. 1949.

Ney, John. *Palm Beach.* Little, Brown. 1966.

Nolan, David. *Fifty Feet in Paradise.* Harcourt, Brace Jovanovich. 1984.

Pierson, Ransdell. *The Queen of Mean: The Unauthorized Biography of Leona Helmsley.* Bantam Books. 1989.

Pulitzer, Roxanne, with Maxa, Kathleen. *The Prize Pulitzer.* Villard Books. 1987.

Schezen, Roberto, and Johnston, Shirley. *Palm Beach Houses.* Rizzoli International Publications. 1991.

Seaman, Frederic. *The Last Days of John Lennon.* Birch Lane Press. 1991.

Sheeran, James Jennings, and Haas, Pamela J. *The Palm Beach Book of Facts and Firsts.* Palm Beach, Fla: PBSB, Inc. 1989.

Sturges, Preston. *Preston Sturges: His Life in His Words.* Simon and Schuster. 1990.

Swanson, Gloria. *Swanson on Swanson.* Random House. 1980.

Thomas, Dana. *The Plungers and the Peacocks.* William Morrow. 1967.

Trump, Donald, J., with Schwartz, Tony. *Trump: The Art of the Deal.* Random House. 1987.

———,with Leerhsen, Charles. *Trump: Surviving at the Top.* Random House. 1990.

Wallace, Irving; Wallace, Amy; Wallechinsky, David; and Wallace, Sylvia. *The Intimate Sex Lives Lives of Famous People.* Delacorte Press. 1981.

Wallechinsky, David, and Wallace, Irving. *The People's Almanac 2.* Bantam Books. 1978.

Wright, William. *Heiress: The Rich Life of Marjorie Merriweather Post.* New Republic Books. 1978.

Index

395

About the Authors

MURRAY WEISS, an associate editor at the *New York Post*, is an award-winning investigative journalist. During an eighteen-year career with the *Post* and the New York *Daily News*, he has been the recipient of numerous awards selected annually for outstanding reporting by the Associated Press, the New York Press Club and the Society of Silurians. Weiss has written extensively on New York City politics, law enforcement and criminal justice, and organized crime and has appeared frequently as a television and radio analyst and commentator.

BILL HOFFMANN is an award-winning reporter for the *New York Post*. In his fourteen years as a globe-trotting journalist, he has broken countless exclusives covering big city politics, major trials, disasters, and the celebrity beat. He has been a correspondent for Reuters News Service, a frequent guest on radio and television news shows, and a lecturer at New York University.